Practical C++ Programming

Practical C++ Programming

Steve Oualline

O'Reilly & Associates, Inc.
103 Morris Street, Suite A
Sebastopol, CA 95472

Practical C++ Programming
by Steve Oualline

Copyright © 1995 O'Reilly & Associates, Inc. All rights reserved.
Printed in the United States of America.

Editors: Adrian Nye and Dale Dougherty

Production Editor: Nicole Gipson

Printing History:

August 1995: First Edition.

This book is printed on acid-free paper with 85% recycled content, 15% post-consumer waste. O'Reilly & Associates is committed to using paper with the highest recycled content available consistent with high quality.

ISBN: 1-56592-139-9

[11/95]

Table of Contents

Preface

This book is devoted to practical C++ programming. It teaches you not only the mechanics of the language, but also style and debugging. The entire life cycle of a program is discussed, including conception, design, writing, debugging, release, documentation, maintenance, and revision.

Style is emphasized. Creating a good program involves more than just typing code. It is an art in which writing and programming skills blend to form a masterpiece. A well-written program not only functions correctly, but also is simple and easy to understand. Comments allow programmers to include descriptive text in their programs. Clearly written, well-commented programs are highly prized.

A program should be as simple as possible. Avoid the use of clever tricks. Cleverness and complexity can kill programs. This book stresses simple, practical rules. For example, the 15 operator-precedence rules in C++ can be simplified to 2:

1. Multiply and divide before you add and subtract.

2. Put parentheses around everything else.

Consider two programs. One was written by a clever programmer, using all the tricks. The program contains no comments, but it works. The other is nicely commented and well structured, but doesn't work. Which program is more useful? In the long run, the "broken" one is more useful because it can be fixed and maintained easily. Although the clever one works now, sooner or later it will have to be modified. The hardest work you will ever have to do is modifying a cleverly written program.

Scope of This Handbook

This handbook is written for people with no previous programming experience, for programmers who know C and want to upgrade their skills to C++, and for those who already know C++ and want to improve their programming style and reliability. You should have access to a computer and know how to use the basic functions such as the text editor and file system.

Computer languages are best learned by writing and *debugging* programs. Sweating over a broken program at two o'clock in the morning only to find that you typed = where you should have typed == is a very effective teaching tool. Many programming examples are used throughout this book. Most of them contain deliberate errors. You are encouraged to enter the examples into your computer and then run and debug them. This process introduces you to common errors using short programs so you will know how to spot and correct such errors in your own larger programs. (Instructions for obtaining copies of the programs presented in this book are located at the end of this chapter.)

Several dialects of C++ are presented:

* A "generic" UNIX compiler that should work on most UNIX systems
* The GNU C++ compiler, named *g++* (available for most UNIX systems[*])
* Borland's Turbo C++ compiler for MS-DOS
* Borland C++ for MS-DOS/Windows
* Microsoft's Visual C++ for MS-DOS/Windows

As far as standard C++ is concerned there are only minor differences among the various compilers. This book clearly indicates where compiler differences can affect the programmer. Specific instructions are given for producing and running programs using each of these compilers. The book also gives examples of using the programming utility *make* for automated program production.

How This Book Is Organized

You must crawl before you walk. In Part I: *The Basics* you learn how to crawl. These chapters teach you enough to write very simple programs. You start with the mechanics of programming and programming style. Next, you learn how to use variables and very simple decision and control statements.

---

[*] The GNU g++ compiler can be obtained by anonymous FTP from *prep.ai.mit.edu*, or you can contact the Free Software Foundation, Inc., at 675 Massachusetts Avenue, Cambridge, MA 02139, (617) 876-3296.

At this point you will have learned enough to create very simple programs; therefore, in Chapter 7, *The Programming Process*, you embark on a complete tour of the programming process that shows you how real programs are created.

Chapter 1, *What Is C++?*, gives you an overview of C++, describes its history and uses, and explains how the language is organized.

Chapter 2, *The Basics of Program Writing*, explains the basic programming process and gives you enough information to write a very simple program.

Chapter 3, *Style*, discusses programming style. How to comment a program is covered, as well as how to write clear and simple code.

Chapter 4, *Basic Declarations and Expressions*, introduces simple C++ statements. Basic variables and the assignment statement are covered in detail along with the arithmetic operators: +, -, *, /, and %.

Chapter 5, *Arrays, Qualifiers, and Reading Numbers*, covers arrays and more complex variables. The shorthand operators ++, --, *=, =, +=, -=, and %= are described.

Chapter 6, *Decision and Control Statements*, explains simple decision statements including if, else and for. The problem of == versus = is discussed.

Chapter 7, *The Programming Process*, takes you through the steps required for creating a simple program, from specification through release. Structured programming, fast prototyping, and debugging are discussed.

Part II: *Simple Programming*, describes all the other simple statements and operators that are used in programming. You also learn how to organize these statements into simple functions.

Chapter 8, *More Control Statements*, describes additional control statements. Included are while, break, and continue. The switch statement is discussed in detail.

Chapter 9, *Variable Scope and Functions*, introduces local variables, functions, and parameters.

Chapter 10, *The C++ Preprocessor*, describes the C++ preprocessor, which gives you great flexibility in creating code. It also provides a tremendous number of ways for you to screw up. Simple rules that help keep the preprocessor from becoming a problem are described.

Chapter 11, *Bit Operations*, discusses the logical C++ operators that work on bits.

In Part III: *Advanced Types and Classes*, you learn how basic declarations and statements can be used in the construction of advanced types such as structures, unions, and classes. You also learn about the concept of pointers.

Chapter 12, *Advanced Types*, explains structures and other advanced types. The `sizeof` operator and the `enum` type are included.

Chapter 13, *Simple Classes*, introduces the concept of a **class**. This is one of the more powerful features of C++. Classes allow you to group data and the operations that can be preformed on that data into one object.

Chapter 14, *More on Classes*, describes additional operations that can be performed with classes.

Chapter 15, *Simple Pointers*, introduces C++ pointer variables and shows some of their uses.

Advanced programming techniques are explored in Part IV: *Advanced Programming Concepts*. In this section, you explore a number of C++ features that let you create complex, yet easy-to-use objects or classes.

Chapter 16, *File Input/Output*, describes both buffered and unbuffered input/output (I/O). ASCII and binary files are discussed and you are shown how to construct a simple file. Old C-style I/O operations are also included.

Chapter 17, *Debugging and Optimization*, describes how to debug a program, as well as how to use an interactive debugger. You are shown not only how to debug a program, but also how to write a program so that it is easy to debug. This chapter also describes many optimization techniques to make your programs run faster and more efficiently.

Chapter 18, *Operator Overloading*, explains that C++ allows you to extend the language by defining additional meanings for the language's operators. In this chapter, you create a complex type and the operators that work on it.

Chapter 19, *Floating Point*, uses a simple decimal floating-point format to introduce the problems inherent in using floating points, such as roundoff errors, precision loss, overflow, and underflow.

Chapter 20, *Advanced Pointers*, describes advanced use of pointers to construct dynamic structures such as linked lists and trees.

Chapter 21, *Advanced Classes*, shows how to build complex, derived classes out of simple, base ones.

Finally a number of miscellaneous features are described in V: *Other Language Features*.

Chapter 22, *Exceptions*, explains how to handle unexpected conditions within a program.

Chapter 23, *Modular Programming*, shows how to split a program into several files and use modular programming techniques. The make utility is explained in more detail.

Chapter 24, *Templates*, allows you to define a generic function or class that generates a family of functions.

Chapter 25, *Portability Problems*, describes the problems that can occur when *porting* a program (moving a program from one machine to another).

Chapter 26, *Putting It All Together*, details the steps necessary to take a complex program from conception to completion. Information hiding and modular programming techniques, as well as object-oriented programming, are stressed.

Chapter 27, *From C to C++*, describes how to turn C code into C++ code, and addresses many of the traps lurking in C code that bite the C++ programmer.

Chapter 28, *C++'s Dustier Corners*, describes the do/while statement, the comma operator, and the ?: operators.

Chapter 29, *Programming Adages*, lists programming adages that will help you construct good C++ programs.

Appendix A, *ASCII Table*, contains a list of character codes and their values.

Appendix B, *Ranges*, lists the numeric ranges of some C++ variable types.

Appendix C, *Operator Precedence Rules*, lists the rules that determine the order in which operators are evaluated.

Appendix D, *Computing sine Using a Power Series*, contains a program that shows how the computer can compute the value of the sine function.

How to Read This Book If You Already Know C

C++ is built on the C language. If you know C, you will find much of the material presented in Chapters 2 through 12 familiar.

C++ does introduce a number of new features, including:

- An entirely new I/O system. (The basics are described in Chapter 4, *Basic Declarations and Expressions*. The new file system is discussed in detail in Chapter 16, *File Input/Output*.)

- Constant and reference variables. (Described in Chapter 5, *Arrays, Qualifiers, and Reading Numbers*.)

- Function overloading, `inline` functions, reference parameters, and default parameters. (Read Chapter 9, *Variable Scope and Functions.*)

Starting with Chapter 13, *Simple Classes*, you will begin to learn entirely new concepts. Classes are unique to C++ and are one of the more powerful features of the language.

Font Conventions

The following conventions are used in this book:

Italic
> is used for directories and to emphasize new terms and concepts when they are introduced. Italic is also used to highlight comments in examples.

Bold
> is used for C keywords.

`Constant Width`
> is used for programs and the elements of a program and in examples to show the contents of files or the output from commands. A reference in text to a word or item used in an example or code fragment is also shown in constant width font.

`Constant Bold`
> is used in examples to show commands or other text that should be typed literally by the user. (For example, **`rm foo`** means to type "rm foo" exactly as it appears in the text or the example.)

`Constant Italic`
> is used in examples to show variables for which a context-specific substitution should be made. (The variable *`filename`*, for example, would be replaced by some actual filename.)

Quotes
> are used to identify system messages or code fragments in explanatory text.

%
> is the UNIX C shell prompt.

$
> is the UNIX Bourne shell or Korn shell prompt.

#
> is the UNIX superuser prompt (either Bourne or C shell). We usually use this for examples that should be executed only by root.

[ ]

> surround optional values in a description of program syntax. (The brackets themselves should never by typed.)

. . .

> stands for text (usually computer output) that's been omitted for clarity or to save space.

The notation CTRL-X or ^X indicates use of *control* characters. It means hold down the "control" key while typing the character "x". We denote other keys similarly (e.g., RETURN indicates a carriage return).

All examples of command lines are followed by a RETURN unless otherwise indicated.

Obtaining Source Code

You can obtain the source code for the programs presented in this book from O'Reilly & Associates through their Internet server.

The example programs in this book are available electronically in a number of ways: by FTP, Ftpmail, BITFTP, and UUCP. The cheapest, fastest, and easiest ways are listed first. If you read from the top down, the first one that works for you is probably the best. Use FTP if you are directly on the Internet. Use Ftpmail if you are not on the Internet, but can send and receive electronic mail to Internet sites (this includes CompuServe users). Use BITFTP if you send electronic mail via BITNET. Use UUCP if none of the above works.

FTP

To use FTP, you need a machine with direct access to the Internet. A sample session is shown, with what you should type in **boldface**.

```
% ftp ftp.uu.net
Connected to ftp.uu.net.
220 FTP server (Version 6.21 Tue Mar 10 22:09:55 EST 1992) ready.
Name (ftp.uu.net:joe): anonymous
331 Guest login ok, send domain style e-mail address as password.
Password: joe@ora.com (use your user name and host here)
230 Guest login ok, access restrictions apply.
ftp> cd /published/oreilly/nutshell/practcpp
250 CWD command successful.
ftp> binary (Very important! You must specify binary transfer for compressed files.)
200 Type set to I.
ftp> get examples.tar.gz
200 PORT command successful.
150 Opening BINARY mode data connection for examples.tar.gz.
226 Transfer complete.
```

```
ftp> quit
221 Goodbye.
%
```

The file is a compressed *tar* archive; extract the files from the archive by typing:

```
% zcat examples.tar.gz | tar xvf -
```

System V systems require the following *tar* command instead:

```
% zcat examples.tar.gz | tar xof -
```

If *zcat* is not available on your system, use separate *uncompress* and *tar* or *shar* commands.

```
% uncompress examples.tar.gz
% tar xvf examples.tar.gz
```

Ftpmail

Ftpmail is a mail server available to anyone who can send electronic mail to and receive it from Internet sites. This includes any company or service provider that allows email connections to the Internet. Here's how you do it.

You send mail to *ftpmail@online.ora.com*. In the message body, give the FTP commands you want to run. The server will run anonymous FTP for you and mail the files back to you. To get a complete help file, send a message with no subject and the single word "help" in the body.

The following is a sample mail session that should get you the examples. This command sends you a listing of the files in the selected directory and the requested example files. The listing is useful if there's a later version of the examples you're interested in.

```
% mail ftpmail@online.ora.com
Subject:
reply-to janetv@xyz.com      (Where you want files mailed)
open
cd /published/oreilly/nutshell/practcpp
mode binary
uuencode
get examples.tar.gz
quit
.
```

A signature at the end of the message is acceptable as long as it appears after "quit."

BITFTP

BITFTP is a mail server for BITNET users. You send it electronic mail messages requesting files, and it sends you back the files by electronic mail. BITFTP currently serves only users who send it mail from nodes that are directly on BITNET, EARN, or NetNorth. BITFTP is a public service of Princeton University. Here's how it works.

To use BITFTP, send mail containing your ftp commands to BITFTP@PUCC. For a complete help file, send HELP as the message body.

The following is the message body you send to BITFTP:

```
FTP   ftp.uu.net   NETDATA
USER   anonymous
PASS   myname@podunk.edu  Put your Internet email address here (not your BITNET address)
CD /published/oreilly/nutshell/practcpp
DIR
BINARY
GET   examples.tar.gz
QUIT
```

Once you've got the desired file, follow the directions under FTP to extract the files from the archive. Since you are probably not on a UNIX system, you may need to get versions of uudecode, uncompress, atob, and tar for your system. VMS, DOS, and Mac versions are available.

UUCP

UUCP is standard on virtually all UNIX systems and is available for IBM-compatible PCs and Apple Macintoshes. The examples are available by UUCP via modem from UUNET; UUNET's connect-time charges apply.

You can get the examples from UUNET whether you have an account there or not. If you or your company has an account with UUNET, you have a system somewhere with a direct UUCP connection to UUNET. Find that system, and type:

```
uucp uunet\!~/published/oreilly/nutshell/practcpp/examples.tar.gz
        yourhost\!~/yourname/
```

The backslashes can be omitted if you use the Bourne shell (*sh*) instead of *csh*. The file should appear some time later (up to a day or more) in the directory */usr/spool/uucppublic yourname*. If you don't have an account, but would like one so that you can get electronic mail, contact UUNET at 703-204-8000.

It's a good idea to get the file */published/oreilly/ls-lR.Z* as a short test file containing the filenames and sizes of all the files available.

Once you've got the desired file, follow the directions under FTP to extract the files from the archive.

Comments and Questions

Please address comments and questions concerning this book to the publisher:

O'Reilly & Associates, Inc.
103 Morris Street, Suite A
Sebastopol, CA 95472

1-800-998-9938 (in the U.S. or Canada)
1-707-829-0515 (international or local)
1-707-829-0104 (FAX)

Acknowledgments

Thanks to Peg Kovar for her proofreading and editing help. Special thanks to Dale Dougherty for ripping apart my first book and forcing me to put it together correctly. I greatly appreciate the hard work put in by Phil Straite and Gregory Satir. I especially thank all those people who reviewed and edited my book. My thanks also go to the production group at O'Reilly & Associates—Nicole Gipson, project manager and production editor; John Files, Juliette Muellner, and Jane Ellin, production assistants; and Mike Sierra, book design implementor. Finally, special thanks go to all the hard-working programmers out there whose code has taught me so much.

I

The Basics

I

The Basics

1

What Is C++?

> *Profanity is the one language that all*
> *programmers understand.*
>
> —Anonymous

The ability to organize and process information is the key to success in the modern age. Computers are designed to handle and process large amounts of information quickly and efficiently. However, they can't do anything until someone tells them what to do. That's where C++ comes in. C++ is a high-level programming language that allows a software engineer to efficiently communicate with a computer.

C++ is a highly flexible and adaptable language. Since its creation in 1980, it has been used for a wide variety of programs including firmware for micro-controllers, operating systems, applications, and graphics programming. C++ is quickly becoming the programming language of choice. There is a tremendous demand for people who can tell computers what to do, and C++ lets you do so quickly and efficiently.

A Brief History of C++

In 1970 two programmers, Brian Kernighan and Dennis Ritchie, created a new language called C. (The name came about because C was superseded by the old programming language they were using, B.) C was designed with one goal in mind: writing operating systems. The language was extremely simple and flexible and soon was used for many different types of programs. It quickly became one of the most popular programming languages in the world.

C had one major problem, however. It was a procedure-oriented language. This meant that in designing a typical C program, the programmer would start by describing the data and then write procedures to manipulate that data.

Programmers eventually discovered that it made a program clearer and easier to understand if they were able to take a bunch of data and group it together with the operations that worked on that data. Such a grouping is called an *object* or *class*. Designing programs by designing classes is known as *object-oriented design (OOD)*.

In 1980 Bjarne Stroustrup started working on a new language, called "C with Classes." This language improved on C by adding a number of new features, the most important of which was classes. This language was improved, augmented, and finally became C++.

C++ owes its success to the fact that it allows the programmer to organize and process information more effectively than most other languages. Also, it builds on the work already done with the C language. In fact, most C programs can be transformed into C++ programs with little trouble. These programs usually don't use all the new features of C++, but they do work. In this way, C++ allows programmers to build on an existing base of C code.

C++ Organization

C++ is designed as a bridge between the programmer and the raw computer. The idea is to let the programmer organize a program in a way that he or she can easily understand. The compiler then translates the language into something the machine can use.

Computer programs consist of two main parts: data and instructions. The computer imposes little or no organization on these two parts. After all, computers are designed to be as general as possible. The idea is for the programmer to impose his or her own organization on the computer and not the other way around.

The data in a computer is stored as a series of bytes. C++ organizes those bytes into useful data. Data declarations are used by the programmer to describe the information he or she is working with. For example:

```
int total;    // Total number accounts
```

tells C++ that you want to use a section of the computer's memory to store an integer named `total`. You can let the compiler decide what particular bytes of memory to use; that's a minor bookkeeping detail you don't need to worry about.

The variable `total` is a *simple variable*. It can hold only one integer and describe only one total. A series of integers can be organized into an array. Again, C++ will handle the details, imposing that organization on the computer's memory.

```
int balance[100];   // Balance (in cents) for all 100 accounts
```

Finally, there are more complex data types. For example, a rectangle might have a width, a height, a color, and a fill pattern. C++ lets you organize these four attributes into one group called a *structure*.

```
struct rectangle {
    int width;        // Width of rectangle in pixels
    int height;       // Height of rectangle in pixels
    color_type color; // Color of the rectangle
    fill_type fill;   // Fill pattern
};
```

However, data is only one part of a program. You also need instructions. As far as the computer is concerned it knows nothing about the layout of the instructions. It knows only what it's doing for the current instruction and where to get the next instruction.

C++ is a high-level language. It lets you write a high-level statement such as:

```
area = (base * height) / 2.0;     // Compute area of triangle
```

The compiler translates this statement into a series of cryptic machine instructions. This sort of statement is called an *assignment statement*. It is used to compute and store the value of an arithmetic expression.

You can also use *control statements* to control the order of processing. Statements such as the `if` and `switch` statements enable the computer to make simple decisions. Statements can be repeated by using looping statements such as `while` and `for`.

Groups of statements can be wrapped to form *functions*. Thus you only need to write a general-purpose function to draw a rectangle once and then you can reuse that function whenever you want to draw a new rectangle. C++ provides a rich set of *standard functions* that perform common functions such as searching, sorting, input, and output.

A set of related functions can be grouped together to form a *module*, and modules are linked to form *programs*.

One of the major goals of the C++ language is to organize instructions into reusable components. After all, you can write programs much faster if you "borrow" most of your code from somewhere else. Groups of reusable modules can be combined into a *library*. For example, if you need a sort routine, you can use the standard function `qsort` from the library and link it into your program.

A computer divides the world into data and instructions. For a long time, high-level languages such as C kept that dividing line in place. In C you can define data or write instructions, but you can't combine the two.

One of C++'s major innovations is the idea of combining data and instructions together in a construct called a class or object. Object-oriented programming allows you to group data with the operations that can be performed on that data. This concept is taken one step further in C++ by allowing you to derive new classes from existing ones.

This last feature is extremely powerful. It allows you to build complex classes on top of smaller, simpler ones. It also allows you to define a basic, abstract class and then derive specific classes from it. For example, an abstract class of **shape** might be used to define the shapes **rectangle, triangle**, and **circle**.

Organization is the key to writing good programs. In this book, you know that the table of contents is in the front and the index is in the back, because that's the way books are organized. Organization makes this book easier to use.

The C++ language lets you organize your programs using a simple yet powerful *syntax*. This book goes beyond the C++ syntax and teaches you style rules that enable you to create highly readable and reliable programs. By combining a powerful syntax with a good programming style you can create powerful programs that perform complex and wonderful operations.

How to Learn C++

The only way to learn how to program is to write programs. You'll learn a lot more by writing and *debugging* programs than you ever will by reading this book. This book contains many programming exercises, and you should try to do as many of them as possible. When doing the exercises keep good programming style in mind. Always comment your programs, even if you're doing the exercises only for yourself. Commenting helps you organize your thoughts, and commenting your own programs is good practice for when you go into the "real world."

Don't let yourself be seduced by the idea that, "I'm only writing these programs for myself, so I don't need to comment them." First of all, code that looks obvious to you when you write it can often be confusing and cryptic when you revisit it a week later. Writing comments also helps you organize your ideas. (If you can write out an idea in English, you are halfway to writing it in C++.)

Finally, programs tend to be around far longer than expected. I once wrote a program that was designed to work only on the computer at Caltech. The program was highly system dependent. As I was the only one who would ever use the program, the program would print the following message if I got the command line wrong:

```
?LSTUIT User is a twit
```

A few years later I was a student at Syracuse University. The secretary at the School of Computer Science needed a program that was similar to my Caltech listing program, so I adapted my program for her use. Unfortunately, I had forgotten about my funny little error message.

Imagine how horrified I was when I came into the Computer Science office and was accosted by the chief secretary. This lady had so much power she could make the dean cringe. She looked at me and said, "User is a twit, huh?" Luckily she had a sense of humor, or I might not be here today.

Sprinkled throughout this book are "broken" programs. Spend the time to figure out why they don't work. Often the problem is very subtle, such as a misplaced semicolon or using = instead of ==. These programs let you learn how to spot mistakes in a small program. That way when you make similar mistakes in a big program, and you *will* make mistakes, you will be trained to spot them.

2

The Basics of Program Writing

The first and most important thing of all, at least for writers today, is to strip language clean, to lay it bare down to the bone.

—Ernest Hemingway

Computers are very powerful tools that can store, organize, and process a tremendous amount of information. However, they can't do anything until someone gives them detailed instructions.

Communicating with computers is not easy. They require instructions that are exact and detailed. Wouldn't life be easier if we could write programs in English? Then we could tell the computer, "Add up all my checks and deposits, and then tell me the total," and the machine would balance our checkbooks.

But English is a lousy language when you must write exact instructions. The language is full of ambiguity and imprecision. Grace Hopper, the grand old lady of computing, once commented on the instructions she found on a bottle of shampoo:

Wash
Rinse
Repeat

She tried to follow the directions, but she ran out of shampoo. (Wash-rinse-repeat. Wash-rinse-repeat. Wash-rinse-repeat. . . .)

Of course, we can try to write in precise English. We'd have to be careful and make sure to spell everything out and be sure to include instructions for every contingency. If we worked really hard, we could write precise English instructions, right?

9

As it turns out, there is a group of people who spend their time trying to write precise English. They're called the government, and the documents they write are called government regulations. Unfortunately, in their effort to make the regulations precise, the government also has made the documents almost unreadable. If you've ever read the instruction book that comes with your tax forms, you know what precise English can be like.

Still, even with all the extra verbiage the government puts in, problems can occur. A few years ago California passed a law requiring all motorcycle riders to wear a helmet. Shortly after this law went into effect a cop stopped a guy for not wearing a helmet. The man suggested the police officer take a closer look at the law.

The law had two requirements: 1) that motorcycle riders have an approved crash helmet and 2) that it be firmly strapped on. The cop couldn't give the motorcyclist a ticket because the man did have a helmet firmly strapped on — to his knee.

So English, with all its problems, is out as a computer language. Now, how do we communicate with a computer?

The first computers cost millions of dollars, while at the same time a good programmer cost about $15,000 a year. Programmers were forced to program in a language where all the instructions were reduced to a series of numbers, called *machine language*. This language could be directly input into the computer. A typical machine-language program looks like:

```
1010 1111
0011 0111
0111 0110
.. and so on for several hundred instructions
```

Whereas machines "think" in numbers, people don't. To program these ancient machines, software engineers would write out their programs using a simple language where each word would stand for a single instruction. This was called *assembly language* because the programmers had to manually translate, or assemble, each line into machine code.

A typical program might look like:

```
Program Translation
MOV A,47 1010 1111
ADD A,B 0011 0111
HALT    0111 0110
.. and so on for several hundred instructions
```

This process is illustrated by Figure 2-1.

Translation was a difficult, tedious, exacting task. One software engineer decided this was a perfect job for a computer, so he wrote a program, called an *assembler*, that would do the job automatically.

Assembly Language	Assembly *(Translation)*	Machine Language Program

MOV A,47
ADD A,B
HALT
...
		1010 1111
		0011 0111
		0111 0110

Figure 2-1. Assembling a program

He showed his new creation to his boss and was immediately chewed out: "How dare you even think of using such an expensive machine for a mere 'clerical' task?" Given the cost of an hour of computer time versus the cost of an hour of programmer's time, this was not an unreasonable attitude.

Fortunately, as time passed the cost of programmers went up and the cost of computers went down. So it became more cost-effective to let the programmers write programs in assembly language and then use a program called an assembler to translate the programs into machine language.

Assembly language organized programs in a way that was easier for the programmers to understand. However, the program was more difficult for the machine to use. The program had to be translated before the machine could execute it. This was the start of a trend. Programming languages became more and more convenient for programmers to use and started requiring more and more computer time to translate them into something useful for computers.

Over the years a series of *high-level languages* has been devised. These languages are attempts to let programmers write in something that is easy for them to understand and that is also precise and simple enough for computers to understand.

Early high-level languages were designed to handle specific types of applications. FORTRAN was designed for number crunching; COBOL, for writing business reports; and PASCAL, for student use. (Many of these languages have far outgrown their initial uses. It is rumored that Nicklaus Wirth has said, "If I had known that PASCAL was going to be so successful, I would have been more careful in its design.")

Later on, Brian Kernighan and Dennis Ritchie developed C and Bjarne Stroustrup turned it into C++.

Programs from Conception to Execution

C++ programs are written in a high-level language using letters, numbers, and the other symbols you find on a computer keyboard. Computers actually execute a very *low-level language* called *machine code* (a series of numbers). So, before a program can be used, it must undergo several transformations.

Programs start out as an idea in a programmer's head. He writes down his thoughts in a file, called a *source file* or *source code*, using a *text editor*. This file is transformed by the *compiler* into an *object file*. Next a program called the *linker* takes the object file, combines it with predefined routines from a *standard library*, and produces an *executable program* (a set of machine-language instructions). In the following sections, you'll see how these various forms of the program work together to produce the final program.

Figure 2-2 shows the steps that must be taken to transform a program written in a high-level language into an executable program.

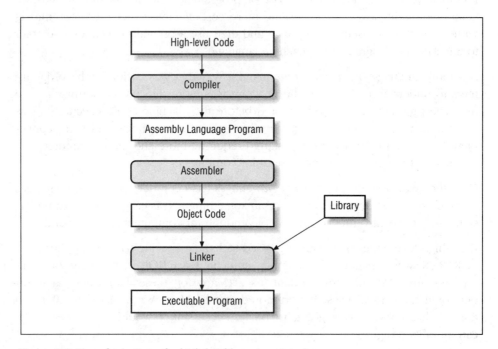

Figure 2-2. Transformation of a high-level language into a program

Wrappers

Fortunately you don't have to run the compiler, assembler, and linker individually. Most C++ compilers use *"wrapper" programs,* which determine which tools need to be run and then run them.

Some programming systems go even farther and provide the developer with an integrated development environment (IDE). The IDE contains an editor, compiler, linker, project manager, debugger, and more in one convenient package. Both Borland and Microsoft provide IDEs with their compilers.

Creating a Real Program

Before you can actually start creating your own programs you need to know how to use the basic programming tools. This section will take you step by step through the process of entering, compiling, and running a simple program.

This section describes how to use two different types of compilers. The first type is the standalone or command-line compiler. This type of compiler is operated in a batch mode from the command line. In other words, you type a command and the compiler turns your source code into an executable program. The other type of compiler is contained in an IDE.

Most UNIX systems use command-line compilers. A few IDE-type compilers are available for UNIX, but they are rare. On the other hand almost all the compilers used with MS-DOS and Windows contain an integrated development environment. For command-line die-hards, these compilers do contain command-line compilers as well.

Creating a Program Using a Command-Line Compiler

In this section you'll go through the step-by-step process needed to create a program using a command-line compiler. Instruction is given for using a generic UNIX compiler, the Free Software Foundation's g++ compiler, Turbo-C++, Borland C++, and Microsoft Visual C++.

However, if you are using a Borland or Microsoft compiler, you might want to skip ahead to the section on using the IDE.

Step 1: Create a Place for Your Program

It is easier to manage things if you create a separate directory for each program you are working on. In this case you'll create a directory called *hello* to hold your hello program.

In UNIX, type:

```
% mkdir hello
% cd hello
```

In MS-DOS, type:

```
C: MKDIR HELLO
C: CD HELLO
```

Step 2: Create the Program

A program starts out as a text file. Example 2-1 shows the hello program in source form.

Example 2-1. Source for the hello.cc program

```
#include <iostream.h>
int main()
{
    cout << "Hello World\n";
    return (0);
}
```

Use your favorite text editor to enter the program. In UNIX your file should be named *hello.cc* and in MS-DOS/Windows the file should be named *HELLO.CPP*.

WARNING

MS-DOS/Windows users should *not* use a word-processing program such as Microsoft Word or WordPerfect to write their programs. Word-processing programs add formatting codes to the file that confuse the compiler. You must use a text editor such as the MS-DOS EDIT program that is capable of editing ASCII files.

Step 3: Run the Compiler

The compiler changes the source file you just created into an executable program. Each compiler has a different command line. The commands for the most popular compilers are listed below.

UNIX CC Compiler (Generic UNIX)

Most UNIX-based compilers follow the same generic standard. The C++ compiler is named CC. To compile our hello program we need the following command:

```
% CC -g -ohello hello.cc
```

The -g option enables debugging. (The compiler adds extra information to the program to make it easier to debug.) The switch -ohello tells the compiler that the program is to be called hello, and the final hello.cc is the name of the source file. See your compiler manual for details on all the possible options. There are several different C++ compilers for UNIX, so your command line may be slightly different.

Free Software Foundation's g++ Compiler

The Free Software Foundation, the GNU people, publishes a number of high-quality programs. (See the glossary entry "Free Software Foundation" for information on how to get their software.) Among their offerings is a C++ compiler called **g++**.

To compile a program using the g++ compiler, use the following command line:

```
% g++ -g -Wall -ohello hello.cc
```

The additional switch **-Wall** turns on all the warnings.

Borland's Turbo C++ in MS-DOS

Borland International makes a low-cost MS-DOS C++ compiler called Turbo-C++. This compiler is ideal for learning. The command line for Turbo-C++ is:

```
C:> tcc -ml -v -N -P -w -ehello hello.cpp
```

The **-ml** tells Turbo-C++ to use the large memory model. (This PC has a large number of different memory models that can be used when creating programs. This book discusses none of them. Instead we take the attitude, "Use large and don't worry about it until you become an expert programmer.")

The **-v** switch tells Turbo-C++ to put debugging information in the program. Warnings are turned on by **-w**; stack checking by **-N**. The compiler will actually compile both C and C++. We force a C++ compile using the **-P** switch. Finally, **-ehello** tells Turbo-C++ to create a program named **hello**, and **hello.cpp** is the name of the source file. See the Turbo-C++ reference manual for a complete list of options.

Borland C++ in MS-DOS and Windows

In addition to Turbo-C++, Borland International also makes a full-featured, professional compiler for MS-DOS/Windows called Borland C++. Its command line is:

```
C:> bcc -ml -v -N -P -w -ehello hello.cpp
```

The command-line options are the same for both Turbo-C++ and Borland C++.

Microsoft Visual C++

Microsoft Visual C++ is another C++ compiler for MS-DOS/Windows. It is not as robust or full featured as its Borland counterpart, but it will compile most of the programs in this book. (Version 1.5 fails to handle templates and exceptions.)

To compile, use the following command line:

```
C:> cl /AL /Zi /W1 hello.cpp
```

The /AL option tells the program to use the large memory model. Debugging is turned on with the /Zi option and warnings with the /Wl option.

Step 4: Execute the Program

Now, when you run the program by typing, for example:

```
hello
```

at the UNIX or MS-DOS prompt, the message:

```
Hello World
```

will appear on the screen.

Creating a Program Using an Integrated Development Environment

Integrated development environments provide a one-stop shop when it comes to programming. They take a compiler, editor, and debugger and wrap them into one neat package for the programmer.

Step 1: Create a Place for Your Program

It is easier to manage things if you create a separate directory for each program you are working on. In this case you'll create a directory called HELLO to hold your hello program.

In MS-DOS, type:

```
C: MKDIR HELLO
C: CD HELLO
```

Step 2: Enter, Compile, and Run Your Program

Each IDE is a little different, so we've included separate instructions for each one.

Turbo-C++

1. Start the Turbo-C++ IDE with the command:

   ```
   C: TC
   ```

2. Use the Options|Compiler|Code Generation command to pull up the Code Generation dialog box as seen in Figure 2-3. Change the memory model to large.

3. Use the Options|Compiler|Entry/Exit command to turn stack checking on, as shown in Figure 2-4.

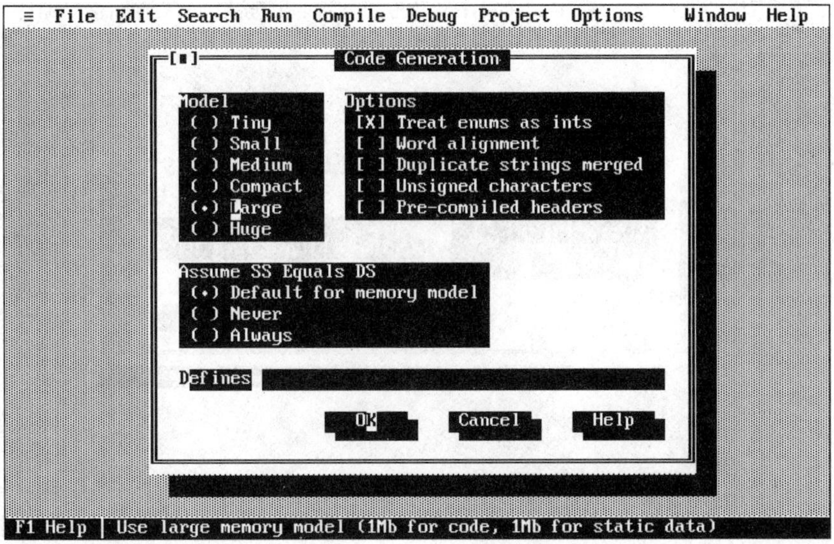

Figure 2-3. Code Generation dialog box

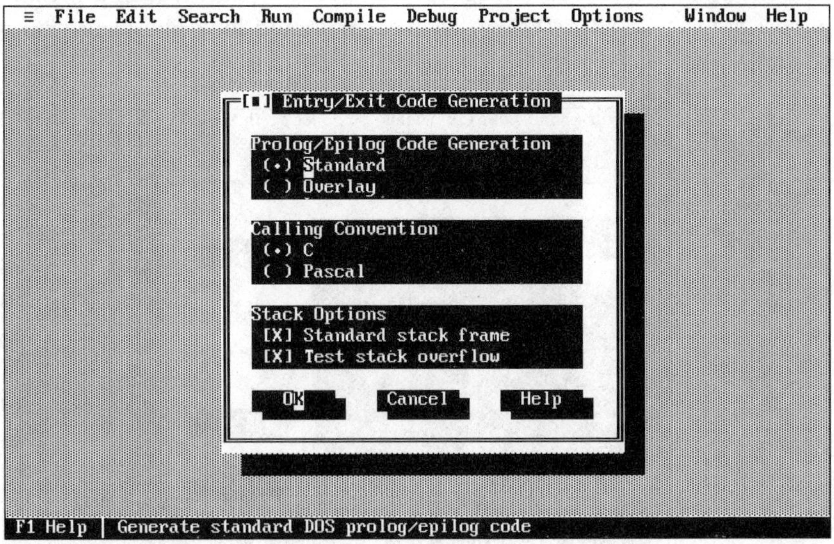

Figure 2-4. Entry/Exit Code Generation dialog box

4. Use the Options|Compiler|Messages|Display command to bring up the Compiler Messages dialog box as seen in Figure 2-5. Select All to display all the warning messages.

5. Use the Options|Save command to save all the options you've used so far.

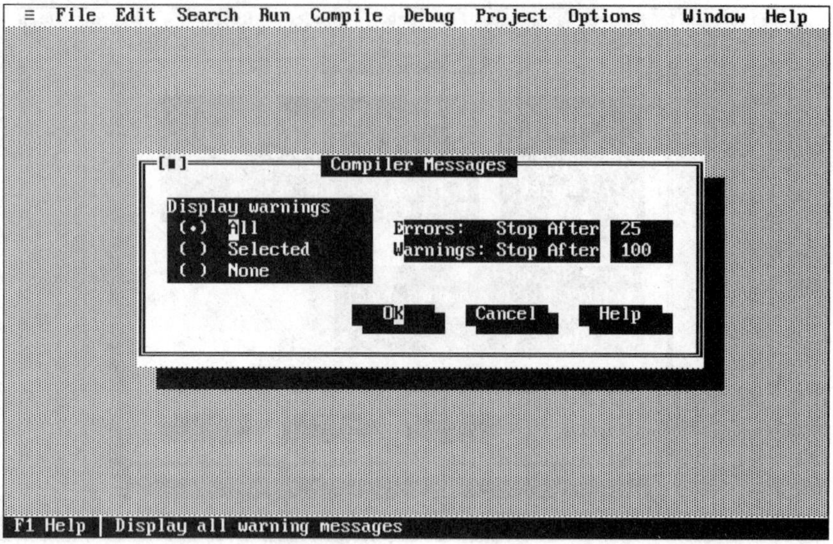

```
≡   File   Edit   Search   Run   Compile   Debug   Project   Options      Window   Help




         ┌─[■]─────────────── Compiler Messages ──────────────┐
         │                                                    │
         │ Display warnings                                   │
         │ (•) All            Errors:    Stop After  25        │
         │ ( ) Selected       Warnings:  Stop After  100       │
         │ ( ) None                                           │
         │                                                    │
         │              ┌───────┐  ┌────────┐  ┌──────┐        │
         │              │  OK   │  │ Cancel │  │ Help │        │
         │              └───────┘  └────────┘  └──────┘        │
         │                                                    │
         └────────────────────────────────────────────────────┘




 F1 Help │ Display all warning messages
```

Figure 2-5. Compiler Messages dialog box

6. Use the Open Project File dialog box to select a project file. In this case your project file is called *HELLO.PRJ*. The screen should look like Figure 2-6 when you're finished.

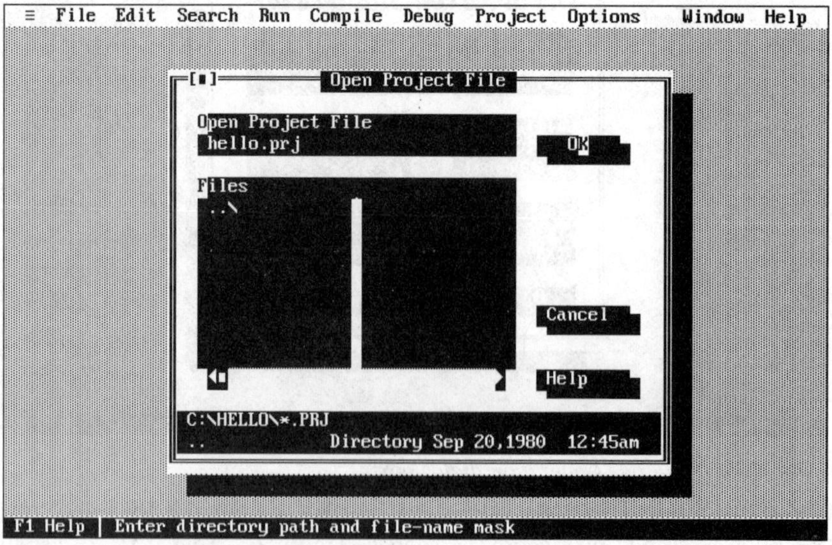

```
≡   File   Edit   Search   Run   Compile   Debug   Project   Options      Window   Help



         ┌─[■]─────────────── Open Project File ──────────────┐
         │                                                    │
         │ Open Project File                                  │
         │ hello.prj                      ┌──────┐            │
         │                                │  OK  │            │
         │ Files                          └──────┘            │
         │ ..\                                                │
         │                                                    │
         │                                                    │
         │                                ┌────────┐          │
         │                                │ Cancel │          │
         │                                └────────┘          │
         │                                ┌──────┐            │
         │                                │ Help │            │
         │ ◄                           ►  └──────┘            │
         │ C:\HELLO\*.PRJ                                      │
         │ ..          Directory Sep 20,1980   12:45am         │
         └────────────────────────────────────────────────────┘



 F1 Help │ Enter directory path and file-name mask
```

Figure 2-6. Open Project File dialog box

7. Press the Insert key to add a file to the project. The file you want to add is *HELLO.CPP* as seen in Figure 2-7.

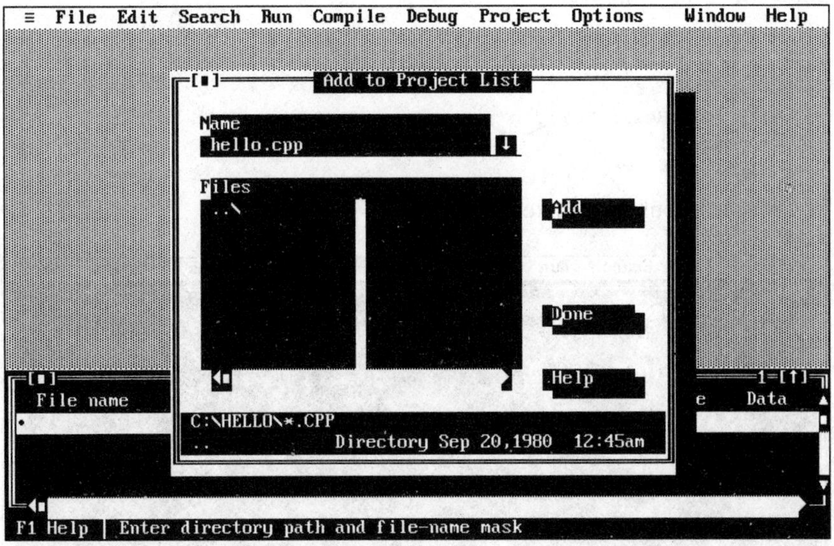

Figure 2-7. Add to Project List dialog box

8. Press ESC to get out of the "add file" cycle.

9. Press the up-arrow key to go up one line. The line with *hello.cpp* should now be highlighted as seen in Figure 2-8.

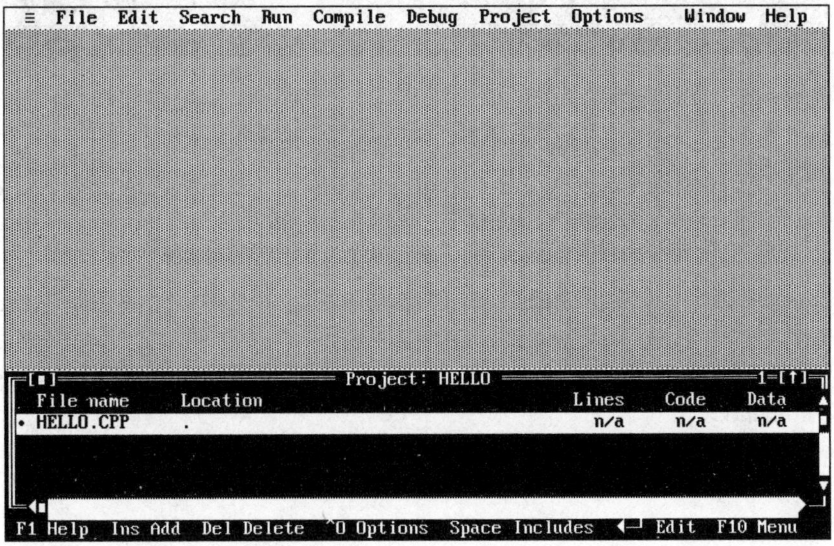

Figure 2-8. "Hello" project

10. Press Return to edit this file.

11. Enter the following code.

```
#include <iostream.h>
int main()
{
    cout << "Hello World\n";
    return (0);
}
```

The results should look like Figure 2-9.

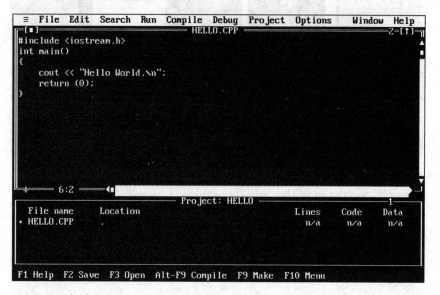

Figure 2-9. Finished project

12. Use the Run I Run command to execute the program.

13. After the program runs, control returns to the IDE. This means that you can't see what your program output. To see the results of the program you must switch to the user screen using the command Window I User.

Pressing any key will return you to the IDE. Figure 2-10 shows the output of the program.

14. When you are finished you can save your program with the File I Save command.

15. To exit the IDE use the File I Quit command.

Figure 2-10. User screen

Borland C++

1. Create a directory called HELLO to hold the files for our hello program. You can create a directory using the Windows' File Manager Program or by typing the following command at the MS-DOS prompt:

   `mkdir \HELLO`

2. From Windows, double-click on the Borland C++ icon to start the IDE. The program begins execution and displays a blank workspace as seen in Figure 2-11.

3. Select the Project|New Project item to create a project for our program. Fill in the "Project Path and Name:" blank with *c:\hello\hello.ide*. For the Target Type select EasyWin[.exe]. The Target Model is set to Large. The results are shown in Figure 2-12.

4. Click on the Advanced button to bring up the Advanced Options dialog. Clear the .rc and .def items as shown in Figure 2-13.

5. Click on OK to return to the New Target dialog.

6. Press `Alt-F10` to bring up node sub-menu shown in Figure 2-14.

7. Select Edit Node Attributes to bring up the dialog shown in Figure 2-15. In the Style Sheet blank, select the item "Debug Info and Diagnostics." Click on OK to return to the main window.

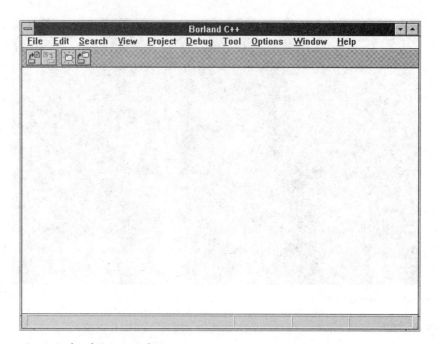

Figure 2-11. Borland C++ initial screen

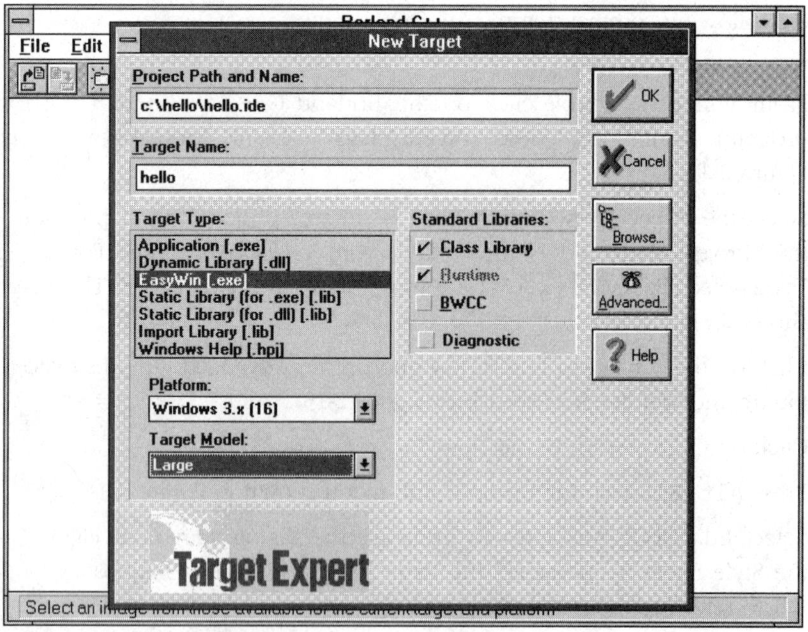

Figure 2-12. New Target dialog box

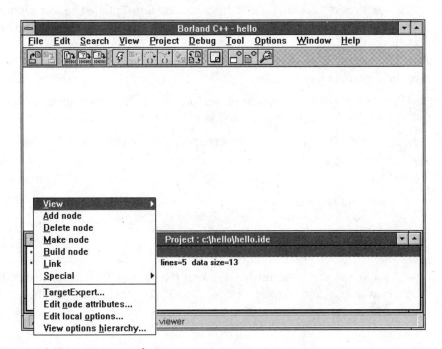

Figure 2-13. Advanced Options dialog box

Figure 2-14. Target Options sub-menu

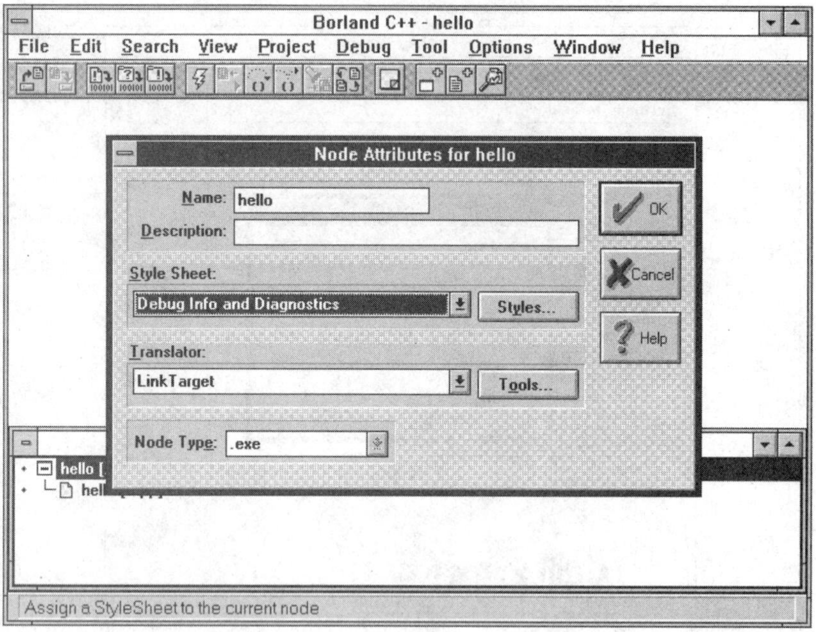

Figure 2-15. Node Attributes dialog box

8. Go to the Project Options dialog by selecting the Options|Project Options item. Go down to the Compiler item and click on the "+" to expand the options.

   Turn on the Test stack overflow option shown in Figure 2-16. Click on OK to save these options.

9. Click on OK to return to the main window. Press the down arrow to select the hello[.cpp] item in the project (see in Figure 2-17).

10. Press Return to start editing the file *hello.cpp*. Type in the following code:

```
#include <iostream.h>
int main()
{
    cout << "Hello World\n";
    return (0);
}
```

When you have finished, your screen will look like Figure 2-18.

11. Compile and run the program by selecting the Debug|Run menu item. The program will run and display "Hello World" in a window, as shown in Figure 2-19.

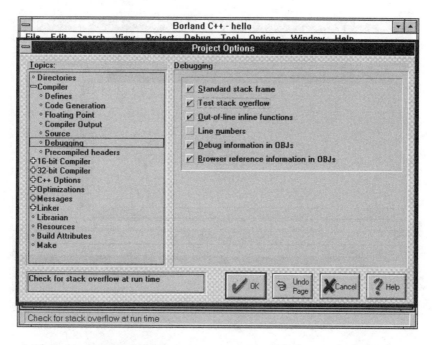

Figure 2-16. Project Options dialog box

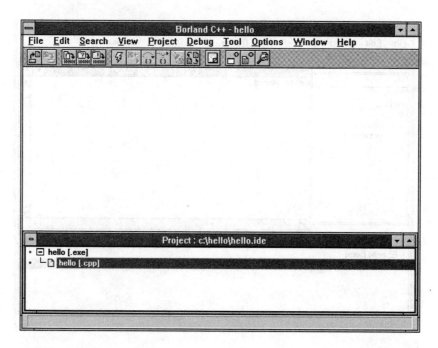

Figure 2-17. Hello Project

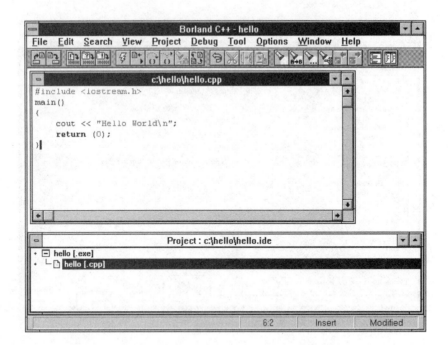

Figure 2-18. "Hello World" program

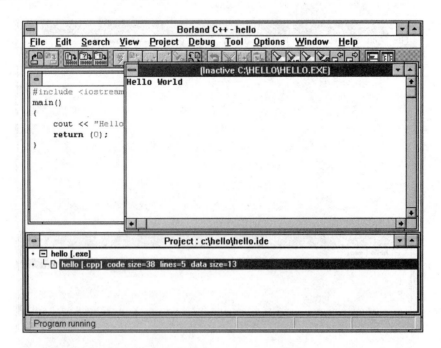

Figure 2-19. "Hello World" after execution

Microsoft Visual C++

1. Create a directory called HELLO to hold the files for our hello program. You can create a directory using the Windows File Manager Program or by typing the following command at the MS-DOS prompt:

```
mkdir \HELLO
```

2. From Windows, double-click on the Visual C++ icon to start the IDE. A blank workspace will be displayed as shown in Figure 2-20.

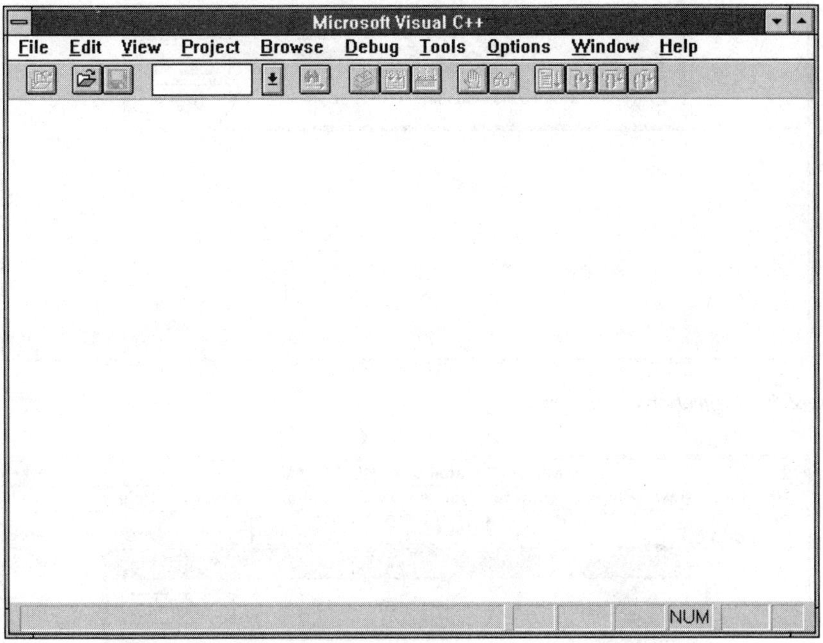

Figure 2-20. Microsoft Visual C++ initial screen

3. Click on Project|New to bring up the New Project dialog shown in Figure 2-21.

   Fill in the Project Name blank with *hello**hello.mak*. Change the Project Type to QuickWin application [.EXE].

4. Visual C++ goes to the Edit dialog to allow you to name the source files in this project (see Figure 2-22). In this case we have only file *hello.cpp*. Click on Add to enter the name in the project and then click on Close to tell Visual C++ that there are no more files in the program.

5. Select Options|Project Options to bring up the Project Options dialog shown in Figure 2-23.

   Click on the Compiler button to change the compiler options.

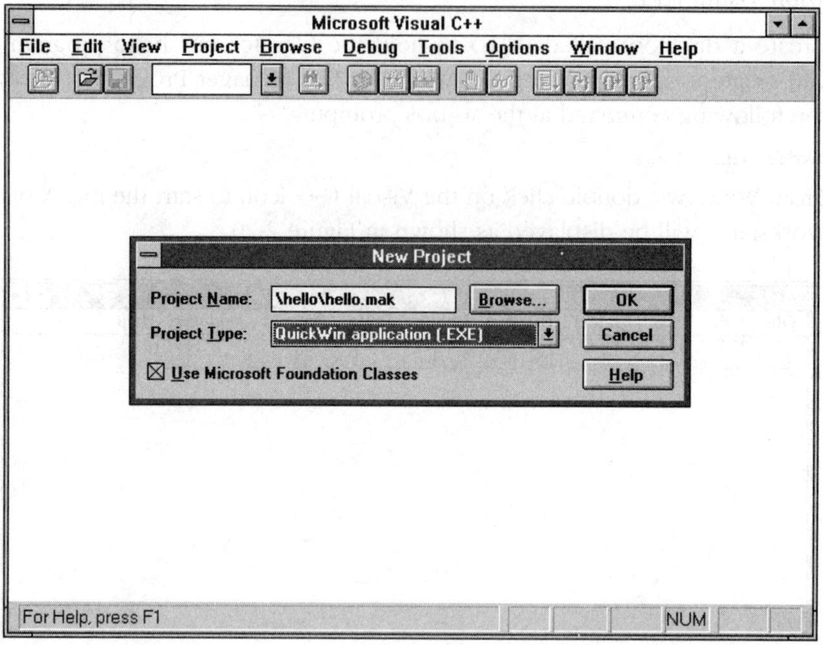

Figure 2-21. Project create screen

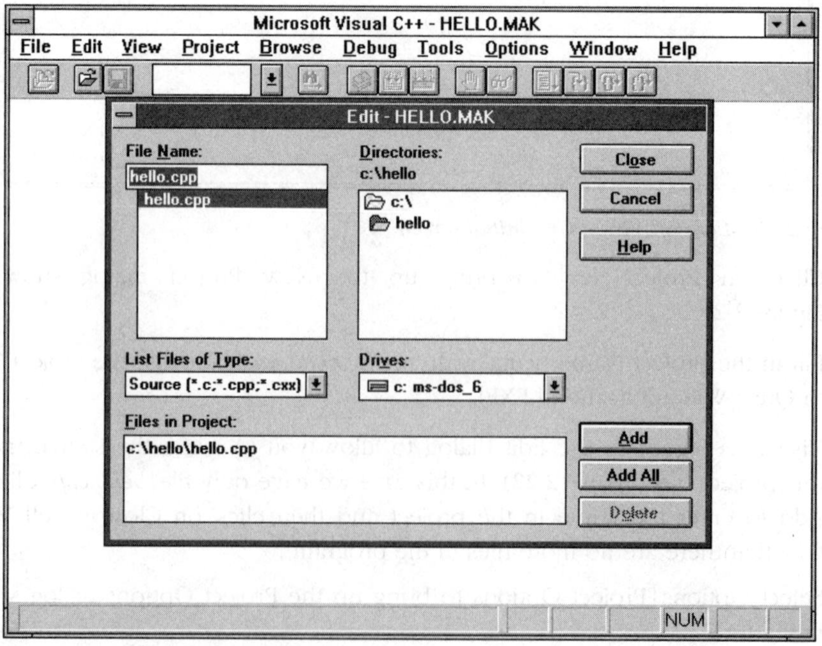

Figure 2-22. Project edit dialog box

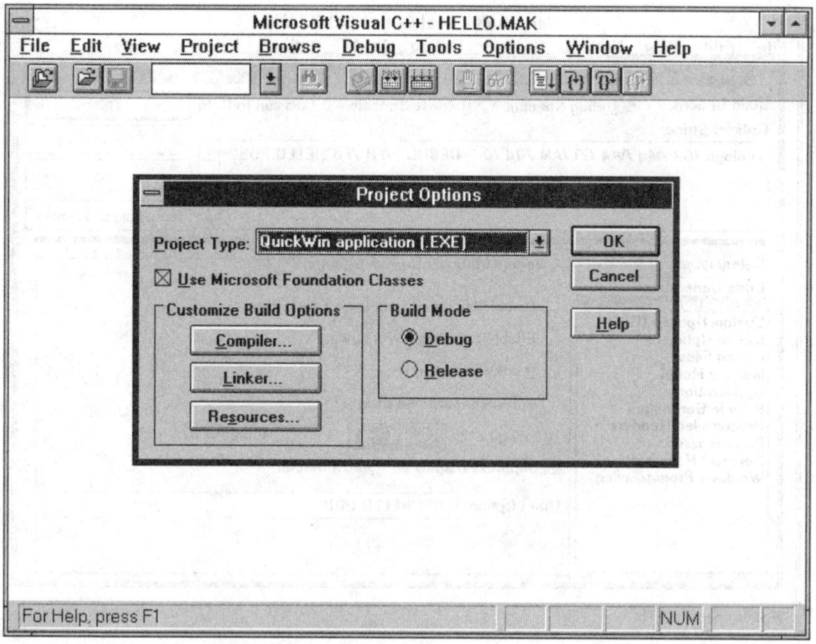

Figure 2-23. Project Options dialog box

6. Go down to the Custom Options item in the Category and change the warning level to 4 as shown in Figure 2-24.

7. Change to the Memory Model category and change the memory model to large (see Figure 2-25).

8. Close the dialog by clicking on the OK button. This brings you back to the Project Options dialog. Click on OK to dismiss this dialog as well.

9. Select "File I New" to start a new program file. Type in the following lines:

```
#include <iostream.h>
int main()
{
    cout << "Hello World\n";
    return (0);
}
```

Your results should look like Figure 2-26.

10. Use the File I Save As menu item to save the file under the name *hello.cpp*.

11. Use the Project I Build command to compile the program. The compiler will output messages as it builds. When it is finished your screen should look like Figure 2-27.

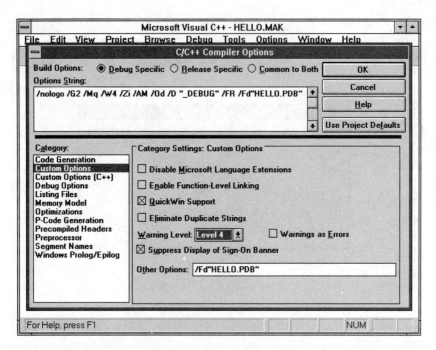

Figure 2-24. Compiler Options dialog box

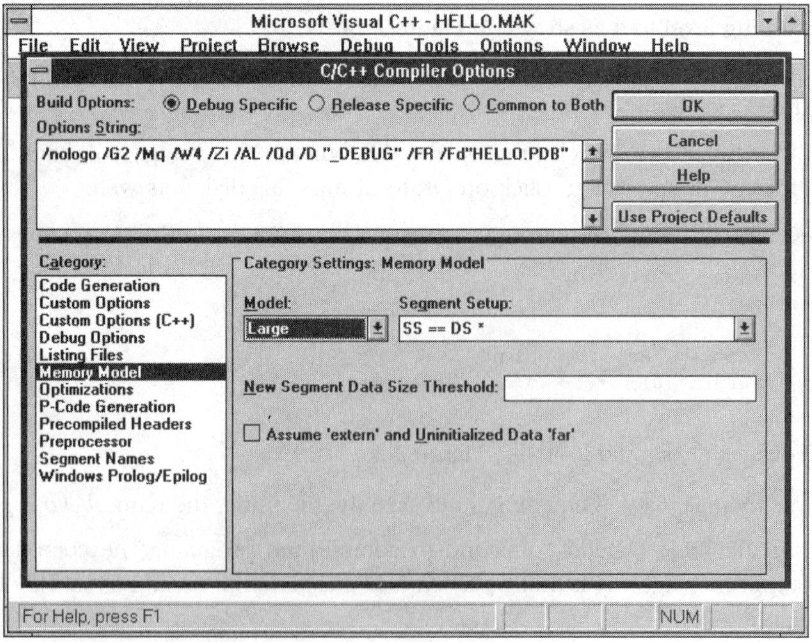

Figure 2-25. Memory Model options

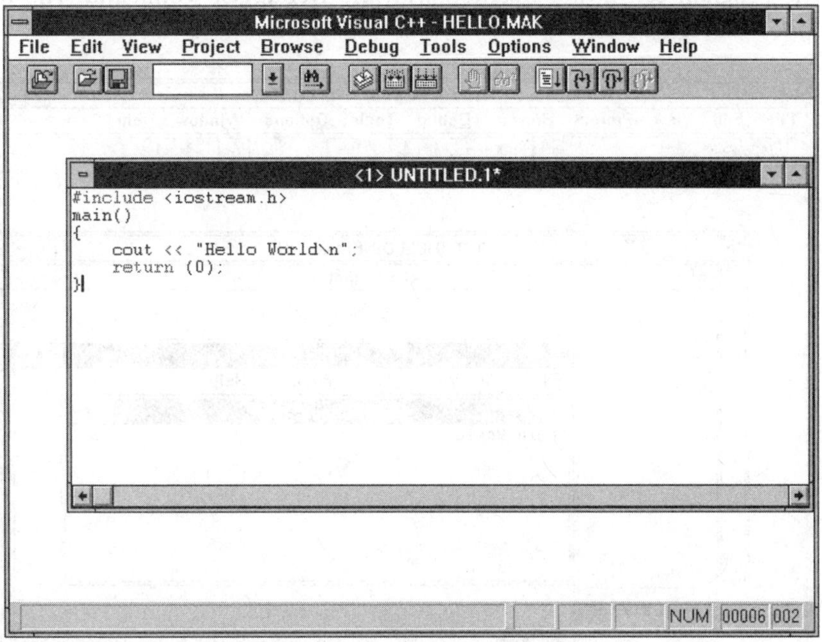

Figure 2-26. Visual C++ with "Hello World" entered

Figure 2-27. Visual C++ build screen

12. The program can now be started with the Debug | Go command. The results appear in Figure 2-28.

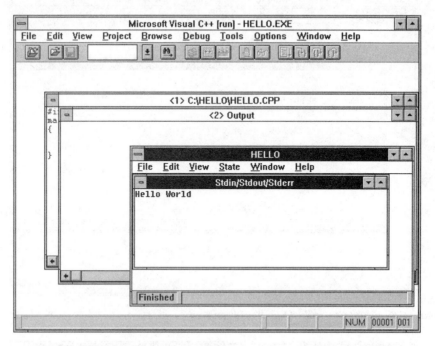

Figure 2-28. "Hello World" results

Getting Help in UNIX

Most UNIX systems have an online documentation system called the "man pages." These can be accessed with the **man** command. (UNIX uses **man** as an abbreviation for "manual.") To get information about a particular subject, use the command:

```
man subject
```

For example, to find out about the classes defined in the **iostream** package, you would type:

```
man iostream
```

The command also has a keyword search mode:

```
man -k keyword
```

To determine the name of every **man** page with the word "output" in its title, use the command:

```
man -k output
```

Getting Help in an Integrated Development Environment

Integrated development environments such as Turbo-C++, Borland C++, and Microsoft C++ have a Help menu item. This item activates a hypertext-based Help system.

Programming Exercises

Exercise 2-1: On your computer, type in the `hello` program and execute it.

Exercise 2-2: Take several programming examples from any source, enter them into the computer, and run them.

3

Style

There is no programming language, no matter how structured, that will prevent programmers from writing bad programs.

—L. Flon

It is the nobility of their style which will make our writers of 1840 unreadable forty years from now.

—Stendhal

This chapter discusses how to use good programming style to create a simple, easy-to-read program. It may seem backward to discuss style before you know how to program, but style is the most important part of programming. Style is what separates the gems from the junk. It is what separates the programming artist from the butcher. You must learn good programming style first, before typing in your first line of code, so everything you write will be of the highest quality.

Contrary to popular belief, programmers do not spend most of their time writing programs. Far more time is spent maintaining, upgrading, and debugging existing code than is ever spent on creating new work. The amount of time spent on maintenance is skyrocketing. From 1980 to 1990 the average number of lines in a typical application went from 23,000 to 1.2 million. The average system age has gone from 4.75 to 9.4 years.

To make matters worse, 74% of the managers surveyed at the 1990 Annual Meeting and Conference of the Software Maintenance Association reported that they "have systems in their department that have to be maintained by specific individuals because no one else understands them."

Most software is built on existing software. I recently completed coding for 12 new programs. Only one of these was created from scratch; the other 11 are adaptations of existing programs.

Programmers believe that the purpose of a program is only to present the computer with a compact set of instructions. This is not true. Programs written only for the machine have two problems:

- They are difficult to correct because sometimes even the author does not understand them.

- Modifications and upgrades are difficult to make because the maintenance programmer must spend a considerable amount of time figuring out what the program does from its code.

Comments

Ideally, a program serves two purposes: First, it presents the computer with a set of instructions and, second, it provides the programmer with a clear, easy-to-read description of what the program does.

Example 2-1 contains a glaring error. It is an error that many programmers still make and one that causes more trouble than any other problem. *The program contains no comments.*

A working but uncommented program is a time bomb waiting to explode. Sooner or later someone will have to modify or upgrade the program, and the lack of comments will make the job ten times more difficult. A well-commented, simple program is a work of art. Learning how to comment is as important as learning how to code properly.

C++ has two flavors of comments. The first type starts with /* and ends with */. This type of comment can span multiple lines as shown:

```
/* This is a single-line comment. */
/*
 * This is a multiline comment.
 */
```

The other form of comment begins with // and goes to the end of the line:

```
// This is another form of comment.
// The // must begin each line that is to be a comment.
```

The advantage of the /* */ comment style is that you can easily span multiple lines, whereas with the // style you have to keep putting the // on each line. The disadvantage of /* */ is that forgetting a */ can really screw up your code.

Which flavor should you use? Whichever one makes your program as clear and as easy to read as possible. Mostly, it's a matter of taste. In this book we use the /* */ style comments for big, multiline comments while the // style is reserved for comments that take up only a single line.

Whatever comment style you decide to use, you *must* comment your programs. Example 3-1 shows how the "hello world" program looks after comments are added.

Example 3-1. hello2/hello2.cc

```
/********************************************************
 * hello -- program to print out "Hello World".        *
 *      Not an especially earth-shattering program.    *
 *                                                      *
 * Author: Steve Oualline                               *
 *                                                      *
 * Purpose: Demonstration of a simple program          *
 *                                                      *
 * Usage:                                               *
 *      Run the program and the message appears         *
 ********************************************************/
#include <iostream.h>
main()
{
    // Tell the world hello
    cout << "Hello World\n";
    return (0);
}
```

In this program, the beginning comments are in a box of asterisks (*) called a *comment box*. This is done to emphasize the more important comments, much like bold characters are used for the headings in this book. Less important comments are not boxed. For example:

```
    // Tell the world hello
    cout << "Hello World\n";
```

To write a program, you must have a clear idea of what you are going to do. One of the best ways to organize your thoughts is to write them down in a language that is clear and easy to understand. Once the process has been clearly stated, it can be translated into a computer program.

Understanding what you are doing is the most important part of programming. I once wrote two pages of comments describing a complex graphics algorithm. The comments were revised twice before I even started coding. The actual instructions

Poor Person's Typesetting

In typesetting you can use font style and size, **bold**, and *italic* to make different parts of your text stand out. In programming, you are limited to a single, monospaced font. However, people have come up with ingenious ways to get around the limitations of the typeface.

Some of the various commenting tricks are:

```
/*********************************************************
 ********************************************************
 ******** WARNING: This is an example of a        ******
 ********    warning message that grabs the       *******
 ********    attention of the programmer.         *******
 ********************************************************
 ********************************************************/

//------------> Another, less important warning<--------

//>>>>>>>>>>>  Major section header  <<<<<<<<<<<<<<<<

/*********************************************************
 * We use boxed comments in this book to denote the    *
 * beginning of a section or program                   *
 ********************************************************/

/*-----------------------------------------------------*\
 * This is another way of drawing boxes                *
\*-----------------------------------------------------*/

/*
 * This is the beginning of a section
 * ^^^^ ^^ ^^^ ^^^^^^^^ ^^ ^ ^^^^^^^
 *
 * In the paragraph that follows we explain what
 * the section does and how it works.
 */

/*
 * A medium-level comment explaining the next
 * dozen or so lines of code.  Even though we don't have
 * the bold typeface we can **emphasize** words.
 */

// A simple comment explaining the next line
```

took only half a page. Because I had organized my thoughts well (and was lucky), the program worked the first time.

Your program should read like an essay. It should be as clear and easy to understand as possible. Good programming style comes from experience and practice. The style described in the following pages is the result of many years of programming experience. It can be used as a starting point for developing your own style. These are not rules, but only suggestions. The only rules are: Make your program as *clear, concise,* and *simple* as possible.

At the beginning of the program is a comment block that contains information about the program. Boxing the comments makes them stand out. The list that follows contains some of the sections that should be included at the beginning of your program. Not all programs will need all sections, so use only those that apply.

Heading

The first comment should contain the name of the program. Also include a short description of what it does. You may have the most amazing program, one that slices, dices, and solves all the world's problems, but it is useless if no one knows what it does.

Author

You've gone to a lot of trouble to create this program. Take credit for it. Also, if someone else must later modify the program, he or she can come to you for information and help.

Purpose

Why did you write this program? What does it do?

Usage

In this section give a short explanation of how to run the program. In an ideal world, every program comes with a set of documents describing how to use it. The world is not ideal. Oualline's law of documentation states: 90% of the time the documentation is lost. Out of the remaining 10%, 9% of the time the revision of the documentation is different from the revision of the program and therefore completely useless. The 1% of the time you actually have documentation and the correct revision of the documentation, the documentation will be written in Japanese.

To avoid falling prey to Oualline's law of documentation, put the documentation in the program.

References

Creative copying is a legitimate form of programming (if you don't break the copyright laws in the process). In the real world, it doesn't matter how you get a working program, as long as you get it; but, give credit where credit is due. In this section you should reference the original author of any work you copied.

File formats

   List the files that your program reads or writes and a short description of their
   format.

Restrictions

   List any limits or restrictions that apply to the program, such as: *The data file
   must be correctly formatted; the program does not check for input errors.*

Revision history

   This section contains a list indicating who modified the program and when
   and what changes have been made. Many computers have a source control
   system (UNIX: RCS and SCCS; MS-DOS/Windows: MKS-RCS, PCVS) that will
   keep track of this information for you.

Error handling

   If the program detects an error, what does it do with the error?

Notes

   Include special comments or other information that has not already been
   covered.

The format of your beginning comments will depend on what is needed for the
environment in which you are programming. For example, if you are a student,
the instructor may ask you to include in the program heading the assignment
number, your name, student identification number, and other information. In
industry, a project number or part number might be included.

Comments should explain everything the programmer needs to know about the
program, but no more. It is possible to overcomment a program. (This is rare, but
it does happen.) When deciding on the format for your heading comments, make
sure there is a reason for everything you include.

Inserting Comments—The Easy Way

If you are using the UNIX editor vi, put the following in your *.exrc* file to make
it easier to construct boxes.

```
:abbr #b /**********************************************
:abbr #e **********************************************/
```

These two lines define vi abbreviations #b and #e, so that typing #b<re-
turn> at the beginning of a block will cause the string:

```
/**************************************************
```

to appear (for beginning a comment box). Typing #e<return> will end a
box. The number of stars was carefully selected so the end of the box is aligned
on a tab stop.

C++ Code

The actual code for your program consists of two parts: variables and executable instructions. Variables are used to hold the data used by your program. Executable instructions tell the computer what to do with the data. C++ classes are a combination of data and the instructions that work on the data. They provide a convenient way of packaging both instructions and data.

A variable is a place in the computer's memory for storing a value. C++ identifies that place by the variable name. Names can be any length and should be chosen so their meaning is clear. (Actually, a limit does exist, but it is so large that you probably will never encounter it.) Every variable in C++ must be declared. (Variable declarations are discussed in Chapter 9, *Variable Scope and Functions*.) The following declaration tells C++ that you are going to use three integer (`int`) variables named `p`, `q`, and `r`:

```
int p,q,r;
```

But what are these variables for? The reader has no idea. They could represent the number of angels on the head of a pin, or the location and acceleration of a plasma bolt in a game of Space Invaders. Avoid abbreviations. Exs. abb. are diff. to rd. and hd. to ustnd. (Excess abbreviations are difficult to read and hard to understand.)

Now consider another declaration:

```
int account_number;
int balance_owed;
```

Now we know that we are dealing with an accounting program, but we could still use some more information. For example, is the `balance_owed` in dollars or cents? It would be much better if we added a comment after each declaration explaining what we are doing.

```
int account_number;    // Index for account table
int balance_owed;      // Total owed us (in pennies)
```

By putting a comment after each declaration we, in effect, create a mini-dictionary where we define the meaning of each variable name. Since the definition of each variable is in a known place, it's easy to look up the meaning of a name. (Programming tools, such as editors, cross-referencers, and `grep`, can also help you quickly find a variable's definition.)

Units are very important. I was once asked to modify a program that converted plot data files from one format to another. Many different units of length were used throughout the program and none of the variable declarations was commented. I tried very hard to figure out what was going on, but it was impossible to determine what units were being used in the program. Finally, I gave up and put the following comment in the program:

```
/**********************************************************
 * Note: I have no idea what the input units are, nor     *
 *       do I have any idea what the output units are,     *
 *       but I have discovered that if I divide  by 3      *
 *       the plots look about the right size.              *
 **********************************************************/
```

One problem many beginning programmers have is that they describe the code, not the variable. For example:

```
int top_limit;      // Top limit is an integer [bad comment]
```

It's obvious from the code that `top_limit` is an integer. What I want to know is what is `top_limit`. Tell me.

```
int top_limit;      // Number of items we can load before losing data
```

You should take every opportunity to make sure your program is clear and easy to understand. Do not be clever. Cleverness makes for unreadable and unmaintainable programs. Programs, by their nature, are extremely complex. Anything you can to do to cut down on this complexity will make your programs better. Consider the following code, written by a very clever programmer.

```
while ('\n' != *p++ = *q++);
```

It is almost impossible for the reader to tell at a glance what this mess does. Properly written this would be:

```
while (1) {
    *destination_ptr = *source_ptr;
    ++destination_ptr;
    ++source_ptr;
    if (*(destination_ptr-1) == '\n')
        break;  // exit the loop if done
}
```

Although the second version is longer, it is much clearer and easier to understand. Even a novice programmer who does not know C++ well can tell that this program has something to do with moving data from a source to a destination.

The computer doesn't care which version is used. A good compiler will generate the same machine code for both versions. It is the programmer who benefits from the verbose code.

Naming Style

Names can contain both uppercase and lowercase letters. In this book we use all lowercase names for variables (e.g., `source_ptr`, `current_index`). All uppercase is reserved for constants (e.g., **MAX_ITEMS**, **SCREEN_WIDTH**). This convention is the classic convention followed by most C and C++ programs.

Many newer programs use mixed-case names (e.g., **RecordsInFile**). Sometimes they use the capitalization of the first letter to indicate information about the variable. For example, **recordsInFile** might be used to denote a local variable while **RecordsInFile** would denote a global variable. (See Chapter 9, *Variable Scope and Functions*, for information about local and global variables.)

Which naming convention you use is up to you. It is more a matter of religion than of style. However, using a consistent naming style is extremely important. In this book we have chosen the first style, lowercase variable names and uppercase constants, and we use it throughout the book.

Coding Religion

Computer scientists have devised many programming styles. These include structured programming, top-down programming, and goto-less programming. Each of these styles has its own following or cult. I use the term "religion" because people are taught to follow the rules blindly without knowing the reasons behind them. For example, followers of the goto-less cult will never use a goto statement, even when it is natural to do so.

The rules presented in this book are the result of years of programming experience. I have discovered that by following these rules, I can create better programs. You do not have to follow them blindly. If you find a better system, by all means use it. (If it really works, drop me a line. I'd like to use it, too.)

Indentation and Code Format

To make programs easier to understand, most programmers indent their programs. The general rule for a C++ program is to indent one level for each new block or conditional. In Example 3-5 there are three levels of logic, each with its own indentation level. The **while** statement is outermost. The statements inside the **while** are at the next level. The statement inside the **if** (**break**) is at the innermost level.

There are two styles of indentation, and a vast religious war is being waged in the programming community as to which is better. The first is the short form:

```
while (! done) {
    cout << "Processing\n";
    next_entry();
}
```

```
    if (total <= 0) {
        cout << "You owe nothing\n";
        total = 0;
    } else {
        cout << "You owe " << total << " dollars\n";
        all_totals = all_totals + total;
    }
```

In this case, most of the curly braces are put on the same line as the statements. The other style puts the curly braces on lines by themselves:

```
    while (! done)
    {
        cout << "Processing\n";
        next_entry();
    }

    if (total <= 0)
    {
        cout << "You owe nothing\n";
        total = 0;
    }
    else
    {
        cout << "You owe " << total << " dollars\n";
        all_totals = all_totals + total;
    }
```

Both formats are commonly used. You should use the format you feel most comfortable with. This book uses the short form.

The amount of indentation is left to the programmer. Two, four, and eight spaces are common. Studies have shown that a four-space indent makes the most readable code. You can choose any indent size as long as you are consistent.

Clarity

A program should read like a technical paper. It should be organized into sections and paragraphs. Procedures form a natural section boundary. You should organize your code into paragraphs. It is a good idea to begin a paragraph with a topic sentence comment and separate it from other paragraphs by a blank line. For example:

```
    // poor programming practice
    temp = box_x1;
    box_x1 = box_x2;
    box_x2 = temp;
    temp = box_y1;
    box_y1 = box_y2;
    box_y2 = temp;
```

A better version would be:

```
/*
 * Swap the two corners
 */

/* Swap X coordinate */
temp = box_x1;
box_x1 = box_x2;
box_x2 = temp;

/* Swap Y coordinate */
temp = box_y1;
box_y1 = box_y2;
box_y2 = temp;
```

Simplicity

Your program should be simple. Some general rules of thumb are:

- A single function should not be longer than one or two pages. (See Chapter 9, *Variable Scope and Functions.*) If it gets longer, it can probably be split into two simpler functions. This rule comes about because the human mind can hold only so much in short-term memory. Three pages is about the most the human mind can wrap itself around in one sitting.

- Avoid complex logic such as multiple nested `ifs`. The more complex your code, the more indentation levels you will need. About the time you start running into the right margin, you should think about splitting your code into multiple procedures and thus decreasing the level of complexity.

- Did you ever read a sentence, like this one, where the author went on and on, stringing together sentence after sentence with the word "and," and didn't seem to understand the fact that several shorter sentences would do the job much better, and didn't it bother you?

  C++ statements should not go on forever. Long statements should be avoided.If an equation or formula looks like it is going to be longer than one or two lines, you probably should split it into two shorter equations.

- Split large single code files into multiple smaller ones. (See Chapter 23, *Modular Programming*, for more information about programming with multiple files.) In general I like to keep my files smaller than 1,500 lines. That way they aren't too difficult to edit and print.

- When using classes (see Chapter 13, *Simple Classes*), put one class per module.

- Finally, the most important rule: Make your program as simple and easy to understand as possible, even if it means breaking some of the rules. The goal is clarity, and the rules given in this chapter are designed to help you accomplish that goal. If the rules get in the way, get rid of them. I have seen one program with a single statement that spanned more than 20 pages. However, because of the specialized nature of the program, this statement was simple and easy to understand.

Consistency and Organization

Good style is only one element in creating a high-quality program. Consistency is also a factor. This book is organized with the table of contents at the front and the index at the back. Almost every book printed has a similar organization. This consistency makes it easy to look up a word in the index or find a chapter title in the table of contents.

Unfortunately the programming community has developed a variety of coding styles. Each has its own advantages and disadvantages. The trick to efficient programming in a group is to pick one style and then use it consistently. That way you can avoid the problems and confusion that arise when programs written in different styles are combined.

Good style is nice, but consistency is better.

Further Reading

In this chapter we have touched only the basics of style. Later chapters expand on this base, adding new stylistic elements as you learn new elements of the language.

Summary

A program should be concise and easy to read. It must serve as a set of computer instructions, but also as a reference work describing the algorithms and data used inside it. Everything should be documented with comments. Comments serve two purposes. First, they describe your program to any maintenance programmer who has to fix it and, second, comments help you remember what you did.

Class discussion 1: Create a style sheet for class assignments. Discuss what comments should go into the programs and why.

Class discussion 2: Analyze the style of an existing program. Is the program written in a manner that is clear and easy to understand? What can be done to improve the style of the program?

Exercise 3-1: Go through all the other programming exercises in this book and write comment blocks for them. This will serve several purposes. First, it will give you practice commenting. Second, it will short-circuit the old programmer's excuse, "But I didn't have time to put in the comments."

4

Basic Declarations and Expressions

A journey of a thousand miles must begin with a single step.

—Lao-zi

If carpenters made buildings the way programmers make programs, the first woodpecker to come along would destroy all of civilization.

—Anonymous

The Elements of a Program

If you are going to construct a building, you need two things: the bricks and a blueprint that tells you how to put them together. In computer programming you also need two things: data (variables) and instructions (code). Variables are the basic building blocks of a program. Instructions tell the computer what to do with the variables.

Comments are used to describe the variables and instructions. They are notes by the author documenting the program so it is clear and easy to read. Comments are ignored by the computer.

In construction, before we can start we must order our materials: "We need 500 large bricks, 80 half-size bricks, and 4 flagstones." Similarly, in C++ you must declare all variables before you can use them. You must name each one of your "bricks" and tell C++ what type of "brick" to use.

After the variables are defined you can begin to use them. In construction the basic structure is a room. By combining many rooms we form a building. In C++ the basic structure is a function. Functions can be combined to form a program.

An apprentice builder does not start out building the Empire State Building. He starts on a one-room house. In this chapter you will concentrate on constructing simple, one-function programs.

Basic Program Structure

The basic elements of a program are the data declarations, functions, and comments. Let's see how these can be organized into a simple C++ program.

The basic structure of a one-function program is:

```
/********************************************************
 * Heading comments                                     *
 ********************************************************/
data declarations
main()
{
    executable statements
    return(0);
}
```

The heading comments tell the programmer all about the program. The *data declarations* describe the data that the program is going to use.

Our single function is named `main`. The name `main` is special, because it is the first function called. Any other functions are called directly or indirectly from `main`. The function `main` begins with:

```
main()
{
```

and ends with:

```
    return(0);
}
```

The line `return(0);` is used to tell the operating system (UNIX or MS-DOS/Windows) that the program exited normally (status=0). A nonzero status indicates an error—the bigger the return value, the more severe the error. Typically 1 is used for most simple errors, such as a missing file or bad command-line syntax.

Now let's take a look at the "Hello World" program (Example 3-3).

At the beginning of the program is a comment box enclosed in /* and */. Following this is the line:

```
#include <iostream.h>
```

This statement signals C++ that you are going to use a set of standard classes called the I/O stream classes. This is a type of data declaration.* Later you use the class cout from this package. (We define a class more completely in Chapter 13, *Simple Classes*, but until we know more we'll treat cout as a "black box" that sends data to the console.)

The main routine contains the instruction:

```
cout << "Hello World\n";
```

which is an executable statement instructing C++ to print the message "Hello World" on the screen. C++ uses a semicolon to end a statement in much the same way we use a period to end a sentence. Unlike with line-oriented languages such as BASIC, the end of a line does not end a statement. The sentences in this book can span several lines—the end of a line is treated as a space separating words. C++ works the same way. A single statement can span several lines. Similarly, you can put several sentences on the same line, just as you can put several C++ statements on the same line. However, most of the time your program is more readable if each statement starts on a separate line.

We are using the standard class cout (console out) to output the message. A standard class is a generally useful C++ object that has already been defined and put in the standard library. A library is a collection of classes, functions, and data that have been grouped together for reuse. The standard library contains classes and functions for input, output, sorting, advanced math, and file manipulation. See your C++ reference manual for a complete list of library functions and standard classes.

"Hello World" is one of the simplest C++ programs. It contains no computations, merely sending a single message to the screen. It is a starting point. Once you have mastered this simple program, you have done a great deal of things right. The program is not as simple as it looks. But once you get it working, you can move on to create more complex code.

Simple Expressions

Computers can do more than just print strings. They can also perform calculations. Expressions are used to specify simple computations. C++ has the five simple operators listed in Table 4-1.

---

* Technically, the statement causes a set of data declarations to be taken from an include file. Chapter 10, *The C++ Preprocessor*, discusses include files.

Table 4-1. Simple Operators

Operator	Meaning
*	Multiply
/	Divide
+	Add
–	Subtract
%	Modulus (remainder after division)

Multiply (*), divide (/), and modulus (%) have precedence over addition (+) and subtraction (–). Parentheses may be used to group terms. Thus:

```
(1 + 2) * 4
```

yields 12, while:

```
1 + 2 * 4
```

yields 9.

The program in Example 4-2 computes the value of the expression **(1 + 2) * 4.**

Example 4-1. Simple Expression

```
main()
{
    (1 + 2) * 4;
    return(0);
}
```

Although we calculate the answer, we don't do anything with it. (This program will generate a "null effect" warning to indicate that there is a correctly written, but useless, statement in the program.)

If we were constructing a building, think about how confused a worker would be if we said, "Take your wheelbarrow and go back and forth between the truck and the building site."

"Do you want me to carry bricks in the wheelbarrow?"

"No. Just go back and forth."

You need to output the results of your calculations.

The cout Output Class

The standard `class` variable `cout` is used to output data to the console. We'll learn what a class is later in Chapter 13, *Simple Classes*. But for now all we have to know is that the operator `<<`[*] tells C++ what to output. So the statement:

```
cout << "Hello World\n";
```

tells C++ to take the string `"Hello World\n"` and write it to the console. Multiple `<<` operators may be used together. For example, both the following lines output the same message:

```
cout << "Hello World\n";
cout << "Hello " << "World\n";
```

Expressions can also be output this way, such as:

```
cout << "Half of " << 64 << " is " << (64 / 2) << "\n";
```

When this is executed it will write:

```
Half of 64 is 32
```

on the console. Note that we had to put a space after the "of" in "Half of." There also is a space on either side of the "is" string. These spaces are needed in the output to separate the numbers from the text. Suppose we didn't put the spaces in and the code looked like:

```
// Problem code
cout << "Half of" << 64 << "is" << (64 / 2) << "\n";
```

At first glance this code looks perfectly normal. There are spaces around each of the numbers. But these spaces are not inside any string, so they will not be output. The result of this code is:

```
Half of64is32
```

Omitting needed spaces is a common first-time programming mistake. Remember, only the text inside the quotation marks will be output.

Variables and Storage

C++ allows you to store values in *variables*. Each variable is identified by a *variable name*.

Additionally, each variable has a *variable type*. The type tells C++ how the variable is going to be used and what kind of numbers (real, integer) it can hold.

---

[*] Technically `<<` is the left shift operator; however, the `cout` class has overloaded this operator and made it the output operator. (See Chapter 16, *File Input/Output*, for a complete discussion of I/O classes and Chapter 18, *Operator Overloading*, for a definition of overloading.)

Names start with a letter or underscore (_) followed by any number of letters, digits, or underscores. Uppercase is different from lowercase, so the names "sam," "Sam," and "SAM" specify three different variables. To avoid confusion, it is better to use different names for variables and not depend on case differences.

Most C++ programmers use all lowercase variable names. Some names, such as int, while, for, and float, have a special meaning to C++ and are considered *reserved words*. They cannot be used for variable names.

The following is an example of some variable names:

```
average      // average of all grades
pi           // pi to 6 decimal places
number_of_students // number of students in this class
```

The following are *not* variable names:

```
3rd_entry    // Begins with a number
all$done     // Contains a "$"
the end      // Contains a space
int          // Reserved word
```

Avoid variable names that are similar. For example the following illustrates a poor choice of variable names:

```
total        // total number of items in current entry

totals       // total of all entries
```

A much better set of names is:

```
entry_total // total number of items in current entry

all_total   // total of all entries
```

Variable Declarations

Before you can use a variable in C++, it must be defined in a *declaration statement*. A variable cannot be used unless it is declared.

A variable declaration serves three purposes:

1. It defines the name of the variable.

2. It defines the type of the variable (integer, real, character, etc.).

3. It gives the programmer a description of the variable.

The declaration of a variable **answer** can be:

```
int answer;     // the result of our expression
```

The keyword **int** tells C++ that this variable contains an integer value. (Integers are defined below.) The variable name is **answer**. The semicolon is used to indicate the statement end, and the comment is used to define this variable for the programmer.

The general form of a variable declaration is:

```
type  name;    // comment
```

Type is one of the C++ variable types (`int`, `float`, etc.) *Name* is any valid variable name. The comment explains what the variable is and what it will be used for. Variable declarations come just before the `main()` line at the top of a program. (In Chapter 9, *Variable Scope and Functions*, you will see how local variables may be declared elsewhere.)

Integers

One variable type is integer. Integers (also known as whole numbers) have no fractional part or decimal point. Numbers such as 1, 87, and –222 are integers. The number 8.3 is not an integer because it contains a decimal point. The general form of an integer declaration is:

```
int  name;    // comment
```

A calculator with an eight-digit display can only handle numbers between 99,999,999 and –99,999,999. If you try to add 1 to 99,999,999, you will get an overflow error. Computers have similar limits. The limits on integers are implementation dependent, meaning they change from computer to computer.

Calculators use decimal digits (0–9). Computers use binary digits (0–1) called *bits*. Eight bits make a *byte*. The number of bits used to hold an integer varies from machine to machine. Numbers are converted from binary to decimal for printing.

On most UNIX machines integers are 32 bits (4 bytes), providing a range of 2,147,483,647 (2^{31}– 1) to –2,147,483,648 ($–2^{31}$). On the PC in Turbo C++, only 16 bits (2 bytes) are used, so the range is 32,767 (2^{15}– 1) to –32,768 ($–2^{15}$).

Question 4-1: *The following will work on a UNIX machine but will fail on a PC.*

```
int zip;      // zip code for current address

.........

zip = 92126;
```

Why does this fail? What will be the result when run on a PC?

Assignment Statements

Variables are given a value through the use of *assignment statements*. Before a variable can be used it must be declared. For example:

```
int answer;     // Result of a simple computation
```

The variable may then be used in an assignment statement, such as:

```
answer = (1 + 2) * 4;
```

The variable **answer** on the left side of the equals sign (=) is assigned the value of the expression (1 + 2) * 4 on the right side. The semicolon ends the statement.

When you declare a variable, C++ allocates storage for the variable and puts an unknown value inside it. You can think of the declaration as creating a box to hold the data. When it starts out it is a mystery box containing an unknown quantity. This is illustrated in Figure 4-1A. The assignment statement computes the value of the expression and drops that value into the box as shown in Figure 4-1B.

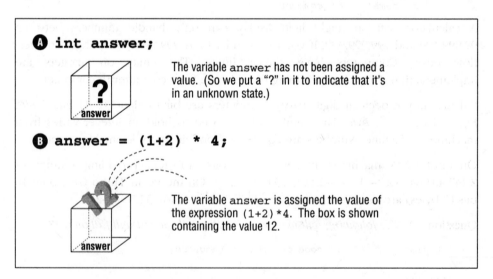

Figure 4-1. Declaration and assignment statements

The general form of the assignment statement is:

```
variable = expression;
```

The equals sign (=) is used for assignment, not equality.

In Example 4-2 the variable `term` is used to store an integer value that is used in two later expressions. Variables, like expressions, can be output using the output operator <<, so we use this operator to check the results.

Example 4-2. tterm/tterm.cc

```
#include <iostream.h>

int term;        // term used in two expressions
main()
{
    term = 3 * 5;
    cout << "Twice " << term << " is " << 2*term << "\n";
    cout << "Three times " << term << " is " << 3*term << "\n";
    return (0);
}
```

Floating Point Numbers

Real numbers are numbers that have a fractional part. Because of the way they are stored internally, real numbers are also known as *floating point numbers*. The numbers 5.5, 8.3, and –12.6 are all floating point numbers. C++ uses the decimal point to distinguish between floating point numbers and integers, so a number such as 5.0 is a floating point number while 5 is an integer. Floating point numbers must contain a decimal point. Numbers such as 3.14159, 0.5, 1.0, and 8.88 are floating point numbers.

Although it is possible to omit digits before the decimal point and specify a number as .5 instead of 0.5, the extra 0 makes it clear that you are using a floating point number. A similar rule applies to 12. versus 12.0. Floating point zero should be written as 0.0.

Additionally, a floating point number may include an exponent specification of the form *e±exp*.

For example, 1.2e34 is shorthand for $1.2*10^{34}$.

The form of a floating point declaration is:

```
float variable;   // comment
```

Again, there is a limit on the range of floating-point numbers the computer can handle. The range varies widely from computer to computer. Floating point accuracy is discussed further in Chapter 19, *Floating Point*.

Floating point numbers may be output using `cout`. For example:

```
cout << "The answer is " << (1.0 / 3.0) << "\n";
```

Floating Point Versus Integer Divide

The division operator is special. There is a vast difference between an integer divide and a floating-point divide. In an integer divide, the result is truncated (any fractional part is discarded). For example, the integer divide value of 19/10 is 1.

If either the divisor or the dividend is a floating-point number, a floating point divide is executed. In this case 19.0/10.0 is 1.9. (19/10.0 and 19.0/10 are also floating-point divides; however, 19.0/10.0 is preferred for clarity.) There are several examples in Table 4-2.

Table 4-2. Expression Examples

Expression	Result	Result Type
1 + 2	3	Integer
1.0 + 2.0	3.0	Floating point
19 / 10	1	Integer
19.0 / 10.0	1.9	Floating point

C++ allows the assignment of an integer expression to a floating-point variable. It will automatically perform the integer-to-floating-point conversion and then make the assignment. A similar conversion is performed when assigning a floating point number to an integer. Floating point numbers are truncated when assigned to integer variables.

Example 4-3. float1/float1.c

```
int    integer;  // an integer
float floating; // a floating point number

main()
{
    floating = 1.0 / 2.0;        // assign floating 0.5
    integer = 1 / 3;             // assign integer 0
    floating = (1 / 2) + (1 / 2); // assign floating 0.0
    floating = 3.0 / 2.0;        // assign floating 1.5
    integer = floating;          // assign integer 1
    return (0);
}
```

Notice that the expression 1/2 is an integer expression resulting in an integer divide and an integer result of 0.

Question 4-2: *Why does Example 4-4 print "The value of 1/3 is 0"? What must be done to this program to fix it?*

Example 4-4. float2/float2.cc

```
#include <iostream.h>

float answer;   // the result of the divide

main()
{
    answer = 1/3;
    cout << "The value of 1/3 is " << answer << "\n";
    return (0);
}
```

Characters

The type `char` represents single characters. The form of a character declaration is:

```
    char variable;    //comment
```

Characters are enclosed in single quotation marks ('). `'A'`, `'a'` and `'!'` are character constants. The backslash character (\) is called the *escape character*. It is used to signal that a special character follows. For example, the character \t can be used to represent the single character "tab." \n is the new-line character. It causes the output device to go to the beginning of the next line, similar to a return key on a typewriter. The character \\ is the backslash itself. Finally, characters can be specified by *nnn* where *nnn* is the octal code for the character. Table 4-3 summarizes these special characters. For a full list of ASCII character codes, see Appendix A.

Table 4-3. Special Characters

Character	Name	Meaning
\b	Backspace	Move the cursor to the left one character
\f	Form feed	Go to top of a new page
\n	New line	Go to the next line
\r	Return	Go to the beginning of the current line
\t	Tab	Advance to the next tab stop (eight-column boundary)
\'	Apostrophe or single quotation mark	The character '
\"	Double quote	The character "
\\nnn	The character *nnn*	The character number *nnn* (octal)
\\NN	The character *NN*	The character number *NN* (hexadecimal)

NOTE

While characters are enclosed in single quotes (`'`), a different data type, the string, is enclosed in double quotes (`"`). A good way to remember the difference between these two types of quotes is that *single* characters are enclosed in *single* quotes. Strings can have any number of characters (including double characters), and they are enclosed in double quotes.

Example 4-5 reverses three characters.

Example 4-5. print3/print3.cc

```
#include <iostream.h>

char char1;     // first character
char char2;     // second character
char char3;     // third character

main()
{
    char1 = 'A';
    char2 = 'B';
    char3 = 'C';
    cout << char1 << char2 << char3 << " reversed is " <<
            char3 << char2 << char1 << "\n";
    return (0);
}
```

When executed, this program prints:

```
ABC reversed is CBA
```

Programming Exercises

Exercise 4-1: Write a program to print your name, Social Security number, and date of birth.

Exercise 4-2: Write a program to print a block E using asterisks (*), where the E is 7 characters high and 5 characters wide.

Exercise 4-3: Write a program to compute the area and circumference of a rectangle 3 inches wide by 5 inches long. What changes must be made to the program so it works for a rectangle 6.8 inches wide by 2.3 inches long?

Exercise 4-4: Write a program to print "HELLO" in big block letters where each letter is 7 characters high and 5 characters wide.

Answers to Chapter Questions

Answer 4-1: The largest number that can be stored in an **int** on a UNIX machine is 2,147,483,647. When using Turbo-C++ the limit is 32,767. The zip code 92126 is larger than 32,767, so it is mangled and the result is 26,590.

This problem can be fixed by using a **long int** instead of just an **int**. The various types of integers are discussed in Chapter 5, *Arrays, Qualifiers, and Reading Numbers.*

Answer 4-2: The problem concerns the division: 1/3. The number 1 and the number 3 are both integers, so this is an integer divide. Fractions are truncated in an integer divide. The expression should be written as:

```
answer = 1.0 / 3.0
```

5

Arrays, Qualifiers, and Reading Numbers

That mysterious independent variable of political calculations, Public Opinion.
—Thomas Henry Huxley

Arrays

So far in constructing our building we have named each brick (variable). That is fine for a small number of bricks, but what happens when we want to construct something larger? We would like to point to a stack of bricks and say, "That's for the left wall. That's brick 1, brick 2, brick 3. . . ."

Arrays allow us to do something similar with variables. An *array* is a set of consecutive memory locations used to store data. Each item in the array is called an *element*. The number of elements in an array is called the *dimension* of the array. A typical array declaration is:

```
// List of data to be sorted and averaged
int     data_list[3];
```

This declares `data_list` to be an array of the three elements `data_list[0]`, `data_list[1]`, and `data_list[2]`, which are separate variables. To reference an element of an array, you use a number called the *index* (the number inside the square brackets []). C++ is a funny language and likes to start counting at 0, so these three elements are numbered 0–2.

NOTE

Common sense tells you that when you declare `data_list` to be three elements long, `data_list[3]` would be valid. Common sense is wrong and `data_list[3]` is illegal.

Example 5-1 computes the total and average of five numbers.

Example 5-1. five/five.cc

```
#include <iostream.h>

float data[5];   // data to average and total
float total;     // the total of the data items
float average;   // average of the items

main()
{
    data[0] = 34.0;
    data[1] = 27.0;
    data[2] = 46.5;
    data[3] = 82.0;
    data[4] = 22.0;

    total = data[0] + data[1] + data[2] + data[3] + data[4];
    average =  total / 5.0;
    cout << "Total " << total << " Average " << average << '\n';
    return (0);
}
```

This program outputs:

```
Total 211.5 Average 42.3
```

Strings

Strings are arrays of characters. The special character `'\0'` (NUL) is used to indicate the end of a string.

Example:

```
char    name[4];

main()
{
    name[0] = 'S';
    name[1] = 'a';
    name[2] = 'm';
    name[3] = '\0';
    return (0);
}
```

This creates a character array four elements long. Note that we had to allocate one character for the end-of-string marker.

String constants consist of text enclosed in double quotes (``"``). You may have already noticed that we've used string constants extensively for output with the cout standard class. C++ does not allow one array to be assigned to another, so you can't write an assignment of the form:

```
name = "Sam";    // Illegal
```

Instead you must use the standard library function strcpy to copy the string constant into the variable. (strcpy copies the whole string including the end-of-string character.) To initialize the variable **name** to "Sam" you would write:

```
#include <string.h>

char     name[4];

main()
{
    strcpy(name, "Sam");    // Legal
    return (0);
}
```

NOTE

The line #include <string.h> is needed to inform C++ that you are using the string function library.

C++ uses variable-length strings. For example, the declaration:

```
#include <string.h>

char string[50];

main()
{
    strcpy(string, "Sam");
```

creates an array (string) that can contain up to 50 characters. The *size* of the array is 50, but the *length* of the string is 3. Any string up to 49 characters long can be stored in string. (One character is reserved for the NULL that indicates the end of the string.)

There are several standard routines that work on string variables. These are listed in Table 5-1.

Table 5-1. String Functions

Function	Description
strcpy(string1, string2)	Copies string2 into string1
strcat(string1, string2)	Concatenates string2 onto the end of string1

Table 5-1. String Functions (Continued)

Function	Description
`length = strlen(string)`	Gets the length of a string
`strcmp(string1, string2)`	0 if string1 `equals` string2; otherwise, nonzero

Example 5-2 illustrates how `strcpy` is used.

Example 5-2. str/sam.cc

```
#include <iostream.h>
#include <string.h>

char name[30];  // First name of someone

main()
{
   strcpy(name, "Sam");
   cout << "The name is " << name << '\n';
   return (0);
}
```

Example 5-3 takes a first name and a last name and combines the two strings. The program works by initializing the variable `first` to the first name (Steve). The last name (Oualline) is put in the variable `last`. To construct the full name, the first name is copied into `full_name`. Then `strcat` is used to add a space. We call `strcat` again to tack on the last name.

The dimension of the string variables is 100 because we know that no one we are going to encounter has a name more than 99 characters long. (If we get a name more than 99 characters long, our program will screw up and split the name in two.)

Example 5-3. name2/man2.cc

```
#include <string.h>
#include <iostream.h>

char first[100];        // first name
char last[100];         // last name
char full_name[100];    // full version of first and last name

main()
{
   strcpy(first, "Steve");      // Initialize first name
   strcpy(last, "Oualline");    // Initialize last name

   strcpy(full_name, first);    // full = "Steve"
                                // Note: strcat not strcpy
   strcat(full_name, " ");      // full = "Steve "
   strcat(full_name, last);     // full = "Steve Oualline"
```

Example 5-3. name2/man2.cc (Continued)

```
    cout << "The full name is " << full_name << '\n';
    return (0);
}
```

The output of this program is:

```
The full name is Steve Oualline
```

Reading Data

So far you've learned how to compute expressions and output the results. You need to have your programs read numbers as well. The output class variable cout uses the operator << to write numbers. The input class variable cin uses the operator >> to read them. For example, the code:

```
cin >> price >> number_on_hand;
```

reads two numbers: **price** and **number_on_hand**. The input to this program should be two numbers, separated by white space. For example, if you type:

```
32 5
```

then **price** gets the value 32 and **number_on_hand** gets 5.

NOTE

This does not give you very precise control over your input. C++ does a reasonable job for simple input. If your program expects a number and you type <enter> instead, the program will skip the <enter> (it's white space) and wait for you to type a number. Sometimes this may lead you to think your program's stuck.

In Example 5-4, we use cin to get a number from the user and then we double it:

Example 5-4. double/double.cc

```
#include <iostream.h>
char  line[100];    // input line from console
int   value;        // a value to double

main()
{
    cout << "Enter a value: ";
    cin >> value;
    cout << "Twice " << value << " is " << value * 2 << '\n';
    return (0);
}
```

This program asks the user for a single number and doubles it. Notice that there is no \n at the end of Enter a value:. This is because we do not want the computer to print a newline after the prompt. For example, a sample run of the program might look like:

```
Enter a value: 12
Twice 12 is 24
```

If we replaced Enter a value: with Enter a value:\n the result would be:

```
Enter a value:
12
Twice 12 is 24
```

Question 5-1: *Example 5-5 is designed to compute the area of a triangle, given its width and height. For some strange reason, the compiler refuses to believe that we declared the variable* width. *The declaration is right there on line two, just after the definition of height. Why isn't the compiler seeing it?*

Example 5-5. comment/comment.cc

```
#include <iostream.h>

int  height;    /* the height of the triangle
int  width;     /* the width of the triangle */
int  area;      /* area of the triangle (computed) */

main()
{
    cout << "Enter width height? ";
    cin >> width >> height;
    area = (width * height) / 2;
    cout << "The area is " << area << '\n';
    return (0);
}
```

The general form of a cin statement is:

```
cin >> variable;
```

This works for all types of simple variables such as int, float, and char.

Reading strings is a little more difficult. To read a string, use the statement:

```
cin.getline(string, sizeof(string));
```

For example:

```
char name[100];    // The name of a person

cin.getline(name, sizeof(name));
```

We discuss the getline and sizeof functions in Chapter 16, *File Input/Output.*

When reading a string, the cin class considers anything up to the end-of-line part of the string. Example 5-6 reads a line from the keyboard and reports the line's length.

Example 5-6. len/len.cc

```
#include <string.h>
#include <iostream.h>

char line[100]; // A line of data

main()
{
    cout << "Enter a line:";
    cin.getline(line, sizeof(line));

    cout << "The length of the line is: " << strlen(line) << '\n';
    return (0);
}
```

When we run this program we get:

```
Enter a line:test
The length of the line is: 4
```

Initializing Variables

C++ allows variables to be initialized in the declaration statement. For example, the following statement declares the integer counter and initializes it to 0.

```
int counter(0);      // number cases counted so far
```

The older C style syntax is also supported:

```
int counter = 0;     // number cases counted so far
```

Arrays can also be initialized in a similar manner. The element list must be enclosed in curly braces ({}). For example:

```
// Product numbers for the parts we are making
int product_codes[3] = {10, 972, 45};
```

This is equivalent to:

```
product_codes[0] = 10;
product_codes[1] = 972;
product_codes[2] = 45;
```

The number of elements in the curly braces ({}) does not have to match the array size. If too many numbers are present, a warning will be issued. If there are not enough numbers, not all the elements are initialized.

If no dimension is given, C++ will determine the dimension from the number of elements in the initialization list. For example, we could have initialized our variable product_codes with the statement:

```
// Product numbers for the parts we are making
int product_codes[] = {10, 972, 45};
```

Strings can be initialized in a similar manner. To initialize the variable name to the string "Sam" we use the statement:

```
char name[] = {'S', 'a', 'm', '\0'};
```

C++ has a special shorthand for initializing strings, by using double quotes (") to simplify the initialization. The previous example could have been written:

```
char name[] = "Sam";
```

The dimension of name is 4, because C++ allocates a place for the '\0' character that ends the string.

C++ uses variable-length strings. For example, the declaration:

```
char string[50] = "Sam";
```

creates an array (string) that can contain up to 50 characters. The size of the array is 50, and the length of the string is 3. Any string up to 49 characters long can be stored in string. (One character is reserved for the NUL that indicates the end of the string.)

NOTE

Our statement initialized only 4 of the 50 values in string. The other 46 elements are not initialized and may contain random data.

Multidimensional Arrays

Arrays can have more than one dimension. The declaration for a two-dimensional array is:

```
type variable[size1][size2]; // comment
```

Example:

```
// a typical matrix
int matrix[2][4];
```

Notice that C++ does **not** follow the notation used in other languages of matrix[10,12].

To access an element of the matrix we use the notation:

```
matrix[1][2] = 10;
```

C++ allows you to use as many dimensions as needed (only limited by the amount of memory available). Additional dimensions can be tacked on.

```
four_dimensions[10][12][9][5];
```

Initializing multidimensional arrays is similar to initializing single-dimension arrays. A set of curly braces {} encloses each element. The declaration:

```
// a typical matrix
int matrix[2][4];
```

can be thought of as a declaration of an array of dimension 2 whose elements are arrays of dimension 4. This array is initialized as follows:

```
// a typical matrix
int matrix[2][4] =
    {
        {1, 2, 3, 4},
        {10, 20, 30, 40}
    };
```

This is shorthand for:

```
matrix[0][0] = 1;
matrix[0][1] = 2;
matrix[0][2] = 3;
matrix[0][3] = 4;

matrix[1][0] = 10;
matrix[1][1] = 20;
matrix[1][2] = 30;
matrix[1][3] = 40;
```

Question 5-2: *Why does the following program print incorrect answers?*

Example 5-7. array/array.cc

```
#include <iostream.h>

int array[3][5] = {      // Two dimensional array
    { 0,  1,  2,  3,  4 },
    {10, 11, 12, 13, 14 },
    {20, 21, 22, 23, 24 }
};

main()
{
    cout << "Last element is " << array[2,4] << '\n';
    return (0);
}
```

When run on a Sun 3/50 this program generates:

```
Last element is 0x201e8
```

Your answers may vary.

Types of Integers

C++ is considered a medium-level language because it allows you to get very close to the actual hardware of the machine. Some languages, such as BASIC, go to great lengths to completely isolate the user from the details of how the processor works. This consistency comes at a great loss of efficiency. C++ lets you give detailed information about how the hardware is to be used.

For example, most machines let you use different-length numbers. Simple BASIC allows the programmer to use only one number type. This simplifies the programming, but BASIC programs are extremely inefficient. C++ allows the programmer to specify many different kinds of integers, so the programmer can make best use of the hardware.

The type specifier **int** tells C++ to use the most efficient size (for the machine you are using) for the integer. This can be 2 to 4 bytes depending on the machine. Sometimes you need extra digits to store numbers larger than are allowed in a normal **int**. The declaration:

```
long int answer;        // the answer of our calculations
```

is used to allocate a long integer. The **long** quantifier informs C++ that you wish to allocate extra storage for the integer. If you are going to use small numbers and wish to reduce storage, use the quantifier **short**.

```
short int year;         // Year including the 19xx part
```

C++ guarantees that the storage for **short** <= **int** <= **long**. In actual practice, **short** almost always allocates 2 bytes; **long**, 4 bytes; and **int**, 2 or 4 bytes. (See Appendix B for numeric ranges.)

Long integer constants end with the character "L." For example:

```
long int var = 1234L;    // Set up a long variable
```

Actually you can use either an uppercase or a lowercase "L." Uppercase is preferred since lowercase easily gets confused with the digit "1."

```
long int funny = 121;    // Is this 12<long> or one hundred twenty-one?
```

The type `short int` uses 2 bytes, or 16 bits. Fifteen bits are used normally for the number and 1 bit for the sign. This gives it a range of –32,768 (-2^{15}) to 32,767 ($2^{15} - 1$). An `unsigned short int` uses all 16 bits for the number, giving it the range of 0 to 65,535 ($2^{16} - 1$). All `int` declarations default to `signed`, so that the declaration:

```
signed long int answer;    // final result
```

is the same as:

```
long int answer;            // final result
```

Finally there is the very short integer, the type `char`. Character variables take up 1 byte. They can also be used for numbers in the range of –128 to 127 or 0 to 255. Unlike integers, they do not default to **signed**; the default is compiler dependent.[*]

Question: Is the following character variable signed or unsigned?

```
char foo;
```

Answers:

a.   It's signed.

b.   It's unsigned.

c.   It's compiler dependent.

d.   If you always specify `signed` or `unsigned` you don't have to worry about problems like this.

Reading and writing very short integers is a little tricky. If you try to use a `char` variable in an output statement, it will be written, *as a character.* You need to trick C++ into believing that the `char` variable is an integer. This can be accomplished with the `int` operator. Example 5-8 shows how to write out a very short integer as a number.

Example 5-8. two2/two2.cc

```
#include <iostream.h>

signed char ch; // Very short integer
                // Range is -128 to 127

main()
{
    cout << "The number is " << int(ch) << '\n';
    return (0);
}
```

We start by declaring a character variable `ch`. This variable is assigned the value `37`. This is actually an integer, not a character, but C++ doesn't care. On the next line we write out the value of the variable. If we tried to write `ch` directly, C++ would treat it as a character. The code `int(ch)` tells C++, "Treat this character as an integer."

---

[*] Turbo-C++ even has a command-line switch to make the default for type **char** either **signed** or **unsigned**.

Reading a very short integer is not possible. You must first read it as a `short int` and then assign it to a very short integer.

Summary of Integer Types

`long int` declarations allow the programmer to explicitly specify extra precision where it is needed (at the expense of memory). `short int` numbers save space but have a more limited range. The most compact integers have type `char`. They also have the most limited range.

`unsigned` numbers provide a way of doubling the range at the expense of eliminating negative numbers. The kind of number you use will depend on your program and storage requirements. The range of the various types of integers is listed in Appendix B.

Types of Floats

The `float` type also comes in various flavors. `float` denotes normal precision (usually 4 bytes). `double` indicates double precision (usually 8 bytes). Double precision gives the programmer twice the range and precision of single-precision (`float`) variables.

The quantifier `long double` denotes extended precision. On some systems this is the same as `double`; on others, it offers additional precision. All types of floating-point numbers are always signed.

On most machines, single-precision floating-point instructions execute faster (but less accurately) than double precision. Double precision gains accuracy at the expense of time and storage. In most cases `float` is adequate; however, if accuracy is a problem, switch to `double` (see Chapter 19, *Floating Point*).

Constant and Reference Declarations

Sometimes you want to use a value that does not change, such as π. The keyword **const** indicates a variable that never changes. To declare a value for **pi** we use the statement:

```
const float PI = 3.1415926;    // The classic circle constant
```

NOTE

By convention variable names use lowercase only while constants use uppercase only. However, there is nothing in the language that requires this, and several programming systems use a different convention.

Constants must be initialized at declaration time and can never be changed. For example, if we tried to reset the value of PI to 3.0 we would generate an error message:

```
PI = 3.0;        // Illegal
```

Integer constants can be used as a size parameter when declaring an array:

```
const int TOTAL_MAX = 50;        // Max. number of elements in the total
                 list
float total_list[TOTAL_MAX];     // Total values for each category
```

NOTE

C++ allows you to use integer expressions when declaring an array. For example, you can say total_list[10] or total_list[7+3]. However, some compilers, such as Borland-C++ Version 3.1, won't allow integer constants in this type of expression. For example:

```
const int first_part = 3;
const int second_part = 7;

float total[3+7];        // Works even in Borland C++ Version 3.1
float total2[first_part + 7];  // Fails in Borland C++ version 3.1
float total3[first_part + second_part];  // Also fails
```

Another special variable type is the **reference** type. A typical reference declaration is:

```
int count;               // Number of items so far
int &actual_count = count;  // Another name for count
```

The special character "&" is used to tell C++ that actual_count is a reference. The declaration causes the names count and actual_count to refer to the same variable. For example, the following two statements are equivalent:

```
count = 5;         // "Actual_count" changes too
actual_count = 5;  // "Count" changes too
```

In other words, a simple variable declaration declares a box to put data in. A reference variable slaps another name on the box, as illustrated in Figure 5-1.

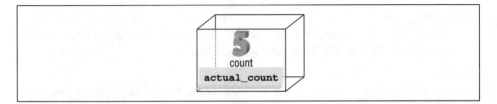

Figure 5-1. Reference variables

This form of the reference variable is not very useful. In fact, in actual programming it is almost never used. In Chapter 9, *Variable Scope and Functions*, you'll see how another form of the reference variable can be very useful.

Qualifiers

As you've seen, C++ allows you to specify a number of qualifiers for variable declarations. Qualifiers may be thought of as adjectives that describe the type that follows. Table 5-2 summarizes the various qualifiers.

Table 5-2. Qualifiers and Simple Types

Special	Class	Size	Sign	Type
volatile	register	long	signed	int
<blank>	static	short	unsigned	float
	extern	double	<blank>	char
	auto	<blank>		<blank>
	<blank>			

Special

The `volatile` keyword is used for specialized programming such as I/O drivers and shared memory applications. It is an advanced modifier whose use is far beyond the scope of this book.

volatile
>   Indicates a special variable whose value may change at any time

<blank>
>   Normal variable

Class

The class of a variable is discussed in detail in Chapter 9, *Variable Scope and Functions*. A brief description of the various classes follows:

register
>   This indicates a frequently used variable that should be kept in a machine register. See Chapter 17, *Debugging and Optimization*.

static
>   The meaning of this word depends on the context. This keyword is described in Chapter 9, *Variable Scope and Functions*, and Chapter 23, *Modular Programming*.

`extern`

> The variable is defined in another file. See Chapter 23 for more information.

`auto`

> A variable allocated from the stack. This keyword is hardly ever used.

<blank>

> Indicates that the default class (`auto`) is selected.

Size

The size qualifier allows you to select the most efficient size for the variable.

`long`

> Indicates a larger than normal integer. (Some nonstandard compilers use `long double` to indicate a very large floating-point variable.)

`short`

> A smaller than normal integer.

`double`

> A double-size floating-point number.

<blank>

> Indicates a normal size number.

Sign

Numbers can be `signed` or `unsigned`. This qualifier applies only to `char` and `int` types. Floating-point numbers are always signed. The default is `signed` for `int` and undefined for characters.

Type

This specifies the type of the variable. Simple types include:

`int`

> Integer

`float`

> Floating-point number

`char`

> Single characters, but can also be used for very short integers

Hexadecimal and Octal Constants

Integer numbers are specified as a string of digits, such as 1234, 88, –123, and so on. These are decimal (base 10) numbers: 174 or 174_{10}. Computers deal with binary (base 2) numbers: 10101110_2. The octal (base 8) system easily converts to and from binary. Each group of three digits ($2^3 = 8$) can be transformed into a single octal digit. Thus 10101110_2 can be written as 10 101 110₂ and changed to the octal 256_8. Hexadecimal (base 16) numbers have a similar conversion, but 4 bits at a time are used. For example, 10010100_2 is 1000 0100, or 84_{16}.

The C++ language has conventions for representing octal and hexadecimal values. Leading zeros are used to signal an octal constant. For example, 0123 is 123 (octal) or 83 (decimal). Starting a number with "0x" indicates a hexadecimal (base 16) constant. So 0x15 is 21 (decimal). Table 5-3 shows several numbers in all three bases.

Table 5-3. Integer Examples

Base 10	Base 8	Base 16
6	06	0x6
9	011	0x9
15	017	0xF

Question 5-3: *Why does the following program fail to print the correct zip code? What does it print instead?*

```
long int zip;        // Zip code

main()
{
    zip = 02137L;        // Use the zip code for Cambridge MA

    cout << "New York's zip code is: " << zip << '\n';
    return(0);
}
```

Operators for Performing Shortcuts

C++ not only provides you with a rich set of declarations, but also gives you a large number of special-purpose operators. Frequently a programmer wants to increment (add 1 to) a variable. Using a normal assignment statement, this would look like:

```
total_entries = total_entries + 1;
```

C++ provides you a shorthand for performing this common task. The ++ operator is used for incrementing.

```
++total_entries;
```

A similar operator, --, can be used for decrementing (subtracting 1 from) a variable.

```
--number_left;
// Is the same as
number_left = number_left - 1;
```

But suppose you want to add 2 instead of 1. Then you can use the following notation:

```
total_entries += 2;
```

This is equivalent to:

```
total_entries = total_entries + 2;
```

Each of the simple operators shown in Table 5-4 can be used in this manner.

Table 5-4. Shorthand Operators

Operator	Shorthand	Equivalent Statement
+=	x += 2;	x = x + 2;
-=	x -= 2;	x = x - 2;
*=	x *= 2;	x = x * 2;
/=	x /= 2;	x = x / 2;
%=	x %= 2;	x = x % 2;

Side Effects

Unfortunately, C++ allows the programmer to use *side effects*. A side effect is an operation that is performed in addition to the main operation executed by the statement. For example, the following is legal C++ code:

```
size = 5;
result = ++size;
```

The first statement assigns size the value of 6. The second statement:

1. Increments size (side effect)

2. Assigns result the value of size (main operation)

But in what order? There are four possible answers:

    1. result is assigned the value of size (5), and then size is incremented.

result is 5 and size is 6.

2. `size` is incremented, and then `result` is assigned the value of `size` (6). `result` is 6 and `size` is 6.

3. The answer is compiler dependent and varies from computer to computer.

4. If you don't write code like this, you don't have to worry about these sorts of questions.

The correct answer is 2: The increment occurs before the assignment. However, 4 is a much better answer. The main effects of C++ are confusing enough without having to worry about side effects.

NOTE

Some programmers highly value compact code. This is a holdover from the early days of computing when storage cost a significant amount of money. It is my view that the art of programming has evolved to the point where clarity is much more valuable than compactness. (Great novels, which a lot of people enjoy reading, are not written in shorthand.)

C++ actually provides two forms of the ++ operator. One is *variable++* and the other is *++variable*. The first:

```
number = 5;
result = number++;
```

evaluates the expression and then increments the number, so `result` is 5. The second:

```
number = 5;
result = ++number;
```

increments first and then evaluates the expression. In this case `result` is 6. However, using ++ or -- in this way can lead to some surprising code:

```
o = --o - o--;
```

The problem with this is that it looks like someone is writing Morse code. The programmer doesn't read this statement, he decodes it. If you never use ++ or -- as part of any other statement, but always put them on a line by themselves, the difference between the two forms of these operators is not noticeable.

NOTE

The prefix form *++variable* is preferred over the suffix form *variable++* because it allows the compiler to generate slightly simpler code.

More complex side effects can confuse even the C++ compiler. Consider the following code fragment:

```
value = 1;
result = (value++ * 5) + (value++ * 3);
```

This expression tells C++ to perform the steps:

1. Multiply value by 5 and add 1 to value.

2. Multiply value by 3 and add 1 to value.

3. Add the results of the two multiples together.

Steps 1 and 2 are of equal priority, unlike the previous example, so *the compiler can execute them in any order it wants to*. Suppose it decides to execute step 1 first, as shown in Figure 5-2.

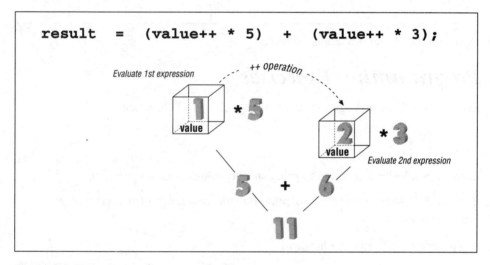

Figure 5-2. Expression evaluation, method 1

But it may execute step 2 first, as shown in Figure 5-3.

By using the first method, we get a result of 11; using the second method the result is 13. The result of this expression is ambiguous. By using the operator ++ in the middle of a larger expression, we created a problem. (This is not the only problem that ++ and -- can cause. We will get into more trouble in Chapter 10, *The C++ Preprocessor.*)

To avoid trouble and keep the program simple, always put ++ and -- on a line by themselves.

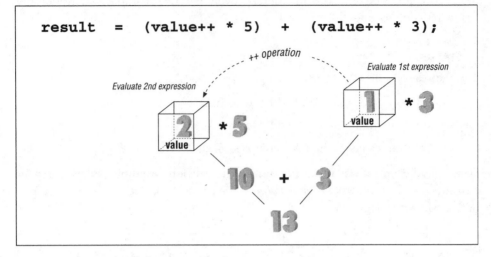

Figure 5-3. Expression evaluation, method 2

Programming Exercises

Exercise 5-1: Write a program that converts Celsius to Fahrenheit.

$$F = \frac{9}{5}C + 32$$

Exercise 5-2: Write a program to calculate the volume of a sphere, $\frac{4}{3}\pi r^3$.

Exercise 5-3: Write a program to print out the perimeter of a rectangle given its height and width.

perimeter $= 2 \cdot$ (width + height)

Exercise 5-4: Write a program that converts miles per hour to kilometers per hour.

miles $=$ (kilometers $\cdot$ 0.6213712)

Exercise 5-5: Write a program that takes hours and minutes as input and outputs the total number of minutes (1 hour 30 minutes = 90 minutes).

Exercise 5-6: Write a program that takes an integer as the number of minutes and outputs the total hours and minutes (90 minutes = 1 hour 30 minutes).

Answers to Chapter Questions

Answer 5-1: The programmer accidentally omitted the end-comment symbol (*/) after the comment for height. The comment continues onto the next line and engulfs the width variable declaration. Example 5-9 shows the program with the comments underlined.

Example 5-9. tempconv.c

```
#include <iostream.h>

int  height;    /* The height of the triangle
int  width;     /* The width of the triangle */
int  area;      /* Area of the triangle (computed) */

main()
{
    cout << "Enter width and height? ";
    cin >> width >> height;
    area = (width * height) / 2;
    cout << "The area is " << area << '\n';
    return (0);
}
```

Answer 5-2: The problem is that the zip code 02137 begins with a zero. That tells C++ that 02137 is an *octal* constant. When we print it, we print in decimal. Because 02137_8 is 8503_{10} the program prints:

```
New York's zip code is: 8503
```

6

Decision and Control Statements

> *Once a decision was made, I did not worry about it afterward.*
> —Harry Truman

Calculations and expressions are only a small part of computer programming. Decision and control statements also are needed, to specify the order in which statements are to be executed.

So far you have constructed *linear programs*, which are programs that execute in a straight line, one statement after another. In this chapter you will see how to change the *control flow* of a program with *branching statements* and *looping statements*. Branching statements cause one section of code to be executed or not, depending on a *conditional clause*. Looping statements are used to repeat a section of code a number of times or until some condition occurs.

if Statement

The `if` statement allows you to put some decision making into your programs. The general form of the `if` statement is:

```
if (condition)
    statement;
```

If the expression is true (nonzero) the statement will be executed. If the expression is zero, the statement will not be executed. For example, suppose you are writing a billing program. At the end, if the customer owes nothing or if he has credit (owes a negative amount) you want to print a message. In C++ this is written:

```
if (total_owed <= 0)
    cout << "You owe nothing.\n";
```

The operator <= is a *relational operator* that represents less than or equal to. This statement reads "if the total_owed is less than or equal to zero, print the message." The complete list of relational operators is found in Table 6-1.

Table 6-1. Relational Operators

Operator	Meaning
<=	Less than or equal to
<	Less than
>	Greater than
>=	Greater than or equal to
==	Equal
!=	Not equal

Multiple relational expressions may be grouped together with *logical operators*. For example, the statement:

```
if ((oper_char == 'Q') || (oper_char == 'q'))
    cout << "Quit\n";
```

uses the *logical OR operator* (||) to cause the if statement to print "Quit" if oper_char is either a lowercase "q" *or* an uppercase "Q." Table 6-2 lists the logical operators.

Table 6-2. Logical Operators

Operator	Usage	Meaning
Logical OR (||)	(*expr1*) || (*expr2*)	True if *expr1* or *expr2* is true
Logical AND (&&)	(*expr1*) && (*expr2*)	True if *expr1* and *expr2* are true
Logical NOT (!)	!(*expr*)	Returns false if *expr* is true or returns true if *expr* is false

Multiple statements after the if may be grouped by putting them inside curly braces ({}). For example:

```
if (total_owed <= 0) {
    ++zero_count;
    cout << "You owe nothing.\n";
}
```

For readability, the statements enclosed in curly braces are usually indented. This allows the programmer to quickly tell which statements are to be conditionally executed. As you will see later, mistakes in indentation can result in programs that are misleading and hard to read.

else Statement

An alternative form of the `if` statement is:

```
if (condition)
    statement;
else
    statement;
```

If the condition is true, the first statement is executed. If it is false, the second statement is executed. In our accounting example, we wrote out a message only if nothing was owed. In real life we probably want to tell the customer how much he owes if there is a balance due.

```
if (total_owed <= 0)
    cout << "You owe nothing.\n";
else
    cout << "You owe " << total_owed << " dollars\n";
```

Note to PASCAL programmers: Unlike PASCAL, C++ requires you to put a semicolon at the end of the statement before the `else`.

Now consider this program fragment:

```
if (count < 10)      // If #1
    if ((count % 4) == 2)    // If #2
        cout << "Condition:White\n";
  else    // (Indentation is wrong)
        cout << "Condition:Tan\n";
```

There are two `if` statements and one `else`. To which `if` does the `else` belong? Pick one:

1. It belongs to `if` #1.

2. It belongs to `if` #2.

3. You don't have to worry about this situation if you never write code like this.

The correct answer is 3. According to the C++ syntax rules, the `else` goes with the nearest `if`, so 2 is syntactically correct. But writing code like this violates the KISS principle (Keep It Simple, Stupid). It is best to write your code as clearly and simply as possible. This code fragment should be written as:

```
if (count < 10) {        // If #1
    if ((count % 4) == 2)    // If #2
        cout << "Condition:White\n";
    else
        cout << "Condition:Tan\n";
}
```

From our original example, it was not clear which `if` statement had the **else** clause; however, adding an extra set of braces improves readability, understanding, and clarity.

How Not to Use strcmp

The function `strcmp` compares two strings and returns zero if they are equal and nonzero if they are different. To check whether two strings are equal, we use the code:

```
// Check for equal
if (strcmp(string1, string2) == 0)
    cout << "Strings equal\n";
else
    cout << "Strings not equal\n";
```

Some programmers omit the comment and the `== 0` clause, leading to the following, confusing code:

```
if (strcmp(string1, string2))
    cout << "......";
```

At first glance, this program obviously compares two strings and executes the `cout` statement if they are equal. Unfortunately, the obvious is wrong. If the strings are equal `strcmp` returns zero, and the `cout` is not executed. Because of this backwards behavior of `strcmp`, you should be very careful in your use of `strcmp` and always comment its use.

Looping Statements

Computers not only do calculations, but also will do them over and over and over. To get a computer to repeat its work, you need a *loop statement.* Looping statements have many uses. For example, loops are used to count the number of words in a document or to count the number of accounts that have past due balances.

while Statement

The `while` statement is used when the program needs to perform repetitive tasks. The general form of a `while` statement is:

```
while (condition)
    statement;
```

The program will repeatedly execute the statement inside the `while` until the condition becomes false (0). (If the condition is initially false, the statement will not be executed.)

For example, Example 6-1 computes all the Fibonacci numbers that are less than 100. The Fibonacci sequence is:

```
1  1  2  3  5  8  . . .
```

The terms are computed from the equations:

```
1
1
2 = 1 + 1
3 = 1 + 2
5 = 3 + 2
etc.
```

In general terms this is:

$$f_n = f_{n-1} + f_{n-2}$$

This is a mathematical equation using math-style variable names (f_n). Mathematicians use this very terse style of naming variables. In programming, terse is dangerous, so we translate these names into something verbose for C++.

fn	translates to	next_number
f_{n-1}	translates to	current_number
f_{n-2}	translates to	old_number

So in C++ code, the equation is expressed as:

```
next_number = current_number + old_number;
```

We want to loop until our current term is 100 or larger. The `while` loop:

```
while (current_number < 100)
```

will repeat our computation and printing until we reach this limit.

In our `while` loop we compute the value of `current_number` and print it. Next we need to advance one term.

This completes the body of the loop. The first two terms of the Fibonacci sequence are 1 and 1. We initialize our first two terms to these values.

Figure 6-1 shows what happens to the variables during the execution of the program. At the beginning `current_number` and `old_number` are 1. We print the value of the current term. Then the variable `next_number` is computed (value 2). Next we advance one term by putting `next_number` into `current_number` and `current_number` into `old_number`. This is repeated until we compute the last term and the `while` loop exits.

Example 6-1 shows this written as C++ code.

Example 6-1. fib/fib.cc

```
#include <iostream.h>
int   old_number;     // previous Fibonacci number
int   current_number; // current Fibonacci number
int   next_number;    // next number in the series

main()
{
    // start things out
    old_number = 1;
    current_number = 1;

    cout << "1\n"; // Print first number

    while (current_number < 100) {

        cout << current_number << '\n';
        next_number = current_number + old_number;

        old_number = current_number;
        current_number = next_number;
    }
    return (0);
}
```

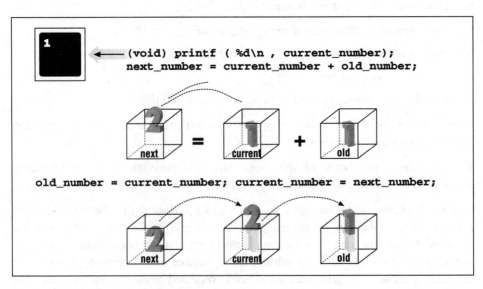

Figure 6-1. Fibonacci execution

Break Statement

We have used a `while` statement to compute Fibonacci numbers less than 100. The loop exits when the condition at the beginning becomes false. Loops also can be exited at any point through the use of a `break` statement.

Suppose you want to add a series of numbers and you don't know how many numbers are to be added together. You need some way of letting the program know it has reached the end of the list. In Program 6-2 you use the number zero (0) to signal the end of the list.

Note that the `while` statement begins with:

```
while (1) {
```

The program will loop forever because the `while` will exit only when the expression 1 is zero. The only way to exit this loop is through a `break` statement.

When we see the end-of-list indicator (zero), we use the statement:

```
if (item == 0)
    break;
```

to exit the loop.

Example 6-2. total/total.cc

```
#include <iostream.h>
int    total;   // Running total of all numbers so far
int    item;    // next item to add to the list

main()
{
    total = 0;
    while (1) {
        cout << "Enter # to add \n";
        cout << "  or 0 to stop:";
        cin >> item;

        if (item == 0)
            break;

        total += item;
        cout << "Total: " << total << '\n';
    }
    cout << "Final total " << total << '\n';
    return (0);
}
```

continue Statement

The `continue` statement is very similar to the **break** statement, except that instead of terminating the loop, it starts executing the body of the loop over from the top. For example, if you modify the previous program to total only numbers larger than 0, you get Example 6-3.

Example 6-3. total2/total2.cc

```
#include <iostream.h>
int    total;      // Running total of all numbers so far
int    item;       // next item to add to the list
int    minus_items; // number of negative items

main()
{
    total = 0;
    minus_items = 0;
    while (1) {
        cout << "Enter # to add\n";
        cout << "  or 0 to stop:";
        cin >> item;

        if (item == 0)
            break;

        if (item < 0) {
            ++minus_items;
            continue;
        }
        total += item;
        cout << "Total: " << total << '\n';
    }

    cout << "Final total " << total << '\n';
    cout << "with " << minus_items << " negative items omitted\n";
    return (0);
}
```

The Assignment Anywhere Side Effect

C++ allows the use of assignment statements almost anyplace. For example, you can put assignment statements inside another assignment statement:

```
// don't program like this
average = total_value / (number_of_entries = last - first);
```

This is the equivalent of saying:

```
// program like this
number_of_entries = last - first;

average = total_value / number_of_entries;
```

The first version buries the assignment of **number_of_entries** inside the expression. Programs should be clear and simple and should not hide anything. The most important rule of programming is *KEEP IT SIMPLE*.

C++ also allows you to put assignment statements in the **while** conditional. For example:

```
// do not program like this
while ((current_number = last_number + old_number) < 100)
    cout << "Term " << current_number << '\n';
```

Avoid this type of programming. Notice how much clearer the logic is in the following version:

```
// program like this
while (1) {
    current_number = last_number + old_number;

    if (current_number >= 100)
        break;

    cout << "Term " << current_number << '\n';
}
```

Question 6-1: *For some strange reason, the program in Example 6-4 thinks that everyone owes a balance of 0 dollars. Why?*

Example 6-4. balance/balance.cc

```
#include <iostream.h>
int    balance_owed;      // amount owed

main()
{
    cout << "Enter number of dollars owed:";
    cin >> balance_owed;

    if (balance_owed = 0)
        cout << "You owe nothing.\n";
    else
        cout << "You owe " << balance_owed << " dollars.\n";

    return (0);
}
```

Sample output:

```
Enter number of dollars owed: 12
You owe 0 dollars.
```

Programming Exercises

Exercise 6-1: Write a program to find the distance between two points.

Exercise 6-2: A professor generates letter grades using Table 6-3.

Table 6-3. Grade Values

% Correct	Grade
0–60	F
61–70	D
71–80	C
81–90	B
91–100	A

Given a numeric grade, print the letter.

Exercise 6-3: Modify the previous program to print out a + or − after the letter grade based on the last digit of the score. The modifiers are listed in Table 6-4.

Table 6-4. Grade-Modification Values

Last digit	Modifier
1–3	−
4–7	<blank>
8–0	+

For example, 81=B−, 94=A, and 68=D+. Note: An F is only an F. There is no F+ or F−.

NOTE

Programmers frequently have to modify code that someone else wrote. A good exercise is to take someone else's Example 6-4 and modify it.

Exercise 6-4: Given an amount (less than $1.00), compute the number of quarters, dimes, nickels, and pennies needed.

Exercise 6-5: A leap year is any year divisible by 4 unless it is divisible by 100, but not 400. Write a program to tell whether a year is a leap year.

Exercise 6-6: Write a program that, given the number of hours an employee worked and his hourly wage, computes his weekly pay. Count any hours over 40 as overtime at time-and-a-half.

Answers to Chapter Questions

Answer 6-1: This program illustrates the most common C++ error and one of the most frustrating. The problem is that C++ allows assignment statements inside of `if` conditionals. The statement:

```
if (balance_owed = 0)
```

uses a single equal sign instead of the double equal. C++ will assign `balance_owed` the value 0 and then test the result (which is zero). If the result were nonzero (true), the `if` clause would be executed. Since the result is zero (false), the `else` clause is executed and the program prints the wrong answer.

The statement

```
if (balance_owed = 0)
```

is equivalent to

```
balance_owed = 0;
if (balanced_owed != 0)
```

The statement should be written:

```
if (balance_owed == 0)
```

This is the most common error that beginning programmers make. It is also one of the most difficult and frustrating to find.

I once taught a course in C programming. One day about a month after the course had ended I saw one of my former students on the street. He greeted me and said, "Steve, I have to tell you the truth. During the class I thought you were going a bit overboard on this = vs. == bug, until now. You see, I just wrote the first C program for my job, and guess what mistake I made."

One trick many programmers use is to put the constant first in any == statement. For example:

```
if (0 == balanced_owed)
```

In this way, if the programmer makes a mistake and puts in = instead of ==, the result is:

```
if (0 = balanced_owed)
```

which causes a compiler error. (You can't assign `balance_owed` to 0.)

7

The Programming Process

It's just a simple matter of programming.
—Any boss who has never written a program

Programming is more than just writing code. Software has a life cycle. It is born, grows up, becomes mature, and finally dies, only to be replaced by a newer, younger product. Understanding this cycle is important because as a programmer you will spend only a small amount of time actually writing new code. Most programming time is spent modifying and debugging existing code. Software does not exist in a vacuum; it must be documented, maintained, enhanced, and sold. In this section we take a look at a small programming project using one programmer. Larger projects that involve many people are discussed in Chapter 23, *Modular Programming*. Although the final code is fewer than a hundred lines, the principles used in its construction can be applied to programs with thousands of lines of code. Figure 7-1 illustrates the software life cycle.

The major steps in making a program are:

- **Requirements**. Programs start when someone gets an idea and assigns you to implement it. The requirement document describes, in very general terms, what is wanted.

- **Specification**. A description of what the program does. In the beginning, a *Preliminary Specification* is used to describe what the program is going to do. Later, as the program becomes more refined, so does the specification. Finally, when the program is finished, the specification serves as a complete description of what the program does.

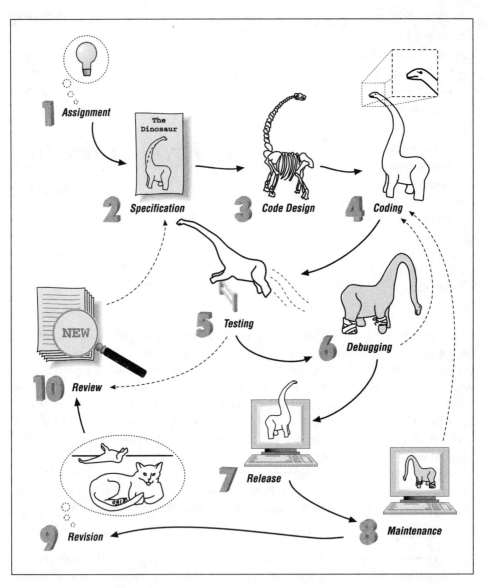

Figure 7-1. Software life cycle

- **Code design**. The programmer does an overall design of the program. The design should include major algorithms, class definitions, module specifications, file formats, and data structures.

  One thing cannot be over-stressed; "*Think before you act.*" Studies have shown that a good design can result in a program that is 1/10 of the size of a poorly designed one. This is especially true when using C++, where designing good objects is critical to writing a good program. (You will find out what objects are in Chapter 13, *Simple Classes*.)

Note: "Think before you act" is good advice not only for coding, but also for life in general.

- **Coding**. The next step is writing the program. This involves first writing a prototype and then filling it in to create the full program.

- **Testing**. The programmer should design a test plan and use it to test the program. It is a good idea, when possible, to have someone else test the program.

- **Debugging**. Unfortunately, very few programs work the first time. They must be corrected and tested again.

- **Release**. The program is packaged, documented, and sent out into the world to be used.

- **Maintenance**. Programs are never perfect. Bugs will be found and will need correction.

- **Revising and updating**. After a program has been working for a while, the users will want changes, such as more features or more intelligent algorithms. At this point a new specification is created and the process starts again.

Setting Up

The operating system allows you to group files in directories. Just as file folders serve as a way of keeping papers together in a filing cabinet, directories serve as a way of keeping files together. In this chapter you will be creating a simple calculator program. All the files for this program will be stored in a directory named calc. To create a directory in UNIX, execute the following commands:

```
% cd ~
% mkdir calc
```

In MS-DOS, type:

```
C:\> cd \
C:\> mkdir calc
```

To tell the operating system which directory you want to use, in UNIX type the command:

```
% cd ~/calc
```

In MS-DOS, type:

```
C:\> cd \calc
C:\CALC>
```

More information on how to organize directories can be found in your operating system documentation.

The Specification

For this chapter we are going to assume that you have been given the assignment to "write a program that acts like a four-function calculator." Typically, the specification you are given is vague and incomplete. It is up to you to refine it into something that exactly defines the program you are going to produce.

The first step is to write a document called *The Preliminary Users' Specification,* which describes what your program is going to do and how to use it. This document does not describe the internal structure of the program or the algorithm you plan to use. A sample specification for the four-function calculator is:

```
Calc
A four-function calculator
Preliminary Specification
Dec. 10, 1994 Steve Oualline
```

Warning: This is a preliminary specification. Any resemblance to any software living or dead is purely coincidental.

Calc is a program that allows the user to turn his $10,000 computer into a $1.98 four-function calculator. The program adds, subtracts, multiplies, and divides simple integers.

When the program is run, it zeros the result register and displays its contents. The user can then type in an operator and number. The result is updated and displayed. The following operators are valid:

Operator	Meaning
+	Addition
-	Subtraction
*	Multiplication
/	Division

Example (user input is in boldface)

```
calc
Result: 0
Enter operator and number: + 123
Result: 123
Enter operator and number: - 23
Result: 100
```

```
Enter operator and number: / 25
Result: 4
Enter operator and number: * 4
Result: 16
```

The preliminary specification serves two purposes. First, you should give it to your boss (or customer) to make sure that what he thought he said and what you thought he said agree. Second, you can circulate it among your colleagues to see whether they have any suggestions or corrections.

This preliminary specification was circulated and received the comments: 1) "How are you going to get out of the program?" and 2) "What happens when you try to divide by 0?"

So a new operator is added:

```
q - quit
```

and we add another paragraph:

```
Dividing by 0 results in an error message and the result register is
left unchanged.
```

IV + III = VII

A college instructor once gave his students an assignment to "write a four-function calculator." One of his students noticed that this was a pretty loose specification and decided to have a little fun. The professor didn't say what sort of numbers had to be used, so the student created a program that worked only with Roman numerals (IV + III = VII). The program came with a complete user manual—written in Latin.

Code Design

After the preliminary specification has been approved, you can start designing code. In the code-design phase, you plan your work. In large programming projects involving many people, the code would be broken up into modules for each programmer. At this stage, file formats are planned, data structures are designed, and major algorithms are decided upon.

This simple calculator uses no files and requires no fancy data structures. What's left for this phase is to design the major algorithm. Outlined in *pseudo-code*, a shorthand halfway between English and real code, it is:

```
Loop
    Read an operator and number
    Do the calculation
```

```
    Display the result
    End-Loop
```

The Prototype

Once the code design is completed, you can begin writing the program. But rather than try to write the entire program at once and then debug it, you will use a method called *fast prototyping*. This consists of writing the smallest portion of the specification you can implement that will still do something. In our case, you will cut the four functions down to a one-function calculator. Once you get this small part working, you can build the rest of the functions onto this stable foundation. Also, the prototype gives the boss something to look at and play around with so he has a good idea of the direction the project is taking. Good communication is the key to good programming, and the more you can show someone, the better. The code for the first version of the four-function calculator is found in Example 7-1.

Example 7-1. calc/calc.cc

```cpp
#include <iostream.h>

int    result;    // the result of the calculations
char   oper_char; // the user-specified operator
int    value;     // value specified after the operator

int main()
{
    result = 0; // initialize the result

    // Loop forever (or till we hit the break statement)
    while (1) {
        cout << "Result: " << result << '\n';

        cout << "Enter operator and number: ";
        cin >> oper_char >> value;

        if (oper_char = '+') {
            result += value;
        } else {
            cout << "Unknown operator " << oper_char << '\n';
        }
    }
    return (0);
}
```

The program begins by initializing the variable **result** to zero. The main body of the program is a loop starting with:

```cpp
    while (1) {
```

This will loop until a **break** statement is reached. The code:

```
cout << "Enter operator and number: ";
cin >> operator >> value;
```

asks the user for an operator and number. These are parsed and stored in the variables **operator** and **value**. (The full set of I/O operations such as << and >> are described in Chapter 16, *File Input/Output*.) Finally, you start checking the operators. If the operator is a plus (+), you perform an addition using the line:

```
if (operator = '+') {
    result += value;
```

So far you only recognize the plus operator. As soon as this works, you will add more operators by adding more **if** statements.

Finally, if an illegal operator is entered, the line:

```
} else {
    cout << "Unknown operator " << operator << '\n';
}
```

writes an error message telling the user he made a mistake.

The Makefile

Once the source has been entered, it needs to be compiled and linked. Up to now we have been running the compiler manually. This is somewhat tedious and prone to error. Also, larger programs consist of many modules and are extremely difficult to compile by hand. Fortunately, both UNIX and Turbo-C++ have a utility called *make* that handles the details of compilation.

For now, just use this example as a template and substitute the name of your program in place of *calc*. The *make* program is discussed in detail in Chapter 23, *Modular Programming*. Basically, *make* looks at the file called *Makefile* for a description of how to compile your program and runs the compiler for you.

For a UNIX system using the generic CC compiler, the *Makefile* should be:

```
    [File: calc1/makefile.unx]
#
# Makefile for many UNIX compilers using the
# "standard" command name CC
#
CC=CC
CFLAGS=-g
all: calc

calc: calc.cc
```

```
        $(CC) $(CFLAGS) -o calc calc.cc

clean:
        rm calc
```

If you are using the Free Software Foundation's g++ compiler, the *Makefile* is:

```
    [File: calc1/makefile.gnu]
#
# Makefile for the Free Software Foundations g++ compiler
#
CC=g++
CFLAGS=-g -Wall
all: calc

calc: calc.cc
        $(CC) $(CFLAGS) -o calc calc.cc

clean:
        rm calc
```

For Turbo-C++, the *Makefile* should be:

```
    [File: calc1/makefile.tcc]
#
# Makefile for Borland's Turbo-C++ compiler
#
CC=tcc
#
# Flags
#           -N  -- Check for stack overflow
#           -v  -- Enable debugging
#           -w  -- Turn on all warnings
#           -ml -- Large model
#
CFLAGS=-N -v -w -ml
all: calc.exe

calc.exe: calc.cpp
        $(CC) $(CFLAGS) -ecalc calc.cpp

clean:
        erase calc.exe
```

For Borland C++, the *Makefile* is the same except the compiler is named *bcc*.

Finally, for Microsoft Visual C++, the *Makefile* is:

```
    [File: calc1/makefile.msc]
#
# Makefile for Microsoft Visual C++
#
CC=cl
#
# Flags
#           AL -- Compile for large model
```

```
#        Zi -- Enable debugging
#        W1 -- Turn on warnings
#
CFLAGS=/AL /Zi /W1
all: calc.exe

calc.exe: calc.cpp
        $(CC) $(CFLAGS)  calc.cpp

clean:
        erase calc.exe
```

NOTE

Microsoft Visual C++ does supply a `make` program as part of its package; however, the *make* command has been renamed to *nmake*.

To compile the program, just execute the command *make*. (Under Microsoft Visual C++ use the command *nmake.) make* determines what compilation commands are needed and execute them.

make uses the modification dates of the files to determine whether or not a compilation is necessary. Compilation creates an object file. The modification date of the object file is later than the modification date of its source. If the source is edited, its modification date is updated, making the object file out of date. *make* checks these dates and, if the source was modified after the object, *make* recompiles the object.

Testing

Once the program is compiled without errors, you can move on to the testing phase. Now is the time to start writing a test plan. This document is simply a list of the steps you perform to make sure the program works. It is written for two reasons.

- If a bug is found, you want to be able to reproduce it.

- If you ever change the program, you will want to retest it to make sure new code did not break any of the sections of the program that were previously working.

The test plan starts out as:

```
Try the following operations

+ 123    Result should be 123
+ 52     Result should be 175
x 37     Error message should be output
```

Running the program you get:

```
Result: 0
Enter operator and number: + 123
Result: 123
Enter operator and number: + 52
Result: 175
Enter operator and number: x 37
Result: 212
```

Something is clearly wrong. The entry "x   37" should have generated an error message but didn't. There is a bug in the program, so you begin the debugging phase. One advantage to making a small working prototype is that you can isolate errors early.

Debugging

First you inspect the program to see if you can detect the error. In such a small program it is not difficult to spot the mistake. However, let's assume that instead of a 21-line program, you have a much larger one containing 5,000 lines. Such a program would make inspection more difficult, so you need to proceed to the next step.

Most systems have C++ debugging programs, but each debugger is different. Some systems have no debugger. In that case you must resort to a diagnostic print statement. (More advanced debugging techniques are discussed in Chapter 17, *Debugging and Optimization*.) The technique is simple: Put a cout where you're sure the data is good (just to make sure it *really* is good). Then put a cout where the data is bad. Run the program and keep putting in cout's until you isolate the area in the program that contains the mistake. The program, with diagnostic cout lines added, looks like:

```
cout << "Enter operator and number: ";
cin >> value >> operator;

cout << "## after cin " << operator << '\n';

if (operator = '+') {
    cout << "## after if " << operator << '\n';
    result += value;
```

NOTE

The ## at the beginning of each cout line flags the line as a debug line. This makes it easy to tell the temporary debug output from the real program output. Also, when you finally find the bug the ## makes it easy to find and remove the debug lines with your editor.

Running the program again results in:

```
Result: 0
Enter operator and number: + 123
Result: 123
Enter operator and number: + 52
## after cin +
## after if +
Result: 175
Enter operator and number: x 37
## after cin x
## after if +
Result: 212
```

From this you see that something is going wrong with the `if` statement. Somehow the variable operator is an `x` going in and a `+` coming out. Closer inspection reveals that you have the old mistake of using `=` instead of `==`. After you fix this bug, the program runs correctly. Building on this working foundation, you add in the code for the other operators, `-`, `*`, and `/`, to create Example 7-2.

Example 7-2. calc3/calc3.c

```
#include <iostream.h>
int    result;    // the result of the calculations
char   oper_char; // the user-specified operator
int    value;     // value specified after the operator
main()
{
    result = 0; // initialize the result

    // loop forever (or until break reached)
    while (1) {
        cout << "Result: " << result << '\n';
        cout << "Enter operator and number: ";

        cin >> oper_char >> value;

        if ((oper_char == 'q') || (oper_char == 'Q'))
            break;

        if (oper_char == '+') {
            result += value;
        } else if (oper_char == '-') {
            result -= value;
        } else if (oper_char == '*') {
            result *= value;
        } else if (oper_char == '/') {
            if (value == 0) {
                cout << "Error: Divide by zero\n";
                cout << "    operation ignored\n";
            } else
                result /= value;
        } else {
            cout << "Unknown operator " << oper_char << '\n';
```

Example 7-2. calc3/calc3.c (Continued)

```
        }
    }
    return (0);
}
```

You expand the test plan to include the new operators and try it again.

```
+ 123     Result should be 123
+ 52      Result should be 175
x 37      Error message should be output
- 175     Result should be zero
+ 10      Result should be 10
/ 5       Result should be 2
/ 0       Divide by zero error
* 8       Result should be 16
q         Program should exit
```

Testing the program, you find much to your surprise that it works. The word "Preliminary" is removed from the specification and the program, test plan, and specification are released.

Maintenance

Good programmers put their programs through a long and rigorous testing process before releasing it to the outside world. Then the first user tries the program and almost immediately finds a bug. This starts the maintenance phase. Bugs are fixed, the program is tested (to make sure the fixes didn't break anything), and the program is released again.

Revisions

Although the program is officially finished, you are not finished with it. After it is in use for a few months, someone will come to us and ask, "Can you add a modulus operator?" So you revise the specifications, add the change to the program, update the test plan, test the program, and release it again.

As time passes, more people will come to you with additional requests for changes. Soon the program has trig functions, linear regressions, statistics, binary arithmetic, and financial calculations. The design is based on the idea of one-character operators. Soon you find yourself running out of characters to use. At this point the program is doing work far beyond what it was initially designed to do. Sooner or later you reach the point where the program needs to be scrapped and a new one written from scratch. At this point you write a new Preliminary Specification and start the process over again.

Electronic Archaeology

Unfortunately, most programmers don't start a project at the design step. Instead they are immediately thrust into the maintenance or revision stage. This means the programmer is faced with the worst possible job: understanding and modifying someone else's code.

Contrary to popular belief, most C++ programs are not written by disorganized orangutans using Zen programming techniques and poorly commented in Esperanto. They just look that way. Electronic archeology is the art of digging through old code to discover amazing things (like how and why the code works).

Your computer can aid greatly in your search to discover the true meaning of someone else's code. Many tools are available for examining and formatting code. (Be careful with your selection of tools, however. Many C tools have yet to be upgraded for C++. See earlier sections on revisions.) Some of these tools include:

- **Cross-references.** These programs have names like **xref**, **cxref**, and **cross**. System V UNIX has the utility **cscope**. They print out a list of variables and where the variables are used.

- **Program indenters.** Programs such as **cb** and **indent** indent a program "correctly" (correct indentation is something defined by the tool maker).

- **Pretty printers.** A pretty printer such as **vgrind** or **cprint** typesets source code for printing on a laser printer.

- **Call graphs.** On System V UNIX the program **cflow** analyzes the structure of the program. On other systems there is a public domain utility, **calls,** that produces call graphs, showing who calls whom and who is called by whom.

- **Class browsers.** A class browser allows you to display the class hierarchy so you can tell what components went into building the class as well as its structure. You'll learn what a class is in Chapter 13, *Simple Classes*.

Which tools should you use? Whichever ones work for you. Different programmers work in different ways. Some techniques for examining code are listed below. Choose the ones that work for you and use them.

Mark Up the Program

Take a printout of the program and make notes all over it. Use red or blue ink so you can tell the difference between the printout and the notes. Use a highlighter to emphasize important sections. These notes are useful; put them in the program as comments, and then make a new printout and start the process over again.

Use the Debugger

The debugger is a great tool for understanding how something works. Most debuggers allow you to step through the program one line at a time, examining variables and discovering how things really work. Once you find out what the code does, make notes and put them in as comments.

Use the Text Editor as a Browser

One of the best tools for going through someone else's code is your text editor. Suppose you want to find out what the variable sc is used for. Use the search command to find the first place sc is used. Search again and find the second. Continue searching until you know what the variable does.

Suppose you find out that sc is used as a sequence counter. Since you're already in the editor, you can easily do a global search-and-replace to change the variable sc to sequence_counter. (Disaster warning: Make sure sequence_counter is not already defined as a variable *before* you make the change. Also make sure you do a *word* replacement or you'll find you replaced sc in places you didn't intend.) Comment the declaration and you're on your way to creating an understandable program.

Add Comments

Don't be afraid to put any information you have, no matter how little, into the comments. Some of the comments I've used include:

```
int state;   // Controls some sort of state machine
int rmxy;    // Something to do with color correction?
```

Finally, there is a catch-all comment:

```
int idn;    // ???
```

which means, "I have no idea what this variable does." Even though the purpose is unknown, it is now marked as something that needs more work.

As you go through someone else's code adding comments and improving style, the structure will become clearer to you. By inserting notes (comments), you make the code better and easier to understand for future programmers.

Suppose you are confronted with the following program written by someone from the "The Terser the Better" school of programming. Your assignment is to figure out what this program does. First you pencil in some comments as shown in Figure 7-2.

```
#include <iostream.h>
#include <stdlib.h>
int    g, l, h, c, n;
char   line[80];
main()
{
    while (1) {
        /*Not Really*/
        g = rand() % 100 + 1;
        l = 0;
        h = 100;
        c = 0;
        while (1) {
            cout << "Bounds " << l << " - " << h << '\n';
            cout << "Value[" << c << "]? ";
            ++c;
            cin >> n;
            if (n == g)
                break;
            if (n < g)
                l = n;
            else
                h = n;
        }
        cout << "Bingo\n";
    }
    return (0);
}
```

(handwritten annotations:) Yuck!!! "l" as var name — Why? — init vars — counter of some sort — adjust bounds l - lower h - higher

Figure 7-2. A terse program

This mystery program requires some work. After going through it and applying the principles described in this section, you get the well-commented, easy-to-understand version shown in Example 7-3.

Example 7-3. guess/good.cc

```
/********************************************************
 * guess -- a simple guessing game                     *
 *                                                      *
 * Usage:                                               *
 *      guess                                           *
 *                                                      *
 *      A random number is chosen between 1 and 100.    *
 *      The player is given a set of bounds and         *
 *      must choose a number between them.              *
 *      If the player chooses the correct number, he wins*
 *      Otherwise, the bounds are adjusted to reflect    *
 *      the players guess and the game continues        *
 *                                                      *
 * Restrictions:                                        *
 *      The random number is generated by the statment  *
 *      rand() % 100.  Because rand() returns a number  *
 *      0 <= rand() <= maxint  this slightly favors     *
```

Example 7-3. guess/good.cc (Continued)

```
 *        the lower numbers.                                      *
 ********************************************************/
#include <iostream.h>
#include <stdlib.h>
int    number_to_guess;   // Random number to be guessed
int    low_limit;         // Current lower limit of player's range
int    high_limit;        // Current upper limit of player's range
int    guess_count;       // Number of times player guessed
int    player_number;     // Number gotten from the player
char   line[80];          // Input buffer for a single line
main()
{
    while (1) {
        /*
         * Not a pure random number; see restrictions
         */
        number_to_guess = rand() % 100 + 1;

        // Initialize variables for loop
        low_limit = 0;
        high_limit = 100;
        guess_count = 0;

        while (1) {
            // Tell user what the bounds are and get his guess
            cout << "Bounds " << low_limit << " - " << high_limit << '\n';
            cout << "Value[" << guess_count << "]? ";

            ++guess_count;

            cin >> player_number;

            // Did he guess right?
            if (player_number == number_to_guess)
                break;

            // Adjust bounds for next guess
            if (player_number < number_to_guess)
                low_limit = player_number;
            else
                high_limit = player_number;

        }
        cout << "Bingo\n";
    }
    return (0);
}
```

Programming Exercises

For each assignment, follow the software life cycle from specification through release.

Exercise 7-1: Write a program to convert English units to metric (e.g., miles to kilometers, gallons to liters, etc.). Include a specification and a code design.

Exercise 7-2: Write a program to perform date arithmetic, such as how many days there are between 6/1/90 and 8/3/92. Include a specification and a code design.

Exercise 7-3: A serial transmission line can transmit 960 characters a second. Write a program that will calculate how long it will take to send a file, given the file's size. Try it on a 400MB (419,430,400 byte) file. Use appropriate units. (A 400MB file takes days.)

Exercise 7-4: Write a program to add an 8% sales tax to a given amount and round the result to the nearest penny.

Exercise 7-5: Write a program to tell whether a number is prime.

Exercise 7-6: Write a program that takes a series of numbers and counts the number of positive and negative values.

II

Simple Programming

8

More Control Statements

Grammar, which knows how to control even kings . . .
—Molière

for Statement

The `for` statement allows you to execute a block of code a specified number of times. The general form of the `for` statement is:

```
for (initial-statement; condition; iteration-statement)
    body-statement;
```

this is equivalent to:

```
initial-statement;
while (condition) {
    body-statement;
    iteration-statement;
}
```

For example, Example 8-1 uses a `while` loop to add five numbers.

Example 8-1. total6/total6w.cc

```
#include <iostream.h>

int total;      // Total of all the numbers
int current;    // Current value from the user
int counter;    // While loop counter

main() {
    total = 0;

    counter = 0;
    while (counter < 5) {
```

Example 8-1. total6/total6w.cc (Continued)

```
        cout << "Number? ";

        cin >> current;
        total += current;

        ++counter;
    }
    cout << "The grand total is " << total << '\n';
    return (0);
}
```

The same program can be rewritten using a `for` statement as seen in Example 8-2.

Example 8-2. total6/total6.cc

```
#include <iostream.h>

int total;      // Total of all the numbers
int current;    // Current value from the user
int counter;    // For loop counter

main() {
    total = 0;
    for (counter = 0; counter < 5; ++counter) {
        cout << "Number? ";

        cin >> current;
        total += current;
    }
    cout << "The grand total is " << total << '\n';
    return (0);
}
```

Note that counter goes from 0 to 4. Normally you count five items as 1, 2, 3, 4, 5. You will get along much better in C++ if you change your thinking to zero-based counting and count five items as 0, 1, 2, 3, 4. (One-based counting is one of the main causes of array overflow errors. See Chapter 5, *Arrays, Qualifiers, and Reading Numbers.*)

Careful examination of the two flavors of this program reveals the similarities between the two versions, as shown in Figure 8-1.

Many older programming languages do not allow you to change the control variable (in this case counter) inside the loop. C++ is not so picky. You can change the control variable anytime you wish—you can jump into and out of the loop and generally do things that would make a PASCAL or FORTRAN programmer cringe. (Even though C++ gives you the freedom to do such insane things, that doesn't mean you should do them.)

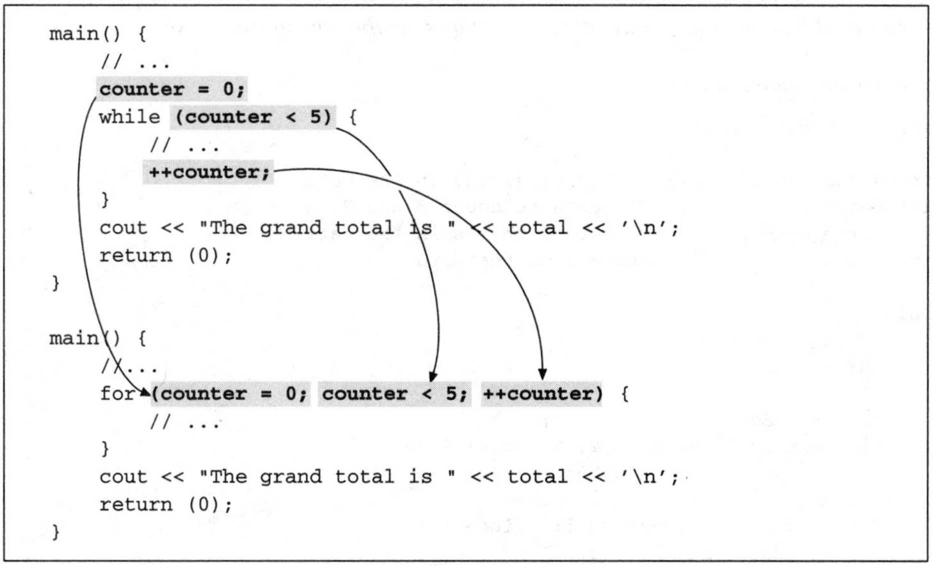

```
main() {
    // ...
    counter = 0;
    while (counter < 5) {
        // ...
        ++counter;
    }
    cout << "The grand total is " << total << '\n';
    return (0);
}

main() {
    // ...
    for (counter = 0; counter < 5; ++counter) {
        // ...
    }
    cout << "The grand total is " << total << '\n';
    return (0);
}
```

*Figure 8-1. Similarities between **while** and for*

Question 8-1: *Example 8-3 contains an error.*

Example 8-3. cent/cent.cc

```
#include <iostream.h>
/*
 * This program produces a Celsius to Fahrenheit conversion
 *    chart for the numbers 0 to 100.
 *
 * Restrictions:
 *    This program deals with integers only, so the
 *    calculations may not be exact.
 */

// The current Celsius temperature we are working with
int celsius;
main() {
    for (celsius = 0; celsius <= 100; ++celsius);
        cout << "Celsius: " << celsius <<
                " Fahrenheit: " << ((celsius * 9) / 5 + 32) << '\n';
    return (0);
}
```

When run, this program prints out:

```
Celsius: 101 Fahrenheit: 213
```

and nothing more. Why?

Question 8-2: *Example 8-4 reads a list of five numbers and counts the number of threes and sevens in the data. Why does it give us the wrong answers?*

Example 8-4. seven/seven.cc.

```
include <iostream.h>

int seven_count;      // Number of sevens in the data
int data[5];          // The data to count 3 and 7 in
int three_count;      // Number of threes in the data
int index;            // Index into the data

main() {
    seven_count = 0;
    three_count = 0;

    cout << "Enter 5 numbers\n";
    cin >> data[1] >> data[2] >> data[3] >>
            data[4] >> data[5];

    for (index = 1; index <= 5; ++index) {
        if (data[index] == 3)
            ++three_count;
        if (data[index] == 7)
            ++seven_count;
    }
    cout << "Threes " << three_count << " Sevens " << seven_count << '\n';
    return (0);
}
```

When we run this program with the data 3 7 3 0 2, the results are:

```
Threes 4 Sevens 1
```

(Your results may vary.)

switch Statement

The `switch` statement is similar to a chain of `if-else` statements. The general form of a `switch` statement is:

```
switch (expression) {
    case constant1:
        statement
        . . . .
        break;

    case constant2:
        statement

        . . . .
        // Fall through

    default:
```

```
        statement
        . . . .
        break;

    case constant3:
        statement
        . . . .
        break;
}
```

The `switch` statement evaluates the value of an expression and branches to one of the `case` labels. Duplicate labels are not allowed, so only one `case` will be selected. The expression must evaluate to a integer, character, or enumeration.

`case` labels can be in any order and must be constants. The `default` label can be put anywhere in the `switch`.

When C++ sees a `switch` statement, it evaluates the expression and then looks for a matching `case` label. If none is found, the `default` label is used. If no `default` is found, the statement does nothing.

A `break` statement inside a `switch` tells the computer to continue the execution after the `switch`. If the `break` is not there, execution continues with the next statement.

NOTE

The `switch` statement is very similar to the PASCAL `case` statement. The main differences are that while PASCAL allows only one statement after the label, C++ allows many. C++ keeps executing until it hits a `break` statement. In PASCAL you can't "fall through" from one `case` to another. In C++ you can.

The calculator program in Chapter 7, *The Programming Process*, contains a series of `if-else` statements.

```
if (operator == '+') {
    result += value;
} else if (operator == '-') {
    result -= value;
} else if (operator == '*') {
    result *= value;
} else if (operator == '/') {
    if (value == 0) {
        cout << "Error: Divide by zero\n";
        cout << "    operation ignored\n";
    } else
        result /= value;
} else {
    cout << "Unknown operator " << operator << '\n';
}
```

This section of code can easily be rewritten as a `switch` statement. In this `switch`, we use a different `case` for each operation. The `default` clause takes care of all the illegal operators.

Rewriting the program using a `switch` statement makes it not only simpler, but also easier to read as seen in Example 8-5.

Example 8-5. calc-sw/calc3.cc

```
#include <iostream.h>
int    result;      // The result of the calculations
char   oper_char;   // The user-specified operator
int    value;       // Value specified after the operator

main()
{
    result = 0;                     // Initialize the result

    // Loop forever (or until break reached)
    while (1) {
        cout << "Result: " << result << '\n';
        cout << "Enter operator and number: ";
        cin >> oper_char >> value;

        if ((oper_char == 'q') || (oper_char == 'Q'))
            break;

        switch (oper_char) {
            case '+':
                result += value;
                break;
            case '-':
                result -= value;
                break;
            case '*':
                result *= value;
                break;
            case '/':
                if (value == 0) {
                    cout << "Error: Divide by zero\n";
                    cout << "    operation ignored\n";
                } else
                    result /= value;
                break;
            default:
                cout << "Unknown operator " << oper_char << '\n';
                break;
        }
    }
    return (0);
}
```

A `break` statement is not required at the end of a `case`. If the `break` is not there, execution will continue with the next statement.

For example:

```
control = 0;

// A not so good example of programming
switch (control) {
        case 0:
                cout << "Reset\n";
        case 1:
                cout << "Initializing\n";
                break;
        case 2:
                cout "Working\n";
}
```

In this case, when `control == 0`, the program prints:

```
Reset
Initializing
```

Case 0 does not end with a `break` statement. After printing "`Reset`" the program falls through to the next statement (case 1) and prints "`Initializing`."

But there is a problem with this syntax. You can't be sure that the program is supposed to fall through from case 0 to case 1, or if the programmer forgot to put in a `break` statement. To clear up this confusion, a `case` section should always end with a `break` statement or the comment "`//fall through`."

```
// A better example of programming
switch (control) {
        case 0:
                cout << "Reset\n";
                // Fall through
        case 1:
                cout << "Initializing\n";
                break;
        case 2:
                cout << "Working\n";
}
```

Because `case 2` is last, it doesn't absolutely need a `break` statement. A `break` would cause the program to skip to the end of the `switch`, but we're already there.

But suppose we modify the program slightly and add another `case` to the `switch`:

```
// We have a little problem
switch (control) {
        case 0:
                cout << "Reset\n";
```

```
                    // Fall through
            case 1:
                    cout << "Initializing\n";
                    break;
            case 2:
                    cout << "Working\n";
            case 3:
                    cout << "Closing down\n";
    }
```

Now when `control` == 2 the program prints:

```
Working
Closing down
```

This is an unpleasant surprise. The problem is caused by the fact that **case 2** is no longer the last **case**. We fall through. (Unintentionally, or otherwise we would have included a `// Fall through` comment.) A **break** is now necessary. If you always put in a **break** statement, you don't have to worry about whether or not it is really needed.

```
    // Almost there
    switch (control) {
            case 0:
                    cout << "Reset\n";
                    // Fall through
            case 1:
                    cout << "Initializing\n";
                    break;
            case 2:
                    cout << "Working\n";
                    break;
    }
```

Finally, we ask the question: What happens when `control` == 5? In this case, since there is no matching **case** or a **default** clause, the entire **switch** statement is skipped.

In this example, the programmer did not include a **default** statement because control will never be anything but 0, 1, or 2. However, variables can get assigned strange values, so we need a little more defensive programming.

```
    // The final version
    switch (control) {
        case 0:
            cout << "Reset\n";
            // Fall through
        case 1:
            cout << "Initializing\n";
            break;
        case 2:
            cout << "Working\n";
            break;
```

```
        default:
            cout << "Internal error, control value " << control <<
                    " impossible\n";
            break;
    }
```

Although a `default` is not required, it should be put in every `switch`. Even though the `default` may be just:

```
    default:
            // Do nothing
            break;
```

it should be included. This indicates that you want to ignore out-of-range data.

switch, break, and continue

The `break` statement has two uses. Used inside a `switch` it causes the program to exit the `switch` statement. Inside of a `for` or `while` loop, it causes a loop exit. The `continue` statement is only valid inside a loop and causes the program to go to the top of the loop.

To illustrate how these statements work, we've produced a new version of the calculator program. The new program prints the result only after valid data is input and has a Help command.

The Help command is special. We don't want to print the result after the Help command, so instead of ending the Help `case` with a `break` we end it with a `continue`. The `continue` forces execution to go to the top of the loop.

When an unknown operator is entered, we print an error message. As with the Help `case`, we use a `continue` statement to skip printing the result.

Finally, there is one special command: quit. This command is handled outside the `switch`. It is handled by the `break` at the top of the loop. Since the `break` is outside the `switch,` it belongs to the `while` loop and causes the program to exit the `while`.

The control flow for this program can be seen in Figure 8-2.

```
#include <iostream.h>
int    result;      // the result of the calculations
char   oper_char;   // operator the user specified
int    value;       // value specified after the operator
main()
{
    result = 0;                      // initialize the result

    // loop forever (or until break reached)
    while (1) {  ◄ - - - - - - - - - - - - - - - - - - - - - - - - - ┐
        cout << "Enter operator and number: ";                       │

        cin >> oper_char >> value;                                   │

        if ((oper_char == 'q') || (oper_char == 'Q'))                │
            break; ──────────────────────────────────────────────┐   │

        switch (oper_char) {                                     │   │
            case '+':                                            │   │
                result += value;                                 │   │
············ break;                                              │   │
            case '-':                                            │   │
                result -= value;                                 │   │
············ break;                                              │   │
            case '*':                                            │   │
                result *= value;                                 │   │
············ break;                                              │   │
            case '/':                                            │   │
                if (value == 0) {                                │   │
                    cout << "Error: Divide by zero\n";           │   │
                    cout << "   operation ignored\n";            │   │
                } else                                           │   │
                    result /= value;                             │   │
············ break;                                              │   │
            case 'h':                                            │   │
            case 'H':                                            │   │
                cout << "Operator   Meaning\n";                  │   │
                cout << "  +        Add\n";                      │   │
                cout << "  -        Subtract\n";                 │   │
                cout << "  *        Multiply\n";                 │   │
                cout << "  /        Divide\n";                   │   │
                continue; - - - - - - - - - - - - - - - - - - - ┘   │
            default:                                                 │
                cout << "Unknown operator " << oper_char << '\n'; │   │
                continue; - - - - - - - - - - - - - - - - - - - - - ┘
        }
······► cout << "Result: " << result << '\n';
    }
    return (0);  ◄──────────────────────────────────────────────────┘
}
```

break inside "switch" · *"continue" (inside switch)* · *"break" (outside switch)*

Figure 8-2. switch/continue

Programming Exercises

Exercise 8-1: Print a checkerboard (8-by-8 grid). Each square should be 5-by-3 characters wide. A 2-by-2 example follows:

```
+-----+-----+
|     |     |
|     |     |
|     |     |
+-----+-----+
|     |     |
|     |     |
|     |     |
+-----+-----+
```

Exercise 8-2: The total resistance of n resistors in parallel is:

$$\frac{1}{R} = \frac{1}{R_1} + \frac{1}{R_2} + \frac{1}{R_3} + \dots + \frac{1}{R_n}$$

Suppose we have a network of two resistors with the values 400Ω and 200Ω. Then our equation would be:

$$\frac{1}{R} = \frac{1}{R_1} + \frac{1}{R_2}$$

Substituting in the value of the resistors we get:

$$\frac{1}{R} = \frac{1}{400} + \frac{1}{200}$$

$$\frac{1}{R} = \frac{3}{400}$$

$$R = \frac{400}{3}$$

So the total resistance of our two-resistor network is 133.3Ω.

Write a program to compute the total resistance for any number of parallel resistors.

Exercise 8-3: Write a program to average n numbers.

Exercise 8-4: Write a program to print out the multiplication table.

Exercise 8-5: Write a program that reads a character and prints out whether or not it is a vowel or a consonant.

Exercise 8-6: Write a program that converts numbers to words. Example: 895 results in "eight nine five."

Exercise 8-7: The number 85 is said "eighty-five" not "eight five." Modify the previous program to handle the numbers 0-100 so all numbers come out as we really say them. Example: 13 ⟹ "thirteen," 100 ⟹ "one hundred."

Answers to Chapter Questions

Answer 8-1: The problem lies with the semicolon (;) at the end of the `for` statement. The body of the `for` statement is between the closing parentheses and the semicolon. In this case it is nothing. Even though the `cout` statement is indented, it is not part of the `for` statement. The indentation is misleading. The C++ compiler does not look at indentation. The program does nothing until the expression

```
centigrade <= 100
```

becomes false (`centigrade == 101`). Then the `cout` is executed.

Answer 8-2: The problem is that we read the number into `data[1]` through `data[5]`. In C++ the range of legal array indices is 0 to <array size>–1 or in this case 0 to 4. `data[5]` is illegal. When we use it strange things happen; in this case the variable `three_count` is changed. The solution is to use only `data[0]` to `data[4]`.

9

Variable Scope and Functions

> *But in the gross and scope of my opinion*
> *This bodes some strange eruption to our state.*
>
> —Shakespeare
> *Hamlet*, Act I, Scene I

So far you have been using only **global variables**. These are variables that can be set or used almost anywhere in the program. In this chapter you learn about other kinds of variables and how to use them. This chapter also tells you how to divide your code into functions. Many aspects of functions are detailed, including function overloading, using functions to build structured programs, and the use of recursive function calls.

Scope and Storage Class

All variables have two attributes, `scope` and `storage class`. The *scope* of a variable is the area of the program where the variable is valid. A *global variable* is valid from the point it is declared to the end of the program. A *local variable's* scope is limited to the block where it is declared and cannot be accessed (set or read) outside that block. A *block* is a section of code enclosed in curly braces ({}). Figure 9-1 illustrates the difference between `local` and `global` variables.

It is possible to declare a `local` variable with the same name as a `global` variable. Normally, the scope of the variable `count` (first declaration in Figure 9-2) would be the whole program. The declaration of a second, local `count` takes precedence over the global declaration inside the small block where the local `count` is declared. In this block, the global `count` is *hidden*. You can also nest `local` declarations and hide `local` variables. These "very local" variables have an even smaller and more local scope than the "normal local" variables. (The clarity

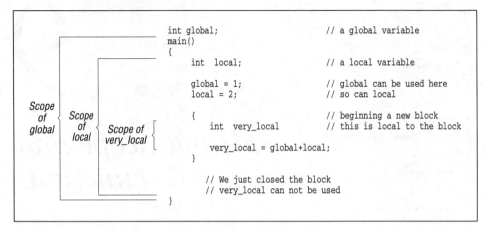

```
                        int global;              // a global variable
                        main()
                        {
                            int local;           // a local variable

                            global = 1;          // global can be used here
                            local = 2;           // so can local

                            {                    // beginning a new block
                                int  very_local  // this is local to the block

                                very_local = global+local;
                            }

                            // We just closed the block
                            // very_local can not be used
                        }
```

Figure 9-1. Local and global variables

of the previous sentence gives you some idea why using nesting to hide local variables does not make your program easy to understand.) Figure 9-2 illustrates a hidden variable.

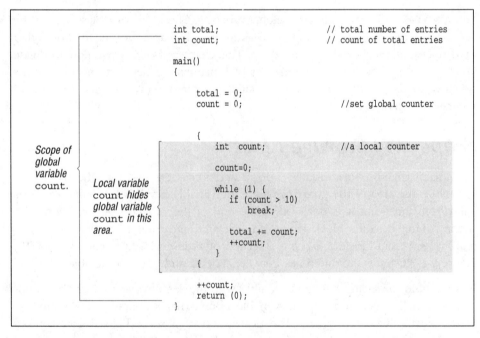

```
                        int total;               // total number of entries
                        int count;               // count of total entries

                        main()
                        {
                            total = 0;
                            count = 0;            //set global counter


                            {
                                int  count;       //a local counter

                                count=0;

                                while (1) {
                                    if (count > 10)
                                        break;

                                    total += count;
                                    ++count;
                                }
                            {

                            ++count;
                            return (0);
                        }
```

Figure 9-2. Hidden variables

The variable **count** is declared both as a local variable and as a global variable. Normally the scope of **count** (global) would be the entire program, but when a variable is declared inside a block, that instance of the variable becomes the active one for the length of the block. The global count has been hidden by the local count for the scope of this block. The shaded area in the figure shows where the scope of count (global) is hidden.

It is not good programming practice to hide variables. The problem is that when you have the statement:

```
count = 1;
```

it is difficult to tell which count you are referring to. Is it the global count, the one declared at the top of main, or the one in the middle of the while loop? It is better to give these variables different names, such as total_count, current_count, and item_count.

The **storage class** of a variable may be either *permanent* or *temporary*. **Global** variables are always permanent. They are created and initialized before the program starts and remain until it terminates. **Temporary** variables are allocated from a section of memory called the *stack* at the beginning of the block. If you try to allocate too many temporary variables you will get a stack overflow error. The space used by the temporary variables is returned to the stack at the end of the block. Each time the block is entered, the temporary variables are initialized.

The size of the stack depends on the system and compiler you are using. On many UNIX systems, the program is automatically allocated the largest possible stack. On other systems, a default stack size is allocated that can be changed by a compiler switch. In Turbo-C++ the stack space must be fewer than 64,000 bytes. This may seem like a lot of space, but several large arrays can eat it up quickly. You should consider making all large arrays permanent.

Local variables are temporary unless they are declared static.

NOTE

static has an entirely different meaning when used with global variables. (It indicates that a variable is local to the current file.) See Chapter 23, *Modular Programming.* For a complete discussion of the many meanings of the word "static," see Table 14-1.

Example 9-1 illustrates the difference between permanent and temporary variables. We have chosen obvious variable names; temporary is a temporary variable while permanent is permanent. C++ initializes temporary each time it is created (at the beginning of the for statement block), while permanent gets initialized only once, at program start-up time.

In the loop both variables are incremented. However, at the top of the loop temporary is initialized to 1.

Example 9-1. perm/perm.cc

```
#include <iostream.h>

main() {
    int counter;      // Loop counter

    for (counter = 0; counter < 3; ++counter) {
        int temporary = 1;
        static int permanent = 1;

        cout << "Temporary " << temporary <<
                " Permanent " << permanent << '\n';
        ++temporary;
        ++permanent;
    }
    return (0);
}
```
The output of this program is:
```
Temporary 1 Permanent 1
Temporary 1 Permanent 2
Temporary 1 Permanent 3
```

NOTE

Temporary variables are sometimes referred to as *automatic variables* because the space for them is allocated automatically. The qualifier `auto` can be used to denote a temporary variable; however, in practice `auto` is almost never used.

Table 9-1 describes the different ways a variable can be declared.

Table 9-1. Declaration Modifiers

Declared	Scope	Storage Class	Initialized
Outside all blocks	Global	Permanent	Once
`static` outside all blocks	Global	Permanent	Once
Inside a block	Local	Temporary	Each time block is entered
`static` inside a block	Local	Permanent	Once

NOTE

The keyword `static` is the most overloaded C++ operator. It means a lot of different things depending on how it is used. For a complete list see Table 14-1.

Functions

Functions allow you to group commonly used code into a compact unit that can be used repeatedly. You have already encountered one function, `main`. It is a special function called at the beginning of the program. All other functions are directly or indirectly called from `main`.

Suppose you want to write a program to compute the area of three triangles. You could write out the formula three times, or you could create a function to do the work and then use that function three times. Each function should begin with a comment block containing the following:

Name
> Name of the function

Description
> Description of what the function does

Parameters
> Description of each parameter to the function

Returns
> Description of the return value of the function

Additional sections may be added such as file formats, references, or notes. Refer to Chapter 3, *Style*, for other suggestions.

The function to compute the area of a triangle begins with:

```
/*******************************************
 * Triangle -- compute area of a triangle  *
 *                                         *
 * Parameters                              *
 *   width -- width of the triangle        *
 *   height -- height of the triangle      *
 *                                         *
 * Returns                                 *
 *   area of the triangle                  *
 *******************************************/
```

The function proper begins with the lines:

```
float triangle(float width, float height)
```

`float` is the function type. This defines the type of data returned by the function. `width` and `height` are the parameters to the function. Parameters are variables local to the function that are used to pass information into the function.

NOTE

The function type is not required by C++. If no function type is declared, the type defaults to `int`. However, if you omit the function type, it is not clear whether you want to have the function default to `int` or you just forgot the function type. To avoid this confusion, always declare the function type and do not use the default.

The function computes the area with the statement:

```
area = width * height / 2.0;
```

What's left is to give the result to the caller. This is done with the **return** statement:

```
return (area)
```

The full triangle function can be seen in Example 9-2.

Example 9-2. tri/tri-sub.cc

```
/********************************************
 * Triangle -- compute area of a triangle  *
 *                                          *
 * Parameters                               *
 *   width -- width of the triangle         *
 *   height -- height of the triangle       *
 *                                          *
 * Returns                                  *
 *   area of the triangle                   *
 ********************************************/

float triangle(float width, float height)
{
    float area; // Area of the triangle

    area = width * height / 2.0;
    return (area);
}
```

The line:

```
size = triangle(1.3, 8.3)
```

is a call to the function `triangle`. When C++ sees this function call it performs the following operations:

```
Triangle's variable width = 1.3
Triangle's height = 8.3

Begin execution of the first line of the function triangle.
```

The technical name for this type of parameter passing is "call by value." The assignment only occurs when the function is called, so data flows through the parameters only one way: in.

The `return` statement is how you get data out of the function. In the triangle example, the function assigns the local variable `area` the value 5.4 and then executes the statement `return (area)`, so the return value of this function is 5.4. This value is assigned to `size`.

```
return(area);          5.4 (The value of area)
// ......
size = triangle(1.3, 8.3)
```

Example 9-3 computes the area of three triangles.

Example 9-3. tri/tri.cc

```
#include <iostream.h>

main()
{
    // Function to compute area of triangle
    float triangle(float width, float height);

    cout << "Triangle #1 " << triangle(1.3, 8.3) << '\n';
    cout << "Triangle #2 " << triangle(4.8, 9.8) << '\n';
    cout << "Triangle #3 " << triangle(1.2, 2.0) << '\n';
    return (0);
}
/*********************************************
 * Triangle -- compute area of a triangle   *
 *                                          *
 * Parameters                               *
 *  width -- width of the triangle          *
 *  height -- height of the triangle        *
 *                                          *
 * Returns                                  *
 *  area of the triangle                    *
 *********************************************/
float triangle(float width, float height)
{
    float area; // Area of the triangle

    area = width * height / 2.0;
    return (area);
}
```

Functions must be declared just like variables. The declaration tells the C++ compiler about the function's return value and parameters. There are two ways of declaring a function. The first is to write the entire function before it's used. The other is to define what's called a *function prototype,* which gives the compiler just enough information to call the function. A function prototype looks like the first line of the function, only the function has no body. For example, the prototype for the **triangle** function is:

```
float triangle(float width, float height);
```

Note the semicolon at the end of the line. This is used to tell C++ that this is a prototype and not a real function.

C++ allows you to leave out the parameter names when declaring a prototype. This function could just as easily have been written:

```
float triangle(float, float);
```

However, this technique is not commonly used. The reason is that it's very easy to create a prototype by simply using the editor to copy the first line of a function and put that line where you want the prototype. (Many times this will be in a header file as described in Chapter 23, *Modular Programming*.) Also, putting the names in the prototype gives anyone reading the program additional useful information.

Functions that have no parameters are declared with a parameter list of **void**. For example:

```
int get_value(void);
```

The **void** construct is a holdover from the old C days when an empty parameter list "()" signaled an old K&R-style C function prototype. Actually, C++ will accept both an empty list and a **void** declaration, but the **void** form is preferred. By putting in the **void** you are saying, "Yes, I know that this function takes no parameters."

The keyword **void** is also used to indicate a function that does not return a value (similar to the FORTRAN **SUBROUTINE** or PASCAL **Procedure**). For example, this function just prints a result, it does not return a value.

```
void print_answer(int answer)
{
    if (answer < 0) {
        cout << "Answer corrupt\n";
        return;
    }
    cout << "The answer is " << answer '\n';
}
```

const Parameters and Return Values

If a parameter is declared **const** then that parameter cannot be changed inside the function. Ordinary parameters can be changed inside functions, but the changes will not be passed back to the calling program.

For example, in the `triangle` function, we never change `width` or `height`. These could easily be declared `const`. Since the return value is also something that cannot be changed, it can be declared `const` as well. The `const` declarations serve to notify the programmer that the parameters do not change inside the functions. If you do attempt to change a `const` parameter, the compiler generates an error. The improved `triangle` function with the `const` declarations can be seen in Example 9-4.

Example 9-4. tri/tri-sub2.cc

```
const float triangle(const float width, const float height)
{
    float area;  // Area of the triangle

    area = width * height / 2.0;
    return (area);
}
```

As it stands now, the `const` declaration for the return value is merely a decoration. In the next section you'll see to how to return references and make the `const` return declaration useful.

Reference Parameters and Return Values

Remember that in Chapter 4, *Basic Declarations and Expressions*, we discussed reference variables. A reference variable is a way of declaring an additional name for a variable. For global and local variables, reference variables are not very useful. However, when used as parameters they take on an entirely new meaning.

Suppose you want to write a subroutine to increment a counter. If you write it like Example 9-5, it won't work.

Example 9-5. value/value.cc

```
#include <iostream.h>
// This function won't work
void inc_counter(int counter)
{
    ++counter;
}

main()
{
    int a_count = 0;       // Random counter

    inc_counter(a_count);
    cout << a_count << '\n';
    return (0);
}
```

Why doesn't it work? Because C++ defaults to call by value. This means that values go in, but they don't come out.

What happens if you convert the parameter counter to a reference? References are just another way of giving the same variable two names. When inc_counter is called, counter becomes a reference to a_count. That means that anything done to counter results in changes to a_count. Example 9-6, using a reference parameter, works properly.

Example 9-6. value/ref.cc

```
#include <iostream.h>
// Works
void inc_counter(int &counter)
{
    ++counter;
}

main()
{
    int a_count = 0;      // Random counter

    inc_counter(a_count);
    cout << a_count << '\n';
    return (0);
}
```

Examining this program we find that it looks a lot like Example 9-5 except for the "&" in front of counter. This "&" tells C++ that counter is a reference and not a normal call-by-value parameter.

Reference declarations can also be used for return values. For example, Example 9-7 finds the biggest element in an array.

Example 9-7. value/big.cc

```
int &biggest(int array[], int n_elements)
{
    int index;  // Current index
    int biggest; // Index of the biggest element

    // Assume the first is the biggest
    biggest = 0;
    for (index = 1; index < n_elements; ++index) {
        if (array[biggest] < array[index])
            biggest = index;
    }

    return (array[biggest]);
}
```

If you wanted to print the biggest element of an array, all you would have to do is:

```
int item_array[5] = {1, 2, 5000, 3, 4}; // An array

cout << "The biggest element is " <<
        biggest(item_array, 5) << '\n';
```

Let's examine this in more detail. First of all, consider what happens when you create a reference variable:

```
int &big_reference = item_array[2]; // A reference to element #2
```

The reference variable **big_reference** is another name for **item_array**[2]. You can now use this reference to print a value:

```
cout << big_reference << '\n';    // Print out element #2
```

But since this is a reference, you can use it on the left side as well:

```
big_reference = 0;        // Zero the largest value of the array
```

The function **biggest** returns a reference. When used on **init_array** it returns a reference to **item_array**[2]. Remember that in the following code, **biggest(item_array, 5)** is **item_array**[2]. The following three code sections all perform equivalent operations. The actual variable, **item_array**[2], does not change; however, the way we refer to it does.

```
// Using the actual data
cout << item_array[2] << '\n';
item_array[2] = 0;

// Using a simple reference
int big_reference = &item_array[2];
cout << big_reference << '\n';
big_reference = 0;

// Using a function that returns a reference
cout << biggest(item_array, 5) << '\n';
biggest(item_array, 5) = 0;
```

Because the version of **biggest** returns a reference, it can be used on the right side of an assignment operation (=). But suppose you don't want that to happen. You can accomplish this by returning a **const** reference.

```
const int &biggest(int array[], int n_elements);
```

This tells C++ that even though you return a reference, the result cannot be changed. Thus, code like

```
biggest(item_array, 5) = 0;                // Now it generates an error
```

is illegal.

Dangling References

You should be careful when using "return by reference." If you're not careful, you can wind up with a reference to a variable that no longer exists. Example 9-8 illustrates this problem.

Example 9-8. ref/ref.cc

```
 1 #include <iostream.h>
 2
 3 const int &min(const int &i1, const int &i2)
 4 {
 5     if (i1 < i2)
 6         return (i1);
 7     return (i2);
 8 }
 9
10 main()
11 {
12     int &i = min(1 + 2, 3 + 4);
13
14     return (0);
15 }
```

Line 3 starts the definition of the function **min**. It returns a reference to the smaller of two integers.

In line 12 we call this function. Before the function **min** is called C++ creates a temporary integer to hold the value of the expression 1 + 2. A reference to this temporary is passed to the **min** function as the parameter **i1**. C++ creates another temporary for the **i2** parameter.

The function **min** is then called and returns a reference to **i1**. But what does **i1** refer to? It refers to a temporary that C++ created in **main**. At the end of the statement C++ can destroy all the temporaries.

Let's look at the call to **min** (line 12) in more detail. Here's a pseudocode version of line 12, including the details that C++ normally hides from the programmer:

```
create integer tmp1, assign it the value 1 + 2
create integer tmp2, assign it the value 3 + 4
bind parameter i1 so it refers to tmp1
bind parameter i2 so it refers to tmp2
call the function "min"
bind main's variable i so it refers to
        the return value (i1-a reference to tmp1)
// At this point i is a reference to tmp1
destroy tmp1
destroy tmp2

//    At this point i still refers to tmp1
//    It doesn't exist, but i refers to it
```

At the end of line 12 we have a bad situation: i refers to a temporary variable that has been destroyed. In other words, i points to something that does not exist. This is called a *dangling reference* and should be avoided.

Array Parameters

So for you've dealt only with simple parameters. C++ treats arrays a little differently. First of all, you don't have to put a size in the prototype declaration. For example:

```
int sum(int array[]);
```

C++ uses a parameter-passing scheme called "call by address" to pass arrays. Another way of thinking of this is that C++ automatically turns all array parameters into reference parameters. This allows any size arrays to be passed. The function sum we just declared may accept integer arrays of length 3, 43, 5,000, or any length.

However, if you want to put in a size you can. C++ allows this although it ignores whatever number you put there. But by putting in the size you alert the people reading your program that this function takes only fixed-size arrays.

```
int sum(int array[3]);
```

For multidimensional arrays you are *required* to put in the size for each dimension except the last one. That's because C++ uses these dimensions to compute the location of each element in the array.

```
int sum_matrix(int matrix1[10][10]);    // Legal
int sum_matrix(int matrix1[10][]);      // Legal
int sum_matrix(int matrix1[][]);        // Illegal
```

Question 9-1: *The function in Example 9-9 should compute the length of a string.[*] Instead it insists that all strings are of length zero. Why?*

Example 9-9. length/length.cc

```
/************************************************************
 * length -- compute the length of a string                *
 *                                                          *
 * Parameters                                               *
 *      string -- the string whose length we want           *
 *                                                          *
 * Returns                                                  *
 *      the length of the string                            *
 ************************************************************/
int  Length(char string[])
{
```

---

[*] This function (when working properly) performs the same function as the library function strlen.

Example 9-9. length/length.cc (Continued)

```
    int index;        // Index into the string

    /*
     * Loop until we reach the end-of-string character
     */
    for (index = 0; string[index] != '\0'; ++index)
        /* do nothing */
    return (index);
}
```

Function Overloading

Let's define a simple function to return the square of an integer:

```
    int square(int value) {
        return (value * value);
    }
```

We also want to square floating point numbers:

```
    float square(float value) {
        return (value * value);
    }
```

Now we have two functions with the same name. Isn't that illegal? In older languages such as C and PASCAL that would be true. In C++ it's not. C++ allows *function overloading*, which means you can define multiple functions with the same names. Thus you can define a `square` function for all types of things: `int`, `float`, `short int`, `double`, and even `char` if we could figure out what it means to square a character.

To keep your code consistent, all functions that use the same name should perform the same basic function. For example you could define the following two `square` functions:

```
    // Square an integer
    int square(int value);

    // Draw a square on the screen
    void square(int top, int bottom, int left, int right);
```

This is perfectly legal C++ code, but it is confusing to anyone who has to read the code.

There is one limitation to function overloading: C++ must be able to tell the functions apart. For example, the following is illegal:

```
    int get_number(void);
    float get_number(void);   // Illegal
```

The problem is that C++ uses the parameter list to tell the functions apart. But the parameter list of the two get_number routines is the same: (void). The result is that C++ can't tell these two routines apart and flags the second declaration as an error.

Default Parameters

Suppose you want to define a function to draw a rectangle on the screen. This function also needs to be able to scale the rectangle as needed. The function definition is:

```
void draw(const rectangle &rectangle; double scale)
```

After using this function for a while, you discover that 90% of the time you don't use the ability of draw to scale. In other words, 90% of the time the scale factor is 1.0.

C++ allows you to specify a default value for scale. The statement:

```
void draw(const rectangle &rectangle; double scale = 1.0)
```

tells C++, "If scale is not specified, make it 1.0." Thus the following are equivalent:

```
draw(big_rectangle, 1.0);    // Explicity specify scale
draw(big_rectangle);         // Let it default to 1.0
```

There are some style problems with default parameters. Study the following code:

```
draw(big_rectangle);
```

Can you tell whether the programmer intended for the scale to be 1.0 or just forgot to put it in? Although sometimes useful, the default parameter trick should be used sparingly.

Unused Parameters

If you define a parameter and fail to use it, most good compilers will generate a warning. For example:

```
void exit_button(Widget &button) {
    cout << "Shutting down\n";
    exit (0);
}
```

generates the message:

```
Warning: line 1.  Unused parameter "button"
```

But what about the times you really don't want to use a parameter? Is there a way to get C++ to shut up and not bother you? There is. The trick is to leave out the name of the parameter.

```
// No warning, but style needs work
void exit_button(Widget &) {
    cout << "Shutting down\n";
    exit (0);
}
```

This is nice for C++, but not so nice for the programmer who has to read your code. We can see that `exit_button` takes a `Widget` & parameter, but what is the parameter? A solution to this problem is to reissue the parameter name as a comment.

```
// Better
void exit_button(Widget & /*button*/) {
    cout << "Shutting down\n";
    exit (0);
}
```

Some people consider this style ugly and confusing. They're right that it's not that easy to read. There ought to be a better way; I just wish I could think of one.

One question you might be asking by now is, "Why would I ever write code like this? Why not just leave the parameter out?"

It turns out that many programming systems make use of *callback functions*. For example, you can tell the X Window System, "When the 'EXIT' button is pushed call the function `exit_button`." Your callback function may handle many buttons, so it's important to know which button is pushed. So X supplies `button` as a parameter to the function.

What happens if you know that only `button` can cause X to call `exit_button`? Well, X is still going to give it to you, you're just going to ignore it. That's why some functions have unused parameters.

inline Functions

Looking back at the `square` function for integers, we see that it is a very short function (one line). Whenever C++ calls a function there is some overhead generated. This includes putting the parameters on the stack, entering and leaving the function, and a stack fix-up after the function returns.

For example, the code:

```
int square(int value) {
    return (value * value);
}
main() {
    // .....
    x = square(x);
```

generates the following assembly code on a 68000 machine (paraphrased).

```
label "int square(int value)"
        link a6,#0                      // Set up local variables

        // The next two lines do the work
        movel a6@(8),d1                 // d1 = value
        mulsl a6@(8),d1                 // d1 = value * d1

        movel d1,d0                     // Put return value in d0
        unlk a6                         // Restore stack
        rts                             // Return(d0)

label "main"
//....
//      x = square(x)
//
        movel a6@(-4),sp@-              // Put the number x on the stack
        jbsr "void square(int value)"
                                        // Call the function

        addqw #4,sp                     // Restore the stack
        movel d0,a6@(-4)                // Store return value in X
// ...
```

As you can see from this code, there are eight lines of overhead for two lines of work. C++ allows you to cut out that overhead through the use of the `inline` function. The `inline` keyword tells C++ that the function is very small. This means that it's simpler and easier for the C++ compiler to put the entire body of the function in the code stream instead of generating a call to the function.

```
inline int square(int value) {
    return (value * value);
}
```

Changing the **square** function:

```
label "main"
// ...
//      x = square(x)
//
        movel d1,a6@(-4)                // d1 = x
        movel a6@(-4),d0                // d0 = x
        mulsl d0,d0                     // d0 = (x * x)

        movel d0,a6@(-4)                // Store result
```

Expanding the function inline has eliminated the eight lines of overhead and results in much faster execution.

The `inline` modifier provides C++ a valuable hint it can use when generating code. `Inline` tells the compiler that the code is extremely small and simple. Like `register`, the `inline` modifier is a hint. If the C++ compiler can't generate a function inline, it will create it as an ordinary function.

Summary of Parameter Types

Table 9-2 lists the various parameter types.

Table 9-2. Parameter Types

Type	Declaration
Call by value	`function(int var)`
	Value is passed into the function and can be changed inside the function, but the changes are not passed to the caller.
Constant call by value	`function(const int var)`
	Value is passed into the function and cannot be changed.
Reference	`function(int &var)`
	Reference is passed to the function. Any changes made to the parameter are reflected in the caller.
Constant reference	`function(const int &var)`
	Value cannot be changed in the function. This form of a parameter is more efficient than "constant call by value" for complex data types. (See Chapter 12, *Advanced Types*.)
Array	`function(int array[])`
	Value is passed in and may be modified. C++ automatically turns arrays into reference parameters.
Call by address	`function(int *var)`
	Passes a pointer to an item. Pointers are covered in Chapter 15, *Simple Pointers*.

Structured Programming Basics

Computer scientists spend a great deal of time and effort studying how to program. The result is that they come up with the absolutely, positively, best programming methodology—a new one each month. Some of these systems include flow charts, top-down programming, bottom-up programming, structured programming, and object-oriented programming.

Now that you have learned about functions, we can talk about using *structured programming techniques* to design programs. This is a way of dividing up or structuring a program into small, well-defined functions. It makes the program easy to write and easy to understand. I don't claim that this system is the absolute best way to program. It happens to be the system that works best for me. If another system works better for you, use it.

Structured programming concentrates on a program's code. Later you'll see how to merge code and data to form classes and begin to perform object-oriented programming.

The first step in programming is to decide what you are going to do. This has already been described in Chapter 7, *The Programming Process*. Next, decide how you are going to structure your data.

Finally, the coding phase begins. When writing a paper, you start with an outline, with each section in the paper described by a single sentence. The details are filled in later. Writing a program is similar. You start with an outline, but this outline is your `main` function. The details can be hidden within other functions. For example, the program in Example 9-10 solves all of the world's problems.

Example 9-10. A global solution

```
main()
{
    void init(void);
    void solve_problems(void);
    void finish_up(void);

    init();
    solve_problems();
    finish_up();
}
```

Of course, some of the details remain to be filled in.

Start by writing the `main` function. It should be less than two pages long. If it grows longer, consider splitting it up into two smaller, simpler functions. The size of the function should be limited to three pages because that is about the maximum amount of information a human being can store in short-term memory at one time. After the `main` function is complete, you can start on the other functions. This type of structured programming is called *top-down programming*. You start at the top (`main`) and work your way down.

Another type of coding is called *bottom-up programming*. This involves writing the lowest-level function first, testing it, and then building on that working set. I tend to use some bottom-up techniques when I'm working with a new standard function that I haven't used before. I write a small function to make sure I really know how the function works and continue from there. This is the approach used in Chapter 7 to construct the calculator program.

In actual practice, both techniques are useful. This results in a mostly top-down, partially bottom-up technique. Computer scientists have a term for this methodology: chaos. The one rule you should follow in programming is, "Use what works best."

Recursion

Recursion occurs when a function calls itself directly or indirectly. Some programming functions lend themselves naturally to recursive algorithms, such as the factorial.

A recursive function must follow two basic rules:

1. It must have an ending point.

2. It must make the problem simpler.

A definition of factorial is:

```
fact(0) = 1
fact(n) = n * fact(n-1)
```

In C++ this is:

```cpp
int fact(int number)
{
    if (number == 0)
        return (1);
    /* else */
    return (number * fact(number-1));
}
```

This satisfies the two rules. First, it has a definite ending point (when **number == 0**). Second, it simplifies the problem because **fact(number-1)** is simpler than **fact(number)**.

Factorial is legal only for **number >= 0**. But what happens if we try to compute **fact(-3)**? The program aborts with a stack overflow or similar message. **fact(-3)** calls **fact(-4)** calls **fact(-5)** and so on. There is no ending point. This is called an *infinite recursion error*.

Many things we do iteratively can be done recursively, such as summing the elements of an array. You can define a function to add elements *m* through *n* of an array as follows:

If you have only one element, then the sum is simple.

Otherwise, it is the sum of the first element and the sum of the rest.

In C++ this is:

```cpp
int sum(int first, int last, int array[])
{
    if (first == last)
        return (array[first]);
    /* else */
        return (array[first] + sum(first + 1, last, array));
}
```

For example:

```
Sum(1 8 3 2) =
    1 + Sum(8 3 2) =
        8 + Sum(3 2) =
            3 + Sum(2) =
                2
            3 + 2 = 5
        8 + 5 = 13
    1 + 13 = 14
Answer = 14
```

Programming Exercises

Exercise 9-1: Write a procedure that counts the number of words in a string. (Your documentation should describe exactly how you define a word.) Write a program to test your new procedure.

Exercise 9-2: Write a function "begins(string1, string2)" that returns true if string1 begins string2. Write a program to test the function.

Exercise 9-3: Write a function count(number, array, length) that will count the number of times number appears in array. The array has length elements. The function should be recursive. Write a test program to go with the function.

Exercise 9-4: Write a function that will take a character string and return a primitive hash code by adding up the value of each character in the string.

Exercise 9-5: Write a function that returns the maximum value of an array of numbers.

Exercise 9-6: Write a function that scans a string for the character "-" and replaces it with "_".

Answers to Chapter Questions

Answer 9-1: The programmer went to a lot of trouble to explain that the for loop did nothing (except increment the index). However, there is no semicolon at the end of the for. C++ keeps reading until it sees a statement (in this case return(index)) and puts that in the for loop. Example 9-11 contains a correctly written version of the program.

Example 9-11. length/rlen.cc

```
int  length(char string[])
{
    int index;      // index into the string

    /*
```

Example 9-11. length/rlen.cc (Continued)

```
    * Loop until we reach the end of string character
    */
    for (index = 0; string[index] != '\0'; ++index)
        /* do nothing */ ;
    return (index);
}
```

10

The C++ Preprocessor

*The speech of man is like embroidered tapestries,
since like them this has to be extended in order to
display its patterns, but when it is rolled up it
conceals and distorts them.*

—Themistocles

The first C compilers had no constants or inline functions. When C was still being developed, it soon became apparent that C needed a facility for handling named constants, macros, and include files. The solution was to create a preprocessor that is run on the programs before they are passed to the C compiler. The preprocessor is nothing more than a specialized text editor. Its syntax is completely different from C's and it has no understanding of C constructs. It is merely a dumb text editor.

The preprocessor was very useful and soon it was merged into the main C compiler. The C++ compiler kept this pre-processor. On some systems, like UNIX, it is still a separate program, automatically executed by the compiler wrapper cc. Some of the newer compilers, like Turbo-C++, have the pre-processor built in.

#define Statement

The `#define` statement can be used to define a constant. For example, the following two lines perform similar functions:

```
#define SIZE 20        // The array size is 20
const int SIZE = 20;   // The array size is 20
```

Actually the line `#define SIZE 20` acts as a command to the preprocessor to *globally change SIZE to 20.* This takes the drudgery and guesswork out of making changes.

All preprocessor commands begin with a hash mark (#) in column 1. C++ is free format. Language elements can be placed anywhere on a line, and the end-of-line is treated just like a space. The preprocessor is not free format. It depends on the hash mark (#) being in the first column. As you will see, the preprocessor knows nothing about C++ and can be (and is) used to edit things other than C++ programs.

WARNING

The preprocessor is not part of the C++ compiler. It uses an entirely different syntax and requires an entirely different mind-set to use it well. Most problems you will see occur when the preprocessor is treated like C++.

Preprocessor directives terminate at the end of the line. In C++ a semicolon (;) ends a statement. The preprocessor directives do not end in a semicolon, and putting one in can lead to unexpected results. A preprocessor directive can be continued by putting a backslash (\) at the end of the line. The simplest use of the preprocessor is to define a replacement macro. For example, the command:

```
#define FOO bar
```

causes the preprocessor to replace the word "FOO" with the word "bar" everywhere "FOO" occurs. It is common programming practice to use all uppercase letters for macro names. This makes it very easy to tell the difference between a variable (all lowercase) and a macro (all uppercase).

The general form of a simple **define** statement is:

```
#define Name Substitute-Text
```

Name can be any valid C++ identifier. *Substitute-Text* can be anything as long as it fits on a single line. The *Substitute-Text* can include spaces, operators, and other characters.

It is possible to use the following definition:

```
#define FOR_ALL for (i = 0; i < ARRAY_SIZE; ++i)
```

and use it like:

```
/*
 * Clear the array
 */
FOR_ALL {
    data[i] = 0;
}
```

It is considered bad programming practice to define macros in this manner. They tend to obscure the basic control flow of the program. In this example, if the programmer wants to know what the loop does, he must search the beginning of the program for the definition of FOR_ALL.

It is even worse to define macros that do large-scale replacement of basic C++ programming constructs. For example, you can define the following:

```
#define BEGIN {
#define END }

    . . .

    if (index == 0)
    BEGIN
        cout << "Starting\n";
    END
```

The problem is that you are no longer programming in C++, but in a half-C++ half-PASCAL mongrel.

The preprocessor can cause unexpected problems because it does not check for correct C++ syntax. For example, Example 10-1 generates an error on line 11.

Example 10-1. big/big.cc

```
 1 #define BIG_NUMBER 10 ** 10
 2
 3 main()
 4 {
 5     // Index for our calculations
 6     int    index;
 7
 8     index = 0;
 9
10     // Syntax error on next line
11     while (index < BIG_NUMBER) {
12         index = index * 8;
13     }
14     return (0);
15 }
```

The problem is in the #define statement on line 1, but the error message points to line 11. The definition in line 1 causes the pre-processor to expand line 11 to look like:

```
while (index < 10 ** 10)
```

Because ** is an illegal operator, this generates a syntax error.

Question 10-1: *The following program generates the answer 47 instead of the expected answer 144. Why? (Hint below.)*

Example 10-2. first/first.cc

```
#include <iostream.h>

#define FIRST_PART      7
#define LAST_PART       5
#define ALL_PARTS       FIRST_PART + LAST_PART

main() {
    cout << "The square of all the parts is " <<
        ALL_PARTS * ALL_PARTS << '\n';
    return (0);
}
```

Hint:

```
CC -E prog.cc
```

sends the output of the preprocessor to the standard output.

In MS-DOS/Windows, the command:

```
cpp prog.cpp
```

creates a file called prog.i containing the output of the preprocessor.

Running the program for Example 10-1 through the preprocessor gives you:

Example 10-3. first/first-ed.out

```
# 1 "first.cc"
# 1 "/usr/local/lib/g++-include/iostream.h" 1 3

// About 900 lines of #include stuff omitted

inline ios& oct(ios& i)
{ i.setf(ios::oct, ios::dec|ios::hex|ios::oct); return i; }

# 1 "first.cc" 2

main() {
    cout << "The square of all the parts is " <<
                7 + 5 * 7 + 5 << '\n';
    return (0);
}
```

NOTE

The output of the C++ preprocessor contains a lot of information, most of which can easily be ignored. In this case, you need to scan the output till you reach the cout line. Examining this line will give you an idea of what caused the error.

Question 10-2: *Example 10-2 generates a warning that* counter *is used before it is set. This is a surprise because the* for *loop should set it. You also get a very strange warning, "null effect," for line 11.*

Example 10-4. max/max.cc

```
 1 // Warning, spacing is VERY important
 2
 3 #include <iostream.h>
 4
 5 #define MAX=10
 6
 7 main()
 8 {
 9     int   counter;
10
11     for (counter = MAX; counter > 0;
12         --counter)
13         cout << "Hi there\n";
14
15     return (0);
16 }
```

Hint: *Take a look at the preprocessor output.*

Question 10-3: *Example 10-3 computes the wrong value for* size. *Why?*

Example 10-5. size/size.cc

```
#include <iostream.h>

#define SIZE    10;
#define FUDGE   SIZE -2;
main()
{
    int size; // Size to really use

    size = FUDGE;
    cout << "Size is " << size << '\n';
    return (0);
}
```

Question 10-4: *The following program is supposed to print the message* "Fatal Error: Abort" *and exit when it receives bad data. But when it gets good data, it exits. Why?*

Example 10-6. dis/die.cc

```
 1 #include <iostream.h>
 2 #include <stdlib.h>  /* ANSI Standard only */
 3
 4 #define DIE \
 5   cerr << "Fatal Error: Abort\n"; exit(8);
 6
 7 main() {
 8     // A random value for testing
 9     int value;
10
11     value = 1;
12     if (value < 0)
13         DIE;
14
15     cerr << "We did not die\n";
16     return (0);
17 }
```

#define versus const

The const keyword is relatively new. Before const, #define was the only way to define constants, so most older code uses #define directives. However, the use of const is preferred over #define for several reasons. First of all, C++ checks the syntax of const statements immediately. The #define directive is not checked until the macro is used. Also, const uses C++ syntax, while #define has a syntax all its own. Finally, const follows normal C++ scope rules, whereas constants defined by a #define directive continue on forever.

In most cases a const statement is preferred over #define. Here are two ways of defining the same constant.

```
#define MAX 10 // Define a value using the pre-processor
               // (This can easily cause problems)

const int MAX = 10; // Define a C++ constant integer
                    // (Safer)
```

The #define directive is limited to defining simple constants. The const statement can define almost any type of C++ constant including things such as structure classes. For example:

```
struct box {
    int width, height;   // Dimensions of the box in pixels
};
```

```
const box pink_box(1.0, 4.5);  // Size of a pink box to be used for
               input
```

The `#define` directive is, however, essential for things such as conditional compilation and other specialized uses.

Conditional Compilation

One problem programmers have is writing code that can work on many different machines. In theory, C++ code is portable; in actual practice many machines have little quirks that must be accounted for. For example, this book covers UNIX, MS-DOS, and Windows compilers. Although they are almost the same, there are some differences, as you will see in Chapter 25, *Portability Problems.*

The preprocessor allows you great flexibility in changing the way code is generated through the use of *conditional compilation.* Suppose you want to put debugging code in the program while you are working on it and then remove the debugging code in the production version. You could do this by including the code in an `#ifdef-#endif` section.

```
#ifdef DEBUG
    cout << "In compute_hash, value " << value << " hash " << hash <<
             "\n";
#endif /* DEBUG */
```

NOTE

You do not have to put the `/* DEBUG */` after the `#endif`, but it is very useful as a comment.

If the beginning of the program contains the directive:

```
#define DEBUG       /* Turn debugging on */
```

the `cout` is included. If the program contains the directive:

```
#undef DEBUG       /* Turn debugging off */
```

the `cout` is omitted.

Strictly speaking the #undef DEBUG is unnecessary. If there is no `#define` DEBUG statement, then DEBUG is undefined. The #undef DEBUG statement is used to indicate explicitly to anyone reading the code that DEBUG is used for conditional compilation and is now turned off.

The directive `#ifdef` will cause the code to be compiled if the symbol is *not* defined.

#else reverses the sense of the conditional. For example:

```
#ifdef DEBUG
    cout << "Test version. Debugging is on\n";
#else /* DEBUG */
    cout << "Production version\n";
#endif /* DEBUG  */
```

A programmer may wish to temporarily remove a section of code. A common method of doing this is to comment out the code by enclosing it in /* */. This can cause problems, as shown by the following example:

```
/***** Comment out this section
    section_report();
    /* Handle the end-of-section stuff */
    dump_table();
**** End of commented out section */
```

This generates a syntax error for the fifth line. Why?

A better method is to use the #ifdef construct to remove the code.

```
#ifdef UNDEF
    section_report();
    /* Handle the end-of-section stuff */
    dump_table();
#endif /* UNDEF */
```

(Of course the code will be included if anyone defines the symbol UNDEF; however, anyone who does should be shot.)

The compiler switch -D*symbol* allows symbols to be defined on the command line. For example, the command:

```
CC -DDEBUG -g -o prog prog.cc
```

compiles the program *prog.c* and includes all the code in #ifdef DEBUG/#endif /* DEBUG */ pairs even though there is no #define DEBUG in the program. The Turbo-C++ equivalent is:

```
tcc -DDEBUG -g -N -eprog.exe prog.c
```

The general form of the option is -D*symbol* or -D*symbol*=*value*. For example, the following sets MAX to 10:

```
CC -DMAX=10 -o prog prog.c
```

Most C++ compilers automatically define some system-dependent symbols. For example, Turbo-C++ defines the symbol __TURBOC__ and MS-DOS defines __MSDOS__. The ANSI standard compiler C defines the symbol __STDC__. C++ compilers define the symbol __cplusplus. Most UNIX compilers define a name for the system (e.g., Sun, VAX, celerity, etc.); however, they are rarely documented. The symbol unix is always defined for all UNIX machines

NOTE

Command-line options specify the initial value of a symbol only. Any `#define` and `#undef` directives in the program can change the symbol's value. For example, the directive:

```
#undef DEBUG
```

results in `DEBUG` being undefined whether or not you use `-DDEBUG`.

#include Files

The `#include` directive allows the program to use source code from another file.

For example, you have been using the directive:

```
#include <iostream.h>
```

in your programs. This tells the preprocessor to take the file *iostream.h* and insert it in the current program. Files that are included in other programs are called *header files*. (Most `#include` directives come at the head of the program.) The angle brackets indicate that the file is a standard header file. In UNIX, these files are usually located in `/usr/include`. In MS-DOS/Windows, they are located in the Turbo-C++ directory (installation dependent).

Standard include files are used for defining data structures and macros used by library routines. For example, `cout` is a standard class that (as you know by now) prints data on the standard output. The `ostream` class definition used by `cout` and its related routines is defined in *iostream.h*.

Sometimes you may want to write your own set of include files. Local include files are particularly useful for storing constants and data structures when a program spans several files. They are especially useful for information sharing when a team of programmers is working on a single project. (See Chapter 23, *Modular Programming*.)

Local include files may be specified by using double quotation marks (") around the filename.

```
#include "defs.h"
```

The filename (`"defs.h"`) can be any valid filename. This can be a simple file, `"defs.h"`; a relative path, called `"../../data.h"`; or an absolute path, called `"/root/include/const.h"`. (In MS-DOS/Windows you should use backslash (\) instead of slash (/) as a directory separator.)

Include files may be nested. This can cause problems. Suppose you define several useful constants in the file *const.h*. If the files *data.h* and *io.h* both include *const.h* and you put the following in your program:

```
#include "data.h"
#include "io.h"
```

you generate errors because the preprocessor sets the definitions in *const.h* twice. Defining a constant twice is not a fatal error; however, defining a data structure or union twice is an error and must be avoided.

One way around this problem is to have *const.h* check to see whether it has already been included and not define any symbols that have already been defined.

Look at the following code:

```
#ifdef _CONST_H_INCLUDED_

/* Define constants */

#define _CONST_H_INCLUDED_
#endif  /* _CONST_H_INCLUDED_ */
```

When *const.h* is included, it defines the symbol _CONST_H_INCLUDED_. If that symbol is already defined (because the file was included earlier), the `#ifdef` conditional hides all the other defines so they don't cause trouble.

NOTE

It is possible to put code in a header file. This is considered poor programming practice. By convention, code goes in `.cc` files and definitions, declarations, macros, and inline functions go in the `.h` files.

Parameterized Macros

So far we have discussed only simple `#defines` or macros. Macros can take parameters. The following macro computes the square of a number:

```
#define SQR(x)  ((x) * (x))     /* Square a number */
```

When used, the macro replaces **x** by the text of its argument. SQR(5) *expands to ((5) * (5))*. It is a good rule always to put parentheses around the parameters of a macro. Example 10-7 illustrates the problems that can occur if this rule is not followed:

Example 10-7. sqr/sqr.cc

```
#include <iostream.h>
#define SQR(x) (x * x)

main()
```

Example 10-7. sqr/sqr.cc (Continued)

```
{
    int counter;      // Counter for loop

    for (counter = 0; counter < 5; ++counter) {
        cout << "x " << counter + 1 <<
                " x squared " << SQR(counter + 1) << '\n';
    }
    return (0);
}
```

Question 10-5: *What does the above program output? (Try running it on your machine.) Why did it output what it did? (Try checking the output of the pre-processor.)*

The keep-it-simple *system of programming prevents us from using the increment (++) and decrement (--) operators except on a line by themselves. When used in an expression, they are considered side effects, and this can lead to unexpected results as illustrated in Example 10-8.*

Example 10-8. sqr-i/sqr-i.cc

```
#include <iostream.h>
#define SQR(x) ((x) * (x))

main()
{
    int counter;      /* Counter for loop */

    counter = 0;
    while (counter < 5)
        cout << "x " << counter + 1 <<
                " x squared " << SQR(++counter) << '\n';
    return (0);
}
```

Why does this not produce the expected output? How much does the counter go up each time.

In the program shown in Example 10-8 the SQR(++counter) *is expanded to* ((++counter) * (++counter)) *in this case. The result is that* counter *goes up by 2 each time through the loop. The actual result of this expression is system dependent.*

Question 10-6: *The following program tells us we have an undefined variable, but our only variable name is* counter. *Why?*

Example 10-9. rec/rec.cc

```
#include <iostream.h>
#define RECIPROCAL (number) (1.0 / (number))
```

Example 10-9. rec/rec.cc (Continued)

```
main()
{
    float    counter;

    for (counter = 0.0; counter < 10.0;
         counter += 1.0) {

        cout << "1/" << counter << " = " <<
                RECIPROCAL(counter) << "\n";
    }
    return (0);
}
```

The # Operator

The # operator is used inside a parameterized macro to turn an argument into a string. For example:

```
#define STR(data) #data
STR(hello)
```

generates

```
"hello"
```

For a more extensive example of how to use this operator see Chapter 26, *Putting It All Together.*

Parameterized Macros Versus Inline Functions

In most cases it is better to use an `inline` function instead of a parameterized macro, to avoid most of the traps caused by parameterized macros. But there are cases where a parameterized macro may be better than an `inline` function. For example, the SQR macro works for both `float` and `int` data types. We'd have to write two `inline` functions to perform the same functions.

```
#define SQR(x) ((x) * (x))   // A parameterized macro
// Works, but is dangerous

// Inline function to do the same thing
inline int sqr(const int x) {
    return (x * x);
}
```

Advanced Features

This book does not cover the complete list of C++ preprocessor directives. Among the more advanced features are an advanced form of the `#if` directive for conditional compilations and the `#pragma` directive for inserting compiler-dependent commands into a file. See your C++ reference manual for more information on these features.

Summary

The C++ preprocessor is a very useful part of the C++ language. It has a completely different look and feel from C++. However, it must be treated apart from the main C++ compiler.

Problems in macro definitions often do not show up where the macro is defined, but result in errors much further down in the program. By following a few simple rules, you can decrease the chances of having problems.

1. Put parentheses around everything. In particular they should enclose `#define` constants and macro parameters.

2. When defining a macro with more than one statement, enclose the code in {}.

3. The preprocessor is not C++. Don't use = or ;.

   ```
   #define X = 5 // Illegal
   #define X 5;   // Illegal
   #define X = 5; // Very illegal

   #define X 5    // Correct
   ```

Finally, be glad. If you got this far, be glad that the worst is over.

Programming Exercises

Exercise 10-1: C++ does not have a Boolean type. Create one using `#define` to define values for BOOLEAN, TRUE, and FALSE.

Exercise 10-2: Write a macro that returns true if its parameter is divisible by 10 and false otherwise.

Exercise 10-3: Write a macro `is_digit` that returns true if its argument is a decimal digit. Write a second macro `is_hex` that returns true if its argument is a hex digit (0–9 A–F a–f). The second macro should reference the first.

Exercise 10-4: Write a preprocessor macro that swaps two integers. (If you're a real hacker, write one that does not use a temporary variable declared outside the macro.)

Answers to Chapter Questions

Answer 10-1: After the program has been run through the preprocessor, the `cout` statement is expanded to look like:

```
cout << "The square of all the parts is " <<  7 + 5 * 7 + 5  << '\n';
```

The equation 7 + 5 * 7 + 5 evaluates to 47. It is a good rule to put parentheses () around all expressions in macros. If you change the definition of `ALL_PARTS` to:

```
#define ALL_PARTS (FIRST_PART + LAST_PART)
```

the program executes correctly.

Answer 10-2: The preprocessor is a very simple-minded program. When it defines a macro, everything past the identifier is part of the macro. In this case, the definition of `MAX` is literally "= 10." When the `for` statement is expanded, the result is:

```
for (counter==10; counter > 0;  --counter)
```

C++ allows you to compute a result and throw it away. For this statement, the program checks to see whether counter is 10 and discards the answer. Removing the = from the definition will correct the problem.

Answer 10-3: As with the previous problem, the preprocessor does not respect C++ syntax conventions. In this case the programmer used a semicolon to end the statement, but the preprocessor included it as part of the definition for `size`. The assignment statement for `size`, expanded, is:

```
size = 10; -2;;
```

The two semicolons at the end do not hurt anything, but the one in the middle is a killer. This line tells C++ to do two things: 1) assign 10 to `size` and 2) compute the value −2 and throw it away (this results in the null effect warning). Removing the semicolons will fix the problem.

Answer 10-4: The output of the preprocessor looks like:

```
void exit();

main() {
    int value;

    value = 1;
    if (value < 0)
        cout << "Fatal Error: Abort\n"; exit(8);

    cout << "We did not die\n";
    return (0);
}
```

The problem is that two statements follow the `if` line. Normally they would be put on two lines. If we properly indent this program we get

Example 10-10. die3/die.cc

```
#include <iostream.h>
#include <stdlib.h>

main() {
    int value;  // A random value for testing

    value = 1;
    if (value < 0)
        cout << "Fatal Error: Abort\n";

    exit(8);

    cout << "We did not die\n";
    return (0);
}
```

From this it is obvious why we always exit. The fact that there were two statements after the `if` was hidden by using a single preprocessor macro. The cure for this problem is to put curly braces around all multistatement macros.

```
#define DIE \
    {cout << "Fatal Error: Abort\n"; exit(8);}
```

Answer 10-5: The answer is that the counter is incremented by two each time through the loop. This is because the macro call:

```
SQR(++counter)
```

is expanded to:

```
((++counter) * (++counter))
```

Answer 10-6: The only difference between a parameterized macro and one without parameters is the parentheses immediately following the macro name. In this case, a space follows the definition of RECIPROCAL, so it is *not* a parameterized macro. Instead it is a simple text replacement macro that replaces RECIPROCAL with:

```
(number) (1.0 / number)
```

Removing the space between RECIPROCAL and (number) corrects the problem.

11

Bit Operations

To be or not to be, that is the question.
—Shakespeare on Boolean algebra

This chapter discusses bit-oriented operations. A bit is the smallest unit of information. Normally it is represented by the values 1 and 0. (Other representations include on/off, true/false, and yes/no.) Bit manipulations are used to control the machine at the lowest level. They allow the programmer to get "under the hood" of the machine. Many higher-level programs will never need bit operations. Low-level coding such as writing device drivers or pixel-level graphic programming requires bit operations. If you plan to program only at a higher level, this chapter may be safely skipped.

Eight bits together form a byte, represented by the C++ data type `char`. A byte might contain the following bits: `01100100`.

This can also be written as the hexadecimal number 0x64. (C++ uses the prefix "0x" to indicate a hexadecimal (base 16) number.) Hexadecimal is convenient for representing binary data because each hexadecimal digit represents 4 binary bits. Table 11-1 gives the hexadecimal (hex) to binary conversion:

Table 11-1. Hex and Binary

Hex	Binary	Hex	Binary
0	0000	8	1000
1	0001	9	1001
2	0010	A	1010
3	0011	B	1011

Table 11-1. Hex and Binary (Continued)

Hex	Binary	Hex	Binary
4	0100	C	1100
5	0101	D	1101
6	0110	E	1110
7	0111	F	1111

So the hexadecimal number 0xAF represents the binary number 10101111.

Bit Operators

Bit, or bitwise, operators allow the programmer to work on individual bits. For example, a short integer holds 16 bits (on most machines). The bit operators treat each of these as an independent bit. By contrast, an add operator treats the 16 bits as a single 16-bit number.

Bit operators allow you to set, clear, test, and perform other operations on bits. The bit operators are listed in Table 11-2.

Table 11-2. Bit Operators

Operator	Meaning
&	Bitwise AND
|	Bitwise OR
^	Bitwise exclusive OR
~	Complement
<<	Shift left
>>	Shift right

These operators work on any integer or character-data type.

The AND Operator (&)

The AND *operator* compares two bits. If they both are 1, the result is 1. The results of the AND operator are defined in Table 11-3.

Table 11-3. AND Operator

Bit1	Bit2	Bit1 & Bit2
0	0	0
0	1	0
1	0	0
1	1	1

When two eight-bit variables (`char` variables) are "ANDed" together, the AND operator works on each bit independently. The following program segment illustrates this operation:

```
int    c1, c2;

c1 = 0x45;
c2 = 0x71;
cout << "Result of " << hex << c1 << " & " << c2 << " = " <<
                (c1 & c2) << dec << '\n';
```

The output of this program is:

```
Result of 45 & 71 = 41
```

This is because:

$$
\begin{array}{lll}
  & c1 = 0x45 & \text{binary } 01000101 \\
\& & c2 = 0x71 & \text{binary } 01110001 \\
\hline
= & 0x41 & \text{binary } 01000001 \\
\end{array}
$$

The bitwise AND (`&`) is similar to the logical AND (`&&`). In the logical AND if both operands are true (nonzero), the result is true (1). In bitwise AND (`&`), if the corresponding bits of both operands are true (1s), then the corresponding bits of the results are true (1s). So the bitwise AND (`&`) works on each bit independently while the logical AND (`&&`) works on the operands as a whole.

However, `&` and `&&` are different operators, as Example 11-1 illustrates:

Example 11-1. and/and.cc

```
#include <iostream.h>

main()
{
    int i1, i2; // Two random integers

    i1 = 4;
    i2 = 2;     // Set values

    // Nice way of writing the conditional
    if ((i1 != 0) && (i2 != 0))
        cout << "Both are not zero #1\n";

    // Shorthand way of doing the same thing
    // Correct C++ code, but rotten style
    if (i1 && i2)
        cout << "Both are not zero #2\n";

    // Incorrect use of bitwise AND resulting in an error
    if (i1 & i2)
        cout << "Both are not zero #3\n";
```

Example 11-1. and/and.cc (Continued)
```
    return (0);
}
```

Question: Why does test #3 fail to print `Both are not zero #3`?

Answer: The operator `&` is a bitwise AND. The result of the bitwise AND is zero.

$$
\begin{array}{rl}
i1=4 & 00000100 \\
i2=2 & 00000010 \\
\hline
\& & 00000000
\end{array}
$$

The result of the bitwise AND is 0, and the conditional is false. If the programmer had used the first form:

```
    if ((i1 != 0) && (i2 != 0))
```

and made the mistake of using `&` instead of `&&`:

```
    if ((i1 != 0) & (i2 != 0))
```

the program would still have executed correctly.

$$
\begin{array}{ll}
(i1 \ != 0) & \text{is true (result = 1)} \\
(i2 \ != 0) & \text{is true (result = 1)}
\end{array}
$$

1 bitwise AND 1 is 1, so the expression is true.

NOTE

Soon after discovering the bug illustrated by this program I told my office mate, "I now understand the difference between AND and AND AND*)*, and he understood me. How we understand language has always fascinated me, and the fact that I could utter such a sentence and have someone understand it without trouble amazed me.

You can use the bitwise AND operator to test whether a number is even or odd. In base 2, the last digit of all even numbers is zero and the last digit of all odd numbers is one. The following function uses the bitwise AND to pick off this last digit. If it is zero (an even number), the result of the function is true.

```
inline int even(const int value)
{
    return ((value & 1) == 0);
}
```

Bitwise OR (|)

The *inclusive* OR *operator* (also known as just the OR operator) compares its two operands. If one or the other bit is a 1, the result is 1. Table 11-4 lists the truth table for the OR operator.

On a byte this would be:

```
        i1=0x47     01000111
        i2=0x53     01010011
    |   57          01010111
```

The Bitwise Exclusive OR (^)

The *exclusive* OR (also known as XOR) *operator* results in a 1 when either of its two operands is a 1, but not both. The truth table for the exclusive OR operator is listed in Table 11-4.

Table 11-4. Exclusive OR

Bit1	Bit2	Bit1 ^ Bit2
0	0	0
0	1	1
1	0	1
1	1	0

On a byte this would be:

```
        i1=0x47     01000111
        i2=0x53     01010011
    ^   14          00010100
```

The Ones Complement Operator (NOT) (~)

The NOT *operator* (also called the invert operator or bit flip) is a unary operator that returns the inverse of its operand, as shown in Table 11-5.

Table 11-5. NOT Operator

Bit	~Bit
0	1
1	0

On a byte this is:

c=	0x45	01000101
~c=	0xBA	10111010

The Left and Right Shift Operators (<<, >>)

The left shift operator moves the data left a specified number of bits. Any bits that are shifted out the left side disappear. New bits coming in from the right are zeros. The right shift does the same thing in the other direction. For example:

	c=0x1C	00011100
c << 1	c=0x38	00111000
c >> 2	c=0x07	00000111

Shifting left by one (x << 1) is the same as multiplying by 2 (x * 2). Shifting left by two (x << 2) is the same as multiplying by 4 (x * 4, or x * 2^2). You can see a pattern forming here. Shifting left by n places is the same as multiplying by 2^n. Why shift instead of multiply? Shifting is faster than multiplication, so

```
i = j << 3;      // Multiply j by 8 (2**3)
```

is faster than:

```
i = j * 8;
```

Or it would be faster if compilers weren't smart enough to turn "multiply by power of two" into "shift."

Many clever programmers use this trick to speed up their programs at the cost of clarity. Don't you do it. The compiler is smart enough to perform the speedup automatically. This means that putting in a shift gains you nothing at the expense of clarity.

The left shift operator multiplies; the right shift divides. So:

```
q = i >> 2;
```

is the same as:

```
q = i / 4;
```

Again, this clever trick should not be used in modern code.

Right Shift Details

Right shifts are particularly tricky. When a variable is shifted to the right, C++ needs to fill the space on the left side with something. For signed variables, C++

uses the value of the sign bit. For unsigned variables, C++ uses zero. Table 11-6 illustrates some typical right shifts.

Table 11-6. Right Shift Examples

	Signed Character	Signed Character	Unsigned Character
Expression	9 >> 2	–8 >> 2	248 >> 2
Binary value >> 2	0000 1010$_2$ >> 2	1111 1000$_2$ >> 2	1111 1000$_2$ >> 2
Result	??00 0010$_2$	??11 1110$_2$ >> 2	??11 1110$_2$ >> 2
Fill	Sign bit (0)	Sign bit (1)	Zero
Final result (binary)	0000 0010$_2$	1111 1110$_2$	0011 1110$_2$
Final result (short int)	2	–2	62

Setting, Clearing, and Testing Bits

A character contains eight bits. Each of these can be treated as a separate flag. Bit operations can be used to pack eight single-bit values in a single byte. For example, suppose you are writing a low-level communications program. You are going to store the characters in an 8K buffer for later use. With each character you will also store a set of status flags. The flags are listed in Table 11-7.

Table 11-7. Communications Status Values

Name	Description
ERROR	True if any error is set
FRAMING_ERROR	A framing error occurred for this character
PARITY_ERROR	Character had the wrong parity
CARRIER_LOST	The carrier signal went down
CHANNEL_DOWN	Power was lost on the communication device

You could store each flag in its own character variable. That would mean that for each character buffered, you would need five bytes of status storage. For a large buffer, that adds up. By instead assigning each status flag its own bit within an eight-bit status character, you cut storage requirements down to 1/5 of the original need.

You can assign the flags the bit numbers listed in Table 11-8.

Table 11-8. Bit Assignments

Bit	Name
0	ERROR
1	FRAMING_ERROR
2	PARITY_ERROR

Table 11-8. Bit Assignments (Continued)

Bit	Name
3	CARRIER_LOST
4	CHANNEL_DOWN

Bits are numbered 76543210 by convention. The constants for each bit are defined in Table 11-9.

Table 11-9. Bit Values

Bit	Binary Value	Hex Constant
7	10000000	0x80
6	01000000	0x40
5	00100000	0x20
4	00010000	0x10
3	00001000	0x08
2	00000100	0x04
1	00000010	0x02
0	00000001	0x01

The definitions could be:

```
// True if any error is set
const int ERROR = 0x01;

// A framing error occurred for this character
const int FRAMING_ERROR = 0x02;

// Character had the wrong parity
const int PARITY_ERROR = 0x04;

// The carrier signal went down
const int CARRIER_LOST = 0x08;

// Power was lost on the communication device
const int CHANNEL_DOWN = 0x10;
```

This method of defining bits is somewhat confusing. Can you tell (without looking at the table) which bit number is represented by the constant `0x10`? Table 11-10 shows how you can use the left shift operator (<<) to define bits.

Table 11-10. The Left Shift Operator and Bit Definition

C++ Representation	Base 2 Equivalent	Result (Base 2)	Bit Number
1 << 0	$00000001_2 << 0$	00000001_2	Bit 0
1 << 1	$00000001_2 << 1$	00000010_2	Bit 1
1 << 2	$00000001_2 << 2$	00000100_2	Bit 2

Table 11-10. The Left Shift Operator and Bit Definition (Continued)

C++ Representation	Base 2 Equivalent	Result (Base 2)	Bit Number
1 << 3	$00000001_2 << 3$	00001000_2	Bit 3
1 << 4	$00000001_2 << 4$	00010000_2	Bit 4
1 << 5	$00000001_2 << 5$	00100000_2	Bit 5
1 << 6	$00000001_2 << 6$	01000000_2	Bit 6
1 << 7	$00000001_2 << 7$	10000000_2	Bit 7

Although it is hard to tell what bit is represented by 0x10, it's easy to tell what bit is meant by 1 << 4.

The flags can be defined as:

```
// True if any error is set
const int ERROR =          (1 << 0);

// A framing error occurred for this character
const int FRAMING_ERROR =   (1 << 1);

// Character had the wrong parity
const int PARITY_ERROR =    (1 << 2);

// The carrier signal went down
const int CARRIER_LOST =    (1 << 3);

// Power was lost on the communication device
const int CHANNEL_DOWN =    (1 << 4);
```

Now that you have defined the bits, you can manipulate them. To set a bit, use the | operator. For example:

```
char    flags = 0;  // Start all flags at 0

    flags |= CHANNEL_DOWN; // Channel just died
```

To test a bit, use the & operator to "mask out" the bits.

```
if ((flags & ERROR) != 0)
    cerr << "Error flag is set\n";
else
    cerr << "No error detected\n";
```

Clearing a bit is a little harder. Suppose you want to clear the bit PARITY_ERROR. In binary this bit is 00000100. You want to create a mask that has all bits set *except* for the bit you want to clear (11111011). This is done with the NOT operator (~). The mask is then ANDed with the number to clear the bit.

```
PARITY_ERROR                00000100
~PARITY_ERROR               11111011
```

flags	00000101
flags & ~PARITY_ERROR	00000001

In C++ this is:

```
flags &= ~PARITY_ERROR; // Who cares about parity
```

Question 11-1: *In the following program, the* HIGH_SPEED *flag works, but the* DIRECT_CONNECT *flag does not. Why?*

```
#include <iostream.h>

const int HIGH_SPEED = (1<<7);      /* modem is running fast */
                                    // we are using a hardwired connection
const int DIRECT_CONNECT = (1<<8);

char flags = 0;                     // start with nothing

main()
{
    flags |= HIGH_SPEED;           // we are running fast
    flags |= DIRECT_CONNECT;       // because we are wired together

    if ((flags & HIGH_SPEED) != 0)
        cout <<"High speed set\n";

    if ((flags & DIRECT_CONNECT) != 0)
        cout <<"Direct connect set\n";
    return (0);
}
```

Bitmapped Graphics

More and more computers now have graphics. For the PC, there are graphics devices like EGA and VGA cards. For UNIX, there is the X windowing system.

In bitmapped graphics, each pixel on the screen is represented by a single bit in memory. For example, Figure 11-1 shows a 14-by-14 bitmap as it appears on the screen and enlarged so you can see the bits.

Suppose we have a small graphic device—a 16-by-16 pixel monochrome display. We want to set the bit at 4, 7. The bitmap for this device is shown as an array of bits in Figure 11-2.

But we have a problem. There is no data type for an array of bits in C++. The closest we can come is an array of bytes. Our 16-by-16 array of bits now becomes a 2-by-16 array of bytes, as shown in Figure 11-3.

To set the pixel at bit number 4,7 we need to set the fourth bit of byte 0,7. To set this bit we would use the statement: `bit_array[0][7] |= (0x80 >> (4));`

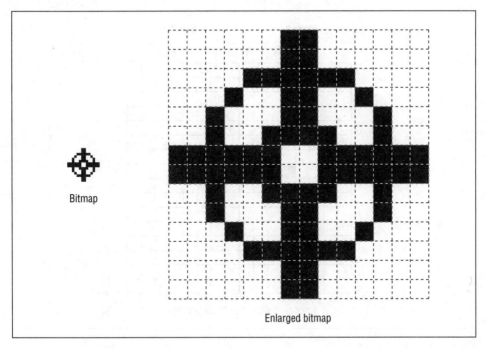

Bitmap

Enlarged bitmap

Figure 11-1. Bitmap, actual size and enlarged

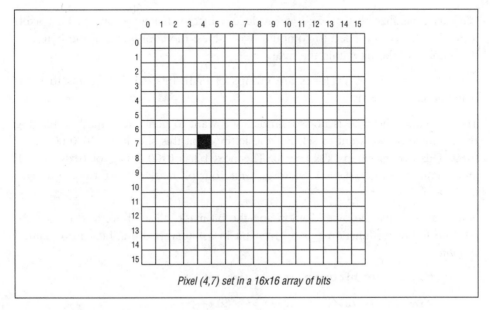

Pixel (4,7) set in a 16x16 array of bits

Figure 11-2. Array of bits

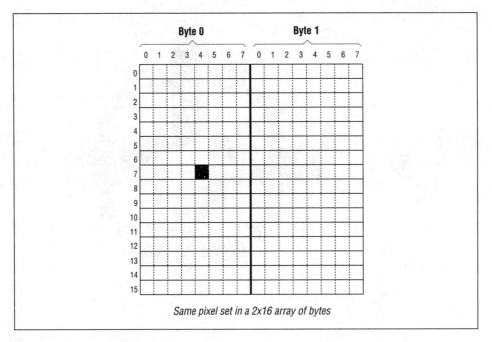

Figure 11-3. Array of bytes

The constant `0x80` is the leftmost bit.

We can generalize this process to produce a macro that turns on the bit (pixel) located at (*x, y*). We need to compute two values: the coordinate of the byte and the number of the bit within the byte.

Our bit address is (*x, y*). Bytes are groups of eight bits, so that means that our byte address is (*x/8, y*).

The bit within the byte is not so simple. We want to generate a mask consisting of the single bit we want to set. For the leftmost bit this should be $1000\ 0000_2$, or 0x80. This occurs when (x%8) == 0. The next bit is $0100\ 0000_2$, or (0x80 >> 1), and occurs when (x%8) == 1. So to generate our bit mask we use the expression (0x80 >> (x%8)).

Now that we have the byte location and the bit mask, all we have to do is set the bit. The following function sets a given bit in a bitmapped graphics array named *graphics*.

```
void inline set_bit(const int x,const int y)
{
    graphics[(x)/8][y] |= (0x80 >> ((x)%8))
}
```

Example 11-2 draws a diagonal line across the graphics array and then prints the array on the terminal.

Example 11-2. graph/graph.cc

```cpp
#include <iostream.h>

const int X_SIZE = 40; // Size of array in the X direction
const int Y_SIZE = 60; // Size of array in the Y direction
/*
 * We use X_SIZE/8 since we pack 8 bits per byte
 */
char graphics[X_SIZE / 8][Y_SIZE];   // The graphics data

/*********************************************************
 * set_bit -- set a bit in the graphics array           *
 *                                                       *
 * Parameters                                            *
 *      x,y -- location of the bit                       *
 *********************************************************/
inline void set_bit(const int x,const int y)
{
    graphics[(x)/8][y] |= (0x80 >>((x)%8));
}

main()
{
    int    loc;        // Current location we are setting
    void   print_graphics(void); // Print the data

    for (loc = 0; loc < X_SIZE; ++loc)
        set_bit(loc, loc);

    print_graphics();
    return (0);
}
/*********************************************************
 * print_graphics -- print the graphics bit array       *
 *                 as a set of X and .'s                *
 *********************************************************/
void print_graphics(void)
{
    int x;      // Current x byte
    int y;      // Current y location
    int bit;    // Bit we are testing in the current byte

    for (y = 0; y < Y_SIZE; ++y) {

        // Loop for each byte in the array
        for (x = 0; x < X_SIZE / 8; ++x) {

            // Handle each bit
            for (bit = 0x80; bit > 0; bit = (bit >> 1)) {
                if ((graphics[x][y] & bit) != 0)
```

Example 11-2. graph/graph.cc (Continued)

```
                    cout << 'X';
                else
                    cout << '.';
            }
        }
        cout << '\n';
    }
}
```

The program defines a bitmapped graphics array:

```
    char graphics[X_SIZE / 8][Y_SIZE];    // The graphics data
```

The constant X_SIZE/8 is used since we have X_SIZE bits across, which translates to X_SIZE/8 bytes.

The main `for` loop:

```
    for (loc = 0; loc < X_SIZE; ++loc)
            set_bit(loc, loc);
```

draws a diagonal line across the graphics array.

Since we do not have a bitmapped graphics device we will simulate it with the subroutine `print_graphics`.

The loop:

```
    for (y = 0; y < Y_SIZE; ++y) {
        ....
```

prints each row. The loop:

```
        for (x = 0; x < X_SIZE / 8; ++x) {
            ...
```

goes through every byte in the row. There are eight bits in each byte handled by the loop:

```
        for (bit = 0x80; bit > 0; bit = (bit >> 1))
```

which uses an unusual loop counter. This loop causes the variable `bit` to start with bit 7 (the leftmost bit). For each iteration of the loop, the bit is moved to the right one bit by `bit = (bit >> 1)`. When we run out of bits, the loop exits.

The loop counter cycles through.

Finally, at the heart of the loops is the code:

Binary	Hex
0000 0000 1000 0000	0x80
0000 0000 0100 0000	0x40

Binary	Hex
0000 0000 0010 0000	0x20
0000 0000 0001 0000	0x10
0000 0000 0000 1000	0x08
0000 0000 0000 0100	0x04
0000 0000 0000 0010	0x02
0000 0000 0000 0001	0x01

```
if ((graphics[x][y] & bit) != 0)
    cout <<"X";
else
    cout << ".";
```

This tests an individual bit and writes "X" if the bit is set or "." if the bit is not set.

Question 11-2: *In the following program, the HIGH_SPEED flag works, but the DIRECT_CONNECT flag does not. Why?In the following program, the HIGH_SPEED flag works, but the DIRECT_CONNECT flag does not. Why?In the following program, the first loop works, but the second one fails. Why?*

Example 11-3. loop/loop.cc

```
#include <iostream.h>
main()
{
    short int i;

    // Works
    for (i = 0x80; i != 0; i = (i >> 1)) {
        cout << "i is " << hex << i << dec << '\n';
    }

    signed char ch;

    // Fails
    for (ch = 0x80; ch != 0; ch = (ch >> 1)) {
        cout << "ch is " << hex << int(ch) << dec << '\n';
    }
    return (0);
}
```

Programming Exercises

Exercise 11-1: Write a set of `inline` functions, `clear_bit` and `test_bit`, to go with the `set_bit` operation defined in Example 11-1. Write a main program to test these macros.

Exercise 11-2: Write a program to draw a 10-by-10 bitmapped square.

Exercise 11-3: Change Example 11-1 so it draws a white line across a black background.

Exercise 11-4: Write a program that counts the number of bits set in an integer. For example, the number 5 (decimal), which is 0000000000000101 (binary), has two bits set.

Exercise 11-5: Write a program that takes a 32-bit integer (**long int**) and splits it into eight 4-bit values. (Be careful of the sign bit.)

Exercise 11-6: Write a program that will take all the bits in a number and shift them to the left end. For example, 01010110 (binary) would become 11110000 (binary).

Answers to Chapter Questions

Answer 11-1: DIRECT_CONNECT is defined to be bit number 8 by the expression (1 << 8); however, the eight bits in a character variable are numbered 76543210. There is no bit number 8. A solution to this problem is to make **flags** a short integer with 16 bits.

Answer 11-2: The problem is that ch is a character (8 bits). The value 0x80 represented in 8 bits is 1000 0000$_2$. The first bit, the sign bit, is set. When a right shift is done on this variable, the sign bit is used for fill, so 1000 0000$_2$ >> 1 is 1100 0000$_2$.

The variable i works even though it is signed because it is 16 bits long. So 0x80 in 16 bits is 0000 0000 1000 0000$_2$. Notice that the bit we've got set is nowhere near the sign bit.

The solution to the problem is to declare ch as an **unsigned** variable.

III

Advanced Types and Classes

12

Advanced Types

> *Total grandeur of a total edifice,*
> *Chosen by an inquisitor of structures.*
> —Wallace Stevens

C++ provides a rich set of data types. Through the use of structures, unions, enum, and class types, the programmer can extend the language with new types.

Structures

Suppose you are writing an inventory program for a warehouse. The warehouse is filled with bins each containing a bunch of parts. All the parts in a bin are identical, so you don't have to worry about mixed bins or partials.

For each bin you need to know:

- The name of the part it holds (character string 30 long).

- The quantity on hand (integer).

- The price (integer cents).

In previous chapters you have used arrays for storing a group of similar data types, but in this example you have a mixed bag: two integers and a string.

Instead of an array, you will use a new data type called a *structure*. In an array, all the elements are of the same type and are numbered. In a structure, each element, or *field,* is named and has its own data type.

The general form of a structure definition is:

```
struct structure-name {
    field-type field-name   // Comment
    field-type field-name   // Comment
    . . . .
} variable-name;
```

For example, you want to define a bin to hold printer cables. The structure definition is:

```
struct bin {
    char    name[30];     // Name of the part
    int     quantity;     // How many are in the bin
    int     cost;         // The cost of a single part (in cents)
} printer_cable_box;      // Where we put the print cables
```

This definition actually tells C++ two things. The first is what a `struct bin` looks like. This statement defines a new data type that can be used in declaring other variables. This statement also declares the variable `printer_cable_box`. Since the structure of a bin has been defined, you can use it to declare additional variables:

```
struct bin terminal_cable_box;  // Place to put terminal cables
```

The *structure-name* part of the definition may be omitted.

```
struct {
    char    name[30];     // Name of the part
    int     quantity;     // How many are in the bin
    int     cost;         // The cost of a single part (in cents)
} printer_cable_box;      // Where we put the print cables
```

The variable `printer_cable_box` is still to be defined, but no data type is created. The data type for this variable is an *anonymous structure*.

The *variable-name* part also may be omitted. This would define a structure type but no variables.

```
struct bin {
    char    name[30];     // Name of the part
    int     quantity;     // How many are in the bin
    int     cost;         // The cost of a single part (in cents)
};
```

In an extreme case, both the *variable-name* and the *structure-name* parts may be omitted. This creates a section of correct but totally useless code.

Once the structure type has been defined you can use it to define variables:

```
struct bin printer_cable_box; // Define the box holding printer cables
```

C++ allows the `struct` to be omitted, so you can use the following declaration:

```
bin printer_cable_box; // Define the box holding printer cables
```

You have defined the variable `printer_cable_box` containing three named fields: `name`, `quantity`, and `cost`. To access them you use the syntax:

```
variable.field
```

For example, if you just found out that the price of the cables went up to $12.95, you would do the following:

```
printer_cable_box.cost = 1295;    // $12.95 is the new price
```

To compute the value of everything in the bin, you can simply multiply the cost by the number of items using the following:

```
total_cost = printer_cable_box.cost * printer_cable_box.quantity;
```

Structures may be initialized at declaration time by putting the list of elements in curly braces ({ }).

```
/*
 * Printer cables
 */
struct bin {
    char    name[30];    // Name of the part
    int     quantity;    // How many are in the bin
    int     cost;        // The cost of a single part (in cents)
};
struct bin printer_cable_box = {
    "Printer Cables",    // Name of the item in the bin
    0,                   // Start with empty box
    1295                 // Cost -- $12.95
};
```

The definition of the structure `bin` and the variable `printer_cable_box` can be combined in one step:

```
struct bin {
    char    name[30];    // Name of the part
    int     quantity;    // How many are in the bin
    int     cost;        // The cost of a single part (in cents)
} printer_cable_box = {
    "Printer Cables",    // Name of the item in the bin
    0,                   // Start with empty box
    1295                 // Cost -- $12.95
};
```

Unions

A structure is used to define a data type with several fields. Each field takes up a separate storage location. For example, the structure

```
struct rectangle {
    int width;
    int height;
};
```

appears in memory as shown in Figure 12-1.

A *union* is similar to a structure; however, it defines a single location that can be given many different field names.

```
union value {
    long int i_value;    // Long integer version of value
    float f_value;       // Floating version of value
}
```

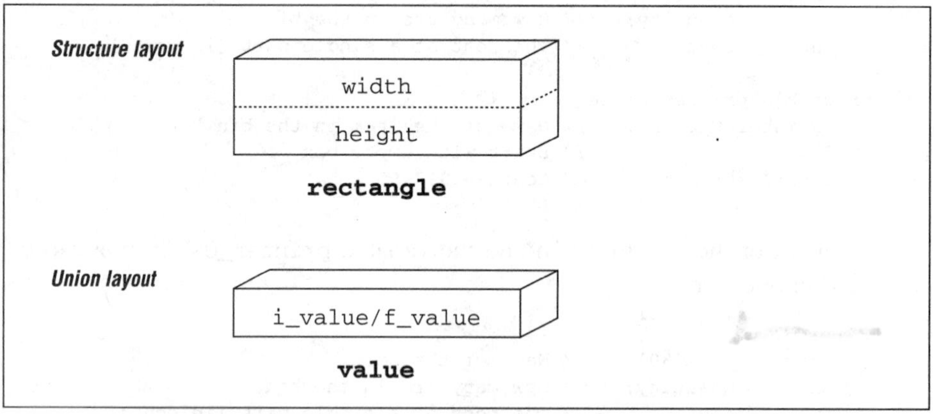

Figure 12-1. Structure and union layout

The fields i_value and f_value share the same space. You might think of a structure as a large box divided up into several different compartments, each with its own name. A union is a box, not divided at all, with several different labels placed on the single compartment inside.

In a structure, the fields do not interact. Changing one field does not change any others. In a union, all fields occupy the same space, so only one may be active at a time. In other words, if you put something in i_value, assigning something to f_value wipes out the old value of i_value.

The following shows how a union may be used:

```
/*
 * Define a variable to hold an integer or
 * a real number (but not both)
 */
union value {
    long int i_value;    // The real number
    float f_value;       // The floating point number
} data;

int i;                   // Random integer
float f;                 // Random floating point number

main()
{
    data.f_value = 5.0;
    data.i_value = 3;    // Data.f_value overwritten

    i = data.i_value;    // Legal

    f = data.f_value;    // Not legal; will generate unexpected results

    data.f_value = 5.5;  // Put something in f_value/clobber i_value
    i = data.i_value;    // Not legal; will generate unexpected results
```

Suppose you want to store the information about a shape. The shape can be any standard shape such as a circle, rectangle, or triangle. The information needed to draw a circle is different from the data needed to draw a rectangle, so you need to define different structures for each shape:

```
struct circle {
    int radius;          // Radius of the circle in pixels
};
struct rectangle {
    int height, width;   // Size of the rectangle in pixels
};
struct triangle {
    int base;            // Length of the triangle's base in pixels
    int height;          // Height of the triangle in pixels
};
```

Now you define a structure to hold the generic shape. The first field is a code that tells you what type of shape you have. The second is a union that holds the shape information:

```
const int SHAPE_CIRCLE    = 0;   // Shape is a circle
const int SHAPE_RECTANGLE = 1;   // Shape is a rectangle
const int SHAPE_TRIANGLE  = 2;   // Shape is a triangle

struct shape {
    int kind;                    // What kind of shape is stored
    union shape_union {          // Union to hold shape information
        struct circle    circle_data;    // Data for a circle
```

```
        struct rectangle rectangle_data;   // Data for a rectangle
        struct triangle  triangle_data;    // Data for a triangle
    } data;
};
```

Graphically you can represent **shape** as a large box. Inside the box is the single integer **kind** and our union **shape_union**. The **union** is a box with three labels on it. The question is which one is the "real" label. You can't tell from looking at the union, but that's why you defined **kind**. It tells us which label to read. The layout of the shape structure is illustrated by Figure 12-2.

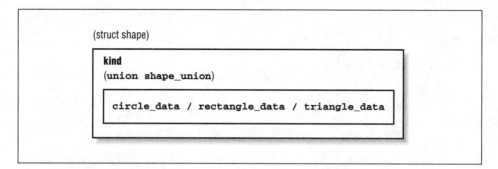

Figure 12-2. "shape" layout

Now you can store a circle in the generic shape:

```
struct shape a_shape;
//...
a_shape.kind = SHAPE_CIRCLE;
a_shape.data.circle_data.radius = 5.0;   // Define the radius of the
                    circle
```

typedef

C++ allows you to define your own variable types through the **typedef** statement. This provides a way for you to extend C++'s basic types. The general form of the **typedef** statement is:

```
typedef type-declaration
```

The *type-declaration* is the same as a variable declaration except a type name is used instead of a variable name. For example:

```
typedef int width; // Define a type that is the width of an object
```

defines a new type, **width**, that is the same as an integer. So the declaration:

```
width box_width;
```

is the same as:

```
int box_width;
```

At first glance, this is not much different from:

```
#define width int

width flag;
```

However, typedefs can be used to define more complex objects which are beyond the scope of a simple #define statement, such as:

```
typedef int group[10];
```

Group is now a new type denoting an array of 10 integers. For example:

```
main()
{
    typedef int group[10];      // Create a new type "group"

    group totals;               // Use the new type for a variable

    // Initialize each element of total
    for (i = 0; i < 10; ++i)
        totals[i] = 0;
```

enum Type

The *enumerated (enum) data type* is designed for variables that can contain only a limited set of values. These values are referenced by name (*tag*). The compiler assigns each tag an integer value internally, such as the days of the week. You could use the directive #define to create values for the days of the week (day_of_the_week) as follows:

```
typedef int day_of_the_week;    // Ddefine the type for days of the week

const int SUNDAY    = 0;
const int MONDAY    = 1;
const int TUESDAY   = 2;
const int WEDNESDAY = 3;
const int THURSDAY  = 4;
const int FRIDAY    = 5;
const int SATURDAY  = 6;

/* Now to use it */
day_of_the_week today = TUESDAY;
```

This method is cumbersome. A better method is to use the **enum** type:

```
enum day_of_the_week {SUNDAY, MONDAY, TUESDAY, WEDNESDAY, THURSDAY,
    FRIDAY, SATURDAY};

/* Now use it */
enum day_of_the_week today = TUESDAY;
```

The general form of an **enum** statement is:

```
enum enum-name {tag-1, tag-2, . . .} variable-name
```

As with structures, the *enum-name* or the *variable-name* may be omitted. The tags may be any valid C++ identifier; however, tags are usually all uppercase.

An additional advantage of using an **enum** type is that C++ will restrict the values that can be used to the ones listed in the **enum** declaration. The following will result in a compiler error:

```
today = 5;   // 5 is not a day_of_the_week
```

One disadvantage of using **enum** is that **enum** variables cannot be used to index an array. The following will result in an error:

```
enum day of the week today = TUESDAY;

// Define string versions of our days of the week
char day_names[7][] = {
    "Sunday",
    "Monday",
    "Tuesday",
    "Wednesday",
    "Thursday",
    "Friday",
    "Saturday"
};

    . . .

    /*
     * The following line generates a warning
     * because today is not an integer
     */
    cout << "Today is " << day_names[today] << '\n';
```

To get around this problem, you need to tell C++ to treat **today** as an integer. This is accomplished through the *cast* or *typecast operation*. The expression **int(today)** tells C++, "I know **today** is not an integer, but treat it like one." To fix the above problem, use the statement:

```
cout << "Today is " << day_names[int(today)] << '\n';
```

Casts are also useful in expressions to make sure the variables have the correct type. In general, you can change the type of almost any expression with the expression:

> *type*(*expression*)

This is particularly useful when working with integers and floating point numbers.

```
int won, lost;      // # games won/lost so far
float   ratio;      // Win/loss ratio

won = 5;
lost = 3;

ratio = won / lost; // Ratio will get 1.0 (a wrong value)

/* The following will compute the correct ratio */
ratio = float(won) / float(lost);
```

C++ also supports the older C-style casting. The syntax for C-style casting is:

> (*type*)*value*

For example:

```
(float)i      // Turn "i" into a floating point number
```

C-style casts are frowned upon because they can easily be ambiguous. For example, in the expression:

```
(float)3 + 5
```

does the (float) apply to 3 to 3 + 5? It's not clear. To make this expression clearer you need to add parentheses:

```
((float)3) + 5
```

As you can see, this form is more complex than C++ casts. Simpler is better, so use C++ casting.[*]

Bit Fields or Packed Structures

So far all the structures you've been using have been *unpacked*. *Packed structures* allow you to declare structures in a way that takes up a minimum of storage. For example, the following structure takes up 6 bytes (on a 16-bit machine):

```
struct item {
    unsigned int list;      // True if item is in the list
```

---

[*] Note: The current C++ Draft Standard describes a number of new casting operations. These are discussed in Chapter 28, *C++'s Dustier Corners*.

```
        unsigned int seen;        // True if this item has been seen
        unsigned int number;      // Item number
    };
```

The storage layout for this structure can be seen in Figure 12-3. Each structure uses 6 bytes of storage (2 bytes for each integer).

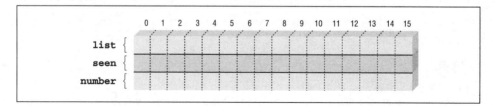

Figure 12-3. Unpacked structure

However, the fields `list` and `seen` can have only two values, 0 and 1, so only 1 bit is needed to represent them. You never plan on having more than 16383 items (0x3fff or 14 bits). You can redefine this structure using bit fields, so, it takes only 2 bytes, by following each field with a colon and the number of bits to be used for that field.

```
struct item {
    unsigned int list:1;     // True if item is in the list
    unsigned int seen:1;     // True if this item has been seen
    unsigned int number:14;  // Item number
};
```

In this example, you tell the compiler to use 1 bit for `list`, 1 bit for `seen` and 14 bits for `number`. Using this method you can pack data into only 2 bytes as seen in Figure 12-4.

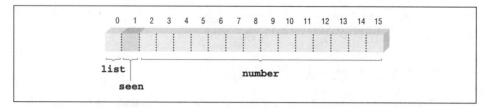

Figure 12-4. Packed structure

Packed structures should be used with care. The machine code to extract data from bit fields is relatively large and slow. Unless storage is a problem, packed structures should not be used.

In Chapter 10, *The C++ Preprocessor*, you needed to store character data and five status flags for 8,000 characters. In this case, using a different byte for each flag would eat up a lot of storage (five bytes for each incoming character). You used bitwise operations to pack the five flags into a single byte. Alternatively, a packed structure could have accomplished the same thing:

```
struct char_and_status {
    char character;      // Character from device
    int error:1;         // True if any error is set
    int framing_error:1;// A framing error occurred
    int parity_error:1; // Character had the wrong parity
    int carrier_lost:1; // The carrier signal went down
    int channel_down:1; // Power was lost on the channel
};
```

Using packed structures for flags is clearer and less error-prone than using bitwise operators. However, bitwise operators allow additional flexibility. You should use the one that is clearest and easiest for you to use.

Arrays of Structures

Structures and arrays can be combined. Suppose you want to record the time a runner completes each lap of a four-lap race. You define a structure to store the time:

```
struct time {
    int hour;   // Hour (24-hour clock)
    int minute; // 0-59
    int second; // 0-59
};

#define MAX_LAPS 4 /* We will have only 4 laps*/

/* The time of day for each lap*/
struct time lap[MAX_LAPS];
```

The statement:

```
struct time lap[MAX_LAPS];
```

defines lap as an array of four elements. Each element consists of a single time structure.

You can use this as follows:

```
/*
 * Runner just past the timing point
 */

lap[count].hour = hour;
lap[count].minute = minute;
lap[count].second = second;
++count;
```

This array can also be initialized at run time.

Initialization of an array of structures is similar to the initialization of multidimensional arrays.

```
struct time start_stop[2] = {
    {10, 0, 0},
    {12, 0, 0}
};
```

Suppose you want to write a program to handle a mailing list. Mailing labels are 5 lines high and 60 characters wide. You need a structure to store names and addresses. The mailing list will be sorted by name for most printouts, and sorted in zip-code order for actual mailings. The mailing list structure looks like:

```
struct mailing {
    char name[60];      // Last name, first name
    char address1[60];// Two lines of street address
    char address2[60];
    char city[40];      // Name of the city
    char state[2];      // Two-character abbreviation
    long int zip;       // Numeric zip code
};
```

You can now declare an array to hold the mailing list:

```
/* Our mailing list */
struct mailing list[MAX_ENTRIES];
```

Programming Exercises

Exercise 12-1: Write a program that will take a list of names and addresses, sort them, and produce a set of mailing labels.

Exercise 12-2: Design a structure to store time and date. Write a function to find the difference between two times in minutes.

Exercise 12-3: Design an airline reservation data structure that contains the following data:

Flight number
Originating airport code (3 characters)
Destination airport code (3 characters)
Departure time
Arrival time

Write a program that lists all the planes that leave from two airports specified by the user.

13

Simple Classes

She thinks that even up in heaven
Her class lies late and snores.

—Cyril Connolly

So far you've used simple variables and structures to hold data and functions to process the data. C++ *classes* allow you to combine data and the functions that use it.

In this chapter you'll see how a class can improve your code by implementing a simple stack two ways: first, using a structure and functions, and then using a class.

Stacks

A *stack* is an algorithm for storing data. Data can be put in the stack using a *push operation*. The *pop operation* removes the data. Data is stored in last-in-first-out (LIFO) order.

You can think of a stack as a stack of papers. When you perform a push operation, you put a new paper on top of the stack. You can push as many times as you want. Each time the new data goes on top of the stack. You get data out of a stack using the pop operation, which takes the top paper off the stack and gives it to the caller.

Suppose you start with an empty stack and put three elements on it, 4, 5, and 8, using three push operations. The first pop would return the top element: 8. The elements 4 and 5 remain in the stack. Popping again will give us 5. You then push another value, 9, on the stack. Popping twice will give us the numbers 9 and 4, in that order. This is illustrated by Table 13-1.

Table 13-1. Stack Operation

Operation	Stack After Operation
Push (4)	4
Push (5)	5 4
Push (8)	8 5 4
Pop (returns 8)	5 4
Pop (returns 5)	4
Push (9)	9 4
Pop (returns 9)	4
Pop (returns 4)	<empty>

Designing a Stack

You start a stack design by designing the data structure. This structure will need a place to put the data (called **data**) and a count of the number of items currently pushed on the stack (called **count**):

```
const int STACK_SIZE = 100;      // Maximum size of a stack

// The stack itself
struct stack {
    int count;                   // Number of items in the stack
    int data[STACK_SIZE];        // The items themselves
};
```

Next you need to create the routines to handle the push and pop operations. The push function stores the item on the stack and then increases the data count.

```
inline void stack_push(struct stack &the_stack, const int item)
{
    the_stack.data[the_stack.count] = item;
    ++the_stack.count;
}
```

Note: This version of the program does not check for stack overflow or other error conditions. Later, in Chapter 14, *More on Classes*, you'll see how you can use this simple stack to make a safer, more complex one.

Popping simply removes the top item and decreases the number of items in the stack.

```
inline int stack_pop(struct stack &the_stack)
{
    // Stack goes down by one
    --the_stack.count;
```

```
        // Then we return the top value
        return (the_stack.data[the_stack.count]);
    }
```

There is one item you've overlooked: initializing the stack. You see you must set up the stack before you can use it. Keeping with the spirit of putting everything in a stack_*xxxx* routine get the **stack_init** function.

```
    inline void stack_init(struct stack &the_stack)
    {
        the_stack.count = 0;        // Zero the stack
    }
```

Notice that you don't need to zero the **data** field in the stack, since the elements of **data** are overwritten by the push operation.

You are now finished. To actually use the stack you declare it with a **struct** statement. Next you must make sure that you initialize it, and then you can push and pop to your heart's content (or at least within the limits of the stack).

```
    struct stack a_stack;     // Declare the stack

    stack_init(a_stack);      // Initialize the stack
    // Stack is ready for use
```

Example 13-1 contains a complete implementation of the structure version of the stack and a short test routine.

Example 13-1. stack_s/stack_s.cc

```
/*********************************************************
 * Stack                                                 *
 *      A set of routines to implement a simple integer  *
 *      stack.                                            *
 *                                                        *
 * Procedures                                             *
 *      stack_init -- initialize the stack                *
 *      stack_push -- put an item on the stack            *
 *      stack_pop -- remove an item from the stack        *
 *********************************************************/
#include <stdlib.h>
#include <iostream.h>

const int STACK_SIZE = 100;     // Maximum size of a stack

// The stack itself
struct stack {
    int count;                  // Number of items in the stack
    int data[STACK_SIZE];       // The items themselves
};

/*********************************************************
 * stack_init -- initialize the stack                    *
```

Example 13-1. stack_s/stack_s.cc (Continued)

```
 *                                                       *
 * Parameters                                            *
 *      the_stack -- stack to initialize                 *
 ********************************************************/
inline void stack_init(struct stack &the_stack)
{
    the_stack.count = 0;          // Zero the stack
}
/********************************************************
 * stack_push -- push an item on the stack              *
 *                                                       *
 * Warning: We do not check for overflow                 *
 *                                                       *
 * Parameters                                            *
 *      the_stack -- stack to use for storing the item   *
 *      item -- item to put in the stack                 *
 ********************************************************/
inline void stack_push(struct stack &the_stack,
                       const int item)
{
    the_stack.data[the_stack.count] = item;
    ++the_stack.count;
}
/********************************************************
 * stack_pop -- get an item off the stack               *
 *                                                       *
 * Warning: We do not check for stack underflow          *
 *                                                       *
 * Parameters                                            *
 *      the_stack -- stack to get the item from          *
 *                                                       *
 * Returns                                               *
 *      the top item from the stack                      *
 ********************************************************/
inline int stack_pop(struct stack &the_stack)
{
    // Stack goes down by one
    --the_stack.count;

    // Then we return the top value
    return (the_stack.data[the_stack.count]);
}

// A short routine to test the stack
main()
{
    struct stack a_stack;         // Stack we want to use

    stack_init(a_stack);

    // Push three values on the stack
    stack_push(a_stack, 1);
```

Example 13-1. stack_s/stack_s.cc (Continued)

```
        stack_push(a_stack, 2);
        stack_push(a_stack, 3);

        // Pop the items from the stack
        cout << "Expect a 3 ->" << stack_pop(a_stack) << '\n';
        cout << "Expect a 2 ->" << stack_pop(a_stack) << '\n';
        cout << "Expect a 1 ->" << stack_pop(a_stack) << '\n';

        return (0);
    }
```

Improved Stack

The structure version of the stack works but has a few drawbacks. The first is that the data and the functions are defined separately, forcing you to pass a **struct stack** variable into each procedure.

There is also the problem of data protection. The fields **data** and **count** are accessible to anyone. The design states that only the stack functions should have access to these fields, but there is nothing to prevent rogue code from modifying them.

A C++ **struct** is a mixed collection of data. The C++ **class** not only holds data like a structure, but also adds a set of functions for manipulating the data and access protection.

Turning the **struct stack** into a **class** you get:

```
    class stack {
        private:
            int count;                  // Number of items in the stack
            int data[STACK_SIZE];       // The items themselves
        public:
            // Initialize the stack
            void init(void);

            // Push an item on the stack
            void push(const int item);

            // Pop an item from the stack
            int pop(void);
    };
```

Let's go into this **class** declaration in more detail. The beginning looks much like a structure definition except that you're using the word **class** instead of **struct**.

```
    class stack {
        private:
```

```
        int count;           // Number of items in the stack
        int data[STACK_SIZE];  // The items themselves
```

This declares two fields: count and data. In a class these items are not called fields; they are called *member variables*. The keyword private indicates the access privileges associated with these two member variables.

There are three levels of access privileges: public, private, and protected. Class members, both data and functions, marked private cannot be used outside the class. They can be accessed only by functions within the class. The opposite of private is public, which indicates members that anyone can access.

Finally, protected is similar to private except that it allows access by derived classes. (We discuss derived classes in Chapter 21, *Advanced Classes*.)

You've finished defining the data for this class. Now you need to define the functions that manipulate the data.

```
    public:
        // Initialize the stack
        void init(void);

        // Push an item on the stack
        void push(const int item);

        // Pop an item from the stack
        int pop(void);
    };
```

This section starts with the keyword public. This tells C++ that you want all these member functions to be available to the outside. In this case, you just define the function prototypes. The code for the function will be defined later.

Next comes the body of the init function. Since this function belongs to the stack class, you prefix the name of the procedure with stack::. (We discuss the scope operator :: in more detail in Chapter 14, *More on Classes*.)

The definition of the init function looks like:

```
    inline void stack::init(void)
    {
        count = 0;  // Zero the stack
    }
```

This procedure zeroes the stack's count. In the structure version of the stack_ init function you must pass the stack in as a parameter. Since this function is part of the stack class, that's unnecessary. This also means that you can access the member variables directly. In other words, instead of having to say the_ stack.count, you just say count.

The functions push and pop are implemented in a similar manner.

```
inline void stack::push(const int item)
{
    data[count] = item;
    ++count;
}

inline int stack::pop(void)
{
    // Stack goes down by one
    --count;

    // Then we return the top value
    return (data[count]);
}
```

The stack class is now complete. All you have to do is use it.

Using a Class

Using a class is much like using a structure. Declaring a class variable is the same, except you use the word **class** instead of **struct**.

```
class stack a_stack;        // Stack we want to use
```

The word **class** is not needed and is frequently omitted.

```
stack a_stack;        // Stack we want to use
```

You access the fields of a structure using a dot, for example:

```
structure.field = 5;
```

Accessing the members of a class is similar, except that the members of a class can be both data and functions. Also, you can access only the members that are public.

To call the **init** member function of the stack class all you need to do is:

```
a_stack.init();
```

The **push** and **pop** member functions can be accessed in a similar manner:

```
a_stack.push(1);
result = a_stack.pop();
```

Example 13-2 contains a class version of the stack.

Example 13-2. stack_c/stack_c.cc

```
/**********************************************************
 * Stack                                                  *
 *      A file implementing a simple stack class          *
 **********************************************************/
```

Example 13-2. stack_c/stack_c.cc (Continued)

```
#include <stdlib.h>
#include <iostream.h>

const int STACK_SIZE = 100;      // Maximum size of a stack

/********************************************************
 * Stack class                                         *
 *                                                     *
 * Member functions                                    *
 *      init -- initialize the stack                   *
 *      push -- put an item on the stack               *
 *      pop -- remove an item from the stack           *
 ********************************************************/
// The stack itself
class stack {
    private:
        int count;               // Number of items in the stack
        int data[STACK_SIZE];    // The items themselves
    public:
        // Initialize the stack
        void init(void);

        // Push an item on the stack
        void push(const int item);

        // Pop an item from the stack
        int pop(void);
};

/********************************************************
 * stack::init -- initialize the stack                 *
 ********************************************************/
inline void stack::init(void)
{
    count = 0;  // Zero the stack
}
/********************************************************
 * stack::push -- push an item on the stack            *
 *                                                     *
 * Warning: We do not check for overflow               *
 *                                                     *
 * Parameters                                          *
 *      item -- item to put in the stack               *
 ********************************************************/
inline void stack::push(const int item)
{
    data[count] = item;
    ++count;
}
/********************************************************
 * stack::pop -- get an item off the stack             *
 *                                                     *
```

Example 13-2. stack_c/stack_c.cc (Continued)

```
 * Warning: We do not check for stack underflow          *
 *                                                        *
 * Returns                                                *
 *     the top item from the stack                        *
 **********************************************************/
inline int stack::pop(void)
{
    // Stack goes down by one
    --count;

    // Then we return the top value
    return (data[count]);
}

// A short routine to test the stack
main()
{
    stack a_stack;        // Stack we want to use

    a_stack.init();

    // Push three values on the stack
    a_stack.push(1);
    a_stack.push(2);
    a_stack.push(3);

    // Pop the items from the stack
    cout << "Expect a 3 ->" << a_stack.pop() << '\n';
    cout << "Expect a 2 ->" << a_stack.pop() << '\n';
    cout << "Expect a 1 ->" << a_stack.pop() << '\n';

    return (0);
}
```

Introduction to Constructors and Destructors

This stack class has one minor inconvenience. The programmer must call the init member function before using the stack. However, programmers are terribly forgetful and sooner or later someone is going to forget to initialize the stack. Wouldn't it be nice if C++ had an automatic way of initializing the stack?

It does. Actually C++ will automatically call a number of member functions. The first you are concerned about is called when the class is created. This is called the *constructor* function and has the same name as the class. For example, the constructor for the **stack** class is named **stack** (also known as **stack::stack** outside the class body).

A variable is created when it is declared. (It can also be created by the **new** operator as you will discuss later in Chapter 20, *Advanced Pointers*.)

You want to have this stack initialized automatically, so you remove the `init` function and replace it with the constructor, `stack::stack`.

```
class stack {
        // ...
    public:
        // Initialize the stack
        stack(void);
        // ...
};

inline stack::stack(void)
{
    count = 0;   // Zero the stack
}
```

You may have noticed that the return type `void` has been omitted in the constructor declaration. Constructors can never return a value so the `void` is not needed. In fact the compiler will complain if it's present.

Since the constructor is called automatically, the program is now simpler. Instead of writing:

```
main()
{
    stack a_stack;       // Stack we want to use

    a_stack.init();
```

you can just write:

```
main()
{
    stack a_stack;       // Stack we want to use

    // Use the stack
```

Also, since you no longer have to count on the programmer putting in the `init` call, the program is more reliable.

Destructors

The constructor is automatically called when the variable is created. The *destructor* is automatically called when the variable is destroyed. This occurs when the variable goes out of scope or when a pointer variable is deleted. (The `delete` is defined in Chapter 20, *Advanced Pointers*.)

The special name for a destructor is the class name with a tilde (~) in front of it. So, for the `stack` class the destructor would be named `~stack`.

Suppose you make the rule that the stack should be empty when the programmer is finished with it. In other words, for every **push** you do, a **pop** must be done. If this doesn't happen, it's an error and you should warn the user.

All you have to do is create a destructor for the stack that checks for an empty stack and issues a warning if the stack is not empty. The destructor looks like:

```
stack::~stack(void)
    if (count != 0)
        cerr << "Error: Destroying a nonempty stack\n";
}
```

Parameterized Constructors

The constructor for a **class** can take parameters. Suppose you want to define a class that holds a person's name and phone number. The data members for this **class** would look like:

```
class person {
    public:
        char name[80];      // Name of the person
        char phone[80];     // Person's phone number
```

You want the constructor for this **class** to automatically initialize both the name and the phone number.

```
    public:
        person(const char i_name[], const char i_phone[]);
    // ... rest of class
};

person::person(const char i_name[], const char i_phone[])
{
    strcpy(name, i_name);
    strcpy(phone, i_phone);
}
```

Now you are ready to use the **class**. When you declare variables of this **class**, you must put two parameters in the declaration. For example:

```
main()
{
    person sam("Sam Jones", "555-1234");
```

Like other functions, constructors can be overloaded. Using the **person** example, you can take care of the case where you have a person with no phone by creating a constructor that takes a name as its only parameter:

```
class person {
    // ... rest of the class
    public:
        person(const char i_name[]);
};
```

```
person::person(const char i_name[])
{
    strcpy(name, i_name);
    strcpy(phone, "No Phone");
}
```

In this case, you have two constructors, one that takes one parameter and one that takes two parameters. You haven't defined a constructor that takes zero parameters, so you can't declare a variable of type **person** without specifying at least one parameter. In other words:

```
person unnamed_source;      // Illegal
```

will generate an error message.

Parameterized Destructors

There is no such thing as a parameterized destructor. Destructors take no parameters and supply no return value. All they do is destroy the variable.

Copy Constructor

The copy constructor is a special constructor that is used to make an exact copy of a class. For example, a copy constructor for the **stack** class would look like:

```
stack::stack(const stack &old_stack)
{
    int i;      // Index used to copy the data

    for (i = 0; i < old_stack.count; ++i) {
        data[i] = old_stack.data[i];
        count = old_stack.count;
}
```

Let's examine this function in more detail. The declaration:

```
stack::stack(const stack &old_stack)
```

identifies this as a copy constructor. The single parameter (**const stack &old_ stack**) identifies this particular constructor as the copy constructor. This function is expected to turn the current class into an exact copy of the parameter.

The code:

```
for (i = 0; i < old_stack.count; ++i) {
    data[i] = old_stack.data[i];
count = old_stack.count;
```

takes all the data from the old stack and puts it into the new stack.

The copy operator can be invoked explicitly as illustrated in the following example:

```
stack a_stack;        // A simple stack

a_stack.push(1);      // Put a couple of elements on the stack
a_stack.push(2);

stack b_stack(a_stack);  // Create a copy of the stack
```

On the face of it, the copy constructor doesn't seem that important. But if you remember, back in Chapter 9, *Variable Scope and Functions*, you discussed the various ways C++ can pass parameters to a function. One of these was call by value. That's where a *copy* of the parameter is made and passed to the function.

When a stack or any other class is passed as a call-by-value parameter, a copy is made of that class using the copy constructor.

In the following code, you've added some commentary to show you the functions that C++ will automatically call behind your back.

```
void use_stack(stack local_stack)
{
    local_stack.push(9);
    local_stack.push(10);
    .. Do something with local_stack
}
```

local_stack::~stack() called

```
main()
{
    stack a_stack;         // Generate a default stack

    a_stack.push(1);
    a_stack.push(2);

    use_stack(a_stack);

    // Prints "2"
    cout << a_stack.pop() << '\n';
```

astack.stack called

local_stack.stack(a_stack) called
(This is part of the parameter-passing mechanism)

As you can see, C++ does a lot of work behind the scenes. It starts when a_stack is declared. C++ calls the default constructor to create a_stack.

The variable a_stack is used, and then passed to the function use_stack. Since a_stack is passed by value, a copy must be made of the stack using the copy constructor local_stack.stack(a_stack).

The function then adds a few items to local_stack. Note: This is a copy of a_stack, so anything you do to local_stack does not affect a_stack. At the end of the function `local_stack` contains four items, 1, 2, 9, 10, and `a_stack` contains two items, 1, 2.

Finally after the function call, you print out the top element of **a_stack,** which is "2".

Automatically Generated Member Functions

Every class has a constructor and a destructor. If the programmer does not write these member functions, C++ will automatically generate them. Also, there are several member functions such as the copy constructor that can be called automatically.

Automatically Generated and Used Functions

class::class()
> Default constructor.

> Automatically generated if no other constructors are defined. The generated code fills the data members of the class with random values.

> Automatically called when a variable of this class is declared with no parameters, such as:

> `class_type var;`

class::class(const class &old_class)
> Copy constructor.

> Automatically generated unless the programmer explicitly defines a copy constructor. The function C++ generates copies all the data members from the old class to the new one.

> Automatically called when passing a call-by-value parameter to a function. This member function may also be called when creating a duplicate of a variable:

> `call_type first_var;`

> `// Call copy constructor to`

> `// make duplicate of first_var`

> `class_type second_var(first_var);`

class::~class()
> Destructor.

> Automatically generated unless the programmer defines one.

Automatically called when a variable is destroyed. This occurs when a variable goes out of scope. (It is also called by the **delete** operator discussed in Chapter 20, *Advanced Pointers.*)

```
class class::operator = (const class &old_class)
```

Assignment operator. (Operator overloading is discussed in Chapter 18, *Operator Overloading.*)

Automatically generated to handle assignment of one class to another. The function C++ generates copies all the data members from the old class to the new one.

```
class_type var1;

class_type var2;

var1 = var2;    // "operator =" called
```

Shortcuts

So far you have used only function prototypes in the classes you've created. It is possible to define the body of the function inside the class itself. Thus:

```
class stack {
    public:
            // .... rest of class

            // Push an item on the stack
            void push(const int item);
};
inline void stack::push(const int item)
{
    data[count] = item;
    ++count;
}
```

can be written as:

```
class stack {
    public:
            // .... rest of class

            // Push an item on the stack
            void push(const int item) {
                data[count] = item;
                ++count;
            }
};
```

The **inline** directive is not required in the second case since all functions declared inside a class are automatically declared inline.

Style

Programming style for classes looks pretty much like the style for structures and functions. Every member variable should be followed by a comment explaining it and every member function should be commented like a function.

However, you comment the prototypes for member functions differently from normal function prototypes. For normal functions you put a full function comment block in front for the prototype. If you did this for the member functions of a class, the comments would obscure the structure of the class. This is one of the few cases when too many comments can cause trouble. So you put a one-line comment in front of each member function prototype and full comments in front of the function itself.

But what about inline-member functions, where the entire body of the function is declared inside the class? How do you comment that? If you put in full comments, you obscure the structure of the class. If you put in one-liners, you omit a lot of useful information. Proper commenting is a balancing act. You need to put in what's useful and leave out what's not.

The solution is to keep the size of the inline-member function small. There are two reasons for this, first all inline functions should be small and, secondly, large functions declared inside a class make the class excessively complex. A good rule of thumb is that if the function requires more than about five lines of code, put a prototype in the class and put the body of the function elsewhere.

The structure of very small member functions should be obvious and thus not require a full-blown comment block. If the function is not obvious and requires extensive comments, you can always put in a prototype and comment the body of the function later in the program.

C++ does not require an access protection declaration (`public`, `private`, or `protected`) before the first *member variable*. The following is perfectly legal:

```
class example {
        int data;
        // ...
};
```

But what is the access protection of `data`? Is it `public`, `private`, or `protected`? If you put in an explicit declaration, then you don't have to worry about questions like this. (For those of you who are curious, the access protection defaults to `private`.)

Finally, C++ will automatically generate some member functions, such as the default constructor, the copy constructor, and the assignment operator. Suppose you have a class that does not specify a copy constructor, such as:

```
// Comments describing the class
// Note: The style of this class leaves something to be desired
class queue {
    private:
        int data[100];     // Data stored in the queue
        int first;         // First element in the queue
        int last;          // Last element in the queue
    public:
        queue();           // Initialize the queue
        void put(int item);// Put an item in the queue
        int get(void);     // Get an item from the queue
};
```

Did the programmer who created this class forget the copy constructor? Will the copy constructor automatically generated by C++ work, or did the programmer design this class knowing that the copy constructor would never be called? These important questions are not answered by the class as written.

All classes have a default constructor, copy constructor, assignment operator, and destructor. If you want to use the one C++ generates automatically, put a comment in the class indicating that the default is being used.

```
// Comments describing the class
class queue {
    private:
        int data[100];     // Data stored in the queue
        int first;         // First element in the queue
        int last;          // Last element in the queue
    public:
        queue();           // Initialize the queue
        // queue(const queue &old_queue)
        //     Use automatically generated copy constructor

        // queue operator = (const queue &old_queue)
        //     Use automatically generated assignment operator

        // ~queue()
        //     Use automatically generated destructor

        void put(int item);// Put an item in the queue
        int get(void);     // Get an item from the queue
};
```

Now it is obvious what member functions the programmer wanted to let C++ generate automatically, and being obvious is very important in any programming project.

The copy constructor automatically generated by C++ is rather simple and limited. It doesn't work in all cases, as you'll see later when you start to construct more complex classes. But what happens when the automatic copy constructor won't work as you desire and you don't want to go to the trouble to create your own?

After all, you may decide that a class will never be copied (or that if it is, it's an error).

One solution is to create a dummy copy constructor that prints an error message and aborts the program:

```
class no_copy {
        // Body of the class
    public:
        // Copy constructor
        no_copy(const no_copy &old_class) {
            cerr <<
              "Error: Copy constructor for 'no_copy' called. Exiting\n";
            exit(8);
        }
};
```

This works, sort of. The problem is that errors are detected at runtime instead of compile time. You want to catch errors as soon as possible, so this solution is at best a hack.

However, you can prevent the compiler from automatically calling the copy constructor. The trick is to declare it private. That's your way of saying to the world, "Yes, there is a copy constructor, but no one can ever use it."

```
class no_copy {
        // Body of the class
    private:
        // There is no copy constructor
        no_copy(const no_copy &old_class);
};
```

Now when the compiler attempts to use the copy constructor you will get an error message like "Error: Attempt to access private member function."

Note: Since the copy constructor is never called, you never have to define the body of this function.

Programming Exercises

Exercise 13-1: Write a parity class. This class allows the program to put any number of items into it and returns TRUE if an even number of items is put in and FALSE if an odd number is used.

Member functions:

```
void parity::put(void);    // Count another element
int parity::test(void);    // Return TRUE(1) if an even number of
                           // puts have been done. Return FALSE(0)
                           // for an odd number.
```

Exercise 13-2: Write a "checkbook" class. You put a list of numbers into this class and get a total out.

Member functions:

```
void check::add_item(int amount);    // Add a new entry to the checkbook
int check::total(void);              // Return the total of all items
```

Exercise 13-3: Write a class to implement a simple queue. A queue is very similar to a stack except the data is removed in first-in-first-out (FIFO) order.

Member functions:

```
void queue::put(int item);   // Insert an item in the queue
int queue::get(void);        // Get the next item from the queue
```

Sample usage:

```
queue a_queue;

a_queue.put(1);     // Queue contains: 1
a_queue.put(2);     // Queue contains: 2
a_queue.put(3);     // Queue contains: 1 2 3

cout << a_queue.get() << '\n';   // Prints 1, queue contains 2 3
cout << a_queue.get() << '\n';   // Prints 2, queue contains 3
```

Exercise 13-4: Define a class that will hold the set of integers from 0 to 31. An element can be set with the **set** member function and cleared with the **clear** member function. It is not an error to set an element that's already set or clear an element that's already clear. The function **test** is used to tell whether an element is set.

Member functions:

```
void small_set::set(int item);     // Set an element in the set
void small_set::clear(int item);   // Clear an element in the set
int small_set::test(void);         // See whether an element is set
```

Sample usage:

```
small_set a_set;

a_set.set(3);     // Set contains [3]
a_set.set(5);     // Set contains [3,5]
a_set.set(5);     // Legal (set contains [3,5])

cout << a_set.test(3) << '\n';    // Prints "1"
cout << a_set.test(0) << '\n';    // Prints "0"

a_set.clear(5);   // Set contains [3]
```

Exercise 13-5: I have a simple method of learning foreign vocabulary words. I write the words down on a list of flash cards. I then go through the stack of flash cards one at a time. If I get a word right, that card is discarded. If I get it wrong, the card goes to the back of the stack.

Write a class to implement this system.

Member functions:

```
struct single_card {
    char *question;        // English version of the word
    char *answer;          // Other language version of the word
};

// Constructor -- takes a list of cards to initialize the flash card
            stack
void flash_card::flash_card(single_card list[]);

// Get the next card
void flash_card::next(single_card &next_card);

void flash_card::right(void);      // The student got the current card
                                       right
void flash_card::wrong(void);      // The student got the current card
                                       wrong
```

14

More on Classes

This method is, to define as the number of a class the class of all classes similar to the given class.

—Bertrand Russell
Principles of Mathematics, **Part II,**
Chapter 11, Section iii, 1903

Friends

In Chapter 13, *Simple Classes*, you defined a basic stack class. Suppose you want to write a function to see whether two stacks are equal. At first glance this is simple. The function looks like Example 14-1.

Example 14-1. stack_c/s_equal.cc

```
/********************************************************
 * stack_equal -- Test to see whether two stacks are    *
 *                equal                                 *
 *                                                      *
 *      s1, s2 -- the two stacks                        *
 *                                                      *
 * Returns                                              *
 *      0 -- stacks are not equal                       *
 *      1 -- stacks are equal                           *
 ********************************************************/
int stack_equal(const stack &s1, const stack &s2)
{
    int index;  // Index into the items in the array

    // Check number of items first
    if (s1.count != s2.count)
        return (0);
```

Example 14-1. stack_c/s_equal.cc (Continued)

```
    for (index = 0; index < s1.count; ++index) {
        if (s1.data[index] != s2.data[index])
            return (0);
    }
    return (1);
}
```

Like many programs, this solution is simple, clear, and *wrong*. The problem is that the member variables `count` and `data` are private. That means you can't access them.

So what do you do? One solution is to make these variables public. That gives the function `stack_equal` access to `count` and `data`. The problem is that it also gives everyone else access, and you don't want that.

Fortunately C++ gives you a way to say, "Let `stack_equal` and only `stack_equal` have access to the private data of the class `stack`." This is accomplished through the `friend` directive. Classes must declare their friends. No function from the outside may access the private data from the class, unless the class allows it.

Example 14-2. stack_c/f_stack.cc

```
// The stack itself
class stack {
    private:
        int count;              // Number of items in the stack
        int data[STACK_SIZE];   // The items themselves
    public:
        // Initialize the stack
        void init(void);

        // Push an item on the stack
        void push(const int item);

        // Pop an item from the stack
        int pop(void);

        friend int stack_equal(const stack &s1, const stack &s2);
};
```

NOTE

`stack_equal` is *not* a member function of the class `stack`. It is a normal, simple function. The only difference is that because the function is a `friend` it has access to private data for any class that calls it friend.

Friend Classes

Friends are not restricted to just functions. One class can be a friend of another. For example:

```
class item {
    private:
        int data;

    friend class set_of_items;
};
class set_of_items {
    // ...
};
```

In this case since the class `set_of_items` is a friend of `item` it has access to all the members of `item`.

Constant Functions

C++ lets you define two types of numbers: constant and nonconstant. For example:

```
int index;       // Current index into the data array
const int DATA_MAX(100);  // Maximum number of items in the array
```

These two items are treated differently. For example, you can change the value of `index` but you can't change `DATA_MAX`.

Now let's consider a class to implement a set of numbers from 0 to 31. The definition of this class is:

```
// Warning: The member functions in this class are incomplete
//          See below for a better definition of this class
class int_set {
    private:
        // ... whatever
    public:
        int_set(void);          // Default constructor
        int_set(const int_set &old_set); // Copy constructor
        void set(int value);    // Set a value
        void clear(int value);  // Clear an element
        int test(int value);    // See whether an element is set
};
```

As with numbers, C++ will let you define two types of sets: constant and nonconstant.

```
int_set var_set;        // A variable set (we can change this)

var_set.set(1);         // Set an element in the set
```

```
// Define a constant version of the set (we cannot change this)
const int_set const_set(var_set);
```

In the `int_set` class there are member functions such as `set` and `clear` that change the value of the set. There is also a function `test` that changes nothing.

Obviously you don't want to allow `set` and `clear` to be used on a constant. However, it is okay to use the `test` member function.

But how does C++ know what can be used on a constant and what can't? The trick is to put the keyword `const` at the end of the function header. This tells C++ that this member function can be used for a constant variable. So if you put `const` *after* the member function `test`, C++ will allow it to be used in a constant. The member functions `set` and `clear` do not have this keyword, so they can't be used in a constant.

```
class int_set {
    private:
        // ... whatever
    public:
        int_set(void);          // Default constructor
        int_set(const int_set &old_set); // Copy constructor
        void set(int value);    // Set a value
        void clear(int value); // Clear an element
        int test(int value) const;   // See whether an element is set
};
```

So in your code you can do the following:

```
int_set var_set;        // A variable set (we can change this)

var_set.set(1);         // Set an element in the set (legal)

// Define a constant version of the set (we cannot change this)
const int_set const_set(var_set);

// In the next statement we use the member function "test" legally
cout << "Testing element 1. Value=" << const_set.test() << '\n';

const_set.set(5);      // Illegal (set is not allowed on a const)
```

Constant Members

Classes may contain constant members. The problem is that constants behave a little differently inside classes than outside. Outside, a constant variable declaration must be initialized. For example:

```
const int data_size = 1024;    // Number of data items in the input
                      stream
```

Inside a class, constants are not initialized when they are declared. For example:

```
class data_list {
    public:
        const int data_size;    // Number of items in the list
    // ... rest of the class
};
```

Constant member variables are initialized by the constructor. It's not as simple as:

```
class data_list {
    public:
        const int data_size;    // Number of items in the list

        data_list(void) {
            data_size = 1024;    // This code won't work
        };
    // ... rest of the class
};
```

Instead, because **data_size** is a constant it must be initialized with a special syntax:

```
        data_list(void) : data_size(1024) {
        };
```

But what happens if you want just a simple constant inside your class? Unfortunately C++ doesn't allow you to do:

```
class foo {
    public:
        const int foo_size = 100;   // Illegal
```

You are left with two choices:

1. Put the constant outside the code:

```
const int foo_size = 100;     // Number of data items in the list

class foo {
```

This makes **foo_size** available to all the world.

2. Use a syntax trick to fool C++ into defining a constant:

```
class foo {
    public:
        enum {foo_size = 100}; // Number of data items in the list
```

This defines **foo_size** as a constant whose value is 100. It does this by actually declaring **foo_size** as a element of an **enum** type and giving it the explicit value 100. Because C++ treats **enums** as integers, this works for defining integer constants.

The drawbacks to the method are that it's tricky, it only works for integers, and it exploits some holes in the C++ syntax that may go away as the language is better defined. Such code can easily cause difficulties for other programmers trying to maintain your code who aren't familiar with the trick.

Static Member Variables

Suppose you want to keep a running count of the number of stacks in use at any given time. One way to do this is to create a global variable `stack_count` that is incremented in the stack constructor and decremented in the destructor.

```
int stack_count = 0; // Number of stacks currently in use

class stack {
    private:
        int count;          // Number of items in the stack
        // ... member variables
    public:
        int data_count;  // Number of items in the stack
        // ... member variables
        stack() {
            // We just created a stack
            ++stack_count;
            count = 0;
        }
        ~stack() {
            // We now have one less stack
            --stack_count;
        }
        // ... other member functions
};
```

Note that `stack_count` is a single global variable. No matter how many different stacks you create, there is one and only one `stack_count`.

Although this system works, it has some drawbacks. The definition of the class `stack` contains everything about the stack, except the variable `stack_count`. It would be nice to put `stack_count` in the class, but if you define it as a member variable, you'll get a new copy of `stack_count` each time you declare a `stack` class variable.

C++ has a special modifier for member variables: `static`. This tells C++ that one and only one variable is to be defined for the class.

```
class stack {
    private:
        static int stack_count; // Number of stacks currently in use
        int count;              // Number of items in the stack
        // ... member variables
    public:
```

```
        stack() {
            // We just created a stack
            ++stack_count;
            count = 0;
        }
        ~stack() {
            // We now have one less stack
            --stack_count;
        }
        // ... other member functions
    };
```

This new version looks almost the same as the global variable version. There is, however, one thing missing: the initialization of **stack_count**. This is done with the statement:

```
    int stack::stack_count = 0; // No stacks have been defined
```

The difference between static and non-static member variables is that if you define three stacks, you create three different **data_count** member variables, but there is one and only one **stack_count**. Member variables belong to the individual stack. Static variables belong to the class.

So if you have:

```
    stack a_stack;
    stack b_stack;
```

Then **a_stack.stack_count** is the same as **b_stack.stack_count**. There is only one **stack_count** for the class **stack**. C++ allows you to access this using the syntax:

```
    <class>::<variable>
```

Thus you can get to **stack_count** with the statement:

```
    cout << "The number of active stacks is " << stack::stack_count << '\n';
```

(Or at least you could if **stack_count** was not private.)

Static Member Functions

The member variable **stack_count** is defined as private. This means that nothing outside the class can access it. You want to know how many stacks are defined, so you need a function to get the value of **stack_count.** A first cut might be:

```
class stack {
        static int stack_count; // Number of stacks currently in use
        // ... member variables
    public:
        // Not quite right
        int get_count(void) {
```

```
                return (stack_count);
        }
        // ... other member functions
};
```

This works, but you need a **stack** type variable to access this function.

```
{
    stack temp_stack;      // Stack for getting the count
    cout << "Current count " << temp_stack.get_count() << '\n';
}
```

Because **get_count** doesn't use any nonstatic data from **stack**, it can be made a *static member function*.

```
class stack {
        static int stack_count; // Number of stacks currently in use
        // ... member variables
    public:
        // Right
        static int get_count(void) {
            return (stack_count);
        }
        // ... other member functions
};
```

You can now access the static member function **get_count** much like you access the static member variable **stack_count**:

```
cout << "The number of active stacks is " << stack::get_count() << '\n';
```

Static member functions are very limited. They can't access nonstatic member variables or functions in the class. They can access static member data, static member functions, and functions and data outside the class.

The Meaning of static

The keyword **static** has many different meanings in C++. Table 14-1 is a complete list of the various ways **static** can be used.

Table 14-1. The Meanings of static

Usage	Meaning
Variable outside the body of any function	The scope of the variable is limited to the file in which it is declared.
Variable declaration inside a function	The variable is permanent. It is initialized once and only one copy is created even if the function is called recursively.
Function declaration	The scope of the function is limited to the file in which it is declared.

Table 14-1. The Meanings of static (Continued)

Usage	Meaning
Member variable	One copy of the variable is created per class (not one per variable).
Member function	Function can only access static members of the class.

Programming Exercises

Exercise 14-1: Two classes share a file. Other areas of the program need to know when this file is busy. Create a function that returns 1 when the file is being used by either of these two classes.

Exercise 14-2: You are asked to write a booking program for the veterinarian: Dr. Able Smith, PHD (Pigs, Horses, Dogs). Define a class type for each animal. Each class should keep track of the number of animals that have been defined using that class in a private static variable. Define a function that returns the total number of animals (all three types combined).

Exercise 14-3: Write a class where each instance of the class can access a stack– not one stack per instance, but one stack period. Any instance of the class can lock the stack for its own exclusive use and unlock it later. Define member functions to perform the lock and unlock functions.

As an added attraction, make the unlock function check to see that the current instance of the class was the same instance that locked the stack in the first place.

Exercise 14-4: You need to supply some I/O routines for handling lines in a file. The basic definition of the line-number class is:

```
class line_number {
    public:
        void goto_line(int line);
        int get_current_line(void);
        long int get_char_pos(void);
}
```

The member functions are defined as:

```
void goto_line(int line);
```

Positions the input file at specified line.

```
int get_current_line(void);
```

Returns the current line number (as set by goto_line).

```
long int get_char_pos(void);
```

Returns the character position of the current line. (This is the tricky one.)

Several `line_number` classes may be in use at any time. The class maintains its own internal list so that it knows which `line_number` classes are in use. When `goto_line` is called, the function will scan the list of `line_number` classes to find the one nearest the given line number and use it to start scanning for the given line number.

For example, suppose there are four active `line_number` variables:

Variable	Position
beginning	Line 0
chapter_start	Line 87
current_heading	Line 112
current_location	Line 52

You wish to move `current_location` to line 90. The `goto_line` function would search the list for the line nearest the new location (in this case `chapter_start`) and use it to jump to line 87. It then would read the file character by character until it saw three end-of-line characters to position itself at line 90.

15

Simple Pointers

The choice of a point of view is the
initial act of culture.
—Ortega y Gasset

There are things and there are pointers to things (Figure 15-1).

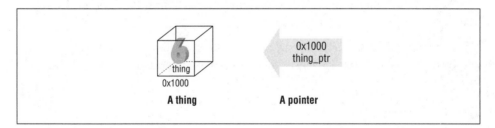

Figure 15-1. A thing and a pointer to a thing

Things can come in any size; some may be big, some may be small. Pointers come in only one size (relatively small).[*]

Throughout this book you use a box to represent a thing. The box may be large or small, but things are always a box. Pointers are represented by arrows.

Most novice programmers get pointers and their contents confused. To limit this problem, all pointer variables in this book end with the extension _ptr. You probably want to follow this convention in your own programs. Although not as common as it should be, this notation is extremely useful.

---

[*] This is not strictly true in Turbo-C++. Because of the strange architecture of the 8086, Turbo-C++ is forced to use both **near** pointers (16 bits) and **far** pointers (32 bits). See the Turbo-C++ manual for details.

Figure 15-1 shows one thing: a variable named `thing`. The name of the variable is written on the box that represents it. This variable contains the value 6. The actual address of this variable is 0x1008. C++ automatically assigns an address to each variable at compile time. The actual addresses differ from machine to machine. Most of the time you don't have to worry about variable addresses, as the compiler takes care of that detail. (After all, you've gotten through 11 chapters of programming without knowing anything about addresses.)

The pointer (`thing_ptr`) points to the variable `thing`. Pointers are also called *address variables* since they contain the addresses of other variables. In this case, the pointer contains the address 0x1008. Since this is the address of `thing`, you say that `thing_ptr` points to `thing`. (You could put another address in `thing_ptr` and force it to point to something else.)

You use "things" and "addresses" in everyday life. For example, you might live in a house (a thing). The street address might be "123 W. Main Street." An address is a small thing that can be written down on a piece of paper. Putting a house on a piece of paper is something else requiring a lot of work and a very large crane.

Street addresses are approximately the same size: one line. Houses come in various sizes. So while "1600 Pennsylvania Ave." might refer to a big house and "8347 Skid Row" might refer to a one-room shack, both addresses are the same size.

Many different address variables can point to the same thing. This is true for street addresses as well. Table 15-1 lists the location of important services in a small town.

Table 15-1. Small-town Directory

Service (Variable Name)	Address (Address Value)	Building (Thing)
Fire department	1 Main Street	City Hall
Police station	1 Main Street	City Hall
Planning office	1 Main Street	City Hall
Gas station	2 Main Street	Ed's Gas Station

In this case you have one, large, multipurpose building that is used by several services. Although there are three address variables (Services), there is only one address (1 Main Street) pointing to one building (City Hall.)

As you will see in this chapter, pointers can be used as a quick and simple way to access arrays. In later chapters you will discover how pointers can be used to create new variables and complex data structures such as linked lists and trees. As you go through the rest of the book, you will be able to understand these data structures as well as create your own.

A pointer is declared by putting an asterisk (*) in front of the variable name in the declaration statement:

```
int thing;       // Define "thing" (see Figure 15-2A)
int *thing_ptr;  // Define "pointer to a thing" (see Figure 15-2B)
```

Table 15-2 lists the operators used in conjunction with pointers.

Table 15-2. Pointer Operators

Operator	Meaning
*	De-reference (given a pointer, get the thing referenced)
&	Address of (given a thing, point to it)

The ampersand operator (&) changes a thing into a pointer. The * changes a pointer into a thing. These operators can easily cause confusion. Let's look at some simple uses of these operators in detail.

thing

A thing. The declaration int thing does *not* contain an asterisk, so thing is not a pointer. Example:

```
thing = 4;// See Figure 15-2C
```

&thing

A pointer to thing. thing is an object. The & (address of) operator gets the address of an object (a pointer), so &thing is a pointer. Example:

```
thing_ptr = &thing;// Point to the thing
                   // (See Figure 15-2A)
*thing_ptr = 5;    // Set "thing" to 5
                   // (See Figure 15-2B)
```

thing_ptr

Thing pointer. The asterisk (*) in the declaration indicates this is a pointer. Also, you have put the extension _ptr onto the name.

*thing_ptr

A thing. The variable thing_ptr is a pointer. The * (de-reference operator) tells C++ to look at the data pointed to, not at the pointer itself. Note: This points to an integer, any integer. It may or may not point to the specific variable thing.

```
*thing_ptr = 5;    // Assign 5 to an integer
                   // We may or may not be pointing
                   //    to the specific integer "thing"
```

The following examples show misuse of pointer operators.

*thing

Illegal. Asks C++ to get the object pointed to by the variable thing. Since thing is not a pointer, this is an invalid operation.

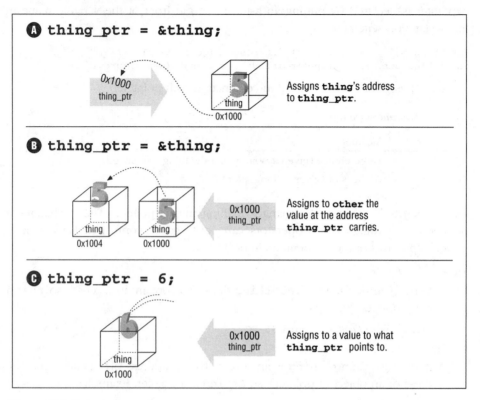

Figure 15-2. Pointer operators

`&thing_ptr`

> Legal, but strange. `thing_ptr` is a pointer. The `&` (address of) operator gets a pointer to the object (in this case `thing_ptr`). The result is a pointer to a pointer. (Pointers to pointers do occur in more complex programs.)

Example 15-1 illustrates a very simple use of pointers. It declares one object, `thing_var`, and a pointer, `thing_ptr`. `thing_var` is set explicitly by the line:

    thing_var = 2;

The line:

    thing_ptr = &thing_var;

causes C++ to set `thing_ptr` to the address of `thing_var`. From this point on, `thing_var` and `*thing_ptr` are the same.

Example 15-1. thing/thing.cc

```
#include <iostream.h>
main()
{
    int   thing_var;  // Define a variable
```

Example 15-1. thing/thing.cc (Continued)

```
    int  *thing_ptr;  // Define a pointer

    thing_var = 2;       // Assigning a value to "thing"
    cout <<Thing " << thing_var << '\n';

    thing_ptr = &thing_var; // Make the pointer point to "thing"
    *thing_ptr = 3;       // thing_ptr points to thing_var so
                          // thing_var changes to 3
    cout << "Thing " << thing_var << '\n';

    // Another way of printing the data
    cout << "Thing " << *thing_ptr << '\n';
    return (0);
}
```

Several pointers can point to the same thing:

```
1:      int       something;
2:
3:      int       *first_ptr;      // One pointer
4:      int       *second_ptr;     // Another pointer
5:
6:      something = 1;             // Give the thing a value
7:
8:      first_ptr = &something;
9:      second_ptr = first_ptr;
```

In line 8 you use the & operator to change a simple variable (something) into a pointer that can be assigned to first_ptr. Because first_ptr and second_ptr are both pointers, you can do a direct assignment in line 9.

After executing this program fragment, you have the situation illustrated by Figure 15-3.

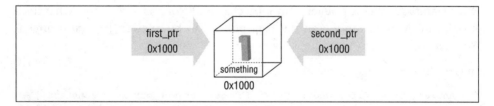

Figure 15-3. Two pointers and a thing

It is most important to note that while you have three variables, there is only one integer (thing). The following are all equivalent:

```
something = 1;
*first_ptr = 1;
*second_ptr = 1;
```

Finally, there is a special pointer called NULL that points to nothing. (The actual numeric value is 0.) The standard include file, *stddef.h*, defines the constant NULL. (Most standard include files that have anything to do with pointers automatically include NULL as well.) The NULL pointer is represented graphically in Figure 15-4.

Figure 15-4. NULL

Constant Pointers

Declaring constant pointers is a little tricky. For example, the declaration:

```
const int result = 5;
```

tells C++ that result is a constant, so

```
result = 10;      // Illegal
```

is illegal. However, the declaration:

```
const char *answer_ptr = "Forty-Two";
```

does *not* tell C++ that the data ("Forty-Two") is a constant. Instead, it tells C++ that answer_ptr is a constant. The pointer cannot be changed, but the data pointed to can. Again you should know the difference between "things" and "pointers to things."

What's answer_ptr? A pointer. Can it be changed? No, it is a constant. What does it point to? A char array. Can the data pointed to by answer_ptr be changed? Yes, it's not constant.

In C++ this is:

```
answer_ptr = "Fifty-One";    // Illegal (answer_ptr is a constant)
*answer_ptr = 'X';           // Legal (*answer_ptr is a char)
```

If you put the const after the *, you tell C++ that the data is constant. For example:

```
char *const name_ptr = "Test";
```

What's name_ptr? A pointer. Can it be changed? Yes. What does it point to? A constant character. Can the data pointed to by name_ptr be changed? No.

```
    name_ptr = "New";           // Legal (name_ptr is not constant)
    *name_ptr = 'B';            // Illegal (*name_ptr is a const char)
```

Finally, you can put const in both places, creating a pointer that cannot be changed to a data item that cannot be changed.

```
const char *const title_ptr = "Title";
```

Pointers and Printing

In C++ you can print the value of a pointer just like you can print the value of a simple variable such as an integer or floating point number. For example:

```
int an_integer = 5;             // A simple integer
int *int_ptr = &an_integer;     // Pointer to an integer

cout << "Integer pointer " << int_ptr << '\n';
```

outputs

```
Integer pointer 0x58239A
```

In this case, the value 0x58239A represents a memory address. This address may vary from program to program.

C++ treats character pointers a little differently from other pointers. A character pointer is treated as a pointer to a string. For example:

```
char some_characters[10] = "Hello";    // A simple set of characters
char *char_ptr = &some_characters[0];  // Pointer to a character

cout << "String pointer " << char_ptr << '\n';
```

outputs

```
String pointer Hello
```

Pointers and Arrays

C++ allows pointer arithmetic. Addition and subtraction are allowed with pointers. Suppose you have the following:

```
char array[10];
char *array_ptr = &array[0];
```

Graphically this is represented in Figure 15-5.

In this example, *array_ptr is the same as array[0], *(array_ptr+1) is the same as array[1], and so on. Note the use of parentheses. (*array_ptr)+1 is *not* the same as array[1]. The +1 is outside the parentheses so it is added after the de-reference. Thus (*array_ptr)+1 is the same as array[0]+1.

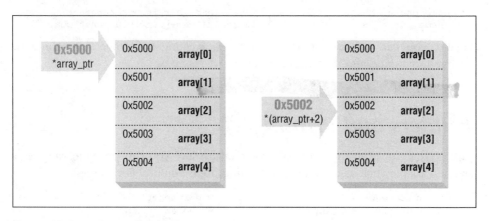

Figure 15-5. Pointers and an array

At first glance this may seem like a complex way of representing simple array indices. You are starting with simple pointer arithmetic. In later chapters you will use more complex pointers to handle more difficult functions efficiently.

Pointers are merely memory addresses. In an array each element is assigned to consecutive addresses. For example, `array[0]` may be placed at address `0xff000024`. Then `array[1]` would be placed at address `0xff000025` and so on. Example 15-2 prints out the elements and addresses of a simple character array. (Note: The I/O manipulators **hex** and **dec** are described in Chapter 16, *File Input/Output.*)

Example 15-2. array-p/array-p.cc

```
#include <iostream.h>
#include <iomanip.h>

const int ARRAY_SIZE  = 10; // Number of characters in array
// Array to print
char array[ARRAY_SIZE] = "012345678";

main()
{
    int index;   /* Index into the array */

    for (index = 0; index < ARRAY_SIZE; ++index) {
        cout << hex;     // Trick to print hex numbers
        cout <<
            "&array[index]=0x" <<  int(&array[index]) <<
            " (array+index)=0x" << int(array+index) <<
            " array[index]=0x" <<  int(array[index]) << '\n',
        cout << dec;
    }
    return (0);
}
```

When run this program prints:

```
&array[index]=0x20090  (array+index)=0x20090  array[index]=0x30
&array[index]=0x20091  (array+index)=0x20091  array[index]=0x31
&array[index]=0x20092  (array+index)=0x20092  array[index]=0x32
&array[index]=0x20093  (array+index)=0x20093  array[index]=0x33
&array[index]=0x20094  (array+index)=0x20094  array[index]=0x34
&array[index]=0x20095  (array+index)=0x20095  array[index]=0x35
&array[index]=0x20096  (array+index)=0x20096  array[index]=0x36
&array[index]=0x20097  (array+index)=0x20097  array[index]=0x37
&array[index]=0x20098  (array+index)=0x20098  array[index]=0x38
&array[index]=0x20099  (array+index)=0x20099  array[index]=0x0
```

Characters usually take up one byte, so the elements in a character array will be assigned consecutive addresses. A short int takes up two bytes, so in an array of short ints the addresses increase by two. Does this mean short_array+1 will not work for anything other than characters? No. C++ automatically scales pointer arithmetic so it works correctly. In this case short_array+1 will point to element number 1.

C++ provides a shorthand for dealing with arrays. Rather than write:

```
array_ptr = &array[0];
```

you can write:

```
array_ptr = array;
```

C++ blurs the distinction between pointers and arrays by treating them the same in many cases. Here you used the variable **array** as a pointer and C++ automatically did the necessary conversion.

Example 15-3 counts the number of elements that are non-zero and stops when a zero is found. No limit check is provided, so there must be at least one zero in the array.

Example 15-3. ptr2/ptr2a.cc

```
#include <iostream.h>

int array[10] = {4, 5, 8, 9, 8, 1, 0, 1, 9, 3};
int index;

main()
{
    index = 0;
    while (array[index] != 0)
        ++index;

    cout << "Number of elements before zero " << index << '\n';
    return (0);
}
```

Rewriting this program to use pointers gives us Example 15-4.

Example 15-4. ptr2/prt2.cc

```
#include <iostream.h>

int array[10] = {4, 5, 8, 9, 8, 1, 0, 1, 9, 3};
int *array_ptr;

main()
{
    array_ptr = array;

    while ((*array_ptr) != 0)
        ++array_ptr;

    cout << "Number of elements before zero " <<
        (array_ptr - array) << '\n';
    return (0);
}
```

The first program uses the expression (`array[index]` != 0). This requires the compiler to generate an index operation, which takes longer than a simple pointer de-reference: (`(*array_ptr)` != 0). The expression at the end of this program, `array_ptr - array`, computes how far `array_ptr` is into the array.

When passing an array to a procedure, C++ will automatically change the array into a pointer. In fact, if you put an & before the array, C++ will issue a warning. Example 15-5 illustrates array passing.

Example 15-5. init-a/init-a.cc

```
const int MAX = 10;

/*********************************************************
 * init_array_1 -- Zero out an array                     *
 *                                                       *
 * Parameters                                            *
 *      data -- the array to zero                        *
 *********************************************************/
void init_array_1(int data[])
{
    int   index;

    for (index = 0; index < MAX; ++index)
        data[index] = 0;
}

/*********************************************************
 * init_array_2 -- Zero out an array                     *
 *                                                       *
 * Parameters                                            *
 *      data_ptr -- pointer to array to zero             *
```

Example 15-5. init-a/init-a.cc (Continued)

```
 ***********************************************************/
void init_array_2(int *data_ptr)
{
    int index;

    for (index = 0; index < MAX; ++index)
        *(data_ptr + index) = 0;
}
#
main()
{
    int   array[MAX];

    // One way of initializing the array
    init_array_1(array);

    // Another way of initializing the array
    init_array_1(&array[0]);

    // Similar to the first method but
    //    function is different
    init_array_2(array);

    return (0);
}
```

Splitting Strings

Suppose you are given a string of the form "Last/First." You want to split this into two strings, one containing the first name and one containing the last name.

Example 15-6 reads in a single line, stripping the newline character from it. The function **strchr** is called to find the location of the slash (/). (The function **strchr** is actually a standard function. You have duplicated it for this example so you can see how it works.)

At this point **last_ptr** points to the beginning character of the last name (with the first tacked on) and **first_ptr** points to a slash. You then split the string by replacing the slash (/) with an end-of-string (NUL or '\0'). Now **last_ptr** points to just the last name and **first_ptr** points to a null string. Moving **first_ptr** to the next character makes **first_ptr** point to the beginning of the first name.

Graphically what you are doing is illustrated in Figure 15-6.

Example 15-6 contains the full program.

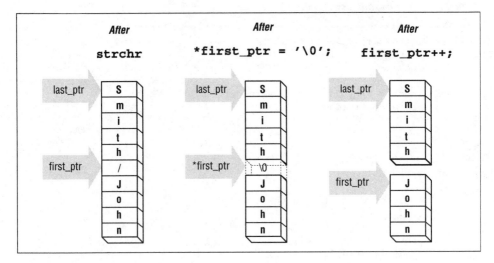

Figure 15-6. Splitting a string

Example 15-6. split/split.cc

```
/**********************************************************
 * Split -- split an entry of the form Last/First        *
 *       into two parts                                   *
 **********************************************************/
#include <iostream.h>
#include <string.h>
#include <stdlib.h>

main()
{
    char line[80];      // The input line
    char *first_ptr;    // Pointer we set to point to the first name
    char *last_ptr;     // Pointer we set to point to the last name

    cin.getline(line, sizeof(line));

    last_ptr = line;    // Last name is at beginning of line

    first_ptr = strchr(line, '/');      // Find slash

    // Check for an error
    if (first_ptr == NULL) {
        cerr << "Error: Unable to find slash in " << line << '\n';
        exit (8);
    }

    *first_ptr = '\0';  // Zero out the slash

    ++first_ptr;        // Move to first character of name

    cout << "First:" << first_ptr << " Last:" << last_ptr << '\n';
```

Example 15-6. split/split.cc (Continued)

```
    return (0);
}
/*********************************************************
 * strchr -- find a character in a string                *
 *      Duplicate of a standard library function,        *
 *      put here for illustrative purposes.              *
 *                                                       *
 * Parameters                                            *
 *      string_ptr -- string to look through             *
 *      find -- character to find                        *
 *                                                       *
 * Returns                                               *
 *      pointer to 1st occurrence of character in string *
 *      or NULL for error                                *
 *********************************************************/
char *strchr(char * string_ptr, char find)
{
    while (*string_ptr != find) {

        // Check for end

        if (*string_ptr == '\0')
            return (NULL);          // Not found

        ++string_ptr;
    }
    return (string_ptr);           // Found
}
```

This program illustrates how pointers and character arrays may be used for simple string processing.

Question 15-1: *Program 15-6 is supposed to print out:*

```
Name: tmp1
```

but instead you get:

```
Name: !_@$#ds80
```

(Your results may vary.) Why does this happen?

Example 15-7. tmp-name/tmp-name.cc

```
#include <iostream.h>
#include <string.h>

/*********************************************************
 * tmp_name -- return a temporary filename               *
 *                                                       *
 * Each time this function is called, a new name will    *
 * be returned                                           *
 *                                                       *
```

Example 15-7. tmp-name/tmp-name.cc (Continued)

```
 *  Returns                                               *
 *       pointer to the new filename                      *
 **********************************************************/
char *tmp_name(void)
{
    char name[30];              // The name we are generating
    static int sequence = 0;    // Sequence number for last digit

    ++sequence; // Move to the next filename

    strcpy(name, "tmp");

    // Put in the sequence digit
    name[3] = sequence + '0';

    // End the string
    name[4] = '\0';

    return(name);
}

int main()
{
    cout << "Name: " << tmp_name() << '\n';
    return(0);
}
```

Pointers and Structures

In Chapter 12, *Advanced Types*, you defined a structure for a mailing list:

```
struct mailing {
    char name[60];      // Last name, first name
    char address1[60];// Two lines of street address
    char address2[60];
    char city[40];
    char state[2];      // Two-character abbreviation
    long int zip;       // Numeric zip code
} list[MAX_ENTRIES];
```

Mailing lists must frequently be sorted in name order and zip-code order. You could sort the entries themselves, but each entry is 226 bytes long. That's a lot of data to move around. A way around this problem is to declare an array of pointers and then sort the pointers:

```
// Pointer to the data
struct mailing *list_ptrs[MAX_ENTRIES];

int current;    // Current mailing list entry

    // ....
```

```
      for (current = 0; current = number_of_entries; ++current)
          list_ptrs = &list[current];
```

```
    // Sort list_ptrs by zip code
```

Now instead of having to move a 226-byte structure around, you are moving 4-byte pointers. This sorting is much faster. Imagine that you had a warehouse full of big heavy boxes and you needed to locate any box quickly. One way of doing this would be to put the boxes in alphabetical order. But that would require a lot of moving, so you assign each location a number, write down the name and number on index cards, and sort the cards by name.

Command-Line Arguments

The procedure **main** actually takes two arguments. They are called **argc** and **argv**. (They don't have to be called **argv** and **argc**; however, 99.99% of C++ programs use these names.)

```
    main(int argc, char *argv[])
    {
```

It's easy to remember which comes first when you realize that they are in alphabetical order.

The parameter **argc** is the number of arguments on the command line (including the program name). The array **argv** contains the actual arguments. For example, if the program **args** were run with the command line:

args this is a test

then:

```
    argc    = 5
    argv[0] = "args"
    argv[1] = "this"
    argv[2] = "is"
    argv[3] = "a"
    argv[4] = "test"
```

NOTE

The UNIX shell expands wildcard characters like *, ?, and [] before sending the command line to the program. See your **sh** or **csh** manual for details.

Turbo-C++ will expand wildcard characters if the file *WILDARG.OBJ* is linked with your program. See the Turbo-C++ manual for details.

Almost all UNIX commands use a standard command-line format. This "standard" has carried over into other environments. A standard UNIX command has the form:

```
command  options file1 file1 file3 ...
```

Options are preceded by a hyphen (-) and are usually a single letter. For example, the option -v might turn on verbose mode. If the option takes a parameter, the parameter follows the letter. For example, the switch —m1024 sets the maximum number of symbols to 1024 and —ooutfile sets the output file name to *outfile*.

You have been given the assignment to write a program that will format and print files. Part of the documentation for the program looks like:

```
print_file [-v] [-l<length>] [-o<name>] [file1] [file2] ...
```

In this line, -v sets verbose options, which turns on a lot of progress information messages. The option -l<length> sets the page size to <length> lines (default = 66) and -o<name> sets the output file to <name> (default = print.out). A list of files to print follows these options ([file1], [file2], etc.). If no files are specified, then print the file print.in.

The while loop cycles through the options. The actual loop is:

```
while ((argc > 1) && (argv[1][0] == '-')) {
```

There is always one argument, the program name. The expression (argc > 1) checks for additional arguments. The first one will be numbered 1. The first character of the first argument is argv[1][0]. If this character is a dash you have an option.

At the end of the loop is the code:

```
        --argc;
        ++argv;
    }
```

This consumes an argument. The number of arguments is decremented to indicate one less option, and the pointer to the first option is incremented, shifting the list to the left one place. (Note: After the first increment, argv[0] no longer points to the program name.)

The switch statement is used to decode the options. Character 0 of the argument is the hyphen (-). Character 1 is the option character, so you use the expression:

```
        switch (argv[1][1]) {
```

to decode the option.

The option -v has no arguments; it just causes a flag to be set.

The -1 option takes an integer argument. The library function atoi is used to convert the string into an integer. From the previous example you know that argv[1][2] starts the string containing the number. This string is passed to atoi.

The option -o takes a filename. Rather than copy the whole string, you set the character pointer out_file to point to the name part of the string. By this time you know that:

```
argv[1][0] = '-'
argv[1][1] = 'o'
argv[1][2] = start of the file name
```

You set out_file to point to the string with the statement:

```
out_file = &argv[1][2];
```

Finally all the options are parsed and you fall through to the processing loop. This merely executes the function do_file for each file argument.

Example 15-8 contains the complete option-decoding program.

Example 15-8. print/print.cc

```
 * Print -- format files for printing                 *
 *****************************************************/
#include <iostream.h>
#include <stdlib.h>

int verbose = 0;                // Verbose mode (default = false)
char *out_file = "print.out";   // Output file name
char *program_name;             // Name of the program (for errors)
int line_max = 66;              // Number of lines per page

/*****************************************************
 * do_file -- dummy routine to handle a file         *
 *                                                   *
 * Parameter                                         *
 *      name -- name of the file to print            *
 *****************************************************/
void do_file(char *name)
{
    cout << "Verbose " << verbose << " Lines " << line_max <<
            " Input " << name << " Output " << out_file << '\n';
}
/*****************************************************
 * Usage -- tell the user how to use this program and *
 *              exit                                 *
 *****************************************************/
void usage(void)
{
    cerr << "Usage is " << program_name << " [options] [file-list]\n";
    cerr << "Options\n";
```

Example 15-8. print/print.cc (Continued)

```
    cerr << "   -v          verbose\n";
    cerr << "   -l<number>  Number of lines\n";
    cerr << "   -o<name>    Set output filename\n";
    exit (8);
}

main(int argc, char *argv[])
{
    // Save the program name for future use
    program_name = argv[0];

    /*
     * Loop for each option
     *    Stop if we run out of arguments
     *    or we get an argument without a dash
     */
    while ((argc > 1) && (argv[1][0] == '-')) {
        /*
         * argv[1][1] is the actual option character
         */
        switch (argv[1][1]) {
            /*
             * -v verbose
             */
            case 'v':
                verbose = 1;
                break;
            /*
             * -o<name>  output file
             *    [0] is the dash
             *    [1] is the "o"
             *    [2] starts the name
             */
            case 'o':
                out_file = &argv[1][2];
                break;
            /*
             * -l<number> set max number of lines
             */
            case 'l':
                line_max = atoi(&argv[1][2]);
                break;
            default:
                cerr << "Bad option " << argv[1] << '\n';
                usage();
        }
        /*
         * Move the argument list up one
         * Move the count down one
         */
        ++argv;
        --argc;
```

Example 15-8. print/print.cc (Continued)

```
    }

    /*
     * At this point all the options have been processed.
     * Check to see if we have no files in the list
     * and, if so, we need to list just standard in
     */
    if (argc == 1) {
        do_file("print.in");
    } else {
        while (argc > 1) {
            do_file(argv[1]);
            ++argv;
            --argc;
        }
    }
    return (0);
}
```

This is one way of parsing the argument list. The use of the `while` loop and `switch` statement is simple and easy to understand. This method does have a limitation. The argument must immediately follow the options. For example, `-o data.out` will work, but `-o data.out` will not. An improved parser would make the program more friendly, but this works for simple programs. (See your system documentation for information on the `getopt` function.)

Programming Exercises

Exercise 15-1: Write a program that uses pointers to set each element of an array to zero.

Exercise 15-2: Write a function that takes a single string as its argument and returns a pointer to the first nonwhite character in the string.

Answers to Chapter Questions

Answer 15-1: The problem is that the variable **name** is a temporary variable. The compiler allocates space for the name when the function is entered and reclaims the space when the function exits. The function assigns **name** the correct value and returns a pointer to it. However, the function is over, so **name** disappears and you have a pointer with an illegal value.

The solution is to declare **name** static. Consequently, it is a permanent variable and will not disappear at the end of the function.

Question 15-2: *After fixing the function, you try using it for two filenames. Example 15-8 should print out:*

```
Name: tmp1
Name: tmp2
```

but it doesn't. What does it print and why?

Example 15-9. tmp2/tmp2.cc

```cpp
#include <iostream.h>
#include <string.h>

/************************************************************
 * tmp_name -- return a temporary filename                 *
 *                                                          *
 * Each time this function is called, a new name will       *
 * be returned                                              *
 *                                                          *
 * Warning: There should be a warning here, but if we       *
 *        put it in we would answer the question.           *
 *                                                          *
 * Returns                                                  *
 *        pointer to the new filename                       *
 ************************************************************/
char *tmp_name(void)
{
    static char name[30];       // The name we are generating
    static int sequence = 0;    // Sequence number for last digit

    ++sequence; // Move to the next file name

    strcpy(name, "tmp");

    // Put in the sequence digit
    name[3] = sequence + '0';

    // End the string
    name[4] = '\0';

    return(name);
}

int main()
{
    char *name1;                // Name of a temporary file
    char *name2;                // Name of a temporary file

    name1 = tmp_name();
    name2 = tmp_name();

    cout << "Name1: " << name1 << '\n';
    cout << "Name2: " << name2 << '\n';
    return(0);
}
```

Answer 15-2: The first call to tmp_name returns a pointer to name. There is only one name. The second call to tmp_name changes name and returns a pointer to it. So you have two pointers, and they point to the same thing, name.

Several library functions return pointers to static strings. A second call to one of these routines will overwrite the first value. A solution to this problem is to copy the values:

```
char name1[100];
char name2[100];

strcpy(name1, tmp_name());
strcpy(name2, tmp_name());
```

IV

Advanced Programming Concepts

16

File Input/Output

I am the heir of all the ages, in the foremost files of time.
—Tennyson

A file is a collection of related data. C++ treats a file as a series of bytes. Many files reside on disk; however, devices such as terminals, printers, and magnetic tapes are also considered files.

The Annotated C++ Reference Manual (Ellis and Stroustrup) is the current widely used standard for C++. This book does *not* contain a specification of the I/O system. A de facto standard has evolved based on the library supplied with the *cfront* compiler from AT&T. The problem is that some of the details may differ from compiler to compiler. For example, Turbo-C++ flushes cout at the end of each line while the SunPro UNIX C++ compiler does not.

The current version of the *ANSI C++ Draft Standard* (September 1994) does contain a detailed description of I/O calls. However, currently no compilers support this, and the standard also is still undergoing revision.

This chapter discusses three different I/O packages. The first is the C++ I/O stream classes. This is the most commonly used I/O system and the one we've been using up to now. Next, we examine the raw I/O routines that give us direct access to the low-level I/O. Finally we look at the C I/O system. Although it is somewhat outdated, C I/O calls still appear in old code. Also, in some cases, the C-style I/O routines are superior to the ones provided with C++.

C++ File I/O

C++ file I/O is based on three classes: the `istream` class for input, the `ostream` class for output, and the `iostream` class for input/output. C++ refers to files as *stream*s since it considers them a stream of bytes. Four class variables are automatically created when you start a program. These are listed in Table 16-1.

Table 16-1. Predefined I/O Class Variables

Variable	Use
cin	Console input (standard input)
cout	Console output (standard output)
cerr	Console error (standard error)
clog	Console log

These variables are defined in the standard include file `<iostream.h>`. Normally `cin` is assigned to the keyboard and `cout`, `cerr`, and `clog` are assigned to the screen. Most operating systems allow you to change these assignments through I/O redirection (see your operating system manual for details).

For example, the command

```
my_prog <file.in
```

runs the program **my_prog** and assigns `cin` to the file *file.in*.

When doing I/O to disk files (except through redirection) you must use the file version of the stream classes. These are `ifstream`, `ofstream`, and `fstream` and are defined in the include file `<fstream.h>`.

NOTE

The `ifstream` class is actually derived from the `istream` class. Similarly, `ofstream` is derived from `ostream` and `fstream` is derived from `iostream`. You'll learn about derived classes in Chapter 21, *Advanced Classes*.

Suppose you want to read a series of 100 numbers from the file *numbers.dat*. You start by declaring the input file variable:

```
ifstream data_file;    // File we are reading the data from
```

Next you need to tell C++ what disk file to use. This is done through the **open** member function:

```
data_file.open("numbers.dat");
```

Now you can read the file using the same statements you've been using to read
cin:

```
for (i = 0; i < 100; ++i)
    data_file >> data_array[i];
```

Finally you need to tell the I/O system that you are done with the file:

```
data_file.close();
```

Closing the file frees resources that can then be used again by the program.

C++ allows the **open** call to be combined with the constructor. For example,
instead of writing:

```
ifstream data_file;      // File we are reading the data from
data_file.open("numbers.dat");
```

you can write:

```
ifstream data_file("numbers.dat");   // File we are reading the data from
```

Additionally, the destructor automatically calls **close**.

But what if the file *numbers.dat* is missing? How can you tell if there is a
problem? The member function **bad** returns "true" if there is a problem, and
"false" otherwise. So to test for problems all you need is:

```
if (data.file.bad()) {
    cerr << "Unable to open numbers.dat\n";
    exit (8);
}
```

A better version of the program for reading numbers is Example 16-1.

Example 16-1. read/read.cc

```
/********************************************************
 * Read -- read in 100 numbers and sum them            *
 *                                                      *
 * Usage:                                               *
 *      read                                            *
 *                                                      *
 * Numbers are in the file "numbers.dat"                *
 *                                                      *
 * Warning: No check is made for a file with fewer than *
 * 100 numbers in it                                    *
 ********************************************************/
#include <iostream.h>
#include <fstream.h>
#include <stdlib.h>

main()
{
    const int DATA_SIZE = 100;  // Number of items in the data
    int data_array[DATA_SIZE];  // The data
```

Example 16-1. read/read.cc (Continued)

```
    ifstream data_file("numbers.dat"); // The input file
    int i;                         // Loop counter

    if (data_file.bad()) {
        cerr << "Error: Could not open numbers.dat\n";
        exit (8);
    }

    for (i = 0; i < DATA_SIZE; ++i)
        data_file >> data_array[i];

    int total;  // Total of the numbers

    total = 0;
    for (i = 0; i < DATA_SIZE; ++i)
        total += data_array[i];

    cout << "Total of all the numbers is " << total << '\n';
    return (0);
}
```

Finally, you have the `getline` member function. It is used to read a full line of data from the input file. This function is defined as:

```
    istream &getline(char *buffer, int len, char delim = '\n')
```

The parameters to this function are:

`buffer`

   A buffer to store the data that has been read.

`len`

   Length of the buffer in bytes. The function reads up to `len` `-1` bytes of data into the buffer. (One byte is reserved for the terminating null character \0.) This parameter is usually `sizeof(buffer)`.

`delim`

   The character used to signal end-of-line.

This function returns a reference to the input file. The function reads up to and including the end-of-line character. The end-of-line character is not stored in the buffer.

Problems can occur if the size specified is too big. C++ provides a convenient way to make sure the size parameter is just right through the use of the `sizeof` operator.

The `sizeof` operator returns the size in bytes of its argument. For example:

```
    long int array[10];     // Each element contains 4 bytes
    char string[30];
```

The sizeof(string) is 30 and sizeof(array) is 40 (4 bytes per long * 10 longs in the array).

NOTE

sizeof is not the same as length. The sizeof operator returns the number of bytes in string (used or not).

Output Files

The functions for output files are similar to input files. For example, the declaration:

```
ofstream out_file("out.dat");
```

creates a file named *out.dat* and lets you write to the file using the file variable out_file.

Actually, the constructor can take two additional parameters. The full definition of the output file constructor is:

```
ofstream::ofstream(const char *name, int mode=ios::out,
                   int prot = filebuf::openprot);
```

The parameters for this function are:

name
>   The name of the file.

mode
>   A set of flags ORed together that determine the open mode. The flag ios::out is required for output files. Other flags are listed in Table 16-2. (The ios:: prefix is used to indicate the scope of the constant. This operator is discussed in more detail in Chapter 21, *Advanced Classes*.)

prot
>   File protection. This is an operating-system-dependent value that determines the protection mode for the file. In UNIX the protection defaults to 0644 (read/write owner, group read, others read). For MS-DOS/Windows this defaults to 0 (normal file).

Table 16-2. Open Flags

Flag	Meaning
ios::app	Append data to the end of the output file.
ios::ate	Go to the end of the file when opened.
ios::in	Open for input (must be supplied to opens for ifstream variables).
ios::out	Open file for output (must be supplied to ofstream opens).

Table 16-2. Open Flags (Continued)

Flag	Meaning
ios::binary	Binary file (if not present, the file is opened as an ASCII file). See the section "Binary I/O" on page 262 for a definition of a binary file.
ios::trunc	Discard contents of existing file when opening for write.
ios::nocreate	Fail if the file does not exist. (Output files only. Input files always fail if there is no file.)
ios::noreplace	Do not overwrite existing file. If a file exists, cause the open to fail.

For example, the statement:

```
ofsteam out_file("data.new",
               ios::out|ios::binary|ios::nocreate|ios::app);
```

appends (ios::app) binary data (ios::binary) to an existing file (ios::nocreate) named *data.new*.

Conversion Routines

So far we have just considered writing characters and strings. In this section, we consider some of the more sophisticated I/O operations: conversions.

To write a number to a printer or terminal you must convert the number to characters. The printer understands only characters, not numbers. For example, the number 567 must be converted to the three characters "5", "6", and "7" to be printed.

The << operator is used to convert data to characters and put them in a file. This function is extremely flexible. It can convert a simple integer into a fixed- or variable-size string as a hex, octal, or decimal number with left or right justification. So far you've been using the default conversion for your output. It serves pretty well, but if you want to control your output exactly, you need to learn about conversion flags.

The member functions setf and unsetf are used to set and clear the flags that control the conversion process. The general form of the functions is:

```
file_var.setf(flags);   // Set flags
file_var.unsetf(flags); // Clear flags
```

Table 16-3 lists the various flags and their meanings.

Table 16-3. I/O Conversion Flags

Flag	Meaning
ios::skipws	Skip leading white-space characters on input.
ios::left	Output is left justified.

Table 16-3. *I/O Conversion Flags (Continued)*

Flag	Meaning
`ios::right`	Output is right justified.
`ios::internal`	Numeric output is padded by inserting a fill character between the sign or base character and the number itself.
`ios::dec`	Output numbers in base 10, decimal format.
`ios::oct`	Output numbers in base 8, octal format.
`ios::hex`	Output numbers in base 16, hexadecimal format.
`ios::showbase`	Print out a base indicator at the beginning of each number. For example: hexadecimal numbers are preceded with "0x".
`ios::showpoint`	Show a decimal point for all floating point numbers whether or not it's needed.
`ios::uppercase`	When converting hexadecimal numbers show the digits A-F as uppercase.
ios::showpos	Put a plus sign before all positive numbers.
`ios::scientific`	Convert all floating point numbers to scientific notation on output.
`ios::fixed`	Convert all floating point numbers to fixed point on output.
`ios::unitbuf`	Buffer output. (More on this later).
`ios::stdio`	Flush stream after each output.

If you want to output a number in hexadecimal format, all you have to do is:

```
number = 0x3FF;
cout << "Dec: " << number << '\n';
cout.setf(ios::hex);
cout << "Hex " << number << '\n';
cout.setf(ios::dec);
```

When run, this program produces the output:

```
Dex 1023
Hex 3ff
```

NOTE

People normally expect the output mode to be decimal, so it is a good idea to reset the mode after each output to avoid later confusion.

When converting numbers to characters the member function:

int *file_var*.width(int size);

determines the minimum characters to use. For example, the number 3 would normally convert to the character string "3" (note the lack of spaces). If the width is set to four, then the result would be "␣␣␣3" where ␣ represents a single space.

The member function:

```
    int file_var.precision(int digits);
```

controls how many digits are printed after the decimal point.

Finally, the function:

```
    char file_var.fill(char pad);
```

determines the file character. This character is used for padding when a number is smaller than the specified width.

NOTE

Some of these flags and parameters are reset after each output call and some are not. Which flags are permanent and which are temporary seems to change from compiler to compiler. In general, don't assume anything is going to remain set and you'll be okay. (Just because you're paranoid doesn't mean the compiler isn't out to get you.)

These functions can be called directly or you can use an *I/O manipulator*. An I/O manipulator is a special function that can be used in an I/O statement to change the formatting. You can think of a manipulator as a magic bullet that when sent through an input or output file changes the state of the file. A manipulator doesn't cause any output; it just changes the state. For example, the manipulator **hex** changes the output conversion to hexadecimal.

```
#include <iostream.h>
#include <iomanip.h>

number = 0x3FF;
cout << "Number is " << hex << number << dec << '\n';
```

The I/O manipulators are defined in the include file **<iomanip.h>**. Table 16-4 contains the full list of I/O manipulators.

Table 16-4. I/O Manipulators

Manipulator	Description
setiosflags(long flags)	Set selected conversion flags.
resetiosflags(long flags)	Reset selected flags.
dec	Output numbers in decimal format.
hex	Output numbers in hexadecimal format.
oct	Output numbers in octal format.
setbase(int base)	Set conversion base to 8, 10, or 16. Sort of a generalized dec, hex, oct.
setw(int width)	Set the width of the output.
setprecision(int precision)	Set the precision of floating point output.

Table 16-4. I/O Manipulators (Continued)

Manipulator	Description
`setfill(char ch)`	Set the fill character.
`ws`	Skip white space on input.
`endl`	Output end-of-line
`ends`	Output end-of-string ('\0').
`flush`	Force any buffered output out. (See Chapter 17, *Debugging and Optimization,* for an explanation of how to use this function).

Example 16-2 shows how some of the I/O manipulators may be used.

Example 16-2. io/io.cc

```
#include <iostream.h>
#include <iomanip.h>
main()
#
{
    int number = 12;    // A number to output
    float real = 12.34; // A real number

    cout << "12345678901234567890123456789 0\n"; // Output ruler
    cout << number << "<-\n";
    cout << setw(5) << number << "<-\n";
    cout << setw(5) << setfill('*') << number << "<-\n";
    cout << setiosflags(ios::showpos|ios::left) << setw(5) <<
            number << "<-\n";

    cout << real << "<-\n";
    cout << setprecision(1) << setiosflags(ios::fixed) << real << "<-\n";
    cout << setiosflags(ios::scientific) << real << "<-\n";
    return (0);
}
```

The output of this program is:

```
12345678901234567890123456789 0
12<-
   12<-
***12<-
+12**<-
12.34<-
12.3<-
1e+01<-
```

Binary and ASCII Files

So far you have limited ourselves to ASCII files. "ASCII" stands for American Standard Code for Information Interchange. It is a set of 95 printable characters and 33 control codes. (A complete list of ASCII codes can be found in Appendix A, *ASCII Table*.) ASCII files are human readable. When you write a program, the *prog.cc* file is ASCII.

Terminals, keyboards, and printers deal with character data. When you want to write a number like 1234 to the screen, it must be converted to four characters (1, 2, 3, 4) and written.

Similarly, when you read a number from the keyboard, the data must be converted from characters to integers. This is done by the >> operator.

The ASCII character "0" has the value 48, "1" the value 49, and so on. When you want to convert a single digit from ASCII to integer, you must subtract this value number:

```
int integer;
char ch;

ch = '5';
integer = ch - 48;
cout << "Integer " << integer << '\n';
```

Rather than remember that "0" is 48, you can just subtract "0":

```
integer = ch - '0';
```

Computers work on binary data. When reading numbers from an ASCII file, the program must process the character data through a conversion routine like the integer conversion routine just defined. This is expensive. Binary files require no conversion. They also generally take up less space than ASCII files. The drawback is they cannot be directly printed on a terminal or printer. (If you've ever seen a long printout coming out of the printer displaying pages with a few characters at the top that look like "!E#(@$%@^Aa^AA^^JHC%^X" then you know what happens when you try to print a binary file.)

ASCII files are portable (for the most part). They can be moved from machine to machine with very little trouble. Binary files are almost certainly nonportable. Unless you are an expert programmer, it is almost impossible to make a portable binary file. (See Chapter 25, *Portability Problems*.)

Which file type should you use? In most cases, ASCII is best. If you have small to medium amounts of data, the conversion time does not seriously affect the performance of your program. (Who cares if it takes 0.5 second to start up instead of 0.3?) ASCII files also make it easy to verify the data.

Only when you are using large amounts of data will the space and performance problems force you to use the binary format.

The End-of-Line Puzzle

Back in the dark ages BC (Before Computers), there existed a magical device called a Teletype Model 33. This amazing machine contained a shift register made out of a motor and a rotor as well as a keyboard ROM consisting solely of levers and springs.

The teletype contained a keyboard, a printer, and a paper tape reader/punch. It could transmit messages over telephones using a modem at the blazing rate of 10 characters a second.

But teletype had a problem. It took 2/10 second to move the printhead from the right side to the left. 2/10 second is two character times. If a second character came while the printhead was in the middle of a return, that character was lost.

The teletype people solved this problem by making end-of-line two characters: <carriage return> to position the printhead at the left margin, and <line feed> to move the paper up one line. That way the <line feed> "printed" while the print-head was racing back to the left margin.

When the early computers came out, some designers realized that using two characters for end-of-line wasted storage (at this time storage was very expensive). Some picked <line feed> for their end-of-line, and some chose <carriage return>. Some of the die-hards stayed with the two-character sequence.

UNIX uses <line feed> for end-of-line. The new-line character \n is `code` 0xA (LF or <line feed>).

MS-DOS/Windows uses the two characters <line feed><carriage return>. Compiler designers had problems in dealing with the old C programs that thought new-line was just <line feed>? The solution was to add code to the I/O library that stripped out the <carriage return> characters from ASCII input files and changed <line feed> to <line feed><carriage return> on output.

In MS-DOS/Windows, whether or not a file is opened as ASCII or binary is important to note. The flag `ios::binary` is used to indicate a binary file:

```
// Open ASCII file for reading
ascii_file.open("name", ios::in);

// Open binary file for reading
binary_file.open("name", ios::in|ios::binary);
```

Question 16-1: *The member function* put *can be used to write out a single byte of a binary file. The following program writes numbers 0 to 127 to a file called test.out.*

It works just fine in UNIX, creating a 128-byte long file; however, in MS-DOS/Windows, the file contains 129 bytes. Why?

Example 16-3. wbin/wbin.cc

```
#include <iostream.h>
#include <fstream.h>
#include <stdlib.h>

main()
{
    int cur_char;    // Current character to write
    ofstream out_file; // Output file

    out_file.open("test.out", ios::out);
    if (out_file.bad()) {
        (cerr << "Cannot open output file\n");
        exit (8);
    }

    for (cur_char = 0; cur_char < 128; ++cur_char) {
        out_file << cur_char;
    }
    return (0);
}
```

Hint: Here is a hex dump of the MS-DOS/Windows file:

```
000:0001 0203 0405 0607 0809 0d0a 0b0c 0d0e
010:0f10 1112 1314 1516 1718 191a 1b1c 1d1e
020:1f20 2122 2324 2526 2728 292a 2b2c 2d2e
030:2f30 3132 3334 3536 3738 393a 3b3c 3d3e
040:3f40 4142 4344 4546 4748 494a 4b4c 4d4e
050:4f50 5152 5354 5556 5758 595a 5b5c 5d5e
060:5f60 6162 6364 6566 6768 696a 6b6c 6d6e
070:6f70 7172 7374 7576 7778 797a 7b7c 7d7e
080:7f
```

UNIX programmers don't have to worry about the C++ library automatically fixing their ASCII files. In UNIX, a file is a file and ASCII is no different from binary. In fact, you can write a half-ASCII/half-binary file if you want to.

Binary I/O

Binary I/O is accomplished through two member functions: **read** and **write**. The syntax for **read** is:

```
in_file.read(data_ptr, size);
```

data_ptr

Pointer to a place to put the data.

size

Number of bytes to be read.

The member function **gcount** returns the number of bytes gotten by the last **read**. This may be less than the number of bytes requested. For example, the **read** might encounter an end-of-file or error:

```
struct {
    int     width;
    int     height;
} rectangle;

in_file.read((char *)(&rectangle), sizeof(rectangle));
if (in_file.bad()) {
    cerr << "Unable to read rectangle\n";
    exit (8);
}
if (in_file.gcount() != sizeof(rectangle)) {
    cerr << "Error: Unable to read full rectangle\n";
    cerr << "I/O error of EOF encountered\n";
}
```

In this example you are reading in the structure **rectangle**. The **&** operator makes **rectangle** into a pointer. The cast "**(char *)**" is needed since **read** wants a character array. The **sizeof** operator is used to determine how many bytes to read in as well as to check that **read** was successful.

The member function **write** has a calling sequence similar to **read**.

```
out_file.write(data_ptr, size);
```

Buffering Problems

Buffered I/O does not write immediately to the file. Instead, the data is kept in a buffer until there is enough for a big write, or until it is flushed. The following program is designed to print a progress message as each section is finished.

```
cout << "Starting";
do_step_1();
cout << "Step 1 complete";
do_step_2();
cout << "Step 2 complete";
do_step_3();
cout << "Step 3 complete\n";
```

Instead of writing the messages as each step completes, **cout** puts them in a buffer. Only after the program is finished does the buffer get flushed, and all the messages come spilling out at once.

The I/O manipulator `flush` forces the flushing of the buffers. Properly written, the above example should be:

```
cout << "Starting" << flush;
do_step_1();
cout << "Step 1 complete" << flush;
do_step_2();
cout << "Step 2 complete" << flush;
do_step_3();
cout << "Step 3 complete\n" << flush;
```

Unbuffered I/O

In buffered I/O, data is buffered and then sent to the file. In unbuffered I/O, the data is immediately sent to the file.

If you drop a number of paperclips on the floor, you can pick them up in buffered or unbuffered mode. In buffered mode, you use your right hand to pick up a paper clip and transfer it to your left hand. The process is repeated until your left hand is full, and then you dump a handful of paperclips into the box on your desk.

In unbuffered mode, you pick up a paperclip and dump it into the box. There is no left-hand buffer.

In most cases buffered I/O should be used instead of unbuffered. In unbuffered I/O, each read or write requires a system call. Any call to the operating system is expensive. Buffered I/O minimizes these calls.

Unbuffered I/O should be used only when reading or writing large amounts of binary data or when direct control of a device or file is required.

Back to the paperclip example — if you were picking up small items like paperclips you would probably use a left-hand buffer. But if you were picking up cannon balls (which are much larger), no buffer would be used.

The `open` system call is used for opening an unbuffered file. The macro definitions used by this call differ from system to system. You are using both UNIX and MS-DOS/Windows, so you have used conditional compilation (`#ifdef` / `#endif`) to bring in the correct files.

```
#include <sys/types.h>
#include <sys/stat.h>
#include <fcntl.h>

#ifdef __MSDOS__        // If we are MS-DOS
#include <io.h>         // Get the MS-DOS include file for raw I/O
#else /* __MSDOS__ */
#include <unistd.h>     // Get the UNIX include file for raw I/O
```

```
#endif /* __MSDOS__ */

int     file_descriptor;

file_descriptor = open(name, flags);        // Existing file
file_descriptor = open(name, flags, mode);//New file
```

file_descriptor

An integer that is used to identify the file for the read, write and close calls. If `file_descriptor` is less than 0 an error occurred.

name

Name of the file.

flags

Defined in the `fcntl.h` header file. Open flags are described in Table 16-5.

Table 16-5. Open Flags

Flag	Meaning
O_RDONLY	Open for reading only
O_WRONLY	Open for writing only
O_RDWR	Open for reading and writing
O_APPEND	Append new data at the end of the file
O_CREAT	Create file (*mode* file required when this flag is present
O_TRUNC	If the file exists, truncate it to 0 length
O_EXCL	Fail if file exists
O_BINARY	Open in binary mode (older UNIX systems may not have this flag)

mode

Protection mode for the file. Normally this is 0666 for most files.

For example, to open the existing file *data.txt* in text mode for reading, you use the following:

```
data_fd = open("data.txt", O_RDONLY);
```

The next example shows how to create a file called *output.dat* for writing only:

```
out_fd = open("output.dat", O_CREAT|O_WRONLY, 0666);
```

Notice that you combined flags using the OR (|) operator. This is a quick and easy way of merging multiple flags.

When any program is initially run, three files are already opened. These are described in Table 16-6.

Table 16-6. Standard Unbuffered Files

File Number	Description
0	Standard in
1	Standard out
2	Standard error

The format of the **read** call is:

```
read_size = read(file_descriptor, buffer, size);
```

read_size

> The actual number of bytes read. A O indicates end-of-file and a negative number indicates an error.

file_descriptor

> File descriptor of an open file.

buffer

> Pointer to the place to read the data.

size

> Size of the data to be read. This is the size of the request. The actual number of bytes read may be less than this. (For example, you may run out of data.)

The format of a write call is:

write_size = write(file_descriptor, buffer, size);

write_size

> Actual number of bytes written. A negative number indicates an error.

file_descriptor

> File descriptor of an open file.

buffer

> Pointer to the data to be written.

size

> Size of the data to be written. The system will try to write this many bytes, but if the device is full or there is some other problem, a smaller number of bytes may be written.

Finally, the close call closes the file:

flag = close(file_descriptor)

flag

> 0 for success, negative for error.

file_descriptor

> File descriptor of an open file.

Example 16-4 copies a file. Unbuffered I/O is used because of the large buffer size. It makes no sense to use buffered I/O to read 1K of data into a buffer (using an `ifstream`) and then transfer it into a 16K buffer.

Example 16-4. copy2/copy2.cc

```
/*****************************************
 * Copy -- copy one file to another      *
 *                                       *
 * Usage                                 *
 *      copy <from> <to>                 *
 *                                       *
 * <from> -- the file to copy from       *
 * <to>   -- the file to copy into       *
 *****************************************/
#include <iostream.h>
#include <stdlib.h>
#include <sys/types.h>
#include <sys/stat.h>
#include <fcntl.h>

#ifdef __MSDOS__        // If we are MS-DOS
#include <io.h>         // Get the MS-DOS include file for raw I/O
#else /* __MSDOS__ */
#include <unistd.h>     // Get the UNIX include file for raw I/O
#endif /* __MSDOS__ */

const int BUFFER_SIZE = (16 * 1024); // Use 16K buffers

main(int argc, char *argv[])
{
    char buffer[BUFFER_SIZE];   // Buffer for data
    int  in_file;               // Input file descriptor
    int  out_file;              // Output file descriptor
    int  read_size;             // Number of bytes on last read

    if (argc != 3) {
        cerr << "Error: Wrong number of arguments\n";
        cerr << "Usage is: copy <from> <to>\n";
        exit(8);
    }
    in_file = open(argv[1], O_RDONLY);
    if (in_file < 0) {
        cerr << "Error: Unable to open " << argv[1] << '\n';
        exit(8);
    }
    out_file = open(argv[2], O_WRONLY | O_TRUNC | O_CREAT, 0666);
    if (out_file < 0) {
        cerr << "Error: Unable to open " << argv[2] << '\n';
        exit(8);
    }
    while (1) {
        read_size = read(in_file, buffer, sizeof(buffer));
```

Example 16-4. copy2/copy2.cc (Continued)

```
        if (read_size == 0)
            break;                  // End of file

        if (read_size < 0) {
            cerr << "Error: Read error\n";
            exit(8);
        }
        write(out_file, buffer, (unsigned int) read_size);
    }
    close(in_file);
    close(out_file);
    return (0);
}
```

Several things should be noted about this program. First of all, the buffer size is defined as a constant, so it is easily modified. Rather than have to remember that 16K is 16,384, the programmer used the expression (16 * 1024). This form of the constant is obviously 16K.

If the user improperly uses the program, an error message results. To help the user get it right, the message tells how to use the program.

You may not read a full buffer for the last read. That is why **read_size** is used to determine the number of bytes to write.

Designing File Formats

Suppose you are designing a program to produce a graph. The height, width, limits, and scales are to be defined in a graph configuration file. You are also assigned to write a user-friendly program that asks the operator questions and writes a configuration file so he or she does not have to learn the text editor. How should you design a configuration file?

One way would be as follows:

    height (in inches)
    width (in inches)
    x lower limit
    x upper limit
    y lower limit
    y upper limit
    x-scale
    y-scale

A typical plotter configuration file might look like:

```
10.0
7.0
0
100
30
300
0.5
2.0
```

This file does contain all the data, but in looking at it, you have trouble identifying what, for example, is the value of the Y lower limit. A solution is to comment the file so the configuration program writes out not only the data, but also a string describing the data.

```
10.0    height (in inches)
7.0     width (in inches)
0       x lower limit
100     x upper limit
30      y lower limit
300     y upper limit
0.5     x-scale
2.0     y-scale
```

Now the file is human readable. But suppose a user runs the plot program and types in the wrong filename, and the program gets the lunch menu for today instead of a plot configuration file. The program is probably going to get very upset when it tries to construct a plot whose dimensions are "BLT on white" versus "Meatloaf and gravy."

The result is that you wind up with egg on your face. There should be some way of identifying this file as a plot configuration file. One method of doing this is to put the words "Plot Configuration File" on the first line of the file. Then, when someone tries to give your program the wrong file, the program will print an error message.

This takes care of the wrong file problem, but what happens when you are asked to enhance the program and add optional logarithmic plotting? You could simply add another line to the configuration file, but what about all those old files? It's not reasonable to ask everyone to throw them away. The best thing to do (from a user's point of view) is to accept old format files. You can make this easier by putting a version number in the file.

A typical file now looks like:

```
Plot Configuration File V1.0
log     Logarithmic or normal plot
10.0    height (in inches)
7.0     width (in inches)
0       x lower limit
```

```
100      x upper limit
30       y lower limit
300      y upper limit
0.5      x-scale
2.0      y-scale
```

In binary files, it is common practice to put an identification number in the first four bytes of the file. This is called the *magic number.* The magic number should be different for each type of file.

One method for choosing a magic number is to start with the first four letters of the program name (e.g., *list*) and convert them to hex: 0x6c607374. Then add 0x80808080 to the number: 0xECE0F3F4.

This generates a magic number that is probably unique. The high bit is set on each byte to make the byte non-ASCII and avoid confusion between ASCII and binary files.

When reading and writing a binary file containing many different types of structures, it is easy to get lost. For example, you might read a name structure when you expected a size structure. This is usually not detected until later in the program. To locate this problem early, the programmer can put magic numbers at the beginning of each structure. Then if the program reads the name structure and the magic number is not correct, it knows something is wrong.

Magic numbers for structures do not need to have the high bit set on each byte. Making the magic number just four ASCII characters makes it easy to pick out the beginning of structures in a file dump.

C-Style I/O Routines

C++ allows you to use the C I/O library in C++ programs. Many times this occurs because someone took a C program and translated it to C++ and didn't want to bother translating the I/O calls. In some cases, the old C library is better and easier to use than the new C++ library. For example, C string-conversion routines such as `sscanf` and `sprintf` are far easier to use than their C++ counterparts.

The declarations for the structures and functions used by the C I/O functions are stored in the standard include file `<stdio.h>`.

The declaration for a file variable is:

```
FILE *file_variable;    /* Comment */
```

Example:

```
#include <stdio.h>

FILE *in_file;  /* File containing the input data */
```

Before a file can be used, it must be opened using the function `fopen`. `fopen` returns a pointer to the file structure for the file. The format for `fopen` is:

```
file_variable = fopen(name, mode);
```

file_variable

>A file variable.

name

>Actual name of the file (*data.txt, temp.dat,* etc.).

mode

>Indicates whether the file is to be read or written. Mode is "w" for writing and "r" for reading.

The function `fclose` closes the file. The format of `fclose` is:

```
status = fclose(file_variable);
```

The variable `status` will be zero if the `fclose` was successful or non-zero for an error.

C provides three preopened files. These are listed in Table 16-7.

Table 16-7. Standard Files

File	Description
stdin	Standard input (open for reading). Equivalent to C++'s `cin`.
stdout	Standard output (open for writing). Equivalent to C++'s `cout`.
stderr	Standard error (open for writing). Equivalent to C++'s `cerr`.
	There is no C file equivalent to C++'s `clog`.

The function `fgetc` reads a single character from a file. If there is no more data in the file the function returns the constant `EOF` (EOF is defined in *stdio.h*). Note that `fgetc` returns an integer, not a character. This is necessary because the EOF flag must be a noncharacter value.

Example 16-5 counts the number of characters in the file *input.txt.*

Example 16-5. copy/copy.cc

```
#include <stdio.h>
#include <stdlib.h>      /* ANSI Standard C file */
#include <iostream.h>

const char FILE_NAME[] = "input.txt";   // Name of the input file

main()
{
    int  count = 0;  // Number of characters seen
```

Example 16-5. copy/copy.cc (Continued)

```
    FILE *in_file;     // Input file

    int ch;            // Character or EOF flag from input

    in_file = fopen(FILE_NAME, "rb");
    if (in_file == NULL) {
        cerr << "Cannot open " << FILE_NAME << '\n';
        exit(8);
    }

    while (1) {
        ch = fgetc(in_file);
        if (ch == EOF)
            break;
        ++count;
    }
    cout << "Number of characters in " << FILE_
            NAME << " is " << count << '\n';

    fclose(in_file);
    return (0);
}
```

A similar function, fputc, exists for writing a single character. Its format is:

> fputc(*character, file*);

The functions fgets and fputs work on one line at a time. The format of the fgets call is:

> *string_ptr* = fgets *(string, size, file)*;

string_ptr

Equal to string if the read was successful, or NULL if EOF or an error is detected.

string

A character array where the function places the string.

size

The size of the character array. fgets reads until it gets a line (complete with ending \n) or it reads size – 1 characters. It then ends the string with a null (\0).

Example:

```
        char    string[100];

        . . .

        fgets(string, sizeof(string), in_file);
```

fputs is similar to fgets except it writes a string instead of reading it. The format of the fputs function is:

string_ptr = fputs*(string, file)*;

The parameters to fputs are similar to the ones for fgets. fputs needs no size because it gets the size of the line to write from the length of the string. (It keeps writing until it hits a null character, \0).

C-Style Conversion Routines

C++ uses the << operator for output. C uses the printf family of functions. A printf call consists of two parts: a format that describes how to print the data and a list of data to print.

The general form of the printf call is:

printf*(format, parameter-1, parameter-2, ...)*;

The *format* string is printed exactly. For example:

printf("Hello World\n");

prints:

Hello World

To print a number, you must put a % conversion in the format string. For example, when C sees %d in the format string, it takes the next parameter from the parameter list (which must be an integer) and prints it.

Figure 16-1 shows how the elements of the printf statement work to generate the final result:

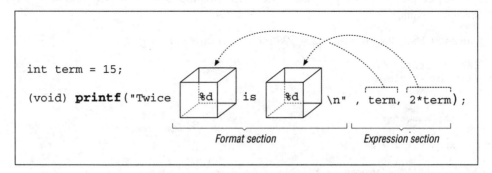

Figure 16-1. printf structure

The conversion %d is used for integers. Other types of parameters use different conversions. For example, if you want to print a floating point number, you need a %f conversion. Table 16-8 lists the conversions.

Table 16-8. C-style Conversions

Conversion	Variable Type
%d	int
%ld	long int
%d	short int
%f	float
%lf	double
%u	unsigned int
%lu	unsigned long int
%u	unsigned short int
%s	char * (string)
%c	char
%o	int (prints octal)
%x	int (prints hexadecimal)
%e	float (in the form *d.ddd*E+*dd*)

Many additional conversions also can be used in the `printf` statement. See your reference manual for details.

The `printf` function does not check for the correct number of parameters on each line. If you add too many, the extra parameters are ignored. If you add too few, C will make up values for the missing parameters. Also C does not type check parameters, so if you use a %d on a floating point number, you will get strange results.

Question 16-2: *Why does 2 + 2 = 5986? (Your results may vary.)*

```
[File: two/two.c]
#include <stdio.h>
main()
{
    int answer;

    answer = 2 + 2;

    printf("The answer is %d\n");
    return (0);
}
```

Question 16-3: *Why does 21 / 7 = 0? (Your results may vary.)*

```
[File: float3/float3.c]
#include <stdio.h>

main()
{
    float result;

    result = 21.0 / 7.0;
    printf("The result is %d\n", result);
    return (0);
}
```

The function `fprintf` is similar to `printf` except that it takes one additional parameter, the file to print to.

```
fprintf(file, format, parameter-1, parameter-2, ...);
```

Another flavor of the `printf` family is the `sprintf` call. The first parameter of `sprintf` is a string. The function formats the output and stores the result in the given string.

```
sprintf(string, format, parameter-1, parameter-2, ...);
```

For example:

```
char string[40];        /* The filename */

/* Current file number for this segment */
int file_number = 0;

sprintf(string, "file.%d", file_number);
++file_number;
out_file = fopen(string, "w");
```

Warning: The return value of `sprintf` differs from system to system. The ANSI standard defines it as the number of characters stored in the string; however, some implementations of UNIX C define it to be a pointer to the string.

Reading is accomplished through the `scanf` family of calls. The `scanf` function has similar sister functions: `fscanf` and `sscanf`. The format for `fscanf` is:

```
number = fscanf(file, format, &parameter-1, . . .);
```

number

Number of parameters successfully converted

file

A file opened for reading

format

Describes the data to be read

parameter-1

  First parameter to be read

WARNING

If you forget to put & in front of each variable for `scanf`, the result can be a "Segmentation violation core dumped" or "Illegal memory access" error. In some cases a random variable or instruction will be modified. This is not common on UNIX machines, but MS-DOS/Windows, with its lack of memory protection, cannot easily detect this problem. In MS-DOS/Windows, omitting & can cause a system crash.

There is one problem with this `scanf`: It's next to impossible to get the end-of-line handling right. However, there's a simple way to get around the limitations of scanf—don't use it. Instead use `fgets` followed by the string version of `scanf`, the function `sscanf`:

```
char line[100];    // Line for data

fgets(line, sizeof(line), stdin);    // Read numbers
sscanf(line, "%d %d", &number1, &number2);
```

Finally, there is a file version of `scanf`, the function `fscanf`. Again this function is extremely difficult and should not be used. Use `fgets` and `sscanf` instead.

C-Style Binary I/O

Binary I/O is accomplished through two routines: `fread` and `fwrite`. The syntax for `fread` is:

```
read_size = fread(data_ptr, 1, size, file);
```

read_size

  Size of the data that was read. If this is less than `size`, then an end-of-file or error occurred.

data_ptr

  Pointer to the data to be read.

size

  Number of bytes to be read.

file

  Input file.

Example:

```
struct {
        int     width;
        int     height;
```

```
    } rectangle;

    if (fread((char *)(&rectangle), 1, sizeof(rectangle), in_file) !=
                                               sizeof(rectangle
            )) {
        fprintf(stderr, "Unable to read rectangle\n");
        exit (8);
    }
```

In this example you are reading in the structure `rectangle`. The & operator makes the structure into a pointer. The cast "`(char *)`" turns &rectangle into the proper parameter type, and the `sizeof` operator is used to determine how many bytes to `fread` in as well as to check that read was successful.

`fwrite` has a calling sequence similar to `fread`:

> *write_size* = fwrite(*data_ptr*, 1, *size*, *file*);

NOTE

To make programming simpler and easier, I always use 1 as the second parameter to `fread` and `fwrite`. For a full description of these functions see your C reference manual.

Question 16-4: *No matter what filename you give the following program, our program can't find it. Why?*

```
[File: fun-file/fun-file.c]
#include <stdio.h>
#include <stdlib.h>

int main()
{
    char            name[100];  /* Name of the file to use  */
    FILE            *in_file;   /* File for input */

    printf("Name? ");
    fgets(name, sizeof(name), stdin);

    in_file = fopen(name, "r");
    if (in_file == NULL) {
        (void) fprintf(stderr, "Could not open file\n");
        exit(8);
    }
    printf("File found\n");
    fclose(in_file);
    return (0);
}
```

Programming Exercises

Exercise 16-1: Write a program that reads a file and counts the number of lines in it.

Exercise 16-2: Write a program to copy a file, expanding all tabs to multiple spaces.

Exercise 16-3: Write a program that reads a file containing a list of numbers and writes two files, one with all the numbers divisible by 3 and another containing all the other numbers.

Exercise 16-4: Write a program that reads an ASCII file containing a list of numbers and writes a binary file containing the same list. Write a program that goes the other way so you can check your work.

Exercise 16-5: Write a program that copies a file and removes all characters with the high bit set (((ch & 0x80) != 0).)

Exercise 16-6: Design a file format to store a person's name, address, and other information. Write a program to read this file and produce a set of mailing labels.

Answers to Chapter Questions

Answer 16-1: The problem is that you are writing an ASCII file, but you wanted a binary file. In UNIX, ASCII is the same as binary, so the program runs fine. In MS-DOS/Windows, the end-of-line issue causes problems. When you write a new-line character (0x0a) to the file, a carriage return (0x0D) is added to the file. (Remember that end-of-line in MS-DOS/Windows is <carriage return><line feed>, or 0x0d, 0x0a.) Because of this editing, you get an extra carriage return (0x0d) in the output file.

To write binary data (without output editing) you need to open the file with the binary option:

```
out_file = fopen("test.out", "wb");
```

Answer 16-2: The `printf` call does not check for the correct number of parameters. The statement:

```
printf("The answer is %d\n");
```

tells the `printf` to print the string "The answer is" followed by the answer. The problem is that the parameter containing the answer was omitted. When this happens `printf` gets the answer from a random location and prints garbage.

Properly written, the `printf` statement is:

```
printf("The answer is %d\n", answer);
```

Answer 16-3: The `printf` call does not check the type of its parameters. You tell the `printf` call to print an integer number (`%d`) and supply it with a floating point parameter (`result`). This mismatch causes unexpected results such as printing the wrong answer.

When printing a floating point number you need a `%f` conversion. Properly written, our `printf` statement is:

```
printf("The answer is %f\n", result);
```

Answer 16-4: The problem is that `fgets` gets the entire line including the new-line character (\n). If you have a file named *sam*, the program reads *sam\n* and tries to look for a file by that name. Because there is no such file, the program reports an error.

The fix is to strip the new-line character from the name:

```
name[strlen(name) - 1] = '\0';    /* Get rid of last character */
```

The error message in this case is poorly designed. True, you did not open the file, but the programmer could supply the user with more information. Are you trying to open the file for input or output? What is the name of the file you are trying to open? You don't even know whether the message you are getting is an error, a warning, or just part of the normal operation. A better error message is:

```
fprintf(stderr, "Error: Unable to open %s for input\n", name);
```

Notice that this message would also help us detect the programming error. When you typed in "sam" the error would be:

```
Error: Unable to open sam
for input
```

This clearly shows us that you are trying to open a file with a new-line in its name.

17

Debugging and Optimization

Bloody instructions which, being learned,
return to plague the inventor.
—Shakespeare, on debugging

Debugging

The hardest part of a program is not the design and writing, but the debugging phase. It is here that you find out how your program really works (instead of how you *think* it works).

To eradicate a bug, you need two things: a way of reproducing the bug and information from the program that lets you locate and correct the problem.

In some cases, finding the bug is easy. You discover the bug yourself, the test department produces a clear and easy test that displays the bug, or the output always comes out bad.

In some cases, especially with interactive programs, reproducing the bug may be 90 percent of the problem. This is especially true when dealing with bug reports sent in by users in the field. A typical call from a user might be:

User:
> That database program you gave me is broken.

Programmer:
> What's wrong?

User:
> Sometimes when I'm doing a sort, it gets things in the wrong order.

Programmer:

What command were you using?

User:

The sort command.

Programmer:

Tell me exactly what you typed, keystroke by keystroke, to get it to fail.

User:

I don't remember it exactly. I was doing a lot of sorts.

Programmer:

If I come over can you show me the bug?

User:

Of course.

Five minutes later the programmer is in the user's office and utters the fatal words, "Show me." The user types away and the program stubbornly works, no matter what the user does to it.

The programmer gives up and goes back to his office only to find a message from the user: "It failed five minutes after you left."

Example 17-1 is a short database lookup program. It asks the user for input and checks the input against a hard-coded list of names. Although it is very simple, the program's structure is typical of much larger and more complex interactive programs.

Example 17-1. base/base.cc

```
/**********************************************************
 * Database -- a very simple database program to         *
 *             look up names in a hard-coded list         *
 *                                                        *
 * Usage:                                                 *
 *     database                                           *
 *             Program will ask you for a name.           *
 *             Enter the name; it will tell you whether*
 *             the name is in the list.                   *
 *                                                        *
 *             A blank name terminates the program.     *
 **********************************************************/
const int STRING_LENGTH = 80;    /* Length of typical string */
#include <iostream.h>
#include <string.h>

main()
{
    char name[STRING_LENGTH];    // A name to look up
```

Example 17-1. base/base.cc (Continued)

```
    int lookup(char *);         // Look up a name

    while (1) {
        cout << "Enter name: ";
        cin.getline(name, sizeof(name));

        // Check for blank name
        if (strlen(name) <= 0)
            break;

        if (lookup(name))
            cout << name << " is in the list\n";
        else
            cout << name << " is not in the list\n";
    }
    return (0);
}
/********************************************************
 * Lookup -- look up a name in a list                   *
 *                                                      *
 * Parameters                                           *
 *      name -- name to look up                         *
 *                                                      *
 * Returns                                              *
 *      1 -- name in the list                           *
 *      0 -- name not in the list                       *
 ********************************************************/
int lookup(char *name)
{
    // List of people in the database
    // Note: Last name is a NULL for end-of-list
    static char *list[] = {
        "John",
        "Jim",
        "Jane",
        "Clyde",
        NULL
    };

    int index;          // Index into list

    for (index = 0; list[index] != NULL; ++index) {
        if (strcmp(list[index], name) == 0)
            return (1);
    }
    return (0);
}
```

A typical execution of this program is:
```
Enter name: Sam
Sam is not in the list
Enter name: John
```

Example 17-1. base/base.cc (Continued)

```
John is in the list
Enter name:
```

When we release this program, the users immediately start complaining about mysterious problems that go away whenever the programmer is around. Wouldn't it be nice to have a little gremlin sitting on the user's shoulder copying down everything he or she types? Unfortunately, gremlins are unavailable; however, we can change this program so it produces a *save file* that contains every keystroke the user typed.

Our program uses the statement:

```
    cin.getline(name, sizeof(name));
```

to read the user data.

Let's write a new routine, **extended_getline,** and use it instead of `getline`. It not only will get a line, but also will save the user's response in a save file.

Example 17-2. xgets/xgets.cc

```
#include <iostream.h>
#include <fstream.h>
/*
 * The main program will open this file if -S is on
 * the command line.
 */
ofstream save_file;              // File to use for saving input
int save_file_open = 0;          // Save file defaults to not open
/********************************************************
 * extended_getline -- get a line from the input file  *
 *              and record it in a save file if needed  *
 *                                                      *
 * Parameters                                           *
 *      line -- the line to read                        *
 *      size -- sizeof(line) -- maximum number of       *
 *                      characters to read              *
 *      file -- file to read data from                  *
 *              (normally stdin)                        *
 *                                                      *
 * Returns                                              *
 *      NULL -- error or end-of-file in read            *
 *      otherwise line (just like getline)              *
 ********************************************************/
istream &extended_getline(char *line, int size, ifstream &file)
{
    istream *result;            /* Result of gets */

    result = &file.getline(line, size);

    // Did someone ask for a save file?
    if (save_file_open) {
```

Example 17-2. xgets/xgets.cc (Continued)

```
        save_file << line << '\n';
    }

    return (*result);
}
```

We also change our main program to handle a new option: "-Sfile" to specify a save file. (Typically uppercase letters are used for debugging and other less used options.) Our new main program is shown in Example 17-3:

Example 17-3. base/base2.cc

```
/********************************************************
 * Data Base -- A very simple database program to      *
 *              look up names in a hard-coded list      *
 *                                                      *
 * Usage:                                               *
 *      database [-S<file>]                             *
 *                                                      *
 *      -S<file>        Specify save file for           *
 *                      debugging purposes              *
 *                                                      *
 *              Program will ask you for a name.        *
 *              Enter the name; it will tell you whether*
 *              the name is in the list.                *
 *                                                      *
 *              A blank name terminates the program.    *
 ********************************************************/
#include <iostream.h>
#include <fstream.h>
#include <stdlib.h>

ofstream save_file;     // Save file if any
int save_file_open = 0; // Save file open flag

char *extended_getline(char *line, int size, istream &file);

main(int argc, char *argv[])
{
    char name[80];        // A name to look up
    char *save_file_name; // Name of the save file

    int lookup(char *name);// look up a name

    while ((argc > 1) && (argv[1][0] == '-')) {
        switch (argv[1][1]) {
            case 'S':
                save_file_name = &argv[1][2];
                save_file.open(save_file_name, ios::out);
                if (save_file.bad())
                    cerr << "Warning: Unable to open save file " <<
                            save_file_name << '\n';
```

Example 17-3. base/base2.cc (Continued)

```
            else
                save_file_open = 1;
            break;
        default:
            cerr << "Bad option: " << argv[1] << '\n';
            exit (8);
    }
    --argc;
    ++argv;
}


while (1) {
    cout << "Enter name: ";
    extended_getline(name, sizeof(name), cin);

    /* ... rest of program ... */
}
return (0);
}
```

Now we have a complete record of what the user typed. Looking at the input, we see that he typed:

```
Sam
 John
```

The second name begins with a space and, although "John" is in the list, "<space>John" is not. In this case we found the error by inspecting the input; however, more complex programs have much more complex input. We could type all that in when debugging, or we could add another feature to **extended_getline** that would add a *playback file* to it. When the playback file is enabled, input will not be taken from the keyboard, but instead will be taken from the file.

Example 17-4. xgets/xgets2.cc

```
#include <iostream.h>
#include <fstream.h>
#
ofstream save_file;      // Save input in this file
int save_file_open = 0; // Save file has been opened
ifstream playback_file; // Playback data from this file
int playback_file_open = 0;// Playback file open flag
/********************************************************
 * extended_getline -- get a line from the input file  *
 *              and record it in a save file if needed  *
 *                                                      *
 * Parameters                                           *
 *      line -- the line to read                        *
 *      size -- sizeof(line) -- maximum number of       *
 *                      characters to read              *
 *      file -- file to read data from                  *
```

Example 17-4. xgets/xgets2.cc (Continued)

```
 *                 (normally stdin)                      *
 *                                                       *
 * Returns                                               *
 *       NULL -- error or end-of-file in read            *
 *       otherwise line (just like getline)              *
 ********************************************************/
istream &extended_getline(char *line, int size, istream &file)
{
    istream *result;            // Rresult of getline

    if (playback_file_open) {
        result = &playback_file.getline(line, size);
        if (file == cin)
            // Echo the input to the standard out
            // so the user sees it
            cout << line << '\n';
    } else
        result = &file.getline(line, size);

    // Did someone ask for a save file?
    if (save_file_open)
        save_file << line << '\n';

    return (*result);
}
```

We also add a playback option to the command line, -Pfile.: This allows us to
automatically "type" the commands that caused the error. Our main program now
looks like Example 17-5.

Example 17-5. base/base3.cc

```
/********************************************************
 * Database -- A very simple database program to        *
 *             look up names in a hard-coded list        *
 *                                                       *
 * Usage:                                                *
 *       database [-S<file>]                             *
 *                                                       *
 *       -S<file>        Specify save file for           *
 *                       debugging purposes              *
 *                                                       *
 *       -P<file>        Specify playback file for       *
 *                       debugging or demonstration      *
 *                                                       *
 *             Program will ask you for a name.          *
 *             Enter the name; it will tell you whether*
 *             the name is in the list.                  *
 *                                                       *
 *             A blank name terminates the program.      *
 ********************************************************/
```

Example 17-5. base/base3.cc (Continued)

```cpp
#include <iostream.h>
#include <fstream.h>
#include <stdlib.h>

ifstream save_file;      // Save file if any
int save_file_open = 0;  // Save file open flag
ofstream playback_file;  // Playback data
int playback_file_open = 0; // True if playback in progress

char *extended_getline(char *line, int size, istream &file);

main(int argc, char *argv[])
{
    char name[80];        // A name to look up
    char *save_file_name; // Name of the save file
    char *playback_file_name; // Name of the playback file

    int lookup(char *name); // lookup a name

    while ((argc > 1) && (argv[1][0] == '-')) {
        switch (argv[1][1]) {
            case 'S':
                save_file_name = &argv[1][2];
                save_file.open(save_file_name, ios::out);
                if (save_file.bad())
                    cerr << "Warning: Unable to open save file " <<
                            save_file_name << '\n';
                else
                    save_file_open = 1;
                break;
            case 'P':
                playback_file_name = &argv[1][2];
                playback_file.open(playback_file_name, ios::in);
                if (playback_file.bad()) {
                    cerr <<
                            "Error: Unable to open playback file " <<
                            playback_file_name << '\n';
                    exit (8);
                }
                playback_file_open = 1;
                break;
            default:
                cerr << "Bad option: " << argv[1] << '\n';
                exit (8);
        }
        --argc;
        ++argv;
    }


    while (1) {
        cout << "Enter name: ";
```

Example 17-5. base/base3.cc (Continued)

```
        extended_getline(name, sizeof(name), cin);

        /* ... rest of program ... */
    }
    return (0);
}
```

Now when a user calls up with an error report, we can tell him, "Try it again with the save-file feature enabled, and then send me a copy of your files." The user then runs the program and saves the input into the file *save.txt*.

```
% database -Ssave.txt
Enter name: Sam
Sam is not in the list
Enter name:  John
John is in the list
Enter name:
```

He sends us the file *save.txt* and we run the error with the playback option enabled.

```
% database -Psave.txt
Enter name: Sam
Sam is not in the list
Enter name:  John
John is in the list
Enter name:
```

We now have a reliable way of reproducing the program. In many cases that's half the battle. Once you can reproduce the problem you can proceed to the next steps: finding it and fixing it.

Once a programmer asked a user to send the programmer a copy of his floppy. An express package arrived the next day containing a Xerox™ photocopy of the floppy. But the user was not completely computer-illiterate: He knew it was a two-sided floppy, so he had photocopied both sides.

Serial Debugging

Before you start debugging, save the old, "working" copy of your program in a safe place. (If you are using a source control system such as SCCS, RCS, or PSVS your last working version should be checked in.) Many times while you are searching for a problem, you may find it necessary to try out different solutions or to add temporary debugging code. Sometimes you will find you've been barking up the wrong tree and need to start over. That's when the last working copy becomes invaluable.

Once you have reproduced the problem, you must determine what caused it to happen. There are several methods for doing this.

Divide and Conquer

The divide and conquer method has already been briefly discussed in Chapter 6, *Decision and Control Statements*. It consists of putting in cout statements where you know the data is good (to make sure it really is good), where the data is bad, and several points in between. This way you can start zeroing in on the section of code that contains the error. More cout statements can further reduce the scope of the error until the bug is finally located.

Debug-Only Code

The divide-and-conquer method uses temporary cout statements. They are put in as needed and taken out after they are used. The pre-processor conditional-compilation directives can be used to put in and take out debugging code. For example:

```
#ifdef DEBUG
    cout << "Width " << width << " Height " << height << '\n';
#endif /* DEBUG */
```

The program can be compiled with DEBUG undefined for normal use so you can define it when debugging is needed.

Debug Command-Line Switch

Rather than using a compile-time switch to create a special version of the program, you can permanently include the debugging code and add a special program switch that will turn on debugging output. For example:

```
if (debug)
    cout << "Width " << width << " Height " << height << '\n';
```

where debug is a variable set if -D is present on the command line.

This has the advantage that only a single version of the program exists. One of the problems with "debug-only" code is that unless the code is frequently used, it can easily become stale and out of date. Frequently a programmer tries to find a bug only to discover that the debug-only code is out of date and needs fixing.

Another advantage of the debug command-line switch is that the user can turn on this switch in the field, save the output, and send it to you for analysis. The runtime switch should be used in all cases instead of conditional compilation, unless there is some reason you do not want the customer to be able to get at the debugging information.

Some programs use the concept of a debug level. Level 0 outputs only minimal debugging information, level 1 more information, and on up to level 9, which outputs everything.

Another debugging technique can be seen in the Ghostscript[*] program by Aladdin Enterprises. This program implements the idea of debugging letters. The command option –Z*xxx* sets the debugging flags for each type of diagnostic output wanted. For example, f is the code for the fill algorithm and p is the code for the path tracer. If I wanted to trace both these sections, I would specify –Zfp.

The option is implemented by the following code:

```
/*
 * Even though we only put 1 zero, C++ will fill in the
 * rest of the arrays with zeros
 */
char debug[128] = {0};     // The debugging flags

main(argc, argv)
int argc;
char *argv[];
{
    while ((argc > 1) && (argv[1][0] == '-')) {
        switch (argv[1][1]) {
            /* .... normal switch .... */

            // Debug switch
            case 'Z':
                debug_ptr = argv[1][2];
                // Loop for each letter
                while (*debug_ptr != '\0') {
                    debug[*debug_ptr] = 1;
                    ++debug_ptr;
                }
                break;
        }
        --argc;
        ++argv;
    }

    /* Rest of program */
}
```

---

[*] Ghostscript is a Postscript™-like interpreter available from the Free Software Foundation for a minimal copying charge. They can be reached at: Free Software Foundation, Inc., 675 Mass Ave., Cambridge, MA 02139; phone (617) 876-3296.

This is used inside the program by:

```
if (debug['p'])
    cout << "Starting new path\n";
```

Ghostscript is a large program (some 25,000 lines) and rather difficult to debug. This form of debugging allows the user to get a great deal of information easily.

Going Through the Output

Enabling debug printout is a nice way of getting information, but many times there is so much data that the information you want can easily get lost.

C++ allows you to *redirect* what would normally go to the screen to a file through the use of the ">file" option. For example:

```
buggy -D9 >tmp.out
```

will run the program buggy with a high level of debug set and send the output to the file *tmp.out.*

The text editor on your system also makes a good file browser. You can use its search capabilities to look for the information you want to find.

Interactive Debuggers

Most compiler manufacturers provide an interactive debugger. They give you the ability to stop the program at any point, examine and change variables, and "single-step" through the program. Because each debugger is different, a detailed discussion is not possible.

However, we are going to discuss one debugger gdb. This program is available for many UNIX machines from the Free Software Foundation. Turbo-C++ has its own built-in debugger. Although the exact syntax used by your debugger may be different, the principles shown here will work for all debuggers.

Basic GDB commands are:

run

> Start execution of a program.

break *line-number*

> Insert a breakpoint at the given line number. When a running program reaches a breakpoint, execution stops and control returns to the debugger.

break *function-name*

> Insert a breakpoint at the first line of the named function. Commonly, the command break in main is used to stop execution at the beginning of the program.

`cont`

Continue execution after a breakpoint.

`print` *expression*

Display the value of an expression.

`step`

Execute a single line in the program. If the current statement calls a function, the function is single stepped.

`next`

Execute a single line in the program, but treat function calls as a single line. This command is used to skip over function calls.

`list`

List the source program.

`where`

Print the list of currently active functions.

`status`

Print a list of breakpoints.

`delete`

Remove a breakpoint.

We have a program that should count the number of threes and sevens in a series of numbers. The problem is it keeps getting the wrong answer for the number of sevens. Our program is shown in Example 17-6.

Example 17-6. seven/count.cc

```
 1 #include <iostream.h>
 2 int seven_count;    /* Number of seven's in the data */
 3 int data[5];        /* The data to count 3 and 7 in */
 4 int three_count;    /* Number of threes in the data */
 5
 6 main() {
 7     int index;  /* Index into the data */
 8     void get_data(int data[]);
 9
10     seven_count = 0;
11     three_count = 0;
12     get_data(data);
13
14     for (index = 1; index <= 5; ++index) {
15         if (data[index] == 3)
16             ++three_count;
17         if (data[index] == 7)
18           ++seven_count;
19     }
20     cout << "Threes " << three_count <<
21           " Sevens " << seven_count << '\n';
```

Example 17-6. seven/count.cc (Continued)

```
22      return (0);
23 }
24 /********************************************************
25  * get_data -- get 5 numbers from the command line    *
26  ********************************************************/
27 void get_data(int data[])
28 {
29     cout << "Enter 5 numbers\n";
30     cin >> data[1] >> data[2] >> data[3] >> data[4] >> data[5];
31 }
```

When we run this program with the data 3 7 3 0 2 the results are:

```
Threes 3 Sevens 3
```

We start by invoking the debugger (GDB) with the name of the program we are going to debug (count). The debugger initializes, outputs the prompt (gdb), and waits for a command.

```
% gdb count
GDB is free software and you are welcome to distribute copies of it
under certain conditions; type "show copying" to see the conditions.
There is absolutely no warranty for GDB; type "show warranty" for details.
GDB 4.12 (m68k-sun-sunos4.0.3),
Copyright 1994 Free Software Foundation, Inc...
(gdb)
```

We don't know where the variable is getting changed, so we'll start at the beginning and work our way through until we get an error. At every step we'll display the variable seven_count just to make sure it's okay.

We need to stop the program at the beginning so we can single-step through it. The command break main tells GDB to set a breakpoint at the first instruction of the function main. The command run tells GDBb to start the program, which will run until it hits the first breakpoint.

```
(gdb) break main
Breakpoint 1 at 0x22c2: file count.cc, line 10.
(gdb)
```

The number 1 is used by GDB to identify the breakpoint. Now we need to start the program:

```
(gdb) run
Starting program: /usr/sdo/count/count

Breakpoint 1, main () at count.cc:10
10          seven_count = 0;
(gdb)
```

The message Breakpoint 1, main... indicates that the program encountered a breakpoint and has now turned control over to debug.

We have reached the point where seven_count is initialized. The command next will execute a single statement, treating function calls as one statement. (The names of the command for your debugger may be different.) We go past the initialization and check to see whether it worked:

```
(gdb) next
11              three_count = 0;
(gdb) print seven_count
$1 = 0
(gdb)
```

It did. We try the next few lines, checking all the time:

```
(gdb) next
12              get_data(data);
(gdb) print seven_count
$2 = 0
(gdb) next
Enter 5 numbers
3 7 3 0 2
14              for (index = 1; index <= 5; ++index) {
(gdb) print seven_count
$3 = 2
(gdb)
```

seven_count somehow changed the value to 2. The last statement we executed was get_data(data); so something is going on in that function. We add a breakpoint at the beginning of get_data, get rid of the one at main, and start the program over with the run command:

```
(gdb) break get_data
Breakpoint 2 at 0x23b2: file count.cc, line 29.
(gdb) info breakpoints
Num Type          Disp Enb Address    What
1   breakpoint    keep y   0x000022c2 in main at count.cc:10
2   breakpoint    keep y   0x000023b2 in get_
              data(int *) at count.cc:29
(gdb) delete 1
(gdb) run
The program being debugged has been started already.
Start it from the beginning? (y or n) Y
Starting program: /usr/sdo/count/count
Breakpoint 2, get_data (data=0x208f8) at count.cc:29
(gdb)
```

We now start single-stepping again until we find the error:

```
Breakpoint 2, get_data (data=0x208f8) at count.cc:29
29              cout << "Enter 5 numbers\n";
(gdb) print seven_count
$5 = 0
(gdb) next
30              cin >> data[1] >> data[2] >> data[3] >> data[4] >> data[5];
(gdb) print seven_count
```

```
    $6 = 0
    (gdb) next
    Enter 5 numbers
    3 7 3 0 2
    31      }
    (gdb) print seven_count
    $7 = 2
    (gdb) list 22
    22          return (0);
    23      }
    24      /**********************************************************
    25       * get_data -- get 5 numbers from the command line       *
    26       **********************************************************/
    27      void get_data(int data[])
    28      {
    29          cout << "Enter 5 numbers\n";
    30          cin >> data[1] >> data[2] >> data[3] >> data[4] >> data[5];
    31      }
```

At line 30 the data was good, but when we reached line 31, the data was bad, so the error is located at line 30 of the program, the cin. We've narrowed the problem down to one statement. By inspection we can see that we are using data[5], an illegal member of the array data.

But why does seven_count go bad? Since data is only five elements long, there is no data[5]. However, the cin >> data[5] has to put the data someplace, so it decided to put it in a random memory location, in this case seven_count.

Debugging a Binary Search

The binary search algorithm is fairly simple. You want to see whether a given number is in an ordered list. Check your number against the one in the middle of the list. If it is the number, you were lucky — stop. If your number was bigger, then you might find it in the top half of the list. Try the middle of the top half. If it was smaller, try the bottom half. Keep trying and dividing the list in half until you find the number or the list gets down to a single number.

Example 17-7 uses a binary search to see whether a number can be found in the file *numbers.dat*.

Example 17-7.   search/search0.cc

```
/**********************************************************
 * Search -- search a set of numbers                     *
 *                                                        *
 * Usage:                                                 *
 *      search                                            *
 *                  You will be asked numbers to look up  *
 *                                                        *
 * Files:                                                 *
```

Example 17-7.   search/search0.cc (Continued)

```
 *        numbers.dat -- numbers 1 per line to search      *
 *                      (Nn ***********************************************
          ********/
#include <iostream.h>
#include <fstream.h>
#include <stdlib.h>
#include <stdio.h>

const int MAX_NUMBERS = 1000;    // Max numbers in file
const char *const DATA_FILE = "numbers.dat"; // File with numbers

int data[MAX_NUMBERS];   // Array of numbers to search
int max_count;           // Number of valid elements in data
#
main()
{
    ifstream in_file;    // Input file
    int middle;          // Middle of our search range
    int low, high;       // Upper/lower bound
    int search;          // Number to search for

    in_file.open(DATA_FILE, ios::in);
    if (in_file.bad()) {
        cerr << "Error: Unable to open " << DATA_FILE << '\n';
        exit (8);
    }

    /*
     * Read in data
     */

    max_count = 0;
    while (1) {
        char line[30];   // Line from the input file

        if (in_file.eof())
            break;

        in_file.getline(line, sizeof(line));

        sscanf(line, "%d", data[max_count]);
        if (data[max_count] == -1)
            break;

        ++max_count;
    }

    while (1) {
        cout << "Enter number to search for or -1 to quit:" ;
        cin >> search;

        if (search == -1)
```

Example 17-7.   search/search0.cc (Continued)

```
            break;

        low = 0;
        high = max_count;

        while (1) {
            middle = (low + high) / 2;

            if (data[middle] == search) {
                cout << "Found at index " << middle << '\n';
            }

            if (low == high) {
                cout << "Not found\n";
                break;
            }

            if (data[middle] < search)
                low = middle;
            else
                high = middle;
        }
    }
    return (0);
}
```

Our data file is:

numbers.dat

```
4
6
14
16
17
-1
```

When we run this program in UNIX, the results are:

```
% search
Segmentation fault (core dumped)
```

When we run this program on MS-DOS, the system locks up and we have to hit
the reset switch. If the program is run in Windows we get an application error (if
we're lucky).

Either way this is not good. It means something went wrong in our program and
the program tried to read memory that wasn't there. The debugger GDB can read
this file and help us determine what happened.

```
% gdb search
GDB is free software and you are welcome to distribute copies of it
under certain conditions; type "show copying" to see the conditions.
```

```
There is absolutely no warranty for GDB; type "show warranty" for details.
GDB 4.12 (m68k-sun-sunos4.0.3),
Copyright 1994 Free Software Foundation, Inc...
(gdb) run
Starting program: /usr/sdo/search/search

Program received signal SIGSEGV, Segmentation fault.
0xec46320 in number ()
(gdb)
```

The debugger tells us we have been killed by a segmentation fault generated from the procedure. But we don't have a procedure **number**! The routine must belong to the C++ library.

We now use the *where* command to find out which function called which function (also known as a *stack trace*):

```
(gdb) where
#0  0xec46320 in number ()
#1  0xec45cc2 in _doscan ()
#2  0xec45b34 in sscanf ()
#3  0x2400 in main () at search.cc:48
(gdb)
```

The current function is printed first, then the function that called it, and so on until we reach the outer function **main**. From this we see that **number** was called by _doscan, which was called by sscanf. We recognize sscanf as a library routine. The other functions must be subroutines called by sscanf. The last function that had control was the call of sscanf, which was made from line 48 of main.

Now we use the *list* command to take a look at the source for this line:

```
(gdb) list 48
43              if (in_file.eof())
44                  break;
45
46              in_file.getline(line, sizeof(line));
47
48              sscanf(line, "%d", data[max_count]);
49              if (data[max_count] == -1)
50                  break;
51
52              ++max_count;
(gdb) quit
The program is running.  Quit anyway (and kill it)? (y or n) Y
```

This is the line that caused the problem.

Another way of finding the problem is to single-step through the program until the error occurs. First list a section of the program to find a convenient place to put the breakpoint, and then start the execution and single-step process.

```
Script started on Mon Oct 31 10:07:19 1994
% gdb search
GDB is free software and you are welcome to distribute copies of it
under certain conditions; type "show copying" to see the conditions.
There is absolutely no warranty for GDB; type "show warranty" for details.
GDB 4.12 (m68k-sun-sunos4.0.3),
Copyright 1994 Free Software Foundation, Inc...
(gdb) list main
18       const char *const DATA_FILE = "numbers.dat";
                 // File with numbers
19
20       int data[MAX_NUMBERS];  // Array of numbers to search
21       int max_count;          // Number of valid elements in data
22       main()
23       {
24           ifstream in_file;   // Input file
25           int middle;         // Middle of our search range
26           int low, high;      // Upper/lower bound
27           int search;         // Number to search for
(gdb) break main
Breakpoint 1 at 0x2318: file search.cc, line 24.
(gdb) run
Starting program: /usr/sdo/search/search

Breakpoint 1, main () at search.cc:24
24           ifstream in_file;   // Input file
(gdb) step
29           in_file.open(DATA_FILE, ios::in);
(gdb) step
30           if (in_file.bad()) {
(gdb) step
39           max_count = 0;
(gdb) step
43               if (in_file.eof())
(gdb) step
46               in_file.getline(line, sizeof(line));
(gdb) step
48               sscanf(line, "%d", data[max_count]);
(gdb) step

Program received signal SIGSEGV, Segmentation fault.
0xec46320 in number ()
(gdb) quit
The program is running.  Quit anyway (and kill it)? (y or n) y
```

This method, too, points at line 48 as the culprit. On inspection we notice that we forgot to put an ampersand (&) in front of the variable for **sscanf**. So we change line 48 from:

```
        sscanf(line, "%d", data[max_count]);
```

to:

```
        sscanf(line, "%d", &data[max_count]);
```

and try again.

NOTE

You might wonder why we use the function **sscanf** when the line:

```
cin >> data[max_data];
```

performs the same function.

The answer is simple. We used **sscanf** to cause problems. Without the pointer error we would have nothing to debug. The **cin** statement is more reliable, and reliable code has no place in a chapter on debugging.

The first number in our list is 4, so we try it. This time our output looks like:

```
Enter number to search for or -1 to quit: 4
Found at index 0
Found at index 0
Not found
Enter number to search for or -1 to quit: ^C
```

The program should find the number, let us know it's at index 0, and then ask for another number. Instead we get two found messages and one not found message. We know that everything is running smoothly up to the time we get the first found message. After that things go downhill.

Getting back into the debugger, we use the **list** command to locate the found message and put a breakpoint there.

```
% gdb search
GDB is free software and you are welcome to distribute copies of it
under certain conditions; type "show copying" to see the conditions.
There is absolutely no warranty for GDB; type "show warranty" for details.
GDB 4.12 (m68k-sun-sunos4.0.3),
Copyright 1994 Free Software Foundation, Inc...
(gdb) list 66,77
66              while (1) {
67                      middle = (low + high) / 2;
68
69                      if (data[middle] == search) {
70                          cout << "Found at index " << middle << '\n';
71                      }
72
73                      if (low == high) {
74                          cout << "Not found\n";
75                          break;
76                      }
77
(gdb) break 70
Breakpoint 1 at 0x249e: file search.cc, line 70.
(gdb) run
Starting program: /usr/sdo/search/search
Enter number to search for or -1 to quit: 4
```

```
Breakpoint 1, main () at search.cc:70
70                    cout << "Found at index " << middle << '\n';
(gdb) step
Found at index 0
73                    if (low == high) {
(gdb) step
78                    if (data[middle] < search)
(gdb) step
81                        high = middle;
(gdb) step
67                    middle = (low + high) / 2;
(gdb) step
69                    if (data[middle] == search) {
(gdb) step
70                        cout << "Found at index " << middle << '\n';
(gdb) step
Found at index 0
73                    if (low == high) {
(gdb) quit
The program is running.  Quit anyway (and kill it)? (y or n) y
```

The program doesn't exit the loop. Instead it continues with the search. Because the number has already been found, this search results in strange behavior. We are missing a break after the cout.

We need to change:

```
if (data[middle] == search) {
    cout << "Found at index " << middle << '\n';
}
```

to:

```
if (data[middle] == search) {
    cout << "Found at index " << middle << '\n';
    break;
}
```

Making this fix, we try the program again:

```
% search
Enter number to search for or -1 to quit: 4
Found at index 0
Enter number to search for or -1 to quit: 6
Found at index 1
Enter number to search for or -1 to quit: 3
Not found
Enter number to search for or -1 to quit: 5
program runs forever (or until we abort it)
```

We have a runaway program. This time instead of setting a breakpoint we just start running the program. After a few seconds pass and we believe that we are stuck in the infinite loop, we stop the program with a control-C (^C). Normally this would abort the program and return us to the shell prompt. Since we are running with the debugger, it returns control to GDB.

```
% gdb search
GDB is free software and you are welcome to distribute copies of it
under certain conditions; type "show copying" to see the conditions.
There is absolutely no warranty for GDB; type "show warranty" for details.
GDB 4.12 (m68k-sun-sunos4.0.3),
Copyright 1994 Free Software Foundation, Inc...
(gdb) run
Starting program: /usr/sdo/search/search
Enter number to search for or -1 to quit: 5
^C
Program received signal SIGINT, Interrupt.
0x2500 in main () at search.cc:79
79                      if (data[middle] < search)
```

Now we can use the single-step command to step through the infinite loop, looking at key values along the way.

```
79                      if (data[middle] < search)
(gdb) print middle
$1 = 0
(gdb) print data[middle]
$2 = 4
(gdb) print search
$3 = 5
(gdb) step
80                          low = middle;
(gdb) step
67                      middle = (low + high) / 2;
(gdb) step
69                      if (data[middle] == search) {
(gdb) step
74                      if (low == high) {
(gdb) step
79                      if (data[middle] < search)
(gdb) step
80                          low = middle;
(gdb) step
67                      middle = (low + high) / 2;
(gdb) step
69                      if (data[middle] == search) {
(gdb) step
74                      if (low == high) {
(gdb) step
79                      if (data[middle] < search)
(gdb) step
80                          low = middle;
(gdb) step
67                      middle = (low + high) / 2;
(gdb) step
69                      if (data[middle] == search) {
(gdb) step
```

```
74                        if (low == high) {
(gdb) step
79                        if (data[middle] < search)
(gdb) step
80                            low = middle;
(gdb) step
67                        middle = (low + high) / 2;
(gdb) step
69                        if (data[middle] == search) {
(gdb) print low
$5 = 0
(gdb) print middle
$6 = 0
(gdb) print high
$7 = 1
(gdb) print search
$8 = 5
(gdb) print data[0]
$9 = 4
(gdb) print data[1]
$10 = 6
(gdb) quit
The program is running.  Quit anyway (and kill it)? (y or n) y
```

The problem is that we have reached a point where:

```
low = 0  middle = 0  high = 1
```

The item we are searching for falls exactly between elements 0 and 1. Our algorithm has an off-by-one error. Obviously the middle element does not match. If it did we'd exit with a **found at** message. So there is no point including the middle element in our new search range. Our code to adjust the interval is:

```
if (data[middle] < search)
    low = middle;
else
    high = middle;
```

It should be:

```
if (data[middle] < search)
    low = middle + 1;
else
    high = middle - 1;
```

The full version of the corrected program is shown in Example 17-8.

Example 17-8. search/search4.cc

```
/************************************************************
 * Search -- search a set of numbers                       *
 *                                                          *
 * Usage:                                                   *
 *      search                                              *
 *              You will be asked numbers to look up        *
```

Example 17-8. search/search4.cc (Continued)

```
 *                                                     *
 * Files:                                              *
 *      numbers.dat -- numbers 1 per line to search    *
 *                         (numbers must be ordered)   *
 ******************************************************/
#include <iostream.h>
#include <fstream.h>
#include <stdlib.h>
#include <stdio.h>

const int MAX_NUMBERS = 1000;    // Max numbers in file
const char *const DATA_FILE = "numbers.dat"; // File with numbers

int data[MAX_NUMBERS];  // Array of numbers to search
int max_count;          // Number of valid elements in data
main()
{
    ifstream in_file;    // Input file
    int middle;          // Middle of our search range
    int low, high;       // Upper/lower bound
    int search;          // Number to search for

    in_file.open(DATA_FILE, ios::in);
    if (in_file.bad()) {
        cerr << "Error: Unable to open " << DATA_FILE << '\n';
        exit (8);
    }

    /*
     * Read in data
     */

    max_count = 0;

    while (1) {
        char line[30];   // Line from the input file

        if (in_file.eof())
            break;

        in_file.getline(line, sizeof(line));

        sscanf(line, "%d", &data[max_count]);
        if (data[max_count] == -1)
            break;

        ++max_count;
    }

    while (1) {
        cout << "Enter number to search for or -1 to quit:" ;
        cin >> search;
```

Example 17-8. search/search4.cc (Continued)

```
        if (search == -1)
            break;

        low = 0;
        high = max_count;

        while (1) {
            if (low >= high) {
                cout << "Not found\n";
                break;
            }
            middle = (low + high) / 2;

            if (data[middle] == search) {
                cout << "Found at index " << middle << '\n';
                break;
            }

            if (data[middle] < search)
                low = middle + 1;
            else
                high = middle - 1;
        }
    }
    return (0);
}
```

Interactive debuggers work well for most programs. Sometimes they need a little help. Consider Example 17-9. We try to debug it and find it fails when point_ number is 735. We want to put a breakpoint before the calculation is made. When the debugger inserts a breakpoint into a program, the program will execute normally until it hits the breakpoint, and then control will return to the debugger. This allows the user to examine and change variables as well as perform other debugging commands. When a cont command is typed, the program will continue execution as though nothing happened. The problem is that there are 734 points before the one we want, and we don't want to stop for each of them.

Example 17-9. debug/cstop.cc

```
float point_color(int point_number)
{
    float correction;            // color correction factor
    extern float red, green, blue;// Current colors

    // Lookup color correction
    extern lookup(int point_number);

    correction = lookup(point_number);
    return (red*correction * 100.0 +
```

Example 17-9. debug/cstop.cc (Continued)

```
            blue*correction * 10.0 +
            green*correction);
}
```

How do we force the debugger to stop only when `point_number` == 735? We can do this by adding the following temporary code:

```
48:    if (point_number == 735)  /* ### Temp code ### */
49:        point_number = point_number;   /* ### Line to stop on ### */
```

Line 49 does nothing useful except serve as a line that the debugger can stop on. We can put a breakpoint on that line with the command `break 49`. The program will process the first 734 points, and then execute line 49, hitting the breakpoint. (Some debuggers have a conditional breakpoint. The advanced GDB command `break 49 if part_number == 735` would also work, however, your debugger may not have such advanced features.)

Runtime Errors

Runtime errors are usually the easiest to fix. Some types of runtime errors are segmentation violation, stack overflow, and divide by 0.

Segmentation violation

This error indicates that the program tried to de-reference a pointer containing a bad value.

Stack overflow

The program tried to use too many temporary variables. Sometimes this means the program is too big or using too many big temporary arrays, but most of the time this is due to infinite recursion problems. Almost all UNIX systems automatically check for this error. Turbo-C++ will check for stack overflow only if the compile time option -N is used.

Divide by 0

Divide by 0 is an obvious error. UNIX masks the problem by reporting an integer divide by zero with the error message `Floating exception (core dumped)`.

In all cases, program execution will be stopped. In UNIX, an image of the running program, called a core file, is written out. This file can be analyzed by the debugger to determine why the program died. Our first run of Example 17-7 resulted in a core dump. (One of the problems with core dumps is that the core files are very big and can fill up a disk quickly.)

One problem with runtime errors is that when they occur, program execution stops immediately. The buffers for buffered files are not flushed. This can lead to some unexpected surprises. Consider Example 17-10.

Example 17-10. debug/flush.cc

```
#include <iostream.h>
main()
{
    int i, j;    /* Two random integers */

    i = 1;
    j = 0;
    cout << "Starting\n";
    cout << "Before divide...";
    i = i / j;  // Divide-by-zero error
    cout << "After\n";
    return(0);
}
```

When run, this program outputs:

```
Starting
Floating exception (core dumped)
```

This might lead you to think the divide had never started, when in fact it had. What happened to the message "Before divide..."? The cout statement executed, and put the message in a buffer, and then the program died. The buffer never got a chance to be emptied.

By putting explicit flush-buffer commands inside the code, we get a truer picture of what is happening, as shown in Example 17-11.

Example 17-11. debug/flush2.cc

```
#include <iostream.h>
main()
{
    int i, j;    /* Two random integers */

    i = 1;
    j = 0;
    cout << "Starting\n";
    cout.flush();
    cout << "Before divide...";
    cout.flush();
    i = i / j;  // Divide-by-zero error
    cout << "After\n";
    cout.flush();
    return(0);
}
```

The flush statement makes the I/O less efficient, but more current.

The Confessional Method of Debugging

The confessional method of debugging is one by which the programmer explains his program to someone: an interested party, an uninterested party, a wall—it doesn't matter whom he explains it to as long he talks about it.

A typical confessional session goes like this:

"Hey, Bill, could you take a look at this? My program has a bug in it. The output should be 8.0 and I'm getting -8.0. The output is computed using this formula – and I've checked out the payment value and rate and the date must be correct, unless there is something wrong with the leap-year code, which—Thank you Bill, you've found my problem."

Bill never said a word.

This type of debugging is also called a *walkthrough*. Getting other people involved brings a fresh point of view to the process, and frequently other people can spot problems you have overlooked.

Optimization

And now a word on optimization: *Don't*. Most programs do not need to be optimized. They run fast enough. Who cares whether an interactive program takes 0.5 seconds to start up instead of 0.2?

To be fair, there are a lot of slow programs out there that can be sped up. This is usually done not by the simple optimization steps shown in this chapter, but by replacing poorly designed core algorithms with more efficient ones.

For a well-written program, the simplest way to get your program to run faster is to get a faster computer. Many times it is cheaper to buy a more powerful machine than it is to optimize a program, because you may introduce new errors into your code. Don't expect miracles from optimization. Usually most programs can only be sped up 10 percent to 20 percent.

Example 17-12 initializes a matrix (two-dimensional array).

Example 17-12. matrix/matrix1.cc

```
const int X_SIZE = 60;
const int Y_SIZE = 30;

int matrix[X_SIZE][Y_SIZE];

void init_matrix(void)
{
    int x, y;     // Current element to initialize
```

Example 17-12.   matrix/matrix1.cc (Continued)

```
    for (x = 0; x < X_SIZE; ++x) {
        for (y = 0; y < Y_SIZE; ++y) {
            matrix[x][y] = -1;
        }
    }
}
```

How can this function be optimized? First we notice we are using two local variables. By using the qualifier **register** on these variables, we tell the compiler that they are frequently used and should be placed in fast registers instead of relatively slow main memory. The number of registers varies from computer to computer. Slow machines like the PC have 2, most UNIX systems have about 11, and supercomputers can have as many as 128. It is possible to declare more register variables than you have registers. C++ will put the extra variables in main memory.

The program now looks like Example 17-13.

Example 17-13.   matrix/matrix2.cc

```
const int X_SIZE = 60;
const int Y_SIZE = 30;

int matrix[X_SIZE][Y_SIZE];

void init_matrix(void)
{
    register int x, y;     // Current element to initialize

    for (x = 0; x < X_SIZE; ++x) {
        for (y = 0; y < Y_SIZE; ++y) {
            matrix[x][y] = -1;
        }
    }
}
```

The outer loop is executed 60 times. This means the overhead associated with starting the inner loop is executed 60 times. If we reverse the order of the loops, we will have to deal with the inner loop only 30 times.

In general, loops should be ordered so the innermost loop is the most complex and the outermost loop is the simplest. Example 17-14 contains the init_matrix function with the loops reordered.

Example 17-14.   matrix/matrix3.cc

```
const int X_SIZE = 60;
const int Y_SIZE = 30;
```

Example 17-14.   matrix/matrix3.cc (Continued)

```
int matrix[X_SIZE][Y_SIZE];

void init_matrix(void)
{
    register int x, y;     // Current element to initialize

    for (y = 0; y < Y_SIZE; ++y) {
        for (x = 0; x < X_SIZE; ++x) {
            matrix[x][y] = -1;
        }
    }
}
```

The Power of Powers of 2

Indexing an array requires a multiply. For example, to execute the line:

```
matrix[x][y] = -1;
```

the program must compute the location where we want to put the -1. To do this, the program must perform the following steps:

1. Get the address of the **matrix**.

2. Compute x * Y_SIZE.

3. Compute y.

4. Add up all three parts to form the address. In C++ this code looks like:

```
*(matrix + (x * Y_SIZE) + y) = -1;
```

However you typically won't write matrix accesses this way because C++ handles the details. But being aware of the details can help you generate more efficient code.

Almost all C++ compilers will convert multiplies by a power of two (2, 4, 8, ...) into shifts, thus taking an expensive operation (multiply) and changing it into an inexpensive operation (shift).

For example:

```
i = 32 * j;
```

is compiled as:

```
i = j << 5; /* 2**5 == 32 */
```

Y_SIZE is 30, which is not a power of two. By increasing Y_SIZE to 32 we waste some memory but get a faster program.

Example 17-15 shows how we can take advantage of a power of two.

Example 17-15. matrix/matrix4.cc

```
const int X_SIZE = 60;
const int Y_SIZE = 32;

int matrix[X_SIZE][Y_SIZE];

void init_matrix(void)
{
    register int x, y;      // Current element to initialize

    for (y = 0; y < Y_SIZE; ++y) {
        for (x = 0; x < X_SIZE; ++x) {
            matrix[x][y] = -1;
        }
    }
}
```

Since we are initializing consecutive memory locations, we can initialize the matrix by starting at the first location and storing a -1 in the next X_SIZE *- Y_SIZE elements. Using this method, we cut the number of loops down to one. The indexing of the matrix has changed from a standard index (matrix[x][y]), requiring a shift and add, into a pointer de-referent (*matrix_ptr) and an increment (++matrix_ptr). In Example 17-16 we've turned our arrays into

Example 17-16. matrix/matrix5.cc

```
const int X_SIZE = 60;
const int Y_SIZE = 30;

int matrix[X_SIZE][Y_SIZE];

void init_matrix(void)
{
    register int index;        // Element counter
    register int *matrix_ptr;    // Current element

    matrix_ptr = &matrix[0][0];
    for (index = 0; index < X_SIZE * Y_SIZE; ++index) {
        *matrix_ptr = -1;
        ++matrix_ptr;
    }
}
```

pointers.But why have both a loop counter and a matrix_ptr? Couldn't we combine the two? In fact we can. In Example 17-17 we've successfully eliminated the loop counter by combining it with the array pointer.

Example 17-17. matrix/matrix6.cc

```
const int X_SIZE = 60;
const int Y_SIZE = 30;
```

Example 17-17.   matrix/matrix6.cc (Continued)

```
int matrix[X_SIZE][Y_SIZE];

void init_matrix(void)
{
    register int *matrix_ptr;    // Current element

    for (matrix_ptr = &matrix[0][0];
            matrix_ptr <= &matrix[X_SIZE - 1][Y_SIZE - 1];
            ++matrix_ptr) {

        *matrix_ptr = -1;
    }
}
```

The function is now well optimized. The only way we could make it better is to manually code it into assembly language. This might make it faster; however, assembly language is highly nonportable and very error-prone.

The library routine **memset** can be used to fill a matrix or array with a single character value. We can use it to initialize the matrix in this program. Frequently used library subroutines such as **memset** are often coded into assembly language and may make use of special processor-dependent tricks to do the job faster than could be done in C++. In Example 17-18 we let the function memset do the work.

Example 17-18.   matrix/matrix7.cc

```
#include <string.h>

const int X_SIZE = 60;
const int Y_SIZE = 30;

int matrix[X_SIZE][Y_SIZE];

void init_matrix(void)
{
    memset(matrix, -1, sizeof(matrix));
}
```

Now our function consists of only a single function call. It seems a shame to have to call a function just to call another function. We have to pay for the overhead of two function calls. It would be better if we called **memset** from the main function. Why don't we rewrite the code using **memset** instead of **init_matrix**? Because he has several hundred **init_matrix** calls and we don't want to do all that editing.

So how do we get rid of the overhead of a function call? By making the function inline.Our final version of the function uses inline to eliminate all the call overhead and can be seen in Example 17-19.

Example 17-19. matrix/matrix8.cc

```
#include <string.h>

const int X_SIZE = 60;
const int Y_SIZE = 30;

int matrix[X_SIZE][Y_SIZE];

inline void init_matrix(void)
{
    memset(matrix, -1, sizeof(matrix));
}
```

Question 17-1: *Why does* memset *successfully initialize the matrix to -1, but— when we try to use it to set every element to 1, we fail?*

```
#include <string.h>

const int X_SIZE = 60;
const int Y_SIZE = 30;

int matrix[X_SIZE][Y_SIZE];

inline void init_matrix(void) {
    memset(matrix, 1, sizeof(matrix));
}
```

How to Optimize

Our matrix initialization function illustrates several optimizing strategies. These are:

Removing invariant code

Code that does not need to be put inside a loop should be put outside the loop. For example:

```
for (i = 0; i < 10; ++i)
    matrix[i] = i + j * 10;
```

can be written as:

```
j_times_10 = j * 10;
for (i = 0; i < 10; ++i)
    matrix[i] = i + j_times_10;
```

Most good optimizing compilers will do this work for you if possible.

Loop ordering

Nested loops should be ordered with the simplest loop outermost and the most complex loops innermost.

Reduction in strength

This is a fancy way of saying use cheap operations instead of expensive ones. Table 17-1 lists the relative cost of common operations.

Table 17-1. Relative Cost of Operations

Operation	Relative Cost
File input and output (<< and >>), including the C functions `printf` and `scanf`.	1,000
`new` and `delete`	800
Trigonometric functions (sin, cos, ...)	500
Floating point (any operation)	100
Integer divide	30
Integer multiply	20
Function call	10
Simple array index	6
Shifts	5
Add/subtract	5
Pointer de-reference	2
Bitwise AND, OR, NOT	1
Logical AND, OR, NOT	1

NOTE

C formatting functions called using `scanf`, `printf`, and `sscanf` are extremely costly because they have to go through the format string one character at a time looking for a format conversion character (`%`). They then have to do a costly conversion between a character string and a number. These functions should be avoided in time-critical sections of code.

Reference parameters

Use constant reference parameters (`const` *type* `&`) instead of constant parameters for structures, unions, and classes.

Powers of 2

Use a power of 2 when doing integer multiply or divide. Most compilers will substitute a shift for the operation.

Pointers

Pointers are faster than indexing an array. They are also more tricky to use.

Inline functions

Using inline functions eliminates the overhead associated with a function call. It also can make the code bigger and a little more difficult to debug. (See case history below.)

Case Study: Inline Functions Versus Normal Functions

I once worked on writing a word-processing program for a large computer manufacturer. We had a function next_char that was used to get the next character
from the current file. It was used in thousands of places throughout the program.
When we first tested the program with next_char written as a function, the
program was unacceptably slow. Analyzing our program we found that 90
percent of the time was spent in next_char. So we changed it to an inline function. The speed doubled; however, our code size went up 40 percent and
required a memory expansion card to work. So the speed was all right, but the
size was unacceptable. We finally had to write the routine as a function in hand-
optimized assembly language to get both the size and the speed to acceptable
levels.

Case Study: Optimizing a Color-Rendering Algorithm

I once was asked to optimize a program that did color rendering for a large
picture. The problem was that the program took eight hours to process a single
picture. This limited us to doing one picture a day.

The first thing I did was run the program on a machine with a floating-point accel-
erator. This brought the time down to about six hours. Next I got permission to
use a high-speed RISC computer that belonged to another project but was
currently sitting idle. That reduced the time to two hours.

I saved six hours solely by using faster machines. No code had changed yet.

Two fairly simple functions were being called only once from the innermost loop.
Rewriting these functions as macros saved about 15 minutes.

Next I changed all the floating-point operations I could from floating-point to
integer. The savings amounted to 30 minutes out of a 1:45 run.

Then I noticed the program was spending about 5 minutes reading an ASCII file
containing a long list of floating-point numbers used in the conversion process.
Knowing that scanf is an extremely expensive function, I cut the initialization
process down to almost nothing by making the file binary. Total runtime was
now down to 1:10.

By carefully inspecting the code and using every trick I knew, I saved another 5
minutes, leaving me 5 minutes short of my goal of an hour per run. At this point

my project was refocused and the program put in mothballs for use at some future date.

Programming Exercises

Exercise 17-1: Take one of your previous programs and run it using the interactive debugger to examine several intermediate values.

Exercise 17-2: Write a matrix-multiply function. Create a test program that not only tests the function, but times it as well. Optimize the program using pointers and determine the time savings.

Exercise 17-3: Write a program to sum the elements in an array. Optimize it.

Exercise 17-4: Write a program that counts the number of bits in a character array. Optimize it through the use of register-integer variables. Time it on several different arrays of different sizes. How much time do you save?

Exercise 17-5: Write your own version of the library function memcpy. Optimize it. Most implementations of memcpy are written in assembly language and take advantage of all the quirks and tricks of the processor. How does your memcpy compare with theirs?

Answers to Chapter Questions

Answer 17-1: The problem is that memset is a *character* fill routine. An integer consists of 2 or 4 bytes (characters). Each byte is assigned the value 1. So a 2-byte integer will receive the value:

```
integer = 0x0101;
```

The 1-byte hex value for -1 is 0xFF. The 2-byte hex value of –1 is 0xFFFF. So we can take two single byte -1 values, put them together and come out with – 1. This works for zero also. Any other number will produce the wrong answer. For example, 1 is 0x01. Two bytes of this is 0x0101, or 257.

18

Operator Overloading

Overloaded, undermanned, ment to flounder, we Euchred God Almighty's storm, bluffed the Eternal Sea!

—Kipling

We all know what happens when we add two integers. But C++ doesn't have a built-in complex type, so it doesn't know how to add two complex numbers. However, through a C++ feature called *operator overloading*, you can "teach" C++ how to handle complex numbers. Operator overloading is used to define a set of functions to add, subtract, multiply and divide complex numbers using the normal operators +, -, *, and /.

In this section we define a complex number class. Let's start by defining the basic C++ complex class. A *complex number* consists of two parts, the real and the imaginary:

```
class complex
{
    protected:
        //
        // Complex numbers consist of two parts
        //
        double real_part;      // The real part
        double imaginary_part; // The imaginary part
        // ...
```

Next we define several member functions. These include the usual constructors and destructors as well as routines to get at the real and imaginary parts of the number.

```
    public:
        // Default constructor initializes the number to (0 + 0i)
        complex(void)
```

```
    {
        real_part = 0;
        imaginary_part = 0;
    }
    // Copy constructor - initialize one complex from another
    complex(const complex& other_complex)
    {
        real_part = other_complex.real_part;
        imaginary_part = other_complex.imaginary_part;
    }
    // Construct a complex from two reals
    // If only real supplied assume the imaginary part is .0
    complex(double init_real, double init_imaginary = 0.0)
    {
        real_part = init_real;
        imaginary_part = init_imaginary;
    }
    // Destructor does nothing
    ~complex() {}

    //
    // Functions to return the parts of the number
    //
    double real(void) const    // "const" is discussed later
    {
        return (real_part);
    }
    double imaginary(void) const
    {
        return (imaginary_part);
    }

    // Define functions to set parts of a number
    void set_real(double real) {
        real_part = real;
    }
    void set_imaginary(double imaginary) {
        imaginary_part = imaginary;
    }

};
```

NOTE

As you may recall, the const appearing after some functions was discussed in Chapter 14, *More on Classes*.

Now we want to use our complex numbers. Declaring variables is simple. Even initializing them with numbers such as (3 + 2i) is easy.

```
complex start;    // Starting point for the graph
complex end(3.0, 2.0);    // Ending point
```

But what happens when we want to add two complex numbers? We need to define a function to do it:

```
// Version 1 of the complex add function
inline complex add(const complex &oper1, const complex &oper2)
{
    complex result(oper1.real() + oper2.real(),
                   oper1.imaginary() + oper2.imaginary());
    return (result);
}
```

A few things should be noted about this function. First, we defined it to take two complex numbers and return a complex number. That way we group additions:

```
// Add three complex numbers
answer = add(first, add(second, third));
```

Constant reference parameters are used (`const complex &`) for our two arguments. This is the most efficient way of passing structures into a function. Finally, because it is such a small function, we've defined it as an inline function for efficiency.

In this function, we explicitly declare a result and return it. We can do both in one step:

```
// Version 2 of the complex add function
inline complex add(const complex &oper1, const complex &oper2)
{
    return (complex(oper1.real() + oper2.real(),
                    oper1.imaginary() + oper2.imaginary()));
}
```

Although it is a little harder to understand, it is more efficient.

It is important to understand what C++ does behind your back. Even such a simple statement as:

```
answer = add(first, second);
```

calls a constructor, an assignment operator, and a destructor–all in that little piece of code.

In version 1 of the **add** function we explicitly allocated a variable for the result. In version 2, C++ automatically creates a temporary variable for the result. This number has no name and doesn't really exist outside the **return** statement.

Creating the temporary variable causes the constructor to be called. The temporary variable is then assigned to **answer**; thus we have a call to the assignment function. After the assignment, C++ no longer has any use for the temporary variable and throws it away by calling the destructor.

Operator Functions

Using the **add** function for complex numbers is a little awkward. It would be nice to be able to convince C++ to automatically call this function whenever we try to add two complex numbers together with the + operator. That's where operator overloading comes in. All we have to do is to write the **add** function as:

```
inline complex operator +(const complex &oper1, const complex &oper2)
{
    return (complex(oper1.real() + oper2.real(),
                    oper1.imaginary() + oper2.imaginary()));
}
```

and C++ handles the rest.

Note: The operator overloading functions should be used carefully. You should try to design them so they follow common-sense rules. That is, + should have something to do with addition; −, with subtraction; and so on. The C++ I/O streams break this rule by defining the shift operators (<< and >>) as input and output operators. This can lead to some confusion, such as:

```
cout << 8 << 2;
```

Does this output "8" followed by "2," or does it output the value of the expression (8 << 2)? Unless you're an expert you can't tell. In this case the numbers "8" and "2" will be output.

You've seen how you can overload the + operator. Now let's explore what other operators you can use.

Binary Arithmetic Operators

Binary operators take two arguments, one on each side of the operator. For example, multiplication and division are binary operators:

```
x * y;
a / b;
```

Unary operators take a single parameter. Unary operators include unary − and the address of (&) operator;

```
-x
&y
```

The binary arithmetic operator functions take two constant parameters and produce a result. One of the parameters must be a class or structure. The result can be anything. For example, the following functions are legal for binary addition:

```
complex operator +(complex v1, complex v2);
complex operator +(complex v1, real v2);
```

```
complex operator +(real v1,    complex v2);
complex operator +(real v1,    real v2);
```

We've had to define a lot of different functions just to support the addition of our complex class. Such diarrhea of the definition is typical when overloading operators.

Table 18-1 lists the binary operators that can be overloaded.

Table 18-1. Binary Operators That Can Be Overloaded

Operator	Meaning
+	Addition
−	Subtraction
*	Multiplication
/	Division
%	Modulus
^	Bitwise exclusive OR
&	Bitwise AND
|	Bitwise OR
<<	Left shift
>>	Right shift

Relational Operators

The relational operators include such things as equals (==) and not equals (!=). Normally they take two constant classes and return either a 0 or a 1. (Actually they can return anything, but that would violate the spirit of relational operators.)

The equality operator for our complex class is:

```
inline int operator == (const complex &oper1, const complex &oper2)
{
    return ((oper1.real() == oper2.real(),
            oper1.imaginary() == oper2.imaginary()));
}
```

Table 18-2 lists the relational operators.

Table 18-2. Relational Operators

Operator	Meaning
==	Equality
!=	Inequality
<	Less than
>	Greater than

Table 18-2. Relational Operators (Continued)

Operator	Meaning
<=	Less than or equal to
>=	Greater than or equal to

Unary operators

Unary operators, such as negative (–), take a single parameter. The negative operator for our complex type is:

```
inline complex operator -(const complex &oper)
{
    return (complex(-oper.real(), -oper.imaginary()));
}
```

Table 18-3 lists the unary operators.

Table 18-3. Unary Operators

Operator	Meaning
+	Positive
–	Negative
*	Dereference
&	Address of
~	Ones complement

Shortcut Operators

Operators such as += and -= are shortcuts for more complicated operators. But what are the return values of += and -=? A very close examination of the C++ standard reveals that these operators return the value of the variable after the increase or decrease. For example:

```
i = 5;
j = i += 2;    // Don't code like this
```

assigns j the value 7. The += function for our complex class is:

```
inline complex &operator +=(complex &oper1, const complex &oper2)
{
    oper1.set_real(oper1.real() + oper2.real());
    oper1.set_imaginary(oper1.imaginary() + oper2.imaginary());
    return (oper1);
}
```

Note that unlike the other operator functions we've defined, the first parameter is not a constant. Also we, return a reference to the first variable, not a new variable or a copy of the first parameter.

Table 18-4 lists the shortcut operators.

Table 18-4. Simple Shortcut Operators

Operator	Meaning
+=	Increase
-=	Decrease
*=	Multiply by
/=	Divide by
%=	Remainder
^=	Exclusive OR into
&=	AND into
|=	OR into
<<=	Shift left
>>=	Shift right

Increment and Decrement Operators

The increment and decrement operators have two forms: prefix and suffix. For example:

```
i = 5;
j = i++;     // j = 5
i = 5;
j = ++i;     // j = 6
```

Both these operators use a function named **operator++**. So how do you tell them apart? The C++ language contains a hack to handle this case. The prefix form of the operator takes one argument, the item to be incremented. The suffix takes two, the item to be incremented and an integer. The actual integer used is meaningless; it's just a position holder to differentiate the two forms of the operation.

If we define ++ for the complex type to mean increment the real part, then our functions to handle the two forms of ++ are:

```
// Prefix      x = ++c
inline complex &operator ++(complex &oper)
{
    oper.set_real(oper.real() + 1.0);
    return (oper);
}

// Suffix      x = c++
inline complex operator ++(complex oper, int)
{
    complex result(oper);   // Result before we incremented
    oper.set_real(oper.real() + 1.0);
```

```
        return (result);
}
```

This is messy. C++ has reduced us to using cute tricks: the unused integer parameter. In actual practice, I never use the suffix version of increment and always put the prefix version on a line by itself. That way, I can avoid most of these problems.

The choice, prefix versus suffix, was decided by looking at the code for the two versions. As you can see, the prefix version is much simpler than the suffix version. So restricting yourself to the prefix version not only simplifies your code, but it also makes the compiler's job a little easier.

Table 18-5 lists the increment and decrement operators.

Table 18-5. Increment and Decrement operators

Operator	Meaning
++	Increment
--	Decrement

Logical Operators

Logical operators include AND (&&), OR (||), and NOT (!). They can be overloaded, but just because you *can* do it doesn't mean you should. In theory, logical operators work only on Boolean values. In practice, because C++ doesn't have a Boolean type, they work on integers. Don't confuse the issue more by overloading them.

Table 18-6 lists the logical operators.

Table 18-6. Logical Operators

Operation	Meaning
||	Logical OR
&&	Logical AND
!	Logical NOT

I/O Operators

You've been using the operators << and >> for input and output. Actually these operators are overloaded versions of the shift operators. This has the advantage of making I/O fairly simple, at the cost of some minor confusion.

We would like to be able to output our complex numbers just like any other data type. To do this we need to define a << operator for it.

We are sending our data to the output stream class **ostream**. The data itself is complex. So our output function is:

```
inline ostream &operator << (ostream &out_file, const complex &number)
{
    out_file << '(' << number.real() << ',' <<
                number.imaginary() << ')';
    return (out_file);
}
```

The function returns a reference to the output file. This enables the caller to string a series of << operations together, such as:

```
complex a_complex(1.2, 3.4);
cout << "The answer is " << a_complex << '\n';
```

The result of this code is:

```
The answer is (1.2, 3.4)
```

Normally the << operator takes two constant arguments. In this case the first parameter is a non-constant **ostream**. This is because the << operator when used for output has side effects, the major one being that the data goes to the output stream. In general, however, it's not a good idea to add side effects to an operator that doesn't already have them.

Input should be just as simple as output. You might think all we have to do is read the numbers (and the related extra characters):

```
// Simple-minded input operation
inline istream &operator >> (istream &in_file, complex &number) {
    double real, imaginary;  // Parts of the number
    char l_paren, comma, r_paren; // Extra chracters output as part of
    in_file >> l_paren >> real >> comma >> imaginary >> r_paren;
    number.set(real, imaginary);
    return (in_file);
}
```

In practice, it's not so simple. First of all, we must call a special member function **ipfx** to tell the I/O system that we are planning a formatted read.

```
inline istream &operator >> (istream &in_file, complex &number)
{
    // ...
    in_file.ipfx(1);     // Tell the I/O system we are reading formatted
```

Next we skip any leading white space.

```
    in_file >> ws;       // Skip white space
```

We should now be pointing to the "(" at the beginning of the number. But before we can read this character, we need to check for trouble and abort if necessary.

```
    if (in_file.bad()) return (in_file);
```

Now, let's grab the "(". Of course, just to make sure, we check to see that we really get a "(" and abort if necessary.

```
in_file >> ch;          // Get character after white space
if (ch != '(') {
    in_file.set(ios::failbit);        // We have an error
    return (in_file);
}
```

The function **set** is used to set a flag indicating that the input operation found a problem. This allows the caller to test to see whether the input worked by calling the **bad** function. (This function can also cause an exception to be thrown. See Chapter 22, *Exceptions*, for more information.)

We have reached the "(". Let's read the real part of the number.

```
in_file >> real;
```

Now we take care of the "," and related white space between the numbers. At each step we check for errors:

```
if (in_file.bad()) return (in_file);
in_file >> ws >> ch;        // Get first character after number
if (in_file.bad()) return (in_file);

if (ch != ',') {
    in_file.set(ios::failbit);
    return (in_file);
}
```

Next is the imaginary part.

```
in_file >> imaginary;
```

Finally, we make sure that the number ends with a ")".

```
in_file >> ws >> ch;
if (in_file.bad()) return (in_file);

if (ch != ')') {
    in_file.set(ios::failbit);
    return (in_file);
}
```

The work's complete, so we store the result and get out.

```
number.set(real, imaginary);
return (in_file);
}
```

The complete version of the complex reader (pun intended) appears in Example 18-1.

Example 18-1

```
inline istream &operator >> (istream &in_file, complex &number)
{
    double real, imaginary;  // Real and imaginary part
    char ch;                 // Random character used to verify input

    number.set(0.0, 0.0);        // Initialize the number (just in case)

    in_file.ipfx(1);     // Tell the I/O system we are reading formatted
    in_file >> ws;       // Skip white space

    if (in_file.bad()) return (in_file);

    in_file >> ch;       // Get character after white space
    if (ch != '(') {
        in_file.set(ios::failbit);      // We have an error
        return (in_file);
    }

    in_file >> real;

    if (in_file.bad()) return (in_file);

    in_file >> ws >> ch;         // Get first character after number

    if (in_file.bad()) return (in_file);

    if (ch != ',') {
        in_file.set(ios::failbit);
        return (in_file);
    }

    in_file >> imaginary;

    in_file >> ws >> ch;
    if (in_file.bad()) return (in_file);

    if (ch != ')') {
        in_file.set(ios::failbit);
        return (in_file);
    }
    number.set(real, imaginary);
    return (in_file);
}
```

Index Operator "[ ]"

The operator [ ] is used by C++ to index arrays. As we will see in Chapter 20, *Advanced Pointers*, this operator is very useful when defining a class that mimics an array. Normally, this function takes two arguments, a class that simulates an array and an index, and returns a reference to an item in the array.

```
double &operator[](array_class &array, int index)
```

We cover the [] operator in more detail in Chapter 23, *Modular Programming*.

new and delete

We'll say very little about overloading the global operators **new** and **delete** at this time. First of all, they aren't introduced until Chapter 20, *Advanced Pointers*, so you don't know what they do. Second, when you know what they do, you won't want to override them.

I've seen only one program where the **new** and **delete** operators were over-ridden (or at least their C equivalents). That program was written by a very clever programmer who liked to do everything a little strangely. The result was code that was a nightmare to debug.

So unless you are a very clever programmer, leave **new** and **delete** alone. And if you are a clever programmer, please leave **new** and **delete** alone anyway. Some day I might have to debug your code.

Exotic Operators

C++ contains a very rich set of operators. Some of these are rarely, if ever, used. These include:

() Allows you to define a default function for a class.

, Comma operator. Allows two expressions to be concatenated. It is rarely used and probably should not be overloaded.

->* Pointer to member. Rarely used.

-> Class member.

All of these operators are discussed in Chapter 28, *C++'s Dustier Corners*.

Operator Member Functions

So far we've been using operator overloading functions just like ordinary functions. They can also be defined as member functions. The only difference is that as member functions the first argument, the class itself, is implied. So, for example, you can write the operator += as an ordinary function or as a member function. Here's the ordinary version that you've already seen.

```
inline complex &operator +=(complex &oper1, const complex &oper2)
{
    oper1.set_real(oper1.real() + oper2.real());
    oper1.set_imaginary(oper1.imaginary() + oper2.imaginary());
    return (oper1);
}
```

Here's the member function:

```
class complex {
    // .....
    public:
        inline complex &operator +=(const complex &oper2)
        {
            real_part += oper2.real();
            imaginary_part += oper2.imaginary();
            return (*this);
        }
```

The only trick used in this function is the keyword `this`. This is a predefined variable that refers to the current object. For example, you can access the data member `real_part` using the statement:

```
real_part += oper2.real();
```

The same statement can be written as:

```
this->real_part += oper2.real();
```

In most cases, you don't need to use `this`. However, in a few, such as the `+=` operator, it comes in handy.

Which flavor of the operator overloading functions should you use? The one that makes your program the clearest and easiest to read. In general, we use the standard functions for the simple operators, such as +, -, *, and /, while I use member functions for the shortcut and unary operators, such as +=, -=, ++, and unary -.

Some overloaded functions only work as member functions. These include the casting operators as well as class specific versions of `new` and `delete`.

Casting

Finally we come to the cast operators. Casting is a way of changing one type to another. For example, let's say that when we cast our `complex` type to a `double`, we want the real part. We can define a cast operator for this function as:

```
class complex:
    public:
        // (We didn't really put this in our complex class)
        double operator double() {return (real_part);}
```

C++ automatically calls this function whenever it wants to turn a `complex` into a `double`.

The trouble is that by defining a cast, you give C++ something else that it can call behind your back. Personally, I like to know whenever C++ calls something, so I avoid creating cast operators. Unless you have a very good reason to define one, don't create a cast operator function.

Full Definition of the Complex Class

Example 18-2 lists the entire complex class. The beginning of the header file summarizes all the functions that are defined. In creating this class I discovered that it consisted of many (29 to be exact) little one- and two-line functions. Commenting each of these with a full-function comment block would obscure the code. In other words, this is one of the few cases (the *very* few) where adding comments would cause confusion, so most of the small functions have no comments.

When creating this class, I noticed that a lot of the functions have a similar structure. For example, += looks a lot like -= and so on. As a matter of fact, I created the -= operator by copying the += functions and editing a little. C++ contains a rich operator set that causes this sort of repetition to happen when you're trying to define a complete set of operators for a class.

Finally, the simple operations are defined in the file *complex.h* while the longer functions are left in the file *complex.cc.*

Example 18-2. complex/complex.h, complex/complex.cc

File: complex.h

```
#ifndef __complex_h__    // Avoid double includes
#define __complex_h__    // Prevent double include

#include <iostream.h>
#include <math.h>

/************************************************************
 * Complex class                                           *
 *                                                         *
 * Members defined                                         *
 *      complex()                  // Default constructor  *
 *      complex(real, imaginary)// Specify two parts       *
 *                              // for construction        *
 *      complex(complex)          // Copy constructor       *
 *                                                         *
 *      real()                    // Get real part          *
 *      imaginary()               // Get imaginary part     *
 *                                                         *
 *      set(real, imaginary)      // Set both parts of #    *
 *      set_real(real)            // Set real part of #     *
 *      set_imaginary(imaginary)// Set imaginary part       *
 *                                                         *
 * Operator member functions                               *
 *                      c -- a complex number              *
 *                      s -- a scalar (double)             *
 *      c = c                                              *
 *      c += c;                                            *
```

Example 18-2. complex/complex.h, complex/complex.cc (Continued)

```
*        c += s;                                               *
*        c -= c;                                               *
*        c -= s;                                               *
*        c /= c;                                               *
*        c /= s;                                               *
*        c *= c;                                               *
*        c *= s;                                               *
*                                                              *
* The following functions don't really make a lot of          *
* sense for complex numbers, but they are defined              *
* for the purpose of illustration                              *
*        c++                                                   *
*        ++c                                                   *
*        c--                                                   *
*        --c                                                   *
*                                                              *
* Arithmetic operators defined                                 *
*        c = c + c;                                            *
*        c = s + c;                                            *
*        c = c + s;                                            *
*        c = c - c;                                            *
*        c = s - c;                                            *
*        c = c - s;                                            *
*        c = c * c;                                            *
*        c = s * c;                                            *
*        c = c * s;                                            *
*        c = c / c;                                            *
*        c = s / c;                                            *
*        c = c / s;                                            *
*        -c                                                    *
*        +c                                                    *
*        ostream << c    // Output function                    *
*        istream >> c    // Input function                     *
****************************************************************/
class complex
{
    private:
        //
        // Complex numbers consist of two parts
        //
        double real_part;       // The real part
        double imaginary_part;  // The imaginary part

    public:
        // Default constructor, zero everything
        complex(void)
        {
            real_part = 0.0;
            imaginary_part = 0.0;
        }

        // Copy constructor
```

Example 18-2. complex/complex.h, complex/complex.cc (Continued)

```
    complex(const complex& other_complex)
    {
        real_part = other_complex.real_part;
        imaginary_part = other_complex.imaginary_part;
    }

    // Construct a complex out of two real numbers
    complex(double init_real, double init_imaginary = 0.0)
    {
        real_part = init_real;
        imaginary_part = init_imaginary;
    }

    // Destructor does nothing
    ~complex() {}

    //
    // Function to return the parts of the number
    //
    double real(void) const
    {
        return (real_part);
    }
    double imaginary(void) const
    {
        return (imaginary_part);
    }

    // Functions to set parts of a number
    void set(double real, double imaginary) {
        real_part = real;
        imaginary_part = imaginary;
    }

    void set_real(double real) {
        real_part = real;
    }

    void set_imaginary(double imaginary) {
        imaginary_part = imaginary;
    }

    complex operator = (const complex& oper2) {
        complex result(oper2);
        return (result);
    }

    complex& operator += (const complex& oper2) {
        real_part += oper2.real();
        imaginary_part += oper2.imaginary();
        return (*this);
    }
```

Example 18-2. complex/complex.h, complex/complex.cc (Continued)

```
    complex& operator += (double oper2) {
        real_part += oper2;
        return (*this);
    }

    complex& operator -= (const complex& oper2) {
        real_part -= oper2.real();
        imaginary_part -= oper2.imaginary();
        return (*this);
    }

    complex& operator -= (double oper2) {
        real_part -= oper2;
        return (*this);
    }

    complex& operator *= (const complex& oper2) {
        // Place to hold the real part of the result
        // while we compute the imaginary part
        double real_result = real_part * oper2.real() -
                             imaginary_part * oper2.imaginary();

        imaginary_part = real_part * oper2.imaginary() +
                         imaginary_part * oper2.real();

        real_part = real_result;
        return *this;
    }

    complex& operator *= (double oper2) {
        real_part *= oper2;
        imaginary_part *= oper2;
        return (*this);
    }

    complex& operator /= (const complex& oper2);

    complex& operator /= (double oper2) {
        real_part /= oper2;
        imaginary_part /= oper2;
        return (*this);
    }

    // c++
    complex operator ++(int) {
        complex result(*this);
        real_part += 1.0;
        return (result);
    }

    // ++c
```

Example 18-2. complex/complex.b, complex/complex.cc (Continued)

```
            complex &operator ++(void) {
                real_part += 1.0;
                return (*this);
            }

            // c--
            complex operator --(int) {
                complex result(*this);
                real_part -= 1.0;
                return (result);
            }

            // --c
            complex &operator --(void) {
                real_part -= 1.0;
                return (*this);
            }
};

inline complex operator + (const complex& oper1, const complex& oper2)
{
    return complex(oper1.real()      + oper2.real(),
                   oper1.imaginary() + oper2.imaginary());
}

inline complex operator + (const complex& oper1, double oper2)
{
    return complex(oper1.real() + oper2,
                   oper1.imaginary());
}

inline complex operator + (double oper1, const complex& oper2)
{
    return complex(oper1 + oper2.real(),
                   oper2.imaginary());
}

inline complex operator - (const complex& oper1, const complex& oper2)
{
    return complex(oper1.real()      - oper2.real(),
                   oper1.imaginary() - oper2.imaginary());
}

inline complex operator - (const complex& oper1, double oper2)
{
    return complex(oper1.real() - oper2,
                   oper1.imaginary());
}

inline complex operator - (double oper1, const complex& oper2)
{
    return complex(oper1 - oper2.real(),
```

Example 18-2. complex/complex.h, complex/complex.cc (Continued)

```
                    -oper2.imaginary());
}

inline complex operator * (const complex& oper1, const complex& oper2)
{
  return complex(
     oper1.real() * oper2.real() - oper1.imaginary() * oper2.imaginary(),
     oper1.real() * oper2.imaginary() + oper1.imaginary() * oper2.real());
}

inline complex operator * (const complex& oper1, const double oper2)
{
  return complex(oper1.real()      * oper2,
                 oper1.imaginary() * oper2);
}

inline complex operator * (const double oper1, const complex& oper2)
{
  return complex(oper1 * oper2.real(),
                 oper1 * oper2.imaginary());
}

extern complex operator / (const complex &oper1, const complex &oper2);

inline complex operator / (const double &oper1, const complex &oper2) {
    return (complex(oper1, 0.0) / oper2);
}

inline complex operator / (const complex &oper1, const double &oper2) {
    return (oper1 / complex(oper2, 0.0));
}

inline int operator == (const complex& oper1, const complex& oper2)
{
  return ((oper1.real() == oper2.real()) &&
          (oper1.imaginary() == oper2.imaginary()));
}

inline int operator != (const complex& oper1, const complex& oper2)
{
  return (!(oper1 == oper2));
}

inline complex operator - (const complex& oper1)
{
  return complex(-oper1.real(), -oper1.imaginary());
}

inline complex operator + (const complex& oper1)
{
  return complex(+oper1.real(), +oper1.imaginary());
}
```

Example 18-2. complex/complex.h, complex/complex.cc (Continued)

```
inline ostream &operator << (ostream &out_file, const complex &number)
{
    out_file << '(' << number.real() << ',' << number.imaginary() << ')';
    return (out_file);
}

extern istream &operator >> (istream &in_file, complex &number);

#endif /* __complex_h__ */        // Avoid double includes
```

File: complex.cc

```
#include "complex.h"

/********************************************************
 * c = c / c -- complex division                       *
 *                                                      *
 * Parameters                                           *
 *      oper1, oper2 -- two operands of the divide      *
 *                                                      *
 * Returns                                              *
 *      result of the divide                            *
 ********************************************************/
complex operator / (const complex& oper1, const complex& oper2)
{
  // Denominator of the result
  double den = fabs(oper2.real()) + fabs(oper2.imaginary());

  // Real part of the oper1 factor
  double oper1_real_den = oper1.real() / den;
  // Imaginary part of the oper1 factor
  double oper1_imag_den = oper1.imaginary() / den;

  // Real part of the oper2 factor
  double oper2_real_den = oper2.real() / den;
  // Imaginary part of the oper2 factor
  double oper2_imag_den = oper2.imaginary() / den;

  // Normalization factor
  double normalization   = oper2_real_den * oper2_real_den +
                           oper2_imag_den * oper2_imag_den;

  return complex((oper1_real_den * oper2_real_den +
                  oper1_imag_den * oper2_imag_den) / normalization,
                 (oper1_imag_den * oper2_real_den -
                  oper1_real_den * oper2_imag_den) / normalization);
}


/********************************************************
 *  c /= c -- complex divide by                        *
 *                                                     *
```

Example 18-2. complex/complex.h, complex/complex.cc (Continued)

```
 *  Parameters                                            *
 *       oper2 -- operator to divide by                   *
 *                                                        *
 *  Returns                                               *
 *       reference to the result of the divide            *
 ********************************************************/
complex& complex::operator /= (const complex& oper2)
{
    // Denominator of the result
    double den = fabs(oper2.real()) + fabs(oper2.imaginary());

    // Denominator -- operator 1 real part
    double oper1_real_den = real_part / den;

    // Denominator -- operator 1 imaginary part
    double oper1_imag_den = imaginary_part / den;

    // Denominator -- operator 2 real part
    double oper2_real_den = oper2.real() / den;

    // Denominator -- operator 2 imaginary part
    double oper2_imag_den = oper2.imaginary() / den;

    // Normalization factor
    double normalization = oper2_real_den * oper2_real_den +
                           oper2_imag_den * oper2_imag_den;
    real_part      = (oper1_real_den * oper2_real_den +
                      oper1_imag_den * oper2_imag_den) / normalization;
    imaginary_part = (oper1_imag_den * oper2_real_den -
                      oper1_real_den * oper2_imag_den) / normalization;
    return (*this);
}


/*********************************************************
 *  istream >> complex -- read a complex number          *
 *                                                        *
 *  Parameters                                            *
 *       in_file -- file to read                          *
 *       number -- place to put the number                *
 *                                                        *
 *  Returns                                               *
 *       reference to the input file                      *
 ********************************************************/
istream &operator >> (istream &in_file, complex &number)
{
    double real, imaginary;  // Real and imaginary part
    char ch;                 // Random character used to verify input

    number.set(0.0, 0.0);        // Initialize the number (just in case)

    in_file.ipfx(1);     // Tell the I/O system we are reading formatted
    in_file >> ws;       // Skip white space
```

Example 18-2. complex/complex.h, complex/complex.cc (Continued)

```
    if (in_file.bad()) return (in_file);

    in_file >> ch;        // Get character after white space
    if (ch != '(') {
        in_file.setf(ios::failbit);      // We have an error
        return (in_file);
    }

    in_file >> real;

    if (in_file.bad()) return (in_file);

    in_file >> ws >> ch;          // Get first character after number

    if (in_file.bad()) return (in_file);

    if (ch != ',') {
        in_file.setf(ios::failbit);
        return (in_file);
    }

    in_file >> imaginary;

    in_file >> ws >> ch;
    if (in_file.bad()) return (in_file);

    if (ch != ')') {
        in_file.setf(ios::failbit);
        return (in_file);
    }
    number.set(real, imaginary);
    return (in_file);
}
```

Question 18-1: *Why does Example 18-3 fail? When run it prints out:*

```
    Copy constructor called
    Copy constructor called
```

over and over. Hint: Review the section "Copy Constructor" in Chapter 13. Thanks to Jeff Hewett for this problem.

Example 18-3. equal/equal.cc

```
1 #include <iostream.h>
2
3 class trouble {
4     public:
5         int data;
6
7         trouble(void);
8         trouble(const trouble &old);
9         trouble operator = (trouble old_trouble);
```

Example 18-3. equal/equal.cc (Continued)

```
10 };
11
12 trouble::trouble(void) {
13     data = 0;
14 }
15
16 trouble::trouble(const trouble &old) {
17     cout << "Copy constructor called\n";
18     *this = old;
19 }
20
21 trouble trouble::operator = (trouble old_trouble) {
22     cout << "Operator = called\n";
23     data = old_trouble.data;
24     return (*this);
25 }
26
27 int main()
28 {
29     trouble trouble1;
30     trouble trouble2(trouble1);
31
32     return (0);
33 }
```

Programming Exercises

Exercise 18-1: Write a class to handle mixed fractions such as "1 1/3." Define addition, subtraction, multiplication, and division operators for these fractions. For example: 1 1/3 + 2 1/2 = 3 5/6.

Exercise 18-2: Write a fixed-point number class to handle numbers. All numbers are of the form DDDDD.D. In other words, all numbers have only a single digit to the right of the decimal point. Use integers to implement this class.

Exercise 18-3: Write a class to implement a sparse integer array. This is much like a simple integer array:

```
int simple_array[100];
```

But unlike a simple array, the indices can go from 0 to 1,000,000. That's the bad news. The good news is that at most 100 elements will be set at any time. The rest of the elements will be zero.

Exercise 18-4: Write a time class. Implement functions to add, subtract, read, and print times.

Exercise 18-5: Write a date class that allows you to add, subtract, read, and print simple dates of the form MM/DD. Assume year is not a leap year.

Exercise 18-6: (Advanced) Write a full-date class that allows you to add, subtract, read, and print dates of the form MM/DD/YY.

Answers to Chapter Questions

Answer 18-1: The copy constructor calls the **operator** = function. The parameter list to this function is:

```
trouble trouble::operator = (trouble old_trouble) {
```

The parameter to this function is being passed as a call-by-value parameter. When C++ sees this type of parameter it calls the copy constructor to put the parameter on the stack.

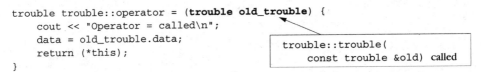

```
trouble trouble::operator = (trouble old_trouble) {
    cout << "Operator = called\n";
    data = old_trouble.data;
    return (*this);
}
```

trouble::trouble(
        const trouble &old) called

So we have an infinite loop. The copy constructor calls the **operator** = function. C++ sees the call-by-value parameter and calls the copy constructor, which calls **operator** = and causes the copy constructor to be called. This keeps up until the system runs out of stack space or the user gets disgusted and aborts the program.

The solution is to pass the parameter to **operator** = as a reference. This not only is more efficient, but also works.

```
trouble trouble::operator = (const trouble &old_trouble) {
```

19

Floating Point

1 is equal to 2 for sufficiently large values of 1.
—Anonymous

Computers handle integers very well. The arithmetic is simple, exact, and fast. Floating point is the opposite. Computers do floating-point arithmetic only with great difficulty.

This chapter discusses some of the problems that can occur with floating point. In order to address the principles involved in floating-point arithmetic, we have defined a simple decimal floating-point format. We suggest you put aside your computer and work through these problems using pencil and paper so you can see firsthand the problems and pitfalls that occur.

The format used by computers is very similar to the one defined in this chapter, except that instead of using base 10, computers use base 2, 8, or 16. However, all the problems demonstrated here on paper can occur in a computer.

Floating-Point Format

Floating point numbers consist of three parts: a sign, a fraction, and an exponent. Our fraction is expressed as a four-digit decimal. The exponent is a single-decimal digit. So our format is:

$$\pm f.fff \times 10^{\pm e}$$

where:

±   is the sign (plus or minus).

f.fff is the four-digit fraction.

±e   is the single-digit exponent.

Zero is $+0.000 \times 10^{+0}$. We represent these numbers in "E" format: $\pm f.fff\text{E}\pm e$.

This format is similar to the floating-point format used in many computers. The IEEE has defined a floating-point standard (#742), but not all machines use it.

Table 19-1 shows some typical floating-point numbers.

Table 19-1. Floating-Point Examples

Notation	Number
+1.000E+0	1.0
+3.300E+5	33000.0
-8.223E-3	-0.008223
+0.000E+0	0.0

The floating-point operations defined in this chapter follow a rigid set of rules. To minimize errors we make use of a *guard digit.* That is an extra digit added to the end of the fraction during computation. Many computers use a guard digit in their floating-point units.

Floating Addition/Subtraction

To add two numbers like 2.0 and 0.3, the computer must perform the following steps:

1. Start with the numbers.

    +2.000E+0   The number is 2.0

    +3.000E-1   The number is 0.3

2. Add guard digits to both numbers.

    +2.0000E+0   The number is 2.0

    +3.0000E-1   The number is 0.3

3. Shift the number with the smallest exponent to the right one digit and increment its exponent. Continue until the exponents of the two numbers match.

    +2.0000E+0   The number is 2.0

    +0.3000E-0   The number is 0.3

4. Add the two fractions. The result has the same exponent as the two numbers.

+2.0000E+0   The number is 2.0

+0.3000E-0   The number is 0.3

+2.3000E+0   Result 2.3

5. Normalize the number by shifting it left or right until there is just one non-zero digit to the left of the decimal point. Adjust the exponent accordingly. A number like +0.1234E+0 would be normalized to +1.2340E-1. Because the number +2.3000E+0 is already normalized, we do nothing.

6. Finally, if the guard digit is greater than or equal to 5, round the next digit up. Otherwise, truncate the number.

+2.3000E+0   Round last digit

+2.300E+0   Result 2.3

7. For floating-point subtraction, change the sign of the second operand and add.

Multiplication

When we want to multiply two numbers such as 0.12 × 11.0, the following rules apply.

1. Add the guard digit.

+1.2000E-1   The number is 0.12

+1.1000E+1   The number is 11.0

2. Multiply the two fractions and add the exponents. (1.2 × 1.1 = 1.32) (−1 + 1 = 0)

+1.2000E-1   The number is 0.12

+1.1000E+1   The number is 11.0

+1.3200E+0   The result is 1.32

3. Normalize the result. If the guard digit is less than or equal to 5, round the next digit up. Otherwise, truncate the number.

+1.3200E+0   The number is 1.32

Notice that in multiply, you didn't have to go through all that shifting. The rules for multiplication are a lot shorter than those for add. Integer multiplication is a lot slower than integer addition. In floating point, multiplication speed is a lot closer to that of addition.

Division

To divide numbers like 100.0 by 30.0, we must perform the following steps.

1. Add the guard digit.

    +1.0000E+2   The number is 100.0

    +3.0000E+1   The number is 30.0

2. Divide the fractions, and subtract the exponents.

    +1.0000E+2   The number is 100.0

    +3.0000E+1   The number is 30.0
    _____

    +0.3333E+1   The result is 3.333

3. Normalize the result.

    +3.3330E+0   The result is 3.333

4. If the guard digit is less than or equal to 5, round the next digit up. Otherwise, truncate the number.

    +3.333E+0   The result is 3.333

Overflow and Underflow

There are limits to the size of the number a computer can handle. What are the results of the following calculation?

    9.000E+9 × 9.000E+9

Multiplying it out, we get:

    8.1×10^{19}

However, we are limited to a single-digit exponent, too small to hold 19. This is an example of *overflow* (sometimes called exponent overflow). Some computers generate a trap when this occurs, thus interrupting the program and causing an error message to be printed. Others are not so nice and generate a wrong answer (like 8.100E+9). Computers that follow the IEEE floating-point standard generate a special value called +Infinity.

Underflow occurs when the numbers become too small for the computer to handle. Example:

    1.000E-9 × 1.000E-9

The result is:

    1.0×10^{-18}

Because −18 is too small to fit into one digit, we have underflow.

Roundoff Error

Floating point is not exact. Everyone knows that 1 + 1 is 2, but did you know that 1/3 + 1/3 = 2/3? This can be shown by the following floating-point calculations:

2/3 as floating point is 6.667E-1

1/3 as floating point is 3.333-1

> +3.333E-1

> +3.333E-1

> ─────────────────────

> +6.666E-1, or 0.6666

which is not:

> +6.667E-1

Every computer has a similar problem with its floating point. For example, the number 0.2 has no exact representation in binary floating point.

Floating point should never be used for money. Because we are used to dealing with dollars and cents, it is tempting to define the amount $1.98 as:

```
float amount = 1.98;
```

However, the more calculations you do with floating point, the bigger the roundoff error. Banks, credit cards, and the IRS tend to be very fussy about money. Giving the IRS a check that's almost right is not going to make them happy. Money should be stored as an integer number of pennies.

Accuracy

How many digits of the fraction are accurate? At first glance you might be tempted to say all four digits. Those of you who have read the previous section on roundoff error might be tempted to change your answer to three.

The answer is: The accuracy depends on the calculation. Certain operations, such as subtracting two numbers that are close to each other, generate inexact results. Consider the following equation:

```
1 - 1/3 - 1/3 - 1/3
```

1.000E+0

−3.333E-1

-3.333E-1
_____

-3.333E-1

or:

1.000E+0

-3.333E-1

-3.333E-1

-3.333E-1
_____

0.0010E+0, or 1.000E-3

The correct answer is 0.000E+0 and we got 1.000E-3. The very first digit of the fraction is wrong. This is an example of the problem called roundoff error that can occur during floating-point operations.

Minimizing Roundoff Error

There are many techniques for minimizing roundoff error. Guard digits have already been discussed. Another trick is to use `double` instead of `float`. This gives you approximately twice the accuracy as well as twice the range. It also pushes away the minimization problem twice as far. But roundoff errors still can creep in.

Advanced techniques for limiting the problems caused by floating point can be found in books on numerical analysis. They are beyond the scope of this text. The purpose of this chapter is to give you some idea of what sort of problems can be encountered.

Floating point by its very nature is not exact. People tend to think of computers as very accurate machines. They can be, but they also can give wildly wrong results. You should be aware of the places where errors can slip into your program.

Determining Accuracy

There is a simple way of determining how accurate your floating point is (for simple calculations). The method used in the following program is to add 1.0 + 0.1, 1.0 + 0.01, 1.0 + 0.001, and so on until the second number gets so small that it makes no difference in the result.

The old C language specified that all floating-point numbers were to be done in `double`. C++ removed that restriction, but because many C++ compilers are really front-ends to a C complier, frequently C++ arithmetic is done in `double`. This means that the expression:

```
float number1, number2;
```

. . .

```
while (number1 + number2 != number1)
```

is equivalent to:

```
while (double(number1) + double(number2) != double(number1))
```

If you use the 1 + 0.001 trick, the automatic conversion of `float` to `double` may give a distorted picture of the accuracy of your machine. (In one case, 84 bits of accuracy were reported for a 32-bit format.) Example 19-1 computes the accuracy of both floating point as used in equations and floating point as stored in memory. Note the trick used to determine the accuracy of the floating-point numbers in storage.

Example 19-1. float/float.cc

```
#include <iostream.h>
#include <iomanip.h>

main()
{
    // Two numbers to work with
    float number1, number2;
    float result;              // Result of calculation
    int   counter;             // Loop counter and accuracy check

    number1 = 1.0;
    number2 = 1.0;
    counter = 0;

    while (number1 + number2 != number1) {
        ++counter;
        number2 = number2 / 10.0;
    }
    cout << setw(2) << counter << " digits accuracy in calculations\n";

    number2 = 1.0;
    counter = 0;

    while (1) {
        result = number1 + number2;
        if (result == number1)
            break;
        ++counter;
        number2 = number2 / 10.0;
    }
    cout << setw(2) << counter << " digits accuracy in storage\n";
```

Example 19-1. float/float.cc (Continued)

```
    return (0);
}
```

Running this on a Sun-3/50 with an MC68881 floating-point chip, we get:

```
20 digits accuracy in calculations
 8 digits accuracy in storage
```

This program only gives an approximation of the floating-point precision arithmetic. A more precise definition can be found in the standard include file *float.h.*

Precision and Speed

A variable of type `double` has about twice the precision of a normal `float` variable. Most people assume that double-precision arithmetic takes longer than single-precision. This is not always the case. Let's assume we have one of the older compilers that does everything in `double`.

For the equation:

```
float answer, number1, number2;

answer = number1 + number2;
```

C++ must perform the following steps:

1. Convert `number1` from single to double precision

2. Convert `number2` from single to double precision

3. Double-precision add

4. Convert result into single precision and store in `answer`

If the variables were of type `double`, C++ would only have to perform the steps:

1. Double-precision add

2. Store result in `answer`

As you can see, the second form is a lot simpler, requiring three fewer conversions. In some cases, converting a program from single precision to double precision makes it run *faster.*

NOTE

Because C++ specifies that floating point can be done in `double` or `float`, you can't be sure of anything. Changing all `floats` into `doubles` may make the program run faster, slower, or the same. The only thing you can be sure of when using floating point is that the results are unpredictable.

Many computers, including the PC and Sun/3 series machines, have a special chip called a floating-point processor that does all the floating-point arithmetic. Actual tests using the Motorola 68881 floating-point chip (which is used in the Sun/3) as well as floating point on the PC show that single precision and double precision run at the same speed.

Power Series

Many trigonometry functions are computed using a *power series*. For example, the series for sine is:

$$\sin(x) = x - \frac{x^3}{3!} + \frac{x^5}{5!} - \frac{x^7}{7!} + \dots$$

The question is, how many terms do we need to get four-digit accuracy? Table 19-2 contains the terms for $\sin(\pi/2)$.

Table 19-2. Terms for sin(π/2)

	Term	Value	Total
1	x	1.571E+0	
2	$\frac{x^3}{3!}$	6.462E-1	9.248E-1
3	$\frac{x^5}{5!}$	7.974E-2	1.005E+0
4	$\frac{x^7}{7!}$	4.686E-3	9.998E-1
5	$\frac{x^9}{9!}$	1.606E-4	1.000E+0
6	$\frac{x^{11}}{11!}$	3.604E-6	1.000E+0

From this we conclude that five terms are needed. However, if we try to compute $\sin(\pi)$ we get Table 19-3.

Table 19-3. Terms for sin(π)

	Term	Value	Total
1	x	3.142E+0	
2	$\frac{x^3}{3!}$	5.170E+0	-2.028E+0
3	$\frac{x^5}{5!}$	2.552E-0	5.241E-1
4	$\frac{x^7}{7!}$	5.998E-1	-7.570E-2

Table 19-3. Terms for sin(π) (Continued)

	Term	Value	Total
5	$\dfrac{x^9}{9!}$	8.224E-2	6.542E-3
6	$\dfrac{x^{11}}{11!}$	7.381E-3	-8.388E-4
7	$\dfrac{x^{13}}{13!}$	4.671E-4	-3.717E-4
8	$\dfrac{x^{15}}{15!}$	2.196E-5	-3.937E-4
9	$\dfrac{x^{17}}{17!}$	7.970E-7	-3.929E-4
10	$\dfrac{x^{19}}{19!}$	2.300E-8	-3.929E-4

π needs nine terms. So, different angles require a different number of terms. (A program for computing the sine to four-digit accuracy showing intermediate terms is included in Appendix D.)

Compiler designers have a dilemma when it comes to designing a sine function. If they know ahead of time the number of terms to use, they can optimize their algorithms for that number of terms. However, they lose accuracy for some angles. So a compromise must be struck between speed and accuracy.

Don't assume that because the number came from the computer, it is accurate. The library functions can generate bad answers—especially when working with excessively large or small values. Most of the time you will not have any problems with these functions, but you should be aware of their limitations.

Finally, there is the question of what is sin(1,000,000)? Our floating-point format is good for only four digits. The sine function is cyclical. That is, sin(0) = sin(2π) = sin(4π). Therefore, sin(1,000,000) is the same as sin(1,000,000 mod 2π).

Because our floating-point format is good to only four digits, sin(1,000,000) is actually sin(1,000,000   1,000). Since 1,000 is bigger than 2π, the error renders meaningless the result of the sine.

Programming Exercises

Exercise 19-1: Write a class that uses strings to represent floating-point numbers in the format used in this chapter. The class should have functions to read, write, add, subtract, multiply, and divide floating-point numbers.

I attended a physics class at Cal Tech taught by two professors. One was giving a lecture on the sun when he said, "... and the mean temperature of the inside of the sun is 13,000,000 to 25,000,000 degrees." At this point the other instructor broke in and asked, "Is that Celsius or Kelvin (absolute zero or Celsius −273)?"

The first lecturer turned to the board for a minute and then said, "What's the difference?" The moral of the story is that when your calculations have a possible error of 12,000,000, a difference of 273 doesn't mean very much.

Exercise 19-2: Create a class to handle fixed-point numbers. A fixed-point number has a constant (fixed) number of digits to the right of the decimal point.

20

Advanced Pointers

A race that binds
Its body in chains and calls them Liberty,
And calls each fresh link progress.
—Robert Buchanan

One of the more useful and complex features of C++ is its use of pointers. With pointers you can create complex data structures such as linked lists and trees. Figure 20-1 illustrates some of these data structures.

Up to now all your data structures have been allocated by the compiler as either permanent or temporary variables. With pointers you can create and allocate *dynamic data structures,* which can grow or shrink as needed. In this chapter you will learn how to use some of the more common dynamic data structures.

Pointers, Structures, and Classes

Structures and classes may contain pointers, or even a pointer to another instance of the same structure. In the following example:

```
class item {
    public:
        int value;
        item *next_ptr;
};
```

the structure `item` is illustrated by Figure 20-2.

The operator `new` allocates storage for a variable and returns a pointer. It is used to create new things out of thin air (actually out of an area of memory called the

355

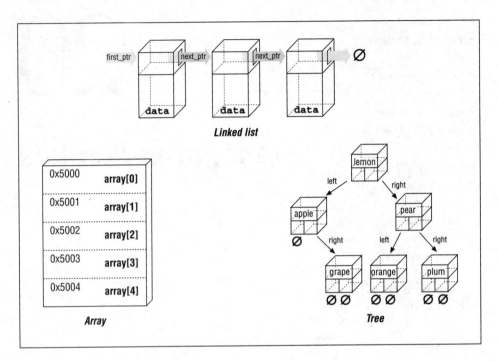

Figure 20-1. Examples of pointer use

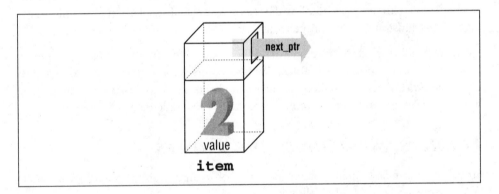

Figure 20-2. Item

heap). Up to now we've used pointers solely to point to named variables. So if we used a statement like:

```
int data;
int *number_ptr;

number_ptr = &data;
```

the thing we are pointing to has a name (**data**). The operator **new** creates a new, unnamed variable and returns a pointer to it. The "things" created by **new** can only be referenced through pointers, never by name.

In the following example, we use **new** to allocate an integer from the heap. The variable **element_ptr** will point to our new integer.

```
int *element_ptr;    // Pointer to an integer

element_ptr = new int;    // Get an integer from the heap
```

The operator **new** takes a single argument: the type of the item to be allocated. According to the latest C++ standard, if **new** runs out of memory it should throw an exception and abort the program. (See Chapter 22, *Exceptions*, for information on how to handle this.) On older C++ systems, when **new** runs out of memory, it returns a null pointer.

Suppose we are working on a complex database that contains (among other things) a mailing list. We want to keep our storage use to a minimum, so we only want to allocate memory for a person if he or she exists. Creating an array of **class person** would allocate the data statically and use up too much space. So we will allocate space as needed. Our structure for a person is:

```
class person {
    public:
        char    name[30];          // Name of the person
        char    address[30];       // Where he lives
        char    city_state_zip[30]; // Part 2 of address
        int     age;               // His age
        float   height;            // His height in inches
}
```

We want to allocate space for this person. Later the pointer to this record will be put in the database.

To create a new person, we use the following:

```
struct person *new_ptr;

new_ptr = new person;
```

The operator **new** can also allocate more complex data types such as arrays. Example 20-1 allocates storage for a character array 80 bytes long (`'\0'` included). The variable **string_ptr** points to this storage.

Example 20-1

```
main()
{
    char *string_ptr;

    string_ptr = new char[80];
```

All we've done is substitute a simple type (such as **person**) with an array specification (**char[80]**).

delete Operator

The operator **new** gets memory from the heap. To return the memory to the heap you use the operator **delete**. The general form of the **delete** operator is:

```
delete pointer;        // Where pointer is a pointer to a simple object
pointer = NULL;
```

where **pointer** is a pointer previously allocated by **new**. If the **new** operator allocated an array, then you must use the form:

```
delete pointer[];      // Where pointer is a pointer to an array
pointer = NULL;
```

NOTE

The reason there are two forms of the **delete** operator is because there is no way for C++ to tell the difference between a pointer to an object and a pointer to an array of objects. The **delete** operator relies on the programmer using "**[]**" to tell the two apart.

Strictly speaking, the line:

```
pointer = NULL;
```

is unnecessary. However, it is a good idea to "null out" pointers after they are deleted. That way, you don't try use a pointer to deleted memory, and also you help prevent any attempts to delete the same memory twice.

The following is an example using **new** to get storage and **delete** to dispose of it.

```
const DATA_SIZE = (16 * 1024);

void copy(void)
{
    char *data_ptr;     // Pointer to large data buffer

    data_ptr = new char[DATA_SIZE];      // Get the buffer

    /*
     * Use the data buffer to copy a file
     */
    delete[] data_ptr;
    data_ptr = NULL;
}
```

But what happens if we forget to free the memory? The buffer becomes dead. That is, the memory management system thinks it's being used, but no one is using it. (The technical term for this is a "memory leak.") If the `delete` statement is removed from the function `copy` then each successive call eats up another 16K of memory.

The other problem that can occur is using memory that has been freed. When `delete` is used, the memory is returned to the memory pool and can be reused. Using a pointer after a `delete` call is similar to an array index out-of-bounds error. You are using memory that belongs to someone else. This can cause unexpected results or program crashes.

Linked List

Suppose you are writing a program to send a list of names to another computer using a communications line. The operator types in the names during the day, and then after work you dial up the other computer and send the names. The problem is, you don't know ahead of time how many names are going to be typed. By using a *linked-list* data structure, you can create a list of names that can grow as more names are entered. With a linked list you can also easily insert names into the middle of the list (which would be slow and difficult with an array). Also, as you will see later, linked lists can be combined with other data structures to handle extremely complex data.

A linked list is a chain of items where each item points to the next item in the chain. Think about the treasure hunt games you played when you were a kid. You were given a note that said, "Look in the mailbox." You raced to the mailbox and found the next clue, "Look in the big tree in the back yard," and so on until you found your treasure (or you got lost). In a treasure hunt each clue points to the next one.

Figure 20-3 graphically illustrates a linked list.

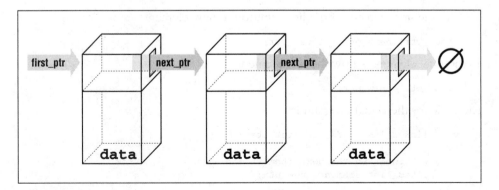

Figure 20-3. Linked list

The class declarations for a linked list are:

```
class linked_list {
    public:
        class linked_list_element {
            public:
                char    data[30];              // Data in this element
            private:
                linked_list_element *next_
                ptr; // Pointer to next element
            friend class linked_list;
        };

    public:
        linked_list_element *first_ptr;   // First element in the list

        // Initialize the linked list
        linked_list(void) {first_ptr = NULL;}

        // ... Other member functions
};
```

The variable `first_ptr` points to the first element of the list. In the beginning, before we insert any elements into the list (it is empty), this variable is initialized to NULL.

Figure 20-4 illustrates how a new element can be added to the beginning of a linked list. Now all we have to do is translate this into C++ code.

To do this in C++, we execute the following steps:

1. Create the item we are going to add.

```
new_ptr = new linked_list;
```

2. Store the item in the new element.

```
(*new_ptr).data = item;
```

3. Make the first element of the list point to the new element.

```
(*new_ptr).next_ptr = first_ptr;
```

4. The new element is now the first element.

```
first_ptr = new_ptr;
```

The code for the actual program is:

```
void linked_list::add_list(int item)
{
    // Pointer to the next item in the list
    linked_list_element *new_ptr;

    new_ptr = new linked_list;
```

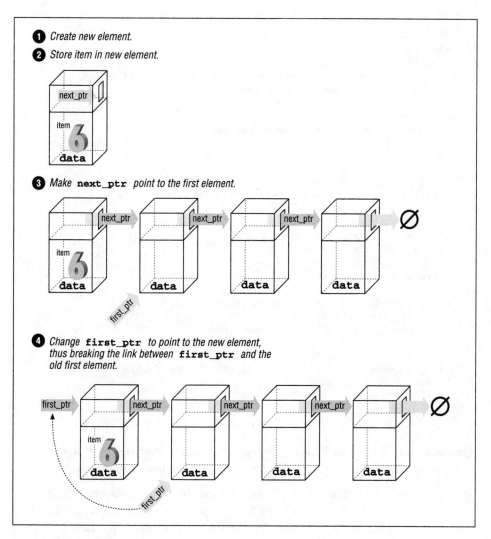

Figure 20-4. New element

```
        strcpy((*new_ptr).data, item);
        (*new_ptr).next_ptr = first_ptr;
        first_ptr = new_ptr;
}
```

Now that we can put things in a list, let's use that ability. We'll now write a short function to search the list till we find a key item or we run out of data. Example 20-2 contains the new find function.

Example 20-2. find/find.cc

```
#include <iostream.h>
#include <string.h>
#include "linked.h"
/***********************************************************
 * Find -- look for a data item in the list               *
 *                                                         *
 * Parameters                                              *
 *      name -- name to look for in the list               *
 *                                                         *
 * Returns                                                 *
 *      1 if name is found                                 *
 *      0 if name is not found                             *
 ***********************************************************/
int linked_list::find(char *name)
{
    /* Current structure we are looking at */
    linked_list_element *current_ptr;

    current_ptr = first_ptr;

    while ((strcmp(current_ptr->data, name) != 0) &&
           (current_ptr != NULL))
        current_ptr = current_ptr->next_ptr;

    /*
     * If current_ptr is null, we fell off the end of the list and
     * didn't find the name
     */
    return (current_ptr != NULL);
}
```

Question 20-1: *Why does running this program sometimes result in a bus error? Other times it will report "found" (return 1) for an item that is not in the list.*

In our `find` program we had to use the cumbersome notation (`*current_ptr).data` to access the data field of the structure. C++ provides a shorthand for this construct using the `->` operator. The dot (.) operator means the field of a structure, and the structure pointer operator (`->`) indicates the field of a structure pointer.

The following two expressions are equivalent:

```
(*current_ptr).data = value;
current_ptr->data = value;
```

Ordered Linked Lists

So far we have only added new elements to the head of a linked list. Suppose we want to add elements in order. Figure 20-5 is an example of an ordered linked list.

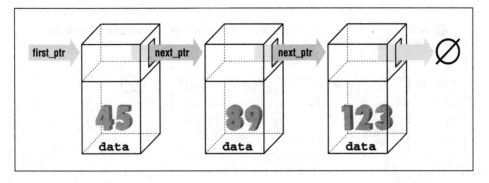

Figure 20-5. Ordered list

Figure 20-6 shows the steps necessary to add a new element, "53," to the list.

The following member function implements this algorithm. The first step is to locate the insertion point. The **first_ptr** points to the first element of the list. The program moves the variable **before_ptr** along the list until it finds the proper place for the insertion. The variable **after_ptr** is set to point to the previous value. The new element will be inserted between these elements.

```
void linked_list::enter(int item)
{
    list *before_ptr; // Insert before this element
    list *after_ptr;  // Insert after this element

    /*
     * Warning: This routine does not take
     *   care of the case where the element is
     *   inserted at the head of the list
     */

    before_ptr = first_ptr;
    while (1) {
        insert_ptr = before_ptr;
        insert_ptr = insert_ptr->next_ptr;

        // Did we hit the end of the list?
        if (insert_ptr == NULL)
            break;

        // Did we find the place?
        if (item >= insert_ptr->data)
            break;
    }
```

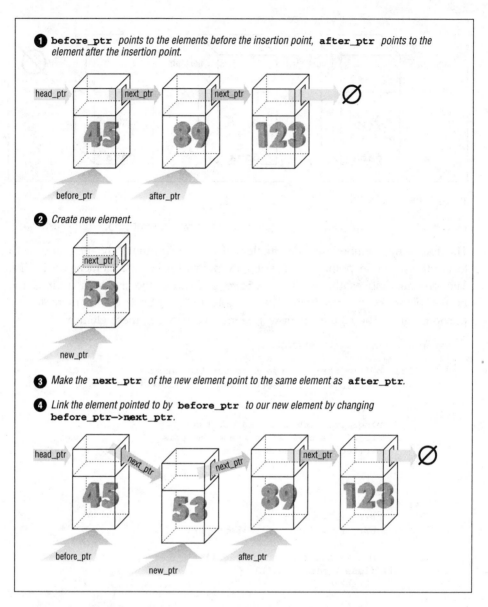

1. `before_ptr` *points to the elements before the insertion point,* `after_ptr` *points to the element after the insertion point.*

2. *Create new element.*

3. *Make the* `next_ptr` *of the new element point to the same element as* `after_ptr`.

4. *Link the element pointed to by* `before_ptr` *to our new element by changing* `before_ptr->next_ptr`.

Figure 20-6. Adding element "53" to an ordered list

Now we know where to insert the new element. All we must do is insert it. We start at the element before the new one (`before_ptr`). This element should point to the new element, so:

```
before_ptr->next_ptr = new_ptr;
```

Next is the new element (`new_ptr`). It needs to point to the element after it, or `after_ptr`. This is accomplished with the code:

```
new_ptr->next_ptr = after_ptr;
```

The element `after_ptr` needs to point to the rest of the chain. Because it already does, we leave it alone. The full code for inserting the new element is:

```
    // Create new item
    new_ptr = new list;
    new_ptr->data = item;

    // Link in the new item
    before_ptr->next_ptr = new_ptr;
    new_ptr->next_ptr = after_ptr;
}
```

Double-linked List

A double-linked list contains two links. One link points forward to the next element; the other points backward to the previous element. Double-linked lists are useful where the program needs to go through the list both forward and backward.

The classes for a double-linked list are:

```
class double_list {
    private:
        class double_list_element {
            public:
                int data;                    // Data item
            private:
                double_list_element *next_ptr;     // Forward link
                double_list_element *previous_ptr;// Backward link
            friend class double_list;
        };
    public:
        double_list_element *head_ptr;    // Head of the list

        double_list(void) {head_ptr = NULL;}

        // ... Other member functions
```

This is shown graphically in Figure 20-7.

To insert an item into the list, we first locate the insertion point:

```
void double_list::enter(int item)
{
    double_list_elememt *insert_ptr; // Insert before this element

    /*
     * Warning: This routine does not take
```

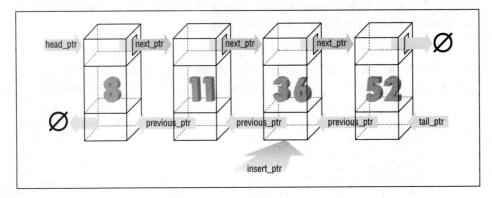

Figure 20-7. Double-linked list

```
 *    care of the case where the element is
 *    inserted at the head of the list
 *    or the end of the list
 */

insert_ptr = head_ptr;
while (1) {
    insert_ptr = insert_ptr->next;

    // Have we reached the end?
    if (insert_ptr == NULL)
        break;

    // Have we reached the right place?
    if (item >= insert_ptr->data)
        break;
}
```

Notice that we do not have to keep track of the variable `after_ptr`. The pointer `insert_ptr->previous_ptr` is used to locate the previous element. To insert a new element, we must adjust two sets of pointers. First we create the new element:

```
// Create new element
new_ptr = new double_list;
```

Next we set up the forward pointer for the new item:

```
new_ptr->next_ptr = insert_ptr;
```

Graphically this is represented by Figure 20-8.

Next we connect the link to the previous element using the code:

```
new_ptr->previous_ptr = insert_ptr->previous_ptr;
```

Graphically, this is represented in Figure 20-9.

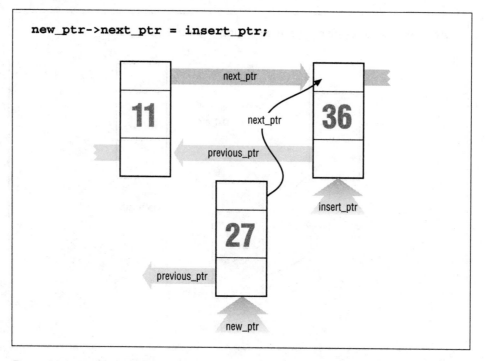

Figure 20-8. Double-linked list insert, part #1

The links are set up for the new element. Now all we have to do is break the old links between items 11 and 36 and connect them to the new item (27).

Getting to item 11 is a bit of a trick. We only have a pointer to item 36 (insert_ ptr). However, if we follow the previous link back (insert_ptr->previous_ ptr), we get the item (11) that we want. Now all we have to do is fix the next_ ptr for this item.

The C++ code for this is surprisingly simple:

```
insert_ptr->previous_ptr->next_ptr = new_ptr;
```

Visually we can see this operation in Figure 20-9.

We have only one remaining link to fix: the **previous_ptr** of the **insert_ptr**. In C++ the code looks like:

```
insert_ptr->previous_ptr = new_ptr;
```

Graphically this operation is represented by Figure 20-11.

In summary, to insert a new item in a double-linked list, you must set four links:

1. The new item's previous pointer:

```
new_ptr->previous_ptr = insert_ptr->previous_ptr;
```

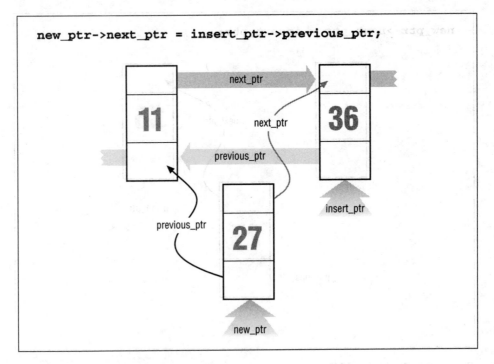

```
new_ptr->next_ptr = insert_ptr->previous_ptr;
```

Figure 20-9. Double-linked list insert, part #2

2. The new item's next pointer:

   ```
   new_ptr->next_ptr = insert_ptr;
   ```

3. The previous pointer of the item that will follow the new item:

   ```
   insert_ptr->previous_ptr->next_ptr = new_ptr;
   ```

4. The next pointer of the item that will precede the new item:

   ```
   insert_ptr->previous_ptr = new_ptr;
   ```

Trees

Suppose we want to create an alphabetized list of the words that appear in a file. We could use a linked list, but searching a linked list is slow because we must check each element until we find the correct insertion point. By using a data type called a *tree,* we can reduce the number of comparisons tremendously.

A *binary tree structure* looks like Figure 20-12.

Each box is called a *node* of the tree. The box at the top is the *root* and the boxes at the bottom are the *leaves.* Each node contains two pointers: a left pointer and a right pointer, which point to the left and right subtrees.

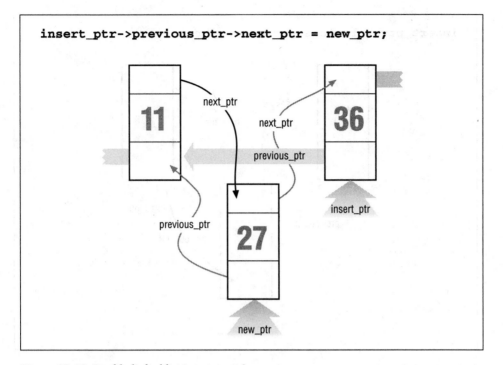

`insert_ptr->previous_ptr->next_ptr = new_ptr;`

Figure 20-10. Double-linked list insert, part 3

The structure for a tree is:

```
class tree {
      class node {
          public:
              char *data;       // Word for this tree
          private:
              node *right;      // Tree to the right
              node *left;       // Tree to the left
          friend class tree;
      };
    public:
      node *root;   // Top of the tree (the root)

      tree(void) {root = NULL;};
      // ... Other member function
};
```

Trees are often used for storing a symbol table (a list of variables used in a program). In this chapter we will use a tree to store a list of words and then to

---

* Programming trees are written with the root at the top and the leaves at the bottom. Common sense tells you that this is upside down. In case you haven't noticed, common sense has very little to do with programming.

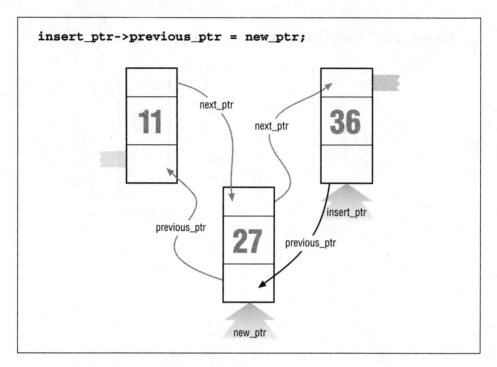

```
insert_ptr->previous_ptr = new_ptr;
```

Figure 20-11. Double-linked list insert, Part 4

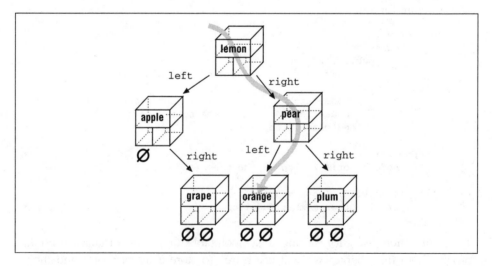

Figure 20-12. Tree

print the list alphabetically. The advantage of a tree over a linked list is that searching a tree takes considerably less time.

In this example, each node stores a single word. The left subtree stores all the words less than the current word, and the right subtree stores all the words greater than the current word.

For example, Figure 20-13 shows how we descend the tree to look for the word "orange." We would start at the root, "lemon." Because "orange" > "lemon," we would descend the right link and go to "pear." Because "orange" < "pear," we descend the left link, where we find "orange."

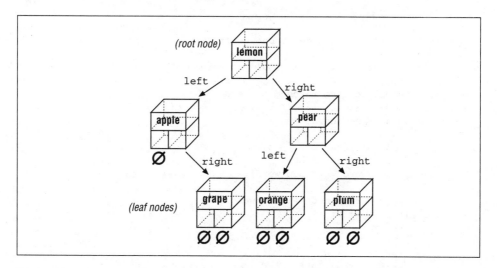

Figure 20-13. Tree search

Recursion is extremely useful with trees. Our rules for recursion are 1) the function must make things simpler and 2) there must be some endpoint.

The algorithm for inserting a word in a tree is:

1. If this is a null tree (or subtree), create a one-node tree with this word.

2. If this node contains the word, do nothing.

3. Otherwise, enter the word in the left or right subtree, depending on the value of the word.

Does this algorithm satisfy our recursion rules? The function has two definite endpoints:

1. A match is found.

2. We have a null node.

Otherwise, we enter the word into a subtree (which is simpler than the whole tree).

To see how this works, consider what happens when we insert the word "fig" into the tree. First we check the word "fig" against "lemon." "Fig" is smaller, so we go to "apple." Because "fig" is bigger, we go to "grape." Because "fig" is smaller than "grape," we try the left link. It is NULL, so we create a new node.

This code makes use of a new function: strdup. This function creates a copy of a string on the heap and returns a pointer to the new string. The string may later be returned to the heap using the delete operator.[*]

The function to enter a value into a tree is:

```
void tree::enter_one(node *&node, char *word)
{
    int  result;        // Result of strcmp

    // See if we have reached the end
    if (node == NULL) {
        node = new node;

        node->left = NULL;
        node->right = NULL;
        node->word = strdup(word);
    }
    result = strcmp(node->word, word);
    if (result == 0)
        return;

    if (result < 0)
        enter(node->right, word);
    else
        enter(node->left, word);
}
```

And the function to kick it off is:

```
void tree::enter(char *word) {
    enter_one(root, word);
};
```

This function passes a pointer to the root of the tree to enter_one. If the root is NULL, enter_one creates the node. Because we are changing the value of a pointer, we must pass *a reference to the pointer.*

---

[*] The function strdup is not part of the proposed ANSI standard for C++. It is, however, available in all the compilers I've seen. It appears to be part of an unwritten standard.

Printing a Tree

Despite the complex nature of a tree structure, it is easy to print. Again we use recursion. The printing algorithm is:

1. For the null tree, print nothing.

2. Print the data that comes before this node (left tree).

3. Print this node.

4. Print the data that comes after this node (right tree).

The code for printing the tree is:

```
void tree::print_one(node *top)
{
    if (top == NULL)
        return;                    // Short tree

    print_tree(top->left);
    cout << top->word << '\n';
    print_tree(top->right);
}
void tree::print(void) {
    print_one(root);
}
```

The Rest of the Program

Now that we have the data structure defined, all we need to complete the program is a few more functions. The main function checks for the correct number of arguments and then calls the scanner and the **print_tree** routine.

The scan function reads the file and breaks it into words. It uses the standard macro **isalpha**. The macro returns 1 if its argument is a letter and 0 otherwise. It is defined in the standard include file **ctype.h**. After a word is found, the function **enter** is called to put the word in the tree. **strdup** creates the space for a string on the heap and then returns the pointer to it.

Example 20-3 is the listing of *words.cc*.

Example 20-3. words/words.cc

```
/**********************************************************
 * Words -- scan a file and print out a list of words     *
 *             in ASCII order                             *
 *                                                        *
 * Usage:                                                 *
 *     words <file>                                       *
 **********************************************************/
#include <iostream.h>
```

Example 20-3. words/words.cc (Continued)

```cpp
#include <fstream.h>
#include <ctype.h>
#include <string.h>
#include <stdlib.h>

class tree {
    private:
        // The basic node of a tree
        class node {
            private:
                node    *right;     // Tree to the right
                node    *left;      // Tree to the left
            public:
                char    *word;      // Word for this tree

                friend class tree;
        };

        // The top of the tree
        node *root;

        // Enter a new node into a tree or subtree
        void enter_one(node *&node, char *word);

        // Print a single node
        void print_one(node *top);
    public:
        tree(void) {root = NULL;}

        // Add a new word to the tree
        void enter(char *word) {
            enter_one(root, word);
        }

        // Print the tree
        void print(void) {
            print_one(root);
        }
};

static tree words;      // List of words we are looking for

/************************************************************
 * Scan -- scan the file for words                          *
 *                                                          *
 * Parameters                                               *
 *      name -- name of the file to scan                    *
 ************************************************************/
void scan(char *name)
{
    char word[100];     // Word we are working on
    int  index;         // Index into the word
```

Example 20-3. words/words.cc (Continued)

```
    int  ch;              // Current character
    ifstream in_file;     // Input file

    in_file.open(name, ios::in);
    if (in_file.bad()) {
        cerr << "Error: unable to open " << name << '\n';
        exit(8);
    }
    while (1) {
        // Scan past the white space
        while (1) {
            ch = in_file.get();

            if (isalpha(ch) || (ch == EOF))
                break;
        }

        if (ch == EOF)
            break;

        word[0] = ch;
        for (index = 1; index < sizeof(word); ++index) {
            ch = in_file.get();
            if (!isalpha(ch))
                break;
            word[index] = ch;
        }
        // Put a null on the end
        word[index] = '\0';

        words.enter(word);
    }
}


main(int argc, char *argv[])
{
    if (argc != 2) {
        cerr <<  "Error: wrong number of parameters\n";
        cerr <<  "        on the command line\n";
        cerr << "Usage is:\n";
        cerr <<  "    words 'file'\n";
        exit(8);
    }
    scan(argv[1]);
    words.print();
    return (0);
}


/**********************************************************
 * tree::enter_one -- enter a word into the tree          *
 *                                                        *
```

Example 20-3. words/words.cc (Continued)

```
 * Parameters                                               *
 *      new_node -- current node we are looking at          *
 *      word -- word to enter                               *
 ***********************************************************/
void tree::enter_one(node *&new_node, char *word)
{
    int  result;          // Result of strcmp

    // See if we have reached the end
    if (new_node == NULL) {
        new_node = new node;

        new_node->left = NULL;
        new_node->right = NULL;
        new_node->word = strdup(word);
    }
    result = strcmp(new_node->word, word);
    if (result == 0)
        return;

    if (result < 0)
        enter_one(new_node->right, word);
    else
        enter_one(new_node->left, word);
}


/**********************************************************
 * tree::print_one -- print out the words in a tree       *
 *                                                        *
 * Parameters                                             *
 *      top -- the root of the tree to print              *
 ***********************************************************/
void tree::print_one(node *top)
{
    if (top == NULL)
        return;                        // Short tree

    print_one(top->left);
    cout << top->word << '\n';
    print_one(top->right);
}
```

Question 20-2: *I once made a program that read the dictionary into memory using a tree structure and then used it in a program that searched for misspelled words. Although trees are supposed to be fast, this program was so slow you would think I used a linked list. Why?*

Hint: *Graphically construct a tree using the words "able," "baker," "cook," "delta," and "easy" and look at the result.*

Data Structures for a Chess Program

A classic problem in artificial intelligence is the game of chess. So far, in spite of all our advances in computer science, no one has been able to create a program that plays chess better than the best grand masters.

We are going to design a data structure for a chess-playing program. In chess there are several moves you can make. Your opponent has many responses, to which you have many answers, and so on back and forth for several levels of moves.

Our data structure is beginning to look like a tree. But this is not a binary tree, because we have more than two branches for each node (Figure 20-14).

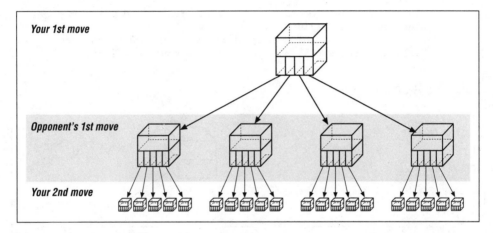

Figure 20-14. Chess tree

We are tempted to use the following data structure:

```
class chess {
    public:
        class board_class board; // Current board position
        class next_class {
            class move_class move;        // Our next move
            class chess *chess_ptr;
                // Pointer to the resulting position
        } next[MAX_MOVES];
};
```

The problem is that the number of moves from any given position varies dramatically. For example, in the beginning you have lots of pieces running around.*

---

* Trivia question: What are the 21 moves you can make in chess from the starting position? (You can move each pawn up one (8 moves) or two (8 more), and the knights can move out to the left and right (4 more) (8+8+4=20).) What's the 21st move?

Things like rooks, queens, and bishops can move any number of squares in a straight line. When you reach the end game (in an evenly matched game), each side probably has only a few pawns and one major piece. The number of possible moves has been greatly reduced.

We want to be as efficient in our storage as possible because a chess program stresses the limits of our machine. We can reduce storage requirements by changing the next-move array into a linked list. The resulting structure is:

```
class next_class {
    class move_class move;         // Our next move
    class next_class *chess_ptr;   // Pointer to the resulting position
};

struct chess {
    class board_class board;        // Current board position
    class next_class *list_
              ptr;      // List of moves we can make from here
    class next_class this_move;     // The move we are making
};
```

Graphically, this looks like Figure 20-15.

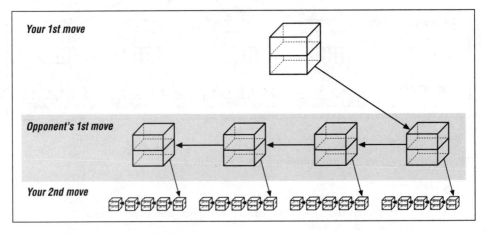

Figure 20-15. Revised chess structure

The new version adds a little complexity, but saves a great deal of storage.

Programming Exercises

Exercise 20-1: Write a cross-reference program.

Exercise 20-2: Write a function to delete an element of a linked list.

Exercise 20-3: Write a function to delete an element of a double-linked list.

Exercise 20-4: Write a function to delete an element of a tree.

Answers to Chapter Questions

Answer 20-1: The problem is with the statement:

```
while ((current_ptr->data != value) &&
       (current_ptr != NULL))
```

current_ptr->data is checked *before* we check to see whether current_ptr is a valid pointer (!= NULL). If it is NULL we can easily check a random memory location that could contain anything. The solution is to check current_ptr before checking what it is pointing to:

```
while (current_ptr != NULL) {
    if (current_ptr->data == value)
        break;
```

Answer 20-2: The problem was as follows: because the first word in the dictionary was the smallest, every other word used the right-hand link. In fact, because the entire list was ordered, only the right-hand link was used. Although this was defined as a tree structure, the result was a linked list. See Figure 20-16.

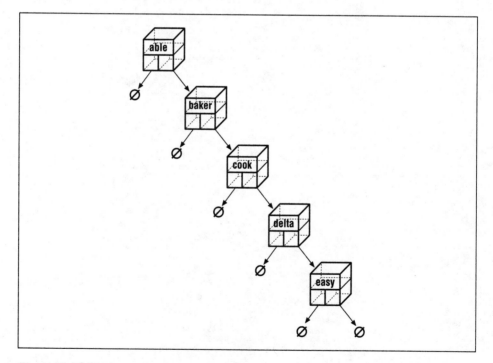

Figure 20-16. Dictionary tree

Some of the more advanced books on data structures, such as Knuth's *Algorithms + Data Structures = Programs*, discuss ways of preventing this by balancing a binary tree.

Trivia Answer: You give up. That's right, the 21st move is to resign.

21

Advanced Classes

> *The ruling ideas of each age have ever been the ideas of its ruling class.*
>
> —Karl Marx
> *Manifesto of the Communist Party*

Derived Classes

The **stack** class that was defined in Example 13-1 contains one major limitation: it does not check for bad data. For example, there is nothing that prevents the user from pushing too many things onto the stack.

We need to define a new bounds-checking stack (**b_stack**). This new stack does everything a simple stack does but also includes bounds checking. C++ allows you to build new classes on old ones. In this case we will be building our bounds-checking stack (**b_stack**) on the existing simple stack (**stack**). Technically we will be using the class **stack** as a *base class* to create a new *derived class*, the bounds-checking stack.

We start by telling C++ that we are creating **b_stack** out of **stack**.

```
class b_stack: public stack {
```

The keyword **public** tells C++ to make all the members of **stack** accessible to the outside world. If we declared **stack** as **private** then the **public** and **protected** members of **stack** would be accessible only inside **b_stack**.

This declaration tells C++ that we are going to use **stack** as a base for **b_stack**. Figure 21-1 shows how C++ views this combination.

Now we need to define the new version of the **push** member function. We first check to see whether there's room in the stack. If there's no more room, we print

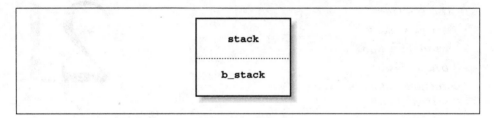

Figure 21-1. Derived class b_stack and base class stack

an error message and abort the program. Otherwise we push the item onto the stack. Here's a limited version of push.

```
inline void b_stack::b_push(const int item)
{
    if (count >= STACK_SIZE) {
        cout << "Error: Push overflows stack\n";
        exit(8);
    }
    // This calls the push member function of the stack class
    push(item);
}
```

We have been very careful in selecting the name of this member function. It is called **b_push** instead of push for a reason. We would like to call it push, but then the code:

```
inline void b_stack::push(const int item)
{
    if (count >= STACK_SIZE) {
        cout << "Error: Push overflows stack\n";
        exit(8);
    }
    // The next line wrongly calls b_stack::push (this function),
    //    not stack::push
    push(item);
}
```

would call the member function push in the class **b_stack** *not* stack's push as we want. The result is that we call **b_stack's** push, which performs a limit check and then calls push. This push belongs to **b_stack**, so we perform a bounds check and call push, and so on. The result is that push will call itself over and over until the system runs out of stack space.

This is not want we want. We want to tell C++ that we want to call the push in **stack**. This can be accomplished by using the scope operator "::". The new version of **b_stack::push** looks like:

```
inline void b_stack::push(const int item)
{
    if (count >= STACK_SIZE) {
```

```
                cout << "Error: Push overflows stack\n";
                exit(8);
            }
            stack::push(item);
        }
```

The full definition for both the **stack** and **b_stack** classes is shown in
Example 21-1.

Example 21-1. stack_c/stack_d1.cc

```
/**********************************************************
 * Stack                                                  *
 *       a file implementing a simple stack class         *
 **********************************************************/
#include <stdlib.h>
#include <iostream.h>

const int STACK_SIZE = 100;      // Maximum size of a stack

/**********************************************************
 * Stack class                                            *
 *                                                        *
 * Member functions                                       *
 *       stack -- initialize the stack                    *
 *       push -- put an item on the stack                 *
 *       pop -- remove an item from the stack             *
 **********************************************************/
// The stack itself
class stack {
    protected:
        int count;               // Number of items in the stack
    private:
        int data[STACK_SIZE];    // The items themselves
    public:
        // Initialize the stack
        stack(void);
        // ~stack() -- default destructor
        // Copy constructor defaults

        // Push an item on the stack
        void push(const int item);

        // Pop an item from the stack
        int pop(void);
};

/**********************************************************
 * stack::stack -- initialize the stack                   *
 **********************************************************/
inline stack::stack(void)
{
    count = 0;   // Zero the stack
}
```

Example 21-1. stack_c/stack_d1.cc (Continued)

```
/**********************************************************
 * stack::push -- push an item on the stack              *
 *                                                        *
 * Warning: We do not check for overflow                  *
 *                                                        *
 * Parameters                                             *
 *      item -- item to put in the stack                 *
 **********************************************************/
inline void stack::push(const int item)
{
    data[count] = item;
    ++count;
}
/**********************************************************
 * stack::pop -- remove item from stack                  *
 *                                                        *
 * Warning: We do not check for stack underflow           *
 *                                                        *
 * Returns                                                *
 *      the top item from the stack                      *
 **********************************************************/
inline int stack::pop(void)
{
    // Stack goes down by one
    --count;

    // Then we return the top value
    return (data[count]);
}

/**********************************************************
 * b_stack -- bound checking stack                       *
 *                                                        *
 * Member function                                        *
 *      push -- push an item on the stack                *
 *      pop -- remove an item from the stack             *
 **********************************************************/
class b_stack: public stack {
    public:
        // b_stack -- default constructor
        // ~b_stack -- default destructor
        // Copy constructor defaults

        // Push an item on the stack
        void push(const int item);

        // Remove an item from the stack
        int pop(void);
};
/**********************************************************
 * b_stack::push -- push an item on the stack            *
 *                                                        *
```

Example 21-1. stack_c/stack_d1.cc (Continued)

```
 * Parameters                                              *
 *       item -- item to put in the stack                  *
 **********************************************************/
inline void b_stack::push(const int item)
{
    if (count >= STACK_SIZE) {
        cerr << "Error: Push overflows stack\n";
        exit (8);
    }
    stack::push(item);
}
/**********************************************************
 * b_stack::pop -- get an item off the stack              *
 *                                                        *
 * Returns                                                *
 *       the top item from the stack                      *
 **********************************************************/
inline int b_stack::pop(void)
{
    if (count <= 0) {
        cerr << "Error: Pop causes stack underflow\n";
        exit (8);
    }
    return (stack::pop());
}
```

Even though these two classes are relatively simple, they illustrate some important features of the C++ language. First we have declared `count` as a `protected` member variable. This means that this variable can be used only within the class `stack` and in any classes derived from `stack`, such as `b_stack`. The `b_stack` functions `push` and `pop` can use `count` to do their work. However, anyone outside of `stack` and `b_stack` cannot use the variable.

Because `b_stack` is derived from `stack`, you can use a `b_stack` type variable wherever a `stack` type variable is used. In the following example, we create a `b_stack` named `bound_stack` that is used as a parameter to the function `push_things`, which takes a normal, unbounded stack as a parameter.

```
    void push_things(stack &a_stack) {
        a_stack.push(1);
        a_stack.push(2);
    }

    // ...
    b_stack bounded_stack; // A random stack
    // ....
    push_things(bounded_stack);
```

The function push_things takes a stack as a parameter. Even though the variable bounded_stack is a b_stack type variable, C++ turns it into a stack when push_things is called.

One way to explain this is that although bounded_stack is of type b_stack, when it is used by push_things the function is looking through a peephole that allows it to see only the stack part of the variable as shown in Figure 21-2.

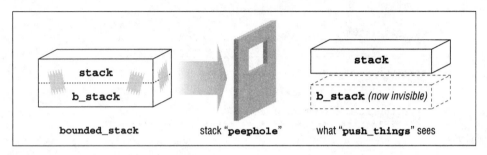

Figure 21-2. How "push_things" sees a b_stack

Let's improve the basic stack so that instead of always allocating a fixed-size stack, we allocate the stack dynamically. The new stack starts with:

```
class stack {
    private:
        int *data;      // Pointer to the data in the stack
    protected:
        int count;      // Current item on the stack
    public:
        stack(const unsigned int size) {
            data = new int[size];
            count = 0;
        };
        virtual ~stack(void) {
            delete data;
            data = NULL;
        }
    // ...
```

(We discuss the keyword virtual later in this chapter.)

This stack is more flexible. To use the new stack we must give it a size when we declare the stack variable. For example:

```
stack big_stack(1000);
stack small_stack(10);
stack bad_stack; // Illegal, size required
```

Back to the bound-checking stack. Somehow we need to call the base class constructor (stack) with a parameter.

The way we do this is to put the base-constructor unitization just after the declaration of the constructor for the derived class:

But this flexibility creates some problems for the bound-checking stack: the constructor for **stack** contains a parameter. How is the bound-checking stack to initialize the simple stack?

The solution is to use a syntax similar to initializing a constant data member.

```
class b_stack: public stack {
    private:
        const unsigned int stack_size;    // Size of the simple stack
    public:
        b_stack(const unsigned int size) : stack(size),
                                            stack_size(size) {
        }
```

In this example, the base class is **stack** and the derived class is **b_stack**. The constructor for **b_stack** takes a single parameter, the size of the stack. It needs to pass this parameter to **stack**. The line:

```
b_stack::b_stack(cont unsigned int size) : stack(size),
```

does this through the **stack(size)** syntax.

NOTE

Because the new version of **stack** uses dynamic memory (**new** and **delete**), it is *vital* that we define the "big four" member functions: the constructor, the destructor, the copy constructor, and the assignment operator (**=**).

Virtual Functions

Today there are many different ways of sending a letter. We can mail it by the United States Postal Service, send it via Federal Express, send it Certified Mail, or even fax it. All of these methods get the letter to the person (most of the time), but they differ in cost and speed.

Let's define a class to handle the sending of a letter. We start by defining an address class and then use this class to define addresses for the sender and the receiver. (The definition of the address class is "just a simple matter of programming" and is left to the reader.)

```
class mail {
    public:
        address sender; // Who's sending the mail (return address)?
        address receiver; // Who's getting the mail?

        // Send the letter
```

```
        void send_it(void) {
        // ... Some magic happens here
        };
    };
```

There is, however, one little problem with this class. We're depending on "magic" to get our letters sent. The process for sending a letter is different depending on which service we are using. One way to handle this is to have send_it call the appropriate routine depending on what service we are using:

```
void mail::send_it(void) {
    switch (service) {
        case POST_OFFICE:
            put_in_local_mailbox();
            break;
        case FEDERAL_EXPRESS:
            fill_out_waybill();
            call_federal_for_pickup();
            break;
        case UPS:
            put_out_ups_yes_sign();
            give_package_to_driver();
            break;
        //... and so on for every service in the universe
```

This solution is a bit clunky. Our mail class must know about all the mailing services in the world. Also consider what happens when we add another function to the class:

```
class mail {
    public:
        // Returns the cost of mailing in cents
        int cost(void) {
        // ... more magic
        }
```

Do we create another big switch statement? If we do, we'll have two big switch statements to worry about. What's worse, the sending instructions and cost for each service are now spread out over two functions. It would be nice if we could group all the functions for the Postal Service in one class, all of Federal Express in one class, and so on.

For example, a class for the Postal Service might be:

```
class post_office: public mail{
    public:
        // Send the letter
        void send_it(void) {
            put_in_local_mailbox();
        };
        // Cost returns cost of sending a letter in cents
        int cost(void) {
                // Costs 32 cents to mail a letter
```

```
        return (32);    // WARNING: This can easily become dated
    }
};
```

Now we have the information for each single service in a single class. The information is stored in a format that is easy to understand. The problem is that it is not easy to use. For example, let's write a routine to send a letter:

```
void get_address_and_send(mail &letter)
{
    letter.from = my_address.
    letter.to = get_to_address();
    letter.send();
}
//...
    class post_office simple_letter;
    get_address_and_send(simple_letter);
```

The trouble is that `letter` is a `mail` class, so when we call `letter.send()` we call the **send** of the base class `mail`. What we need is a way of telling C++, "Please call the **send** function of the derived class instead of the base class."

The `virtual` keyword identifies a member function that can be overridden by a member function in the derived class. If we are using a derived class, then C++ will look for members in the derived class and then in the base class, in that order. If we are using a base class variable (even if the actual instance is a derived class), then C++ will search only the base class for the member function. The exception is when the base class defines a `virtual` function. In this case, the derived class is searched and then the base class.

Table 21-1 illustrates the various search algorithms.

Table 21-1. Member Function Search Order

Class Type	Member Function Type	Search Order
Derived	Normal	Derived->base
Base	Normal	Base
Base	virtual	Derived->base

Example 21-2 illustrates the use of `virtual` functions.

Example 21-2. virt/virt.cc

```
// Illustrates the use of virtual functions

#include <iostream.h>

class base {
    public:
        void a(void) { cout << "base::a called\n"; }
```

Example 21-2. virt/virt.cc (Continued)

```
        virtual void b(void) { cout << "base::b called\n"; }
        virtual void c(void) { cout << "base::c called\n"; }
};

class derived: public base {
    public:
        void a(void) { cout << "derived::a called\n"; }
        void b(void) { cout << "derived::b called\n"; }
};

void do_base(base &a_base)
{
    cout << "Call functions in the base class\n";

    a_base.a();
    a_base.b();
    a_base.c();
}

main()
{
    derived a_derived;

    cout << "Calling functions in the derived class\n";

    a_derived.a();
    a_derived.b();
    a_derived.c();

    do_base(a_derived);
    return (0);
}
```

The derived class contains three member functions. Two of them are self-defined: a and b. The third, c, is inherited from the base class. When we call a, C++ looks at the derived class to see whether that class defines the function. In this case it does, so the line:

```
    a_derived.a();
```

outputs:

```
    derived::a called
```

When b is called the same thing happens, and we get:

```
    derived::b called
```

It doesn't matter whether the base class defines a and b or not. C++ calls the derived class and goes no further.

However, the derived class doesn't contain a member function named c. So when we reach the line:

```
a_derived.c();
```

C++ tries to find c in the derived class and fails. Then it tries to find the member function in the base class. In this case it succeeds and we get:

```
base::c called
```

Now let's move on to the function do_base. Because it takes a base class as it's arguments, C++ restricts its search for member functions to the base class. So the line:

```
a_base.a();
```

outputs

```
base::a called
```

But what happens when the member function b is called? This is a `virtual` function. That tells C++ that the search rules are changed. C++ first checks whether there is a b member function in the derived class, and then C++ checks the base class. In the case of b, there is a b in the derived class, so the line:

```
a_base.b();
```

outputs:

```
derived::b called
```

The member function c is also a `virtual` function. Therefore, C++ starts by looking for the function in the derived class. In this case it's not defined there, so C++ then looks in the base class. It is defined there, so we get:

```
base::c called
```

Now getting back to our mail. We need a simple base class that describes the basic mailing functions for each different type of service.

```cpp
class mail {
    public:
        address sender; // Who is sending the mail (return address)?
        address receiver; // Who is getting the mail?

        // Send the letter
        virtual void send_it(void) {
            cout << "Error: send_it not defined in derived class.\n"
            exit (8);
        };
        // Cost of sending a letter in pennies
        virtual int cost(void) {
            cout << "Error: cost not defined in derived class.\n"
```

```
            exit (8);
        };
    };
```

Now we can define a derived class for each different type of service. For example:

```
class post_office: public mail {
    public:
        void send_it(void) {
            put_letter_in_box();
        }
        int cost(void) {
            return (29);
        }
};
```

Now we can write a routine to send a letter and not have to worry about the details. All we have to do is call **send_it** and let the `virtual` function do the work.

The `mail` class is an abstraction that describes a generalized mailer. To associate a real mailing service, we need to use it as the base for a derived class. But what happens if the programmer forgets to put the right member functions in the derived class? For example:

```
class federal_express: public mail {
    public:                       `
        void send_it(void) {
            put_letter_in_box();
        }
        // Something is missing
};
```

When we try to find the cost of sending a letter via Federal Express, C++ will notice that there's no `cost` function in `federal_express` and call the one in `mail`. The `cost` function in `mail` knows that it should never be called, so it spits out an error message and aborts the program. Getting an error message is nice, but getting it at compilation rather than during the run would be better.

C++ allows you to specify `virtual` functions that *must* be overridden in a derived class. For this example, the new, improved, abstract mailer is:

```
class mail {
    public:
        address sender; // Who is sending the mail (return address)?
        address receiver; // Who is getting the mail?

        // Send the letter
        virtual void send_it(void) = 0;
        // Cost of sending a letter in pennies
        virtual int cost(void) = 0;
};
```

The "= 0" tells C++ that these member functions are *pure virtual functions*. That is, they can never be called directly. Any class containing one or more pure virtual functions is called an *abstract class*. If you tried to use an abstract class as an ordinary type, such as:

```
void send_package(void) {
     mail a_mailer;    // Attempt to use an abstract class
```

you would get a compile-time error.

Virtual Classes

Let's design some classes to handle a tax form. In the upper right corner of each form is a blank for your name, address, and Social Security number. All the forms contain this same information, so we'll define a class for this corner of the form.

```
class name {
    public:
         char *name;    // Name of the taxpayer
         //... Rest of the class
};
```

Now let's use this class to design another class for the 1040 form.

```
class form_1040: public name {
    public:
         int income;    // Wages, tips, and other income
         // ...
};
```

Our class structure so far is illustrated by Figure 21-3.

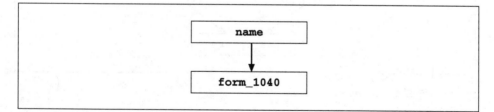

Figure 21-3. 1040 class structure

Unfortunately our tax returns consist of more than one form. For deductions we need Schedule A, so let's define a class for it.

```
class schedule_a: public name {
    public:
         int home_interest;    // Interest deduction for home mortgage
         // ... Rest of class
};
```

Putting the two forms together, we get a simple return.

```
class tax_return: public form_1040, schedule_a {
    //... Rest of class
};
```

Figure 21-4 illustrates this class structure.

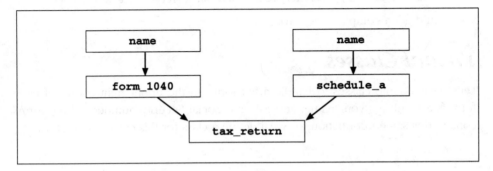

Figure 21-4. Tax return structure

The problem with this structure is that we have two **name** classes. But the taxpayer's name doesn't change from one form to another. What we want is the class structure shown in Figure 21-5.

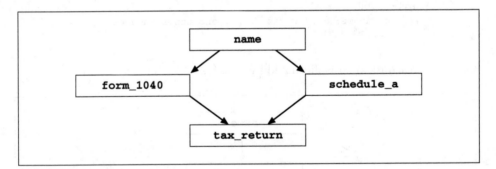

Figure 21-5. Better tax return structure

Declaring a base class **virtual** tells C++ to combine common base classes. Redefining tax_return using **virtual** base classes we get:

```
class form_1040: virtual public name {
    public:
        int income;    // Wages, tips, and other income
        // ...
};

class schedule_a: virtual public name {
    public:
        int home_interest;    // Interest deduction for home mortgage
```

```
            // ... Rest of class
    };

    class tax_return: public form_1040, schedule_a {
        //... Rest of class
    };
```

Notice that the class **name** is used as the base for two derived classes; derived classes cause their base class's constructor to be called to initialize the class. Does this mean that the constructor for **name** will be called twice? The answer is no. C++ is smart enough to know that **name** is used twice and to ignore the second initialization.

Function Hiding in Derived Classes

Example 21-3 defines a base class with the overloaded function do_it, which comes in both an integer version and a floating-point version. The program also defines a derived class that contains the single integer do_it.

Example 21-3. doit/doit.cc

```
class simple {
    public:
        int do_it(int i, int j) {return (i*j);}
        float do_it(float f) {return (f*2);}
};
class derived: public simple {
    public:
        int do_it(int i, int j) {return (i+j);}
};
```

Clearly, when we are using the **derived** class and we call the integer version of do_it, we are calling the one in the derived class. But what happens if we call the floating-point version? The derived class has no floating point do_it. Normally, if we don't have a member function in the derived class, C++ will look to the base class.

However, since a version of do_it is defined in the derived class, C++ will look to the derived class for *all* flavors of do_it. In other words, if one form of do_it is defined in the derived class, then that locks out all forms of the function.

```
    main() {
        derived test;      // Define a class for our testing
        int i;             // Test variable
        float f;           // Test variable

        i = test.do_it(1, 3);   // Legal; returns 4 (1 + 3)
        f = test.do_it(4.0);    // Illegal; "do_it(float)" not defined in
                                // the class "derived"
```

Constructors and Destructors in Derived Classes

Constructors and destructors behave differently from normal member functions especially when used with derived classes. When a derived-class variable is created, the constructor for the base class is called first, followed by the constructor for the derived class.

Example 21-4 defines a simple base class and uses it to create a derived class.

Example 21-4. cons/class.cc

```
#include <iostream.h>

class base_class {
    public:
        base_class() {
            cout << "base_class constructor called\n";
        }
        ~base_class() {
            cout << "base_class destructor called\n";
        }
};
class derived_class:public base_class {
    public:
        derived_class() {
            cout << "derived_class constructor called\n";
        }
        ~derived_class() {
            cout << "derived_class destructor called\n";
        }
};
```

Now when we execute the code:

```
    derived_class *sample_ptr = new derived_class;
```

the program prints:

```
    base_class constructor called
    derived_class constructor called
```

After the variable is destroyed, the destructors are called. The destructor for the derived class is called first, followed by the destructor for the base class. So when we destroy the variable with the statement:

```
    delete sample_ptr;
    sample_ptr = NULL;
```

we get:

```
    derived_class destructor called
    base_class destructor called
```

But C++ has a surprise lurking for us. Remember that derived classes can operate as base classes. For example:

```
base_class *base_ptr = new derived_class;
```

is perfectly legal. However, there is a problem when the variable is deleted:

```
delete base_ptr;
base_ptr = NULL;
```

You see, `base_ptr` is a pointer to a `base class`. At this point all the code can see is the `base class`. There is no way for C++ to know that there is a `derived class` out there. So when the variable is deleted, C++ *fails to call the derived class constructor.*

The output of the **delete** statement is:

```
base_class destructor called
```

We have just tricked C++ into deleting a class without calling the proper destructor.

We need some way to tell C++, "Hey, there is a derived class out there and you might want to call its destructor." The way we do this is to make the destructor for the base class a `virtual` function.

```
class base_class {
    public:
        base_class() {
            cout << "base_class constructor called\n";
        }
        virtual ~base_class() {
            cout << "base_class destructor called\n";
        }
};
```

The keyword `virtual` normally means, "Call the function in the derived class instead of the one in the base class." For the destructor, it has a slightly different meaning. When C++ sees a `virtual` destructor, it will call the destructor of the derived class and then call the destructor of the base class.

So with the `virtual` destructor in place, we can safely delete the `base_class` variable and the program will output the proper information:

```
derived_class destructor called
base_class destructor called
```

Question 21-1: *Why does Example 21-5 fail when we delete the variable* `list_ptr`? *The program seems to get upset when it tries to call* `clear` *at line 17.*

Example 21-5. blow/blow.cc

```
 1 #include <iostream.h>
 2 #include <stdlib.h>
 3
 4 class list {
 5     private:
 6       int item;        // Current item number
 7
 8     public:
 9       virtual void clear() = 0;
10
11       void next_item(void) {
12           ++item;
13       }
14
15       list(void) {
16           item = 0;
17       }
18
19       virtual ~list() {
20           clear();
21       }
22 };
23
24 class list_of_integers : public list {
25     public:
26         int array[100];    // Place to store the items
27
28       void clear(void) {
29           int i;       // Array index
30
31           for (i = 0; i < 100; ++i)
32               array[i] = 0;
33       }
34 };
35
36 main()
37 {
38     list_of_integers *list_ptr = new list_of_integers;
39
40     // Cause problems
41     delete list_ptr;
42     list_ptr = NULL;
43     return (0);
44 }
```

Summary

Since programming began, programmers have been trying to find ways of building re-usable code. C++, through the use of derived classes, allows you to build classes on top of existing code. This provides a great deal of flexibility and makes the code easier to organize and maintain.

Programming Exercises

Exercise 21-1: Combine the checkbook class of Example 13-2 with the queue class of Example 13-2 to implement a checkbook class that can print out the last ten entries of your checkbook.

Exercise 21-2: Define a "string-match" base class.

```
class string_matcher {
    public:
        // Returns true if string matches, false if not
        int match(const char *const string);
    ...
```

Define derived classes that match words, numbers, and blank strings.

Exercise 21-3: Define a base class **shape** that can describe any simple shape such as a square, circle or equilateral triangle. The size of all these shapes can be reduced to a single dimension.

Define derived classes for each of the three shapes.

Create a **virtual** function in the base class that returns the area of each shape.

Note: You will need to more precisely define what dimensions are stored in the base class. (Is the size in the base class for circle, the radius, or the diameter?)

Exercise 21-4: Write a base class called **person** that describes a person of either gender. Define two derived classes called **man** and **woman** that define gender specific items. Write pure **virtual** functions in the base class for operations that are common to both sexes yet are handled in different ways by each of them.

Exercise 21-5: Write a base class **number** that holds a single integer value and contains one member function, **print_it**. Define three derived classes to print the value in hex, octal, and decimal.

Answers to Chapter Questions

Answer 21-1: Remember that destructors are called in the order of derived class first and then base class. In this case, the destructor for the derived class, **list_of_integers**, is called to destroy the class. The class is *gone*.

Next, the destructor for the base class **list** is called. It calls the function **clear**. This a pure **virtual** function, so C++ must call the **clear** function in the derived class. But the derived class is **gone**. There is no **clear** function. This makes C++ very upset and it aborts the program. (Actually, only good compilers will cause a program to abort. Others may do something really strange to your program.)

You should never call pure `virtual` functions from a destructor.

V

Other Language Features

22

Exceptions

How glorious it is — and also how painful — to be an exception.
—Alfred de Musset

Airplanes fly from one place to another and 99.9% of the time there's no trouble. But when there is trouble such as a stuck wheel or an engine fire, pilots are trained to handle the emergency.

Let's examine in detail what happens during an airborne emergency such as an engine catching fire. This is an exception to normal flight. A fire alarm goes off in the cockpit.

This catches the pilots' attention and they start going through the fire-emergency procedure. This is an extensive list of things to do in case of fire. The airline prepared this list ahead of time and the pilots have the list memorized. The pilots do what's necessary to handle the exception: activate the fire extinguisher, shut down the engine, land very quickly, etc.

Let's break down this procedure into C++ pseudocode. When the pilots take off they are going to try to fly the plane from one point to another without problems. The C++ "code" for this is:

```
try {
    fly_from_point_a_to_point_b();
}
```

The `try` keyword indicates that we are going to attempt an operation that may cause an exception.

But what happens when we get an exception? We need to handle it. The C++ code for this is:

```
catch (fire_emergency &fire_info) {
    active_extinguisher(fire_info.engine);
    turn_off(fire_info.engine);
    land_at_next_airport();
}
```

The keyword `catch` indicates that this section of code handles an exception. In this case the exception handled is a **fire_emergency**. This is the *type* of emergency. It could be a fire in engine number 1, engine number 2, or engine number 3 (assuming a three-engine plane). *Which* engine is on fire is stored in the variable `fire_info`.

The **fire_emergency** class describes what type of fire occurred. Its definition is:

```
class fire_emergency {
    public:
        int engine;    // Which engine is on fire
        // Other information about the fire
};
```

We've covered everything but the actual detection of the fire. Buried within each engine is a fire sensor. The code for this sensor is:

```
// Watch for fire in engine #2
void sensor_2(void) {
    while (engine_running()) {
        if (engine_on_fire()) {
            fire_emergency fire_info;

            fire_info.engine = 2;
            throw(fire_info);
        }
    }
}
```

When this code senses a fire, it puts the information in a **fire_emergency** variable named `fire_info` and triggers an exception with the `throw` statement.

When the `throw` statement is executed, normal processing is stopped. After all, when a fire occurs, normal flying is stopped. Execution is transferred to the `catch` statement for the **fire_emergency**.

To summarize, *exception handling* consists of:

- A description of a possible problem, in this case the **fire_emergency** class.

- A section of code in which the exception may occur, which is enclosed in a `try` statement. In this case, the statement is **fly_from_point_a_to_point_b()**.

- Something that causes an exception and triggers the emergency procedures through a `throw` statement.

- Exception-handling code inside a `catch` block.

Stack Exceptions

In Chapter 21, *Advanced Classes*, we defined a stack with bounds checking. If the user attempted to push too much data on the stack or to pop too much off, the class would issue an error message and abort. This is not a good way to handle an exception. Think of how the pilots would feel if the plane displayed an error message and shut down every time there was a fire.

The first thing we need to do is decide what type of exceptions we are going to handle and describe them as classes. In our stack example, the only exception we expect is an out-of-bounds error. We'll describe this error with a simple string. The class for an out-of-bounds error is:

```
const int WHAT_MAX = 80;         // Longest possible error message
class bound_err {
    public:
        char what[WHAT_MAX];     // What caused the error

        // Initialize the bound error with a message
        bound_err(char *_what) {
            // WARNING: This does not check for "_what" being too long
            strcpy(what, _what);
        }
        // bound_err(bound_err) -- default copy constructor
        // ~bound_err -- default destructor
};
```

Exception checking starts with the keyword `try`. This tells C++ that exceptions may be generated in the section of code that follows and that they will be handled immediately after the `try` block. For example, if we are trying to perform a big stack operation, the code might look like:

```
try {
    do_big_stack_operation();
};
```

Immediately after the `try` block, we need to tell C++ what problems we will handle, by using a `catch` statement. The syntax for this statement is:

```
catch (problem_type &parameter) {
    statements;
}
```

The *problem_type* is the class that describes what happened. For the out-of-bounds error, the `catch` statement looks like:

```
catch (bound_err &what_happened) {
    cerr << "Error: Bounds exceeded\n";
    cerr << "Reason: " << what_happened.what << '\n';
}
```

Several `catch` statements may be used to catch different types of exceptions. If an exception is not caught, it is considered an *unexpected exception* and will cause a call to the unexpected-exception handler, which aborts the program by default. If you want to catch all exceptions, use "..." for the exception type. For example:

```
catch (bound_err &what_happened) {
    // .... Body of catch
}
catch (...) {
    cerr << "Something strange happened\n";
}
```

Now we need to update our old stack program and replace all the "error-message-and-abort" code with `throw` statements. The new procedure for **push** now looks like:

```
inline void b_stack::push(const int item)
{
    if (count >= STACK_SIZE) {
        bound_err overflow("Push overflows stack");
        throw overflow;
    }
    stack::push(item);
}
```

Actually we don't need a special variable for overflow. The code can be consolidated. In the previous example we used two statements to explicitly show what is going on. The following code performs the same operation:

```
inline void b_stack::push(const int item)
{
    if (count >= STACK_SIZE) {
        throw bound_err("Push overflows stack");
    }
    stack::push(item);
}
```

The basic function definition we've been using so far tells C++, "Expect any exception to be thrown at any time." The **push** function can only throw a **bound_err** exception. C++ allows you to list all the possible exceptions in a function by putting a `throw` directive at the end of the function declaration:

```
inline void b_stack::push(const int item) throw(bound_err) {
```

But what happens if we throw an exception that's not in the list of exceptions? C++ will turn this into a call to the function unexpected().

Example 22-1 contains a new version of the bound-checking stack with exceptions.

Example 22-1. stack_c/stack_el.cc

```
/********************************************************
 * Stack                                                *
 *       a file implementing a simple stack class       *
 ********************************************************/
#include <stdlib.h>
#include <iostream.h>

const int STACK_SIZE = 100;     // Maximum size of a stack

/********************************************************
 * Stack class                                          *
 *                                                      *
 * Member functions                                     *
 *       stack -- initialize the stack                  *
 *       push -- put an item on the stack               *
 *       pop -- remove an item from the stack           *
 ********************************************************/
// The stack itself
class stack {
    protected:
        int count;              // Number of items in the stack
    private:
        int data[STACK_SIZE];   // The items themselves
    public:
        // Initialize the stack
        stack(void);
        // ~stack() -- default destructor
        // Copy constructor defaults

        // Push an item on the stack
        void push(const int item);

        // Pop an item from the stack
        int pop(void);
};

/********************************************************
 * stack::stack -- initialize the stack                 *
 ********************************************************/
inline stack::stack(void)
{
    count = 0;  // Zero the stack
}
/********************************************************
 * stack::push -- push an item on the stack             *
 *                                                      *
```

Example 22-1. stack_c/stack_el.cc (Continued)

```
 * Warning: We do not check for overflow                   *
 *                                                         *
 * Parameters                                              *
 *       item -- item to put in the stack                  *
 ********************************************************/
inline void stack::push(const int item)
{
    data[count] = item;
    count++;
}
/********************************************************
 * stack::pop -- get an item off the stack                 *
 *                                                         *
 * Warning: We do not check for stack underflow            *
 *                                                         *
 * Parameters                                              *
 *       the_stack -- stack to initialize                  *
 *                                                         *
 * Returns                                                 *
 *       the top item from the stack                       *
 ********************************************************/
inline int stack::pop(void)
{
    // Stack goes down by one
    count--;

    // Then we return the top value
    return (data[count]);
}

const int WHAT_MAX = 80;          // Largest possible error message
/********************************************************
 * bound_err -- a class used to handle out-of-bounds     *
 *              exceptions.                               *
 ********************************************************/
class bound_err {
    public:
        char what[WHAT_MAX];      // What caused the error

        // Initialize the bound error with a message
        bound_err(char *_what) {
            if (strlen(_what) < (WHAT_MAX -1))
                strcpy(what, _what);
            else
                strcpy(what, "Internal error: _what is too long");
        }
        // bound_err(bound_err) -- default copy constructor
        // ~ bound_err -- default destructor
};


/********************************************************
 * b_stack -- bound-checking stack                         *
```

Example 22-1. stack_c/stack_el.cc (Continued)

```
 *                                                       *
 * Member function                                       *
 *      push -- push an item on the stack                *
 *      pop -- remove an item from the stack             *
 ********************************************************/
class b_stack: public stack {
    public:
        // b_stack -- default constructor
        // ~b_stack -- default destructor
        // Copy constructor defaults

        // Push an item on the stack
        void push(const int item) throw(bound_err);

        // Remove an item from the stack
        int pop(void) throw(bound_err);
};
/********************************************************
 * b_stack::push -- push an item on the stack           *
 *                                                       *
 * Parameters                                            *
 *      item -- item to put in the stack                 *
 ********************************************************/
inline void b_stack::push(const int item) throw(bound_err)
{
    if (count >= STACK_SIZE) {
        bound_err overflow("Push overflows stack");
        throw overflow;
    }
    stack::push(item);
}
/********************************************************
 * b_stack::pop -- get an item off the stack            *
 *                                                       *
 * Returns                                               *
 *      the top item from the stack                      *
 ********************************************************/
inline int b_stack::pop(void) throw(bound_err)
{
    if (count <= 0) {
        throw bound_err("Pop causes stack underflow");
    }
    return (stack::pop());
}

b_stack test_stack;     // Define a stack for the bounds checking

void push_a_lot(void) {
    int i;          // Push counter

    for (i = 0; i < 5000; i++) {
        test_stack.push(i);
```

Example 22-1. stack_c/stack_el.cc (Continued)

```
    }
}

main()
{
    try {
        push_a_lot();
    }
    catch (bound_err &err) {
        cerr << "Error: Bounds exceeded\n";
        cerr << "Reason: " << err.what << '\n';
        exit (8);
    }
    catch (...) {
        cerr << "Error: Unexpected exception occurred\n";
        exit (8);
    }
    return (0);
}
```

Runtime Library Exceptions

The exception-handling mechanism is relatively new. The draft ANSI C++ standard defines the exceptions that should be thrown by the routines in the runtime library. However, these "standard" exceptions are so new they are still being refined and updated. There are lots of details still to be worked out.

Compiler makers need time to catch up to the standard. At the time of this writing, the currently available C++ compilers generate few if any exceptions in their runtime library, and none generates "standard" exceptions. This situation will change as the ANSI standard gets better defined and compilers improve. About the best advice I can give you is to read your compiler's reference manual and watch out!

Programming Exercises

Exercise 22-1: Add code to the queue class of Example 13-2 that will trigger an exception when too many items are put in the queue.

Exercise 22-2: Take the fraction class from Example 18-3 and add code to generate an exception when a divide by zero occurs. Also add code to generate an exception when a bad number is read.

Exercise 22-3: Update the checkbook class of Example 13-2 so it generates an exception when your balance goes below zero.

Exercise 22-4: Write a function `count_letter` that takes a single character. This function will count the number of consonants and vowels. If a nonletter is given to the function, it generates an exception.

23

Modular Programming

Many hands make light work.
—John Heywood

So far, we have been dealing with small programs. As programs grow larger and larger, they should be split into sections, or *modules*. C++ allows programs to be split into multiple files, compiled separately, and then combined (linked) to form a single program.

In this chapter, we go through a programming example, discussing the C++ techniques needed to create good modules. You also are shown how to use *make* to put these modules together to form a program.

Modules

A module is a collection of functions or classes that perform related functions. For example, there could be a module to handle database functions such as lookup, enter, and sort. Another module could handle complex numbers, and so on.

Also, as programming problems get big, more and more programmers are needed to finish them. An efficient way of splitting up a large project is to assign each programmer a different module. That way each programmer only has to worry about the internal details of his or her own code.

In this chapter, we discuss a module to handle *infinite arrays*. The functions in this package allow the user to store data into an array without worrying about its size. The infinite array grows as needed (limited only by the amount of memory in the computer). The infinite array will be used to store data for a histogram but can also be used to store things such as line numbers from a cross reference program or other types of data.

413

Public and Private

Modules are divided into two parts, *public* and *private*. The public part tells the user how to call the functions in the module and contains the definitions of data structures and functions that are to be used from outside the module. The public definitions are put in a header file, which is included in the user' program. In the infinite array example, we have put the public declarations in the file *ia.h* (see listing on page 417).

Anything internal to the module is private. Everything that is not directly usable by the outside world should be kept private.

The extern Modifier

The `extern` modifier is used to indicate that a variable or function is defined outside the current file but is used in this file. Example 23-1 illustrates a simple use of the `extern` modifier.

Example 23-1. main.cc and count.cc

```
File: main.cc
#include <iostream.h>
/* Number of times through the loop */
extern int counter;

/* Routine to increment the counter */
extern void inc_counter(void);

main()
{
    int    index; /* Loop index */

    for (index = 0; index < 10; ++index)
        inc_counter();
    cout << "Counter is " << counter << '\n';
    return (0);
}
File: count.cc
/* Number of times through the loop */
int counter = 0;

/* Trivial example */
void inc_counter()
{
    ++counter;
}
```

The function **main** uses the variable **counter**. Because **counter** is not defined in **main**, it is defined in the file *counter.cc*. The **extern** declaration is used by *main.cc* to indicate that `counter` is declared somewhere else, in this case the file *counter.cc*. The modifier `extern` is not used in this file, because this is the "real" declaration of the variable.

Actually, three modifiers can be used to indicate the files in which a variable is defined, as shown in Table 23-1.

Table 23-1. Modifiers

Modifier	Meaning
extern	Variable/function is defined in another file.
<blank>	Variable/function is defined in this file (public) and can be used in other files.
static	Variable/function is local to this file (private).

Notice that the keyword `static` has two meanings. (It is the most overworked modifier in the C++ language. For a complete list of the meanings of `static` see Table 14-1.) For data defined globally, `static` means "private to this file." For data defined inside a function, it means "variable is allocated from static memory (instead of the temporary stack)."

C++ is very liberal in its use of the rules for `static`, `extern`, and <blank> modifiers. It is possible to declare a variable as `extern` at the beginning of a program and later define it as <blank>.

```
extern sam;
int sam = 1;     // This is legal
```

This ability is useful when you have all your external variables defined in a header file. The program includes the header file (and defines the variables as `extern`), and then defines the variable for real.

Another problem concerns declaring a variable in two different files.

File: main.cc

```
int    flag  = 0;     // Flag is off

main()
{
    cout << "Flag is " << flag << '\n';
}
```

File: sub.cc

```
int    flag = 1;       // Flag is on
```

What happens in this case? There are several possibilities:

- `flag` could be initialized to 0 because `main.cc` is loaded first.

- `flag` could be initialized to 1 because the entry in `sub.cc` overwrites the one in `main.cc`.

- The compiler could very carefully analyze both programs, and then pick out the value that is most likely to be wrong.

In this case, there is only one global variable called `flag`. It will be initialized to either 1 or 0 depending on the whims of the compiler. It is entirely possible for the program `main` to print out:

```
flag is 1
```

even though we initialized it to zero. To avoid the problem of hidden initializations, use the keyword `static` to limit the scope of variables to the file in which they are declared.

If we had written:

File: main.cc

```
static int      flag = 0;        // Flag is off

main()
{
        cout << "Flag is " << flag << '\n';
}
```

File: sub.cc

```
static int      flag = 1;        // Flag is on
```

then `flag` in *main.cc* is an entirely different variable from `flag` in *sub.cc*. However, you should still give the variables different names to avoid confusion.

Headers

Information that is shared between modules should be put in a header file. By convention, all header filenames end with ".h". In the infinite array example, we use the file *ia.h*.

The header should contain all the public information, such as:

- A comment section describing clearly what the module does and what is available to the user

- Public class definitions

- Common constants

- Public structures

- Prototypes of all the public functions

- `extern` declarations for public variables

In the infinite array example, more than half the file *ia.h* is devoted to comments. This commenting is not excessive; the real guts of the coding is hidden in the program file *ia.cc*. The *ia.h* file serves both as a program file and as documentation to the outside world.

Notice that there is no mention in the *ia.h* comments about how the infinite array is implemented. At this level, we don't care how something is done, just what functions are available.

Example 23-2. ia/ia.h

```
/*********************************************************
 * Definitions for the infinite array (ia) class        *
 *                                                       *
 * An infinite array is an array whose size can grow     *
 * as needed.  Adding more elements to the array         *
 * will just cause it to grow.                           *
 *-------------------------------------------------------*
 * class infinite_array                                  *
 *    Member functions                                   *
 *        infinite_array(void)  -- default constructor   *
 *        ~infinite_array(void) -- destructor            *
 *        int &operator [](int index)                    *
 *                gets an element of the infinite array  *
 *********************************************************/

// Number of elements to store in each cell of the infinite array
const unsigned int BLOCK_SIZE = 100;

class infinite_array {
    private:
        // The data for this block
        int    data[BLOCK_SIZE];

        // Pointer to the next array
        class infinite_array *next;
    public:
        // Default constructor
        infinite_array(void)
        {
            next = NULL;
            memset(data, '\0', sizeof(data));
        }

        // Default destructor
        ~infinite_array(void);

        // Return a reference to an element of the array
```

Example 23-2. ia/ia.h (Continued)

```
            int &operator[] (const unsigned int index);
};
```

A few things should be noted about this file. Everything in the file is a constant definition, a data structure definition, or an external definition. Any code that is defined is inline. No actual code or storage is defined in the header file.

The Body of the Module

The body of the module contains all the functions and data for that module. Private functions that are not to be called from outside the module should be declared `static`. Variables declared outside of a function that are not used outside the module are declared `static`.

A Program to Use Infinite Arrays

The infinite array module (*ia.cc*) is shown in Figure 23-1. The program uses a simple linked list to store the elements of the array. A linked list can grow longer as needed (until you run out of memory). Each list element, or bucket, can store 100 numbers. To find element 308, the program starts at the beginning, skips past the first three buckets, and then extracts element 8 from the data in the current bucket.

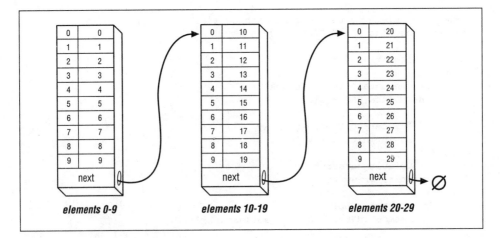

Figure 23-1. Infinite array structure

Example 23-3 contains the code for module *ia.cc*.

Example 23-3. ia/ia.cc

```
/***********************************************************
 * infinite-array -- routines to handle infinite arrays *
 *                                                       *
 * An infinite array is an array that grows as needed.   *
 * There is no index too large for an infinite array     *
 * (unless you run out of memory).                       *
 ***********************************************************/
#include <iostream.h>
#include <stdlib.h>
#include <string.h>

#include "ia.h"                   // Get common definitions

/***********************************************************
 * operator [] -- find an element of an infinite array  *
 *                                                       *
 * Parameters                                            *
 *      index  -- index into the array                   *
 *                                                       *
 * Returns                                               *
 *      reference to the element in the array            *
 ***********************************************************/
int &infinite_array::operator [] (const unsigned int index)
{
    // Pointer to the current bucket
    class infinite_array *current_ptr;

    int current_index;   // Index we are working with

    current_ptr = this;
    current_index = index;

    while (current_index >= BLOCK_SIZE) {
        if (current_ptr->next == NULL) {
            current_ptr->next = new infinite_array;
            if (current_ptr->next == NULL) {
                cerr << "Error: Out of memory\n";
                exit(8);
            }
        }
        current_ptr = current_ptr->next;
        current_index -= BLOCK_SIZE;
    }
    return (current_ptr->data[current_index]);
}

/***********************************************************
 * ~infinite_array -- destroy the infinite array        *
 ***********************************************************/
infinite_array::~infinite_array(void)
```

Example 23-3. ia/ia.cc (Continued)

```
{
    /*
     * Note: We use a cute trick here.
     *
     * Because each bucket in the infinite array is
     * an infinite array itself, when we destroy
     * next, it will destroy all that bucket's "next"s
     * and so on recursively clearing the entire array.
     */
    if (next != NULL) {
        delete next;
        next = NULL;
    }
}
```

The Makefile for Multiple Files

The utility *make* is designed to aid the programmer in compiling and linking programs. Before *make*, the user had to explicitly type compile commands each time there was a change in the program:

```
g++ -Wall -g -ohello hello.cc
```

NOTE

In this chapter we use the commands for the GNU g++ compiler. The C++ compiler on your system may have a different name and a slightly different syntax.

As programs grow, the number of commands needed to create them grows. Typing in a series of 10 or 20 commands is tiresome and error-prone, so programmers started writing *shell scripts* (or, in MS-DOS, *.BAT files*). Then all the programmer had to type was do-it and the computer would compile everything. This was overkill, however, because all the files were recompiled regardless of need.

As the number of files in a project grew, this recompiling became a significant problem. Changing one small file, starting the compilation, and then having to wait until the next day while the computer executed several hundred compile commands was frustrating—especially when only one compile was really needed.

The program *make* was created to do *intelligent compiles*. Its purpose is to first decide what commands need to be executed and then execute them.

The file *Makefile* (upper/lowercase is important in UNIX) contains the rules used by make to decide how to build the program. The *Makefile* contains the following sections:

- Comments
- Macros
- Explicit rules
- Default rules

Any line beginning with a # is a comment.

A macro has the format:

   name = data

Name is any valid identifier. *Data* is the text that will be substituted whenever **make** sees $(*name*).

Example:

```
#
# Very simple Makefile
#
MACRO = Doing All

all:
        echo $(MACRO)
```

Explicit rules tell **make** what commands are needed to create the program. These rules can take several forms. The most common is:

   target: *source* [*source2*] [*source3*]
              command
              [*command*]
              [*command*]
        . . .

Target is the name of a file to create. It is "made," or created, out of the source file *source*. If the *target* is created out of several files, they are all listed.

The command used to create the target is listed on the next line. Sometimes it takes more than one command to create the target. Commands are listed one per line. Each is indented by a tab.

For example, the rule:

```
hello: hello.cc
        g++ -Wall -g -o hello hello.cc
```

tells **make** to create the file *hello* from the file *hello.cc* using the command:

```
g++ -Wall -g -o hello hello.cc
```

Make will create *hello* only if necessary. The files used in the creation of *hello*, arranged in chronological order (by modification times), are shown in Table 23-2.

Table 23-2 . File Modification Times

UNIX	MS-DOS/Windows	Modification Time
hello.cc	HELLO.CPP	Oldest
hello.o	HELLO.OBJ	Old
hello	HELLO.EXE	Newest

If the programmer changes the source file *hello.cc*, the file's modification time will be out of date with respect to the other files. make will sense this and re-create the other files.

Another form of the explicit rule is:

> *source*:
> > *command*
> > [*command*]

In this case, the commands are executed each time make is run, unconditionally.

If the commands are omitted from an explicit rule, make uses a set of built-in rules to determine what command to execute.

For example, the rule:

```
hist.o: ia.h hist.cc
```

tells make to create *hist.o* from *hist.cc* and *ia.h*, using the standard rule for making *<file>.o* from *<file>.cc*. This rule is:

```
g++ $(CFLAGS) -c file.CC
```

(make predefines the macro $(CFLAGS).)

We are going to create a main program *hist.cc* that calls the module *ia.cc*. Both files include the header *ia.h*, so they depend on it. The UNIX *Makefile* that creates the program *hist* from *hist.cc* and *ia.cc* is listed in Example 23-4.

Example 23-4. ia/Makefile

```
# Make file needs debugging
CFLAGS = -g -Wall
SRC = ia.cc hist.cc
OBJ = ia.o  hist.o

all: hist

hist: $(OBJ)
        g++ $(CFLAGS) -o hist $(OBJ)
```

Example 23-4. ia/Makefile (Continued)

```
hist.o:ia.h hist.cc
        g++ $(CFLAGS) -c hist.cc

ia.o:ia.h ia.cc
        g++ $(CFLAGS) -c ia.cc

clean:
        rm hist io.o hist.o
```

The macro SRC is a list of all the C++ files. OBJ is a list of all the object (.o) files. The lines:

```
    hist: $(OBJ)
            g++ $(CFLAGS) -o hist $(OBJ)
```

tell make to create *hist* from the object files. If any of the object files are out of date, make will re-create them.

The line:

```
    hist.o:ia.h
```

tells make to create *hist.o* from *ia.h* and *hist.cc* (*hist.cc* is implied). Because no command is specified, the default is used.

Example 23-5 shows the Makefile for MS-DOS/Windows, using Turbo-C++.

Example 23-5. ia/Makefile.dos

```
#
# Makefile for Borland's Turbo-C++ compiler
#
CC =tcc
#
# Flags
#        -N  -- Check for stack overflow
#        -v  -- Enable debugging
#        -w  -- Turn on all warnings
#        -ml -- Large model
#        -A  -- Force ANSI compliance
#
CFLAGS = -N -v -w -ml -A
#
SRCS = hist.c ia.c
OBJS = hist.obj ia.obj

ia: $(OBJS)
        $(CC) $(CFLAGS) -oia.exe $(OBJS)

hist.obj: hist.cpp ia.h
        $(CC) $(CFLAGS) -c hist.cpp
```

Example 23-5. ia/Makefile.dos (Continued)

```
ia.obj: ia.c ia.h
        $(CC) $(CFLAGS) -c ia.cpp
```

This file is similar to the UNIX *Makefile* except that Turbo-C++ make does not provide any default rules.

There is one big drawback with make. It only checks to see whether the files have changed, not the rules. If you have compiled all your program with CFLAGS=-g for debugging and need to produce the production version (CFLAGS = -O), make will *not* recompile.

The command touch changes the modification date of a file. (It doesn't change the file, it just makes the operating system think it did.) If you touch a source file such as *hello.cc* and then run make, the program will be re-created. This is useful if you have changed the compile-time flags and want to force a re-compilation.

Make provides a rich set of commands for creating programs. Only a few have been discussed here.[*]

Using the Infinite Array

The histogram program (hist) is designed to use the infinite array package. It takes one file as its argument. The file contains a list of numbers between 0 and 99. Any number of entries may be used. The program prints a histogram showing how many times each number appears. (A histogram is a graphic representation of the frequency of data.)

This file contains a number of interesting programming techniques.

The first one is: Let the computer do the work whenever possible. For example, don't program like this:

```
const int LENGTH_X = 300;    // Width of the box in dots
const int LENGTH_Y = 400;    // Height of the box in dots
const int AREA = 12000;      // Total box area in dots
```

In this case, the programmer has decided to multiply 300 x 400 to compute the area. He would be better served by letting the computer do the multiplying:

```
const int LENGTH_X = 300;    // Width of the box in dots
const int LENGTH_Y = 400;    // Height of the box in dots

const int AREA = (LENGTH_X * LENGTH_Y);  // Total box area in dots
```

---

[*] If you are going to create programs that require more than 10 or 20 source files, it is suggested you read the book *Managing Projects with make* (O'Reilly & Associates, Inc.).

That way, if either LENGTH_X or LENGTH_Y is changed, AREA changes automatically. Also, the computer is more accurate in its computations. (If you noticed, the programmer made an error: his AREA is too small by a factor of 10.)

In the histogram program, the number of data points in each output line is computed by the definition:

```
const float FACTOR = ((HIGH_BOUND - LOW_BOUND) / ((float) (NUMBER_OF_LINES-
            1)));
```

The user should be helped whenever possible. In the hist program, if the user does not type the correct number of parameters on the command line, a message appears telling what is wrong and how to correct it.

The program uses the library routine memset to initialize the counters array. This routine is highly efficient for setting all values of an array to zero. The line:

```
    memset(counters, '\0', sizeof(counters));
```

zeros the entire array counters. sizeof(counters) makes sure that all the array is zeroed. Example 23-6 contains a program that uses the infinite array for storing data used to produce a histogram.

Example 23-6. ia/hist.cc

```
File: hist.cc
/********************************************************
 * hist -- generate a histogram of an array of numbers  *
 *                                                      *
 * Usage                                                *
 *      hist <file>                                     *
 *                                                      *
 * Where                                                *
 *      file is the name of the file to work on         *
 ********************************************************/
#include <iostream.h>
#include <fstream.h>
#include <iomanip.h>

#include <stdlib.h>
#include <string.h>

#include "ia.h"

/*
 * The following definitions define the histogram
 */
const int NUMBER_OF_LINES = 50; // # lines in the result
const int LOW_BOUND       = 0;  // Lowest number we record
const int HIGH_BOUND      = 99; // Highest number we record
/*
 * if we have NUMBER_OF_LINES data to
 * output then each item must use
```

Example 23-6. ia/hist.cc (Continued)

```
 * the following factor
 */
const int FACTOR =
  ((HIGH_BOUND - LOW_BOUND + 1) / NUMBER_OF_LINES);

// Number of characters wide to make the histogram
const int WIDTH = 60;

// Array to store the data in
static infinite_array data_array;
// Number of items in the array
static int data_items;

main(int argc, char *argv[])
{
    void  read_data(char *name);// Get the data into the array
    void  print_histogram(void);// Print the data

    if (argc != 2) {
        cerr << "Error: Wrong number of arguments\n";
        cerr << "Usage is:\n";
        cerr << "  hist <data-file>\n";
        exit(8);
    }
    data_items = 0;

    read_data(argv[1]);
    print_histogram();
    return (0);
}
/*********************************************************
 * read_data -- read data from the input file into      *
 *              the data array                           *
 *                                                       *
 * Parameters                                            *
 *      name -- the name of the file to read             *
 *********************************************************/
void  read_data(char *name)
{
    ifstream in_file(name); // Input file
    int data;               // Data from input

    if (in_file.bad()) {
        cerr << "Error: Unable to open " << name << '\n';
        exit(8);
    }
    while (!in_file.eof()) {
        in_file >> data;

        // If we get an eof we ran out of data in last read
        if (in_file.eof())
          break;
```

Example 23-6. ia/hist.cc (Continued)

```
            data_array[data_items] = data;
            ++data_items;
        }
}
/************************************************************
 * print_histogram -- print the histogram output          *
 ************************************************************/
void  print_histogram(void)
{
    // Upper bound for printout
    int    counters[NUMBER_OF_LINES];
    int low;                // Lower bound for printout
    int    out_of_range = 0;// Number of items out of bounds
    int    max_count = 0;// Biggest counter
    float scale;           // Scale for outputting dots
    int    index;           // Index into the data

    memset(counters, '\0', sizeof(counters));

    for (index = 0; index < data_items; ++index) {
        int data; // Data for this point

        data = data_array[index];

        if ((data < LOW_BOUND) || (data > HIGH_BOUND))
            ++out_of_range;
        else {
            // Index into counters array
            int    count_index;

            count_index = int (float(data - LOW_BOUND) / FACTOR);

            ++counters[count_index];
            if (counters[count_index] > max_count)
                max_count = counters[count_index];
        }
    }

    scale = float(max_count) / float(WIDTH);

    low = LOW_BOUND;

    for (index = 0; index < NUMBER_OF_LINES; ++index) {
        // Index for outputting the dots
        int    char_index;
        int    number_of_dots;    // Number of * to output

        cout << setw(2) << index << ' ' <<
                setw(3) << low << "-" <<
                setw(3) << low + FACTOR - 1 << " (" <<
                setw(4) << counters[index] << "): ";
```

Example 23-6. ia/hist.cc (Continued)

```
            number_of_dots = int(float(counters[index]) / scale);
            for (char_index = 0; char_index < number_of_dots;
                ++char_index)
                cout << '*';
            cout << '\n';
            low += FACTOR;
        }
    cout << out_of_range << " items out of range\n";
}
```

A sample run of this program produces:

```
%   hist   test
0:  0-  2 ( 100): ************************
1:  2-  4 ( 200): ************************************************
2:  4-  6 ( 100): ************************
3:  6-  8 ( 100): ************************
4:  8- 10 (   0):
5: 10- 12 ( 100): ************************
6: 12- 14 (  50): ************
7: 14- 16 ( 150): ************************************
8: 16- 18 (  50): ************
9: 18- 20 (  50): ************
10: 20- 22 ( 100): ************************
11: 22- 24 ( 100): ************************
12: 24- 26 (  50): ************
13: 26- 28 ( 100): ************************
14: 28- 30 (  50): ************
15: 30- 32 ( 100): ************************
16: 32- 34 (  50): ************
17: 34- 36 (   0):
18: 36- 38 ( 100): ************************
19: 38- 40 (   1):
20: 40- 42 ( 150): ************************************
21: 42- 44 (  50): ************
22: 44- 46 ( 250): ************************************************************
23: 46- 48 ( 100): ************************
24: 48- 51 ( 150): ************************************
25: 51- 53 ( 100): ************************
26: 53- 55 (  50): ************
27: 55- 57 ( 200): ************************************************
28: 57- 59 (  50): ************
29: 59- 61 (  50): ************
30: 61- 63 (  50): ************
31: 63- 65 ( 150): ************************************
32: 65- 67 ( 100): ************************
33: 67- 69 (   0):
34: 69- 71 ( 199): ************************************************
35: 71- 73 ( 200): ************************************************
36: 73- 75 ( 100): ************************
37: 75- 77 (  50): ************
38: 77- 79 ( 100): ************************
```

```
39: 79- 81 ( 100): ************************
40: 81- 83 ( 200): **************************************************
41: 83- 85 ( 100): ************************
42: 85- 87 (   0):
43: 87- 89 (   0):
44: 89- 91 (  50): ************
45: 91- 93 ( 150): ************************************
46: 93- 95 ( 100): ************************
47: 95- 97 (  50): ************
48: 97- 99 ( 100): ************************
49: 99-101 (   0):
500 items out of range
```

Dividing a Task into Modules

Unfortunately, computer programming is more of an art than a science. There are no hard and fast rules that tell you how to divide a task into modules. Knowing what makes a good module and what doesn't comes with experience and practice.

This section describes some general rules for module division and how they can be applied to real-world programs. The techniques described here have worked well for me. You should use whatever works for you.

Information is a vital part of any program. The key to a program is your decision about what information you want to use and what processing you want to perform on it. Be sure to analyze the information flow before you begin the design.

Design the modules to minimize the amount of information that has to pass between them. If you look at the organization of the Army, you'll see that it is divided up into modules. There is the infantry, artillery, tank corps, and so on. The amount of information that passes between these modules is minimized. For example, if an infantry sergeant wants the artillery to bombard an enemy position, he calls up artillery command and says, "There's a pillbox at location Y-94. Get rid of it." The artillery command handles all the details of deciding which battery to use, how much firepower to allocate based on the requirements of other fire missions, maintaining supplies, and many more details.*

Programs should be organized the same way. Information that can be kept inside a module should be. Minimizing the amount of intermodule communication cuts down on communication errors as well as limiting maintenance problems that occur when a module is upgraded.

---

* This is a very general diagram of the division of an ideal army. The system used by the United States Army is more complex and so highly classified that even the generals don't know how it works.

Module Division Example: Text Editor

You are already familiar with using a text editor. It is a program that allows the user to display and change text files. The main piece of information is the text file we are editing. Most editors are display oriented and continually display about 24 lines of the current file on the screen.

Finally, one more piece of information is needed: the editing commands. The commands are typed in by the user. This information must be parsed so the computer can understand it. Then it can be executed. The individual commands are small and perform similar functions (`delete  line` is very much like `delete character`). Imposing a standard structure on the command execution modules improves readability and reliability. A block diagram of the editor can be seen in Figure 23-2.

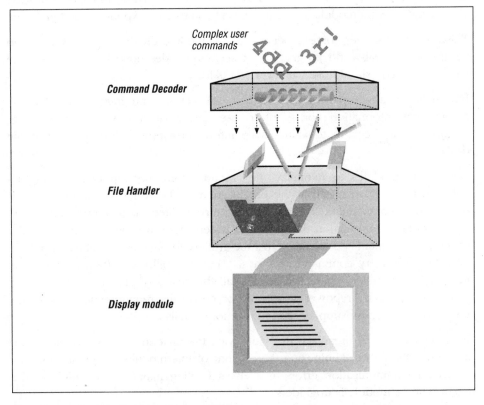

Figure 23-2.. Module division of the text editor

There is minimal communication between the modules. The display section needs to know only two things: 1) where the cursor is and 2) what the file currently looks like. All the file module needs to do is read the file, write the file, and keep track of changes. Even the way the changes are made can be minimized. All editing commands, no matter how complex, can be broken down into a series of inserts and deletes. It is the responsibility of the command module to take the complex user commands and turn them into simple inserts and deletes that the file handler can process. Information passing between the modules is minimal. No information passes between the command decoder and the display module.

A word processor is just a fancy text editor. Where a simple editor only has to worry about ASCII characters (one font, one size), a word processor must be able to handle many different sizes and shapes.

Compiler Construction

In a compiler, the information being processed is C++ code. The job of the compiler is to transform that information from C++ source to machine-dependent object code. There are several stages in this process. First the code is run through the preprocessor to expand macros, take care of conditional compilation, and read include files. Next the processed file is passed to the first stage of the compiler, the lexical analyzer.

The lexical analyzer takes as its input a stream of characters and returns a series of *tokens*. A token is a computer-science term meaning word or operator. For example, let's look at the English command:

```
Open the door.
```

There are 14 characters in this command. Lexical analysis would turn this into three words and a period. These tokens are then passed to the parser where they are assembled into sentences. At this stage a symbol table is started so that the parser can have some idea what variables are being used by the program.

Now the compiler knows what the program is supposed to do. The optimizer looks at the instructions and tries to figure out how to make them more efficient. This step is optional and is omitted unless the -O flag is specified on the command line.

The code generator turns the high-level statements into machine-specific assembly code. In assembly language, each assembly-language statement corresponds to one machine instruction. The assembler turns assembly language into binary code that can be executed by the machine. The general information flow of a compiler is diagrammed in Figure 23-3.

Lexical analysis and parsing are very common and used in a wide variety of programs. The utility *lex* can generate the lexical analyzer module for a program, given a description of the tokens used by the program. Another utility, *yacc*, can generate the parser module. These programs are described in the book *lex & yacc* (O'Reilly & Associates).

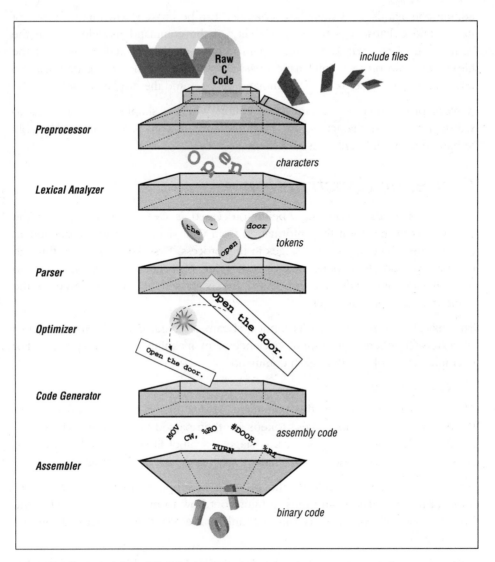

Figure 23-3. Compiler modules

Spreadsheet

A simple spreadsheet takes a matrix of numbers and equations and displays the results on screen. The information managed by this program is the equations and the data.

The core of a spreadsheet is the equations. To change the equations into numbers, we need to go through lexical analysis and parsing, just like a compiler.

But unlike a compiler, we don't generate machine code. Instead, we interpret the equations and compute the results.

Results are passed off to the display manager, which puts them on the screen. Add to this an input module that allows the user to edit and change the equations, and you have a spreadsheet, as shown in Figure 23-4.

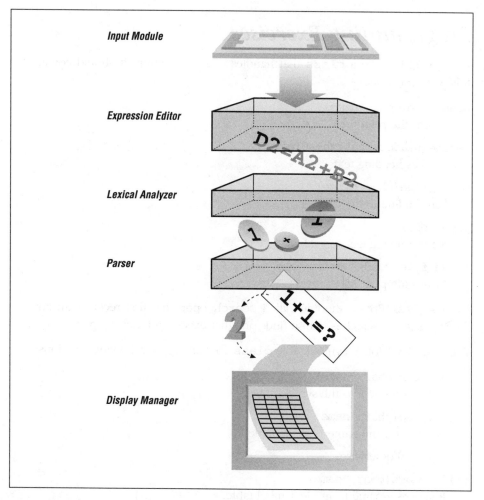

Figure 23-4. Spreadsheet layout

Module Design Guidelines

Although there are no hard and fast rules when it comes to laying out the modules for a program, here are some general guidelines.

- The number of public functions in a module should be small.

- The information passed between modules should be small.

- All the functions in a module should perform related jobs.

- Modules should contain no more than 1,500 lines. With more lines, they become difficult to edit, print, and understand.

Programming Exercises

Exercise 23-1: Write a `class` that handles page formatting. It should contain the following functions:

`open_file(char *name)`
> Opens the print file.

`define_header(char *heading)`
> Defines heading text.

`print_line(char *line)`
> Sends a line to the file.

`page(void)`
> Starts a new page.

`close_file(void)`
> Closes the print file.

Exercise 23-2: Write a module called `search_open` that first receives an array of filenames that it searches until it finds one that exists, and then it opens that file.

Exercise 23-3: Write a symbol table `class` containing the following functions:

`void enter(char *name)`
> Enters a name into the symbol table.

`int lookup(char *name)`
> Returns 1 if the name is in the table;
>
> returns 0 otherwise.

`void remove(char *name)`
> Removes a name from the symbol table.

Exercise 23-4: Take the *words* program from Chapter 20, *Advanced Pointers*, and combine it with the infinite array module to create a cross-reference program. (As an added bonus, teach it about C++ comments and strings to create a C++ cross-referencer.)

24

Templates

> *Thou cunning'st pattern of excelling nature.*
> —Shakespeare
> *Othello,* Act V

What Is a Template?

Templates are a relatively new addition to C++. They allow you to write generic classes and functions that work for several different data types.

Templates will be a very useful part of the C++ language, when they grow up. The problem is that although the *Draft ANSI C++ Standard* specifies the complete syntax for templates, it says nothing about how to implement them. The result is that each compiler maker has implemented templates differently, so programs that use templates tend to be nonportable.

Templates: The Hard Way

Suppose we want to define a function **max** to return the maximum of two items. Actually, we don't want to define just one **max** function, but a family of functions: one to find the maximum of two **int**s, one for **float**s, one for **char**s, and so on.

We start by defining a parameterized macro to generate the code for the function. This is called the *definition stage.* The macro looks like:

```
#define make_max(type) type max(type d1, type d2) { \
    if (d1 > d2)                                     \
        return (d1);                                 \
    return (d2);                                     \
}
```

NOTE

Each line except the last one ends in a backslash (\). A `#define` macro spans a single line, so the backslash turns our five lines into one. By putting the backslashes in the same column we can easily tell if we miss one.

This macro generates no code. It merely provides the definition that is used in the next phase to generate the functions we want. This is called the *generation phase*.

```
define_max(int);
define_max(float);
define_max(char);
```

Finally, somewhere in the code we use the functions we've just defined. (This is called the *use phase*, of course.)

```
main(void) {
    float f = max(3.5, 8.7);
    int   i = max(100, 800);
    char ch = max('A', 'Q');
```

Figure 24-1 shows the source code for the `#define` style templates and the code generated by them.

This method works adequately for simple functions like **max**. It doesn't work well for larger functions. One drawback to this system is that we must invoke the macro **define_max** for each data type we want to use. It would be nice if C++ would call **define_max** automatically.

Templates allow you to define a generic function. C++ then uses this template to generate a specific *instance* of the function as needed. For example, to define the function **max** as a template, we write:

```
template<class kind>
kind max(kind d1, kind d2) {
    if (d1 > d2)
        return (d1);
    return (d2);
}
```

NOTE

The construct `<class kind>` tells C++ that the word `kind` can be replaced by any type. (Note: The keyword `class` is used in this context to indicate that `kind` can be any type: not only classes, but simple types as well.)

The `template` declaration corresponds to the definition of the parameterized macro. Like the parameterized macro, it generates no code; it merely provides a definition for the next phase.

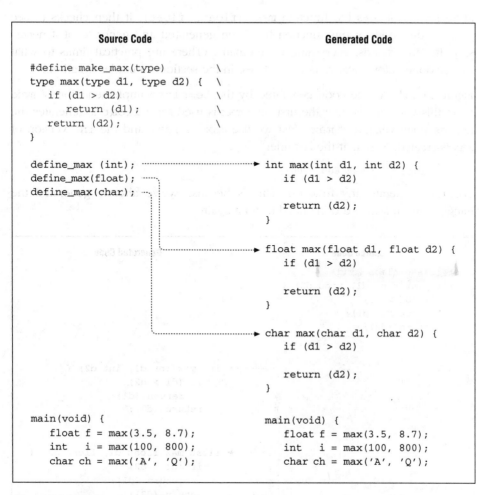

Figure 24-1. *Code generated by #define style templates*

Now we can use the template, much like we used the functions defined by the parameterized macro:

```
main(void) {
    float f = max(3.5, 8.7);
    int   i = max(100, 800);
    char ch = max('A', 'Q');
    int   i2 = max(600, 200);
```

You may have noticed that we skipped the **generation phase**. That's because C++ automatically performs the generation for us. In other words, C++ looks at the line:

```
    float f = max(3.5, 8.7);
```

and sees that it uses the function `max (float, float)`. It then checks to see whether the code for this function has been generated and generates it if necessary. In other words, everything is automatic. (There are practical limits to what can be done automatically, as you will see in the section on implementation.)

Figure 24-2 shows the code generated by the `template` implementation of `max`. From this you can see that the first time `max` is used for a `float` it generates the floating point version of `max`. Next we use `max` for `int`, and the `int` version of `max` is created. Note that the last line:

```
int  i2 = max(600, 200);
```

does not generate any function. This is because we've already generated the integer version `max` and don't need to do it again.

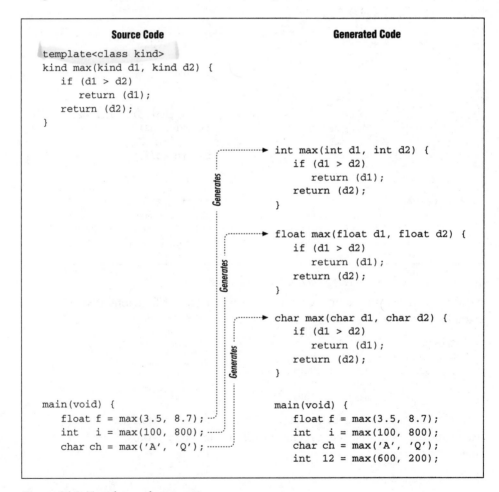

Figure 24-2. Template code generation

Function Specialization

Templates go a bit further than simple code generation. They can handle special cases as well.

Suppose we want to use the function **max** to compare strings as well:

```
char *name1 = "Able";
char *name2 = "Baker";

cout << max(name1, name2) << '\n';
```

We have a problem, because strings are represented by a character pointer (**char** *). The comparison:

```
if (d1 > d2)
```

compares the value of the *pointers*, not the data that's pointed to. What we want to do is tell C++, "Use the normal comparison except when the data type is a string, and then use **strcmp**."

This is done through a process called *specialization.* We declare a special version of the **max** function just for strings:

```
char *max(char *d1, char *d2) {
    if (strcmp(d1, d2) < 0)
        return (d1);
    return (d2);
}
```

When C++ first sees the use of the function **max** it looks through the list of simple functions before it looks through its list of templates. Thus when we have:

```
cout << max(name1, name2) << '\n';
```

C++ will find the simple function **max(char *, char *)** before trying to expand the template **max(kind d1, kind d2)**.

Example 24-1 illustrates the use of template functions.

Example 24-1. max-t/max.cc .

```
#include <iostream.h>
#include <string.h>

// A template for the "max" function

template<class kind>
kind max(kind d1, kind d2) {
    if (d1 > d2)
        return (d1);
    return (d2);
}
```

Example 24-1. max-t/max.cc (Continued).

```
// A specialization for the "max" function
//    because we handle char * a little differently
char *max(char *d1, char *d2) {
    if (strcmp(d1, d2) > 0)
        return (d1);
    return (d2);
}

main()
{
    // Let's test max
    cout << "max(1, 2) " << max(1, 2) << '\n';
    cout << "max(2, 1) " << max(2, 1) << '\n';

    cout << "max(\"able\", \"baker\") " << max("able", "baker") << '\n';
    cout << "max(\"baker\", \"able\") " << max("baker", "able") << '\n';
    return (0);
}
```

Class Templates

Class templates are a little more complex than function templates. Declaring them is easy. They are defined just like function templates. Example 24-2 shows the stack class from Chapter 13, *Simple Classes*, written as a template.

Example 24-2. max-t/stack1.cc .

```
#include <stdlib.h>
#include <iostream.h>

const int STACK_SIZE = 100;     // Maximum size of a stack

/********************************************************
 * Stack class                                         *
 *                                                     *
 * Member functions                                   *
 *      stack -- initialize the stack                 *
 *      push -- put an item on the stack              *
 *      pop -- remove an item from the stack          *
 ********************************************************/
// The stack itself
template<class kind>
class stack {
    private:
        int count;              // Number of items in the stack
        kind data[STACK_SIZE];  // The items themselves
    public:
        // Initialize the stack
        stack(void) {
            count = 0;  // Zero the stack
        }
```

Example 24-2. max-t/stack1.cc (Continued).

```
        // Push an item on the stack
        void push(const kind item) {
            data[count] = item;
            ++count;
        }

        // Pop an item from the stack
        kind pop(void) {
            // Stack goes down by one
            --count;

            // Then we return the top value
            return (data[count]);
        }
};
```

There is a problem, however. To use this class we need to declare an instance of this class. In the past, we've been able to declare a stack with the statement:

```
stack a_stack;      // This won't work
```

The problem is that **stack** is now a generic template. The stack can now contain anything. When C++ sees this declaration, it's going to ask, "A stack of what?" We must specify the type of data we are storing. The new declaration is:

```
stack<int> a_stack;     // A stack of integers
```

The **<int>** tells C++ to use "**int**" for "**kind**" throughout the stack. We can now use the new class variable:

```
a_stack.push(1);
x = a_stack.pop();
```

In the **stack** class, we defined all the member functions inside the class definition. We could just as well have specified the procedures outside the class. To do so, we must put the template clause **template<class kind>** in front of each procedure and put the template parameter (**<kind>**) in the name of the class. For example, the **pop** routine would look like:

```
/***********************************************************
 * stack::push -- push an item on the stack               *
 *                                                         *
 * Warning: We do not check for overflow                   *
 *                                                         *
 * Parameters                                              *
 *      item -- item to put on the stack                   *
 ***********************************************************/
template<class kind>
inline void stack<kind>::push(const kind item)
{
```

```
        data[count] = item;
        ++count;
}
```

Class Specialization

You can think of a class template such as

```
    template <class kind>stack { ...
```

as instructions that tell C++ how to generate a set of classes named `stack<int>`, `stack<double>`, `stack<float>`, and so on. C++ will also generate automatically the member functions: `stack<int>::push`, `stack<double>::push`, and `stack<float>::push`.

However, if you explicitly declare a member function yourself, C++ will use your definition before generating its own. Suppose we want to have a stack store strings (`char *`). We don't want to store the pointers; we want to store the actual strings. To do this, we need a special version of the `push` function that duplicates the string before pushing it onto the stack:

```
    inline void stack<char *>::push(const char * item)
    {
        data[count] = strdup(item);
        ++count;
    }
```

Note that we didn't use `template<class kind>` at the beginning of the function. The `template` keyword tells C++: "This is a generic class. Generate specific versions from it." With no `template,` we are telling C++: "This is the real thing. Use it directly."

Implementation Difficulties

The Annotated C++ Reference Manual by Ellis and Stroustrup is considered the default standard of the C++ language. It contains a complete definition of the syntax for `templates`. However, it does not explain how compilers should implement them.

As you shall see, implementing `templates` is not easy. For example, suppose we put the `stack` template in a module. The file *stack.h* defines the class and the file *stack.cc* defines the member functions. (We will assume that none of the member functions are inline.)

Now we want to use the template for a floating-point stack (`stack<float>`) in the file *main.cc*. Figure 24-3 shows the source-code layout.

This is where the compiler implementors start pulling their hair out.

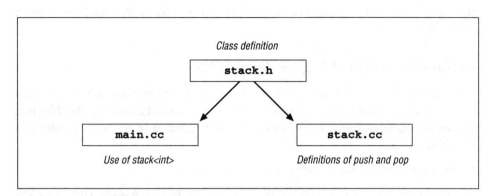

*Figure 24-3. Source-code layout for using a **stack** template*

We know that in *main.cc,* we're going to use stack<int>. As a matter of fact, the file *stack.h* defined prototypes for the two member functions push and pop. So when the compiler sees stack<int>, it should automatically generate the code for push and pop.

But *how?* The bodies of these two member functions are tucked away in the file *stack.cc.* The compiler is working on *main.cc.* It doesn't know anything about any other file, so it doesn't know how to generate push<int> and pop<int>.

But couldn't the compiler generate push<int> and pop<int> when it compiles *stack.cc?* Yes, if it knew that someone had declared a stack<int> variable. But the only one who did that is *main.cc* and the compiler isn't working on that file just now. Managers call this situation "technically challenging." Programmers call it "a nightmare."

The problems associated with template generation are not simple to solve. Different compiler makers have chosen different approaches. The problem is that all these approaches are not compatible. Code written for one compiler may not work on another. In some cases, even code written for one version of a compiler might not work in another version.

Templates are the leading edge of C++ compiler technology and, like all new programs, there are just a few bugs to work out. In the following sections, we discuss the various ways compiler makers have attempted to solve the problems associated with templates. Compiler technology and standards are constantly evolving, so the information in this section may not be up to date.

Microsoft's Implementation

As of this publication date, the Microsoft C++ and Visual C++ compilers do not have templates. Although extremely simple, this form of "implementation" is very limited. On the other hand, I've never had any trouble with templates using a Microsoft compiler.

Turbo-C++ and GNU g++ Templates

The Turbo-C++ and the GNU g++ compilers take a similar approach. If you plan to use `stack<float>`, then you must have a `stack<float>` in the file that defines the member functions: *stack.cc*. At the beginning of the *stack.cc* file, you will need the line:

```
typedef stack<float> floating_point_stack;
```

Actually you never have to use the type `floating_point_stack`. The `typedef` is there just to tell the compiler to generate the needed member functions.

Both compilers also have switches that tell the compiler what to do about inline functions that can't be handled inline. Suppose you define the function:

```
template<class kind>
inline kind max(kind d1, kind d2) {
    if (d1 > d2)
        return (d1);
    return (d2);
}
```

in the header file *max.h* and then proceed to use the `max<float>` function in three different files. Also suppose that the function is so complex that the compiler decided to ignore the `inline` directive. (I know that's a lot of supposing, but it's the only way you get to this mess.)

When your three files are compiled, three copies of `max<float>` are generated. The Turbo-C++ linker is smart enough to detect this fact and will throw two of them away. The GNU g++ linker is not so smart, and you'll wind up with three copies of the same routine in your code.

Both Turbo-C++ and GNU provide you with compiler options that help solve this problem. If you put the line:

```
#pragma interface // GNU g++ only option
```

in your code, it tells GNU: "Don't generate the body for any template functions found in this header." Later, in one of your files, you must put the directive:

```
#pragma implementation // GNU g++ only option
```

This tells GNU, "Here's where you generate the function bodies."

Turbo-C++ uses similar pragmas. However, the "interface" directive is:

```
#pragma option -Jgx // Turbo-C++ only option
```

and the "implementation" directive is:

```
#pragma option -Jg // Turbo-C++ only option
```

The options are clunky, nonportable, and difficult to use. They are meant to solve an implementation problem that has not been properly solved yet.

CFront-Based Compilers

CFront is the name of the AT&T C++ to C translator that was the basis of the first C++ compiler. Most C++ compiler makers consider themselves standard if they are compatible with the latest version of CFront.

CFront handles the problem of template generation by putting it off until link time, so you only compile and link the file *main.cc*. At link time, CFront notices that *main.cc* uses `stack<float>`. It then looks for a file named *stack.cc*. (Note: Your file must be named *<class>*.cc.) This file is used to generate the templates.

Although this method seems simple enough, there are a lot of details to take care of. For example, the file *stack.h* is automatically included when the linker tries to compile *stack.cc*. What's worse, if you include it yourself with a `#include "stack.h"`, the compiler gets confused.

The CFront approach is a good attempt at solving the template problem, but there are still many bugs to work out.

Writing Portable Templates

How can you write a portable template? The simple answer is, "Don't use them." However, the best way to create a truly portable template is to write everything as inline functions and put all your functions in a single-header file. As far as I can tell, this method works for every compiler that has templates. It may not be the most efficient way of doing things, but it is the most portable.

Summary

Templates provide a convenient way of writing generic classes and functions. However, implementation of templates is still undergoing refinement. As a practical matter, you may want to wait until the language settles down a little before using them.

Programming Exercises

Exercise 24-1: Write a template `min` that returns the minimum of two values. Make sure you handle strings correctly.

Exercise 24-2: Write a template class to implement an array with bounds checking.

Exercise 24-3: Define a template class that implements a set. The class allows you to set, clear, and test elements. (An integer version of this class was presented in Example 13-2.)

25

Portability Problems

Wherein I spake of most disastrous changes,
Of moving accidents by flood and field,
Of hair-breadth 'scapes i' the
imminent deadly breadth...

—Shakespeare on program porting
Othello, Act 1, Scene 3

You've just completed work on your great masterpiece, a ray-tracing program that renders complex three-dimensional shaded graphics on a Cray supercomputer using 30MB of memory and 5GB of disk space. What do you do when someone comes in and asks you to port this program to an IBM PC with 640K of memory and 100MB of disk space? Killing him is out. Not only is it illegal, but it also is considered unprofessional. Your only choice is to whimper and start the port. It is during this process that you will find that your nice, working program exhibits all sorts of strange and mysterious problems.

C++ programs are supposed to be portable. However, C++ contains many machine-dependent features. Also, because of the vast difference between UNIX and MS-DOS/Windows, system dependencies can frequently be found in many programs. This chapter discusses some of the problems associated with writing truly portable programs as well as some of the traps you might encounter.

Modularity

One of the tricks to writing portable programs is to put all the nonportable code into a separate module. For example, screen handling differs greatly in MS-DOS/Windows and UNIX. To design a portable program, you'd have to write machine-specific screen-update modules.

For example, the HP-98752A terminal has a set of function keys labeled F1–F8. The PC also has a function-key set. The problem is that these keys don't send out the same set of codes. The HP sends "<esc>p<return>" for F1 and the PC sends "<null>". In this case, you would want to write a **get_code** routine that gets a character (or function key string) from the keyboard and translates function keys. Because the translation is different for both machines, a machine-dependent module is needed for each one. For the HP machine, you would put together the program with *main.cc* and *hp-tty.cc*, while for the PC you would use *main.cc* and *pc-tty.cc*.

Word Size

A `long int` is 32 bits, a `short int` is 16 bits,[*] and a normal `int` can be 16 or 32 bits depending on the machine. This can lead to unexpected problems. For example, the following code works on a 32-bit UNIX system, but fails when ported to MS-DOS/Windows:

```
int zip;

zip = 92126;
cout << "Zip code " << zip << '\n';
```

The problem is that on MS-DOS/Windows, **zip** is only 16 bits — too small for 92126. To fix the problem, we declare **zip** as a 32-bit integer:

```
long int zip;

zip = 92126;
cout << Zip code " << zip << '\n';
```

Now zip is 32 bits and can hold 92126.

Byte-Order Problem

A `short int` consists of two bytes. Consider the number 0x1234. The two bytes have the value 0x12 and 0x34. Which value is stored in the first byte? The answer is machine dependent.

This can cause considerable trouble when you try to write portable binary files. Motorola 68000-series machines use one type of byte order (ABCD), while Intel and Digital Equipment Corporation machines use another (BADC).

One solution to the problem of portable binary files is to avoid them. Put an option in your program to read and write ASCII files. ASCII offers the twin advantages of being far more portable as well as human readable.

---

[*] The draft ANSI standard does not specify the actual size of `long int` or `short int`. However, on every machine I know of, a `long int` is 32 bits and a `short int` is 16 bits.

The disadvantage is that text files are larger. Some files may be too big for ASCII. In that case, the magic number at the beginning of a file may be useful. Suppose the magic number is 0x11223344 (a bad magic number, but a good example). When the program reads the magic number, it can check against the correct number as well as the byte-swapped version (0x22114433). The program can automatically fix the file problem:

```
const int MAGIC     = 0x11223344; // File identification number
const int SWAP_MAGIC = 0x22114433; // Magic number byte swapped

ifstream in_file;  // File containing binary data
long int magic;    // Magic number from file

in_file.open("data");

in.file.read((char *)&magic, sizeof(magic));

switch (magic) {
    case MAGIC:
        // No problem
        break;
    case SWAP_MAGIC:
        cout <<"Converting file, please wait\n";
        convert_file(in_file);
        break;
    default:
        cerr << "Error: Bad magic number " << magic << '\n';
        exit (8);
}
```

Alignment Problem

Some computers limit the addresses that can be used for integers and other types of data. For example, the 68000 series requires that all integers start on a two-byte boundary. If you attempt to access an integer using an odd address, you generate an error. Some processors have no alignment rules, while some are even more restrictive, requiring integers to be aligned on a four-byte boundary.

Alignment restrictions are not limited to integers. Floating point numbers and pointers also must be aligned correctly.

C++ hides the alignment restrictions from you. For example, if you declare the following structure on a 68000:

```
struct funny {
    char    flag;    // Type of data following
    long int value;  // Value of the parameter
};
```

C++ allocates storage for this structure as shown on the left in Figure 25-1.

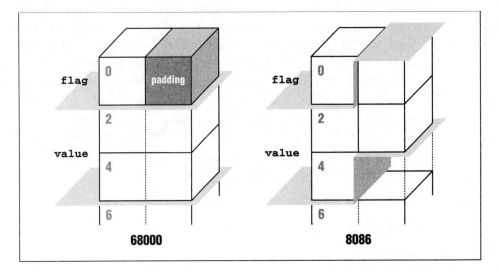

Figure 25-1. Structure on 68000 and 8086 architectures

On an 8086-class machine with no alignment restrictions, this is allocated as shown on the right in Figure 25-1.

The problem is that the size of the structure changes from machine to machine. On a 68000, the structure size is six bytes and on the 8086, it is five. So if you write a binary file containing 100 records on a 68000, it will be 600 bytes long, while on an 8086 it will be only 500 bytes long. Obviously the file is not written the same way on both machines.

One way around this problem is to use ASCII files. As we have said before, there are many problems with binary files. Another solution is to explicitly declare a pad byte:

```
struct new_funny {
        char    flag;    // Type of data following
        char    pad;     // Not used
        long int value;  // Value of the parameter
};
```

The pad character makes the field value align correctly on a 68000 machine while making the structure the correct size on an 8086-class machine.

Using pad characters is difficult and error-prone. For example, although new_ funny is portable between machines with one- and two-byte alignment for 32-bit integers, it is not portable to any machine with a four-byte integer alignment.

NULL-Pointer Problem

Many programs and utilities were written using UNIX on VAX computers. On this computer, the first byte of any program is 0. Many programs written on this computer contain a bug: They use the null pointer as a string.

Example:

```
#define NULL 0

char *string;

string = NULL;
cout << "String is '" << str "'\n";
```

This is actually an illegal use of **string**. Null pointers should never be dereferenced. On the VAX, this error causes no problems. Because byte zero of the program is zero, **string** points to a null string. This is due to luck, not design.

On a VAX, this will print:

```
String is ''
```

On an old Celerity, the first byte of the program is a "Q." When this program is run on a Celerity, it will print:

```
String is 'Q'
```

On other computers, this type of code can generate unexpected results. Many of the utilities ported from a VAX to a Celerity exhibited the "Q" bug.

Filename Problems

UNIX specifies files as `/root/sub/file` while MS-DOS/Windows uses `\root\sub\file`. When porting from UNIX to MS-DOS/Windows, file names must be changed. For example:

```
#ifndef __MSDOS__
#include <sys/stat.h> /* UNIX version of the file */
#else __MSDOS__
#include <sys\stat.h> /* DOS version of the file */
#endif __MSDOS__
```

Question 25-1: *Why does Example 25-1 work on UNIX, but when we run it in MS-DOS/Windows we get the message:*

oot ew   able: file not found

Example 25-1. ifstream in_file

```
#ifndef __MSDOS__
#define NAME "/root/new/table"
#else __MSDOS__
#define NAME "\root\new\table"
#endif __MSDOS__

in_file.open(NAME);
if (in_file.bad()) {
    cout << NAME << ": file not found\n";
    exit(8);
}
```

File Types

In UNIX there is only one file type. In MS-DOS/Windows there are two, text and binary. The flags O_BINARY and O_TEXT are used in MS-DOS/Windows to indicate file type. Older versions of UNIX have no such flags.

One way of handling this problem is to write different **open** calls for each system:

```
#ifndef __MSDOS__
file_descriptor = open("file", O_RDONLY);
#else __MSDOS__
file_descriptor = open("file", O_RDONLY|O_BINARY);
#endif __MSDOS__
```

This is messy. A far better way is to define dummy O_BINARY and O_TEXT flags:

```
#ifndef O_BINARY   /* Do we have an O_BINARY? */
#define O_BINARY 0  /* If not define one (BINARY and TEXT)*/
#define O_TEXT 0    /*  so they don't get in the way */
#endif O_BINARY


 . . .
file_descriptor = open("file", O_RDONLY|O_BINARY);
```

Summary

It is possible to write portable programs in C++. Because C++ runs on many different types of machines that use different operating systems, it is not easy. However, if you keep portability in mind when creating the code, you can minimize the problems.

Porting Four-Letter Words

Portability problems can occur outside of the programming world. When *Practical C Programming* was translated into Japanese the translator had a little trouble with one of the programming problems.

The problem was, "Write a program to translate four-letter words into more polite equivalents."

Trouble is that the Japanese have no concept of four-letter words. In their language, all words are one letter. The translator explained the concept as best he could, but just to drive the point home, he gave some examples of forbidden English words. I'll spare you the X-rated examples.

Answers to Chapter Questions

Answer 25-1: The problem is that C++ uses the backslash (\) as an escape character. The character \r is <return>, \n is <new line>, and \t is <tab>. What we really have for a name is:

```
<return>oot<new line>ew<tab>able
```

The name should be specified as:

```
#define NAME "\\root\\new\\table"
```

NOTE

The `#include` uses a filename, not a C++ string. While you must use double backslashes (\\) in a C++ string, you use single backslashes in an #include. The following two lines are both correct:

```
#define NAME "\\root\\new\\table"
#include "\root\new\defs.h"
```

26

Putting It All Together

For there isn't a job on the top of the earth the beggar don't know, nor do.

—Kipling

In this chapter we create a complete program. Every step of the process is covered, from setting forth the requirements to testing the result.

Requirements

Before we start, we need to decide what it is we are going to do. This is a very important step and is left out of far too many programming cycles.

This chapter's program must fulfill several requirements. First, it must be long enough to demonstrate modular programming, but at the same time be short enough to fit inside a single chapter. Second, it must be complex enough to demonstrate a wide range of C++ features, but be simple enough for a novice C++ programmer to understand.

Finally, it must be useful. This is not so simple to define. What's useful to one person might not be useful to another. We decided to refine this requirement and restate it as "It must be useful to C++ programmers." The program we have selected reads C++ source files and generates simple statistics on the nesting of parentheses, and the ratio of comments to code lines.

The specification for our statistics program is:

```
Preliminary Specification for a C++ Statistics Gathering Program
Steve Oualline
February 10, 1995
```

The program stat gathers statistics about C++ source files and prints them. The command line is:

```
stat <files..>
```

where <files..> is a list of source files. The following shows the output of the program on a short test file.

Example 26-1. stat/stat.out .

```
 1 (0    {0    #include <iostream.h>
 2 (0    {0    /*********************************************************
 3 (0    {0     * calc -- a simple 4-function calculator               *
 4 (0    {0     *********************************************************/
 5 (0    {0    int     result;      // The result of the calculations
 6 (0    {0    char    oper_char;   // User-specified operator
 7 (0    {0    int     value;       // Value specified after the operator
 8 (0    {0    main()
 9 (0    {1    {
10 (0    {1        result = 0;                    // Initialize the result
11 (0    {1
12 (0    {1        // Le (1) {
14 (0    {2            cout << "Result: " << result << '\n';
15 (0    {2            cout << "Enter operator and number: ";
16 (0    {2
17 (0    {2            cin >> oper_char >> value;
18 (0    {2
19 (1    {2            if ((oper_char == 'q') ||
20 (0    {2                (oper_char == 'Q'))
21 (0    {2                break;
22 (0    {2
23 (0    {3            switch (oper_char) {
24 (0    {3                case '+':
25 (0    {3                    result += value;
26 (0    {3                    break;
27 (0    {3                case '-':
28 (0    {3                    result -= value;
29 (0    {3                    break;
30 (0    {3                case '*':
31 (0    {3                    result *= value;
32 (0    {3                    break;
33 (0    {3                case '/':
34 (0    {4                    if (value == 0) {
35 (0    {4                        cout << "Error: Divide by zero\n";
36 (0    {4                        cout << "    operation ignored\n";
37 (0    {3                    } else
38 (0    {3                        result /= value;
39 (0    {3                    break;
40 (0    {3                default:
41 (0    {3                    cout << "Unknown operator " <<
42 (0    {3                            oper_char << '\n';
43 (0    {3                    break;
44 (0    {2            }
45 (0    {1        }
```

Example 26-1. stat/stat.out (Continued).

```
46 (0  {1         return (0);
47 (0  {0  }
Total number of lines: 47
Maximum nesting of () : 2
Maximum nesting of {} : 4
Number of blank lines ................4
Number of comment only lines ..........4
Number of code only lines ............35
Number of lines with code and comments 4
Comment to code ratio 20.5%
```

Code Design

There are several schools of code design. In structured programming, you divide the code up into modules and then divide the module into submodules, divide the sub-modules into sub-submodules, and so on. This is also known as procedure- oriented programming. In *object-oriented programming,* you try to think of the problem as a collection of data that you manipulate through member functions.

There also are other approaches, such as state tables and transition diagrams. All of these have the same basic principle at heart: "Arrange the program's information in the clearest and simplest way possible and then try to turn it into C++ code."

Our program breaks down into several logical modules. First, there is a token scanner, which reads raw C++ code and turns it into tokens. Actually, this function sub-divides into two smaller modules. The first reads the input stream and determines what type of character we have. The second takes in character-type information and uses it to assemble tokens. The other module contains the statistics gathering and a small main program.

Token Module

Our program scans C++ source code and uses the tokens to generate statistics. A token is a group of characters that form a single word, number, or symbol. For example, the line:

```
answer = (123 + 456) / 89;  // Compute some sort of result
```

consists of the tokens:

```
T_ID        The word "answer"
T_OPERATOR  The character "="
T_L_PAREN   Left pParenthesis
T_NUMBER    The number 123
T_OPERATOR  The character "+"
```

```
T_NUMBER     The number 456
T_R_PAREN    Right parenthesis
T_OPERATOR   The divide operator
T_NUMBER     The number 89
T_OPERATOR   The semicolon
T_COMMENT    The // comment
T_NEW_LINE   The end-of-line character
```

Our token module needs to identify groups of characters. For example, an identifier is defined as a letter or underscore, followed by any number of letters or digits. So our tokenizer needs to contain the pseudocode:

```
If the current character is a letter then
    scan until we get a character that's not a letter or digit
```

As you can see from the pseudocode, our tokenizer depends a great deal on character types, so we need a module to help us with the type information.

Character-type Module

The purpose of the character-type module is to read characters and decode their types. Some types overlap. For example, C_ALPHA_NUMERIC includes the C_NUMERIC character set. This module stores most of the type information in an array and requires only a little logic to handle the special types like C_ALPHA_NUMERIC.

Statistics Class

In this program, a statistic is an object that consumes tokens and outputs statistics. We start by defining an abstract class for our statistics. This class is used as the basis for the statistics we are collecting. The class diagram can be seen in Figure 26-1.

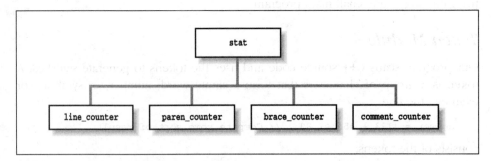

Figure 26-1. Statistics class hierarchy

Our definition of a statistic is "something that uses tokens to collect statistics." These statistics may be printed at the beginning of each line or at the end of the file.

Our four statistics are more specific. For example, the class `paren_counter` counts the nesting of parenthesis as well as the maximum nesting. The current nesting is printed at the beginning of each line (the "(" number). The maximum nesting level is written out at the end of the file.

The other classes are defined in a similar manner. The only trick used here is that we've made the line numbering a statistic. It counts the number of `T_NEW_LINE` tokens and outputs that count at the start of each line.

Coding

The coding process was fairly simple. The only problem that came up was getting the end-of-line correct.

Functional Description

This section describes all the classes and major functions in our program. For a more complete and detailed description, take a look at the listings at the end of this chapter.

char_type Class

The `char_type` class sets the type of a character. For the most part, this is done through a table named `type_info`. Some types, such as `C_ALPHA_NUMERIC`, include two different types of characters, `C_ALPHA` and `C_DIGIT`. Therefore, in addition to our table, we need a little code for the special cases.

input_file Class

This class reads data from the input file one character at a time. It buffers up a line and on command writes the line to the output.

token Class

We want an input stream of tokens. We have an input stream consisting of characters. The main function of this class, `next_token`, turns characters into tokens. Actually, our tokenizer is rather simple, because we don't have to deal with most of the details that a full C++ tokenizer must handle.

The coding for this function is fairly straightforward, except for the fact that it breaks up multiline comments into a series of `T_COMMENT` and `T_NEW_LINE` tokens.

One clever trick is used in this section. The `TOKEN_LIST` macro is used to generate an enumerated list of token types as well as a string array containing the names of each of the tokens. Let's examine how this is done in more detail.

The definition of the `TOKEN_LIST` class is:

```
#define TOKEN_LIST \
    T(T_NUMBER),       /* Simple number (floating point or integer) */ \
    T(T_STRING),       /* String or character constant */                \
    T(T_COMMENT),      /* Comment */                                     \
    T(T_NEWLINE),      /* Newline character */                           \
    T(T_OPERATOR),     /* Arithmetic operator */                         \
    T(T_L_PAREN),      /* Character "(" */                               \
    T(T_R_PAREN),      /* Character ")" */                               \
    T(T_L_CURLY),      /* Character "{" */                               \
    T(T_R_CURLY),      /* Character "}" */                               \
    T(T_ID),           /* Identifier */                                  \
    T(T_EOF)           /* End of File */
```

When invoked, this macro will generate the code:

```
T(T_NUMBER),
T(T_STRING),
// .. and so on
```

If we define a `T` macro, it will be expanded when the `TOKEN_LIST` macro is expanded. We would like to use the `TOKEN_LIST` macro to generate a list of names, so we define the `T` macro as:

```
#define T(x) x          // Define T() as the name
```

Now, our `TOKEN_LIST` macro will generate:

```
T_NUMBER,
T_STRING,
// .. and so on
```

Putting all this together with a little more code, we get a way to generate a `TOKEN_TYPE` enum list:

```
#define T(x) x          // Define T() as the name
enum TOKEN_TYPE {
    TOKEN_LIST
};
#undef T                // Remove old temporary macro
```

Later we redefine `T` so it generates a string:

```
#define T(x) #x         // Define x as a string
```

This allows us to use `TOKEN_LIST` to generate a list of strings containing the names of the tokens:

```
#define T(x) #x         // Define x as a string
const char *const TOKEN_NAMES[] = {
```

```
    TOKEN_LIST
};
#undef T                    // Remove old temporary macro
```

When expanded, this macro generates:

```
const char *const TOKEN_NAMES[] = {
    "T_NUMBER",
    "T_STRING",
    //....
```

Using tricks like this is acceptable in limited cases. However, such tricks should be extensively commented so the maintenance programmer who has to fix your code can understand what you did.

stat Class

stat class is an abstract class that is used as a basis for the four real statistics we are collecting. It starts with a member function to consume tokens. This function is a pure virtual function, which means that any derived classes must define the function take_token.

```
class stat {
    public:
        virtual void take_token(TOKEN_TYPE token) = 0;
```

The function take_token generates statistics from tokens. We need some way of printing them. We print statistics in two places. The first is at the beginning of each line and the second is at the end of the file. Our abstract class contains two virtual functions to handle these two cases:

```
        virtual void line_start(void) {};
        virtual void eof(void) {};
};
```

Unlike take_token, these functions have default bodies–empty bodies, but bodies just the same. What does this mean? Our derived classes *must* define take_token. They *don't* have to define line_start or eof.

line_counter class

The simplest statistic we collect is a count of the number of lines processed so far. This counting is done through the line_counter class. The only token it cares about is T_NEW_LINE. At the beginning of each line it outputs the line number (the current count of the T_NEW_LINE tokens). At the end of file, this class outputs nothing. As a matter of fact, the line_counter class doesn't even define an eof function. Instead, we let the default in the base class (stat) do the "work."

brace_counter class

This class keeps track of the nesting level of the curly braces {}. We feed the class a stream of tokens through the **take_token** member function. This function keeps track of the left and right curly braces and ignores everything else.

```
// Consume tokens,  count the nesting of {}
void brace_counter::take_token(TOKEN_TYPE token) {
    switch (token) {
        case T_L_CURLY:
            ++cur_level;
            if (cur_level > max_level)
                max_level = cur_level;
            break;
        case T_R_CURLY:
            --cur_level;
            break;
        default:
            // Ignore
            break;
    }
}
```

The results of this statistic are printed in two places. The first is at the beginning of each line. The second is at the end of file. We define two member functions to print these statistics:

```
// Output start of line statistics
// namely the current line number
void brace_counter::line_start(void) {
    cout.setf(ios::left);
    cout.width(2);

    cout << '{' <<  cur_level << ' ';

    cout.unsetf(ios::left);
    cout.width();
}

// Output eof statistics
// namely the total number of lines
void brace_counter::eof(void) {
    cout << "Maximum nesting of {} : " << max_level << '\n';
}
```

paren_counter class

This class is very similar to the **brace_counter** class. As a matter of fact, it was created by copying the **brace_counter** class and performing a few simple edits.

We probably should combine the **paren_counter** class and the **brace_counter** class into one class that uses a parameter to tell it what to count. Oh well, something for the next version.

comment_counter class

In this class, we keep track of lines with comments in them, lines with code in them, lines with both, and lines with none. The results are printed at the end of file.

do_file procedure

The `do_file` procedure reads each file one token at a time, and sends them to the `take_token` routine for every statistic class. But how does it know what statistics classes to use? There is a list:

```
static line_counter line_count;        // Counter of lines
static paren_counter paren_count;      // Counter of () levels
static brace_counter brace_count;      // Counter of {} levels
static comment_counter comment_count;  // Counter of comment info

// A list of the statistics we are collecting
static stat *stat_list[] = {
    &line_count,
    &paren_count,
    &brace_count,
    &comment_count,
    NULL
};
```

A couple of things should be noted about this list. Even though `line_count`, `paren_count`, `brace_count`, and `comment_count` are all different types, they are all based on the type `stat`. This means that we can put them in an array called `stat_list`. This design also makes it easy to add another statistic to the list. All we have to do is define a new class and put a new entry in the `stat_list`.

Testing

To test this program, we came up with a small C++ program that contains every different type of possible token. The results are shown in Example 26-2.

Example 26-2. stat/test.cc

```
/*******************************************************
 * This is a mult-line comment                         *
 *      T_COMMENT, T_NEWLINE                            *
 *******************************************************/
const int LINE_MAX = 500;        // T_ID, T_OPERATOR, T_NUMBER

// T_L_PAREN, T_R_PAREN
static void do_file( const char *const name)
{
```

Example 26-2. stat/test.cc (Continued)

```
    // T_L_CURLY
    char *name = "Test"              // T_STRING

    // T_R_CURLY
}
// T_EOF
```

Revisions

As it stands, the program collects a very limited set of statistics. It might be nice to add things like average identifier size, per-procedure statistic, and pre-class statistics. One thing we kept in mind when we designed our program is the need for expendability.

We stopped our statistics collection at four types of statistics because we had fulfilled our mission to demonstrate a reasonable advanced set of C++ constructs. We didn't add more because it would make the program too complex to fit in the chapter. On the whole, the program does its job well.

A Final Warning

Just because you can generate a statistic doesn't mean that it's useful.

Program Files

The ch_type.h file

Example 26-3. stat/ch_type.h

```
/********************************************************
 * char_type -- Character type class                   *
 *                                                      *
 * Member functions:                                    *
 *      type -- returns the type of a character.        *
 *              (Limited to simple types)               *
 *      is(ch, char_type) -- check to see if ch is      *
 *              a member of the given type.             *
 *              (Works for derrived types as well.)     *
 ********************************************************/
class char_type {
    public:
        enum CHAR_TYPE {
            C_EOF,                   // End of file character
            C_WHITE,     // Whitespace or control character
            C_NEWLINE,   // A newline character
```

Example 26-3. stat/ch_type.h (Continued)

```
            C_ALPHA,     // A letter (includes _)
            C_DIGIT,     // A number
            C_OPERATOR,  // Random operator
            C_SLASH,     // The character '/'
            C_L_PAREN,   // The character '('
            C_R_PAREN,   // The character ')'
            C_L_CURLY,   // The character '{'
            C_R_CURLY,   // The character '}'
            C_SINGLE,    // The character '\''
            C_DOUBLE,    // The character '"'
            // End of simple types, more complex, derived types follow
            C_HEX_DIGIT, // Hexidecimal digit
            C_ALPHA_NUMERIC     // Alpha numeric
        };
    private:
        static enum CHAR_TYPE type_

        // Fill in a range of type info stuff
        void fill_range(int start, int end, CHAR_TYPE type);
    public:
        char_type();    // Initialize the data
        // ~char_type   -- default destructor

        // Returns true if character is a given type
        int is(int ch, CHAR_TYPE kind);

        CHAR_TYPE type(int ch);
};
```

The ch_type.cc file

Example 26-4. stat/ch_type.cc

```
/*************************************************************
 * ch_type package                                          *
 *                                                          *
 * The class ch_type is used to tell the type of            *
 * various characters.                                      *
 *                                                          *
 * The main member functions are:                           *
 *      is -- True if the character is the indicated         *
 *              type.                                        *
 *      type -- Return type of character.                    *
 *************************************************************/
#include <iostream.h>

#include "ch_type.h"

// Define the type information array
char_type::CHAR_TYPE char_type::type_info[256];
/*************************************************************
 * fill_range -- fill in a range of types for the          *
```

Example 26-4. stat/ch_type.cc (Continued)

```
 *        character type class                             *
 *                                                         *
 * Parameters                                              *
 *        start, end -- range of items to fill in          *
 *        type -- type to use for filling                  *
 **********************************************************/
void char_type::fill_range(int start, int end, CHAR_TYPE type)
{
    int cur_ch;

    for (cur_ch = start; cur_ch <= end; ++cur_ch) {
        type_info[cur_ch] = type;
    }
}


/**********************************************************
 * char_type::char_type -- initialize the char type table*
 **********************************************************/
char_type::char_type()
{
    fill_range(0, 255, C_WHITE);

    fill_range('A', 'Z', C_ALPHA);
    fill_range('a', 'z', C_ALPHA);
    type_info['_'] = C_ALPHA;

    fill_range('0', '9', C_DIGIT);

    type_info['!'] = C_OPERATOR;
    type_info['#'] = C_OPERATOR;
    type_info['$'] = C_OPERATOR;
    type_info['%'] = C_OPERATOR;
    type_info['^'] = C_OPERATOR;
    type_info['&'] = C_OPERATOR;
    type_info['*'] = C_OPERATOR;
    type_info['-'] = C_OPERATOR;
    type_info['+'] = C_OPERATOR;
    type_info['='] = C_OPERATOR;
    type_info['|'] = C_OPERATOR;
    type_info['~'] = C_OPERATOR;
    type_info[','] = C_OPERATOR;
    type_info[':'] = C_OPERATOR;
    type_info['?'] = C_OPERATOR;
    type_info['.'] = C_OPERATOR;
    type_info['<'] = C_OPERATOR;
    type_info['>'] = C_OPERATOR;

    type_info['/'] = C_SLASH;
    type_info['\n'] = C_NEWLINE;

    type_info['('] = C_L_PAREN;
    type_info[')'] = C_R_PAREN;
```

Example 26-4. stat/ch_type.cc (Continued)

```
    type_info['{'] = C_L_CURLY;
    type_info['}'] = C_R_CURLY;

    type_info['"'] = C_DOUBLE;
    type_info['\''] = C_SINGLE;
}

int char_type::is(int ch, CHAR_TYPE kind)
{
    if (ch == EOF) return (kind == C_EOF);

    switch (kind) {
        case C_HEX_DIGIT:
            if (type_info[ch] == C_DIGIT)
                return (1);
            if ((ch >= 'A') && (ch <= 'F'))
                return (1);
            if ((ch >= 'a') && (ch <= 'f'))
                return (1);
            return (0);
        case C_ALPHA_NUMERIC:
            return ((type_info[ch] == C_ALPHA) ||
                        (type_info[ch] == C_DIGIT));
        default:
            return (type_info[ch] == kind);
    }
};

char_type::CHAR_TYPE char_type::type(int ch) {
    if (ch == EOF) return (C_EOF);
    return (type_info[ch]);
}
```

The token.h file

Example 26-5. stat/token.h

```
/***********************************************************
 * token -- token handling module                         *
 *                                                         *
 * Functions:                                              *
 *      next_token -- get the next token from the input    *
 ***********************************************************/

/*
 * A list of tokens
 *      Note, how this list is used depends on defining the macro T.
 *      This macro is used for defining the tokens types themselves
 *      as well as the string version of the tokens.
 */
#define TOKEN_LIST \
```

Example 26-5. stat/token.h (Continued)

```
    T(T_NUMBER),        /* Simple number (floating point or integer) */ \
    T(T_STRING),        /* String or character constant */             \
    T(T_COMMENT),       /* Comment */                                  \
    T(T_NEWLINE),       /* Newline character */                        \
    T(T_OPERATOR),      /* Arithmetic operator */                      \
    T(T_L_PAREN),       /* Character "(" */                            \
    T(T_R_PAREN),       /* Character ")" */                            \
    T(T_L_CURLY),       /* Character "{" */                            \
    T(T_R_CURLY),       /* Character "}" */                            \
    T(T_ID),            /* Identifier */                               \
    T(T_EOF)            /* End of File */

/*
 * Define the enumerated list of tokens.
 *      This makes use of a trick using the T macro
 *      and our TOKEN_LIST
 */
#define T(x) x          // Define T() as the name
enum TOKEN_TYPE {
    TOKEN_LIST
};
#undef T                // Remove old temporary macro

// A list of the names of the tokens
extern const char *const TOKEN_NAMES[];

const int LINE_MAX = 500;        // Longest possible line

/***********************************************************
 * input_file -- data from the input file                  *
 *                                                         *
 * The current two characters are store in                 *
 *      cur_char and next_char                             *
 *                                                         *
 * The member function read_char moves eveyone up          *
 * one character.                                          *
 *                                                         *
 * The line is buffered and output everytime a newline     *
 * is passed.                                              *
 ***********************************************************/
class input_file: public ifstream {
    private:
        char line[LINE_MAX];     // Current line
        char *char_ptr;          // Current character on the line
    public:
        int cur_char;   // Current character (can be EOF)
        int next_char;  // Next character (can be EOF)

        /*
         * Initialize the input file and read the first 2
         * characters.
         */
```

Example 26-5. stat/token.h (Continued)

```
        input_file(const char *const name) : ifstream(name) {
            if (bad())
                return;
            cur_char = get();
            next_char = get();
            char_ptr = line;
        }


        /*
         * Write the line to the screen
         */
        void flush_line() {
            *char_ptr = '\0';
            cout << line;
            cout.flush();
            char_ptr = line;
        }
        /*
         * Advance one character
         */
        void read_char(void) {
            *char_ptr = cur_char;
            ++char_ptr;

            cur_char = next_char;
            next_char = get();
        }
};

#ifndef TRUE
#define TRUE 1            // Define a simple TRUE/FALSE value
#define FALSE 0
#endif /* TRUE */

/***********************************************************
 * token class                                            *
 *                                                        *
 *      Reads the next token in the input stream          *
 *      and returns its type.                             *
 ***********************************************************/
class token {
    private:
        // True if we are in the middle of a comment
        int in_comment;

        // True if we need to read a character
        // (This hack is designed to get the new lines right)
        int need_to_read_one;

        // Read a /* */ style comment
        TOKEN_TYPE read_comment(input_file &in_file);
    public:
```

Example 26-5. stat/token.h (Continued)

```
        token(void) {
            in_comment = FALSE;
            need_to_read_one = 0;
        }

        // Return the next token in the stream
        TOKEN_TYPE next_token(input_file &in_file);
};
```

The token.cc file

Example 26-6. stat/token.cc

```
/********************************************************
 * token -- token handling module                      *
 *                                                      *
 * Functions:                                           *
 *      next_token -- get the next token from the input *
 ********************************************************/
#include <fstream.h>
#include <stdlib.h>

#include "ch_type.h"
#include "token.h"

/*
 * Define the token name list
 *      This makes use of a trick using the T macro
 *      and our TOKEN_LIST
 */
#define T(x) #x          // Define x as a string
const char *const TOKEN_NAMES[] = {
    TOKEN_LIST
};
#undef T                 // Remove old temporary macro

static char_type char_type;     // Character type information
/********************************************************
 * read_comment -- read in a comment                   *
 *                                                      *
 * Parameters                                           *
 *      in_file -- file to read                         *
 *                                                      *
 * Returns                                              *
 *      Token read.  Can be a T_COMMENT or T_NEW_LINE   *
 *      depending on what we read.                      *
 *                                                      *
 *      Multi-line comments are split into multiple     *
 *      tokens.                                          *
 ********************************************************/
TOKEN_TYPE token::read_comment(input_file &in_file)
{
```

Example 26-6. stat/token.cc (Continued)

```
    if (in_file.cur_char == '\n') {
        in_file.read_char();
        return (T_NEWLINE);
    }
    while (1) {
        in_comment = TRUE;
        if (in_file.cur_char == EOF) {
            cerr << "Error: EOF inside comment\n";
            return (T_EOF);
        }
        if (in_file.cur_char == '\n')
            return (T_COMMENT);
        if ((in_file.cur_char == '*') &&
            (in_file.next_char == '/')) {
            in_comment = FALSE;
            // Skip past the ending */
            in_file.read_char();
            in_file.read_char();
            return (T_COMMENT);
        }
        in_file.read_char();
    }
}
/********************************************************
 * next_token -- read the next token in an input stream *
 *                                                      *
 * Parameters                                           *
 *      in_file -- file to read                         *
 *                                                      *
 * Returns                                              *
 *      next token                                      *
 ********************************************************/
TOKEN_TYPE token::next_token(input_file &in_file)
{

    if (need_to_read_one)
        in_file.read_char();

    need_to_read_one = 0;

    if (in_comment)
        return (read_comment(in_file));

    while (char_type.is(in_file.cur_char, char_type::C_WHITE)) {
        in_file.read_char();
    }
    if (in_file.cur_char == EOF)
        return (T_EOF);

    switch (char_type.type(in_file.cur_char)) {
        case char_type::C_NEWLINE:
            in_file.read_char();
```

Example 26-6. stat/token.cc (Continued)

```
            return (T_NEWLINE);
    case char_type::C_ALPHA:
        while (char_type.is(in_file.cur_char,
                            char_type::C_ALPHA_NUMERIC))
            in_file.read_char();
        return (T_ID);
    case char_type::C_DIGIT:
        in_file.read_char();
        if ((in_file.cur_char == 'X') || (in_file.cur_char == 'x')) {
            in_file.read_char();
            while (char_type.is(in_file.cur_char, char_type::C_HEX_
                in_file.read_char();
            return (T_NUMBER);
        }
        while (char_type.is(in_file.cur_char, char_type::C_DIGIT))
            in_file.read_char();
        return (T_NUMBER);
    case char_type::C_SLASH:
        // Check for  /* characters
        if (in_file.next_char == '*') {
            return (read_comment(in_file));
        }
        // Now check for double slash comments
        if (in_file.next_char == '/') {
            while (1) {
                // Comment starting with // and ending with EOF is lega
                if (in_file.cur_char == EOF)
                    return (T_COMMENT);
                if (in_file.cur_char == '\n')
                    return (T_COMMENT);
                in_file.read_char();
            }
        }
        // Fall through
    case char_type::C_OPERATOR:
        in_file.read_char();
        return (T_OPERATOR);
    case char_type::C_L_PAREN:
        in_file.read_char();
        return (T_L_PAREN);
    case char_type::C_R_PAREN:
        in_file.read_char();
        return (T_R_PAREN);
    case char_type::C_L_CURLY:
        in_file.read_char();
        return (T_L_CURLY);
    case char_type::C_R_CURLY:
        in_file.read_char();
        return (T_R_CURLY);
    case char_type::C_DOUBLE:
        while (1) {
            in_file.read_char();
```

Example 26-6. stat/token.cc (Continued)

```
                // Check for end of string
                if (in_file.cur_char == '"')
                    break;

                // Escape character, then skip the next character
                if (in_file.cur_char == '\\')
                    in_file.read_char();
            }
            in_file.read_char();
            return (T_STRING);
        case char_type::C_SINGLE:
            while (1) {
                in_file.read_char();
                // Check for end of character
                if (in_file.cur_char == '\'')
                    break;

                // Escape character, then skip the next character
                if (in_file.cur_char == '\\')
                    in_file.read_char();
            }
            in_file.read_char();
            return (T_STRING);
        default:
            cerr << "Internal error: Very strange character\n";
            abort();
    }
    cerr << "Internal error: We should never get here\n";
    abort();
    return (T_EOF);      // Should never get here either
}
```

The stat.cc file

Example 26-7. stat/stat.cc

```
/*********************************************************
 * stat                                                  *
 *       Produce statistics about a program              *
 *                                                       *
 * Usage:                                                *
 *       stat [options] <file-list>                      *
 *                                                       *
 *********************************************************/
#include <iostream.h>
#include <fstream.h>
#include <iomanip.h>
#include <stdlib.h>
#include <memory.h>

#include "ch_type.h"
#include "token.h"
```

Example 26-7. stat/stat.cc (Continued)

```
/**********************************************************
 * stat -- general purpose statistic                     *
 *                                                        *
 * Member functions:                                     *
 *      take_token -- receives token and uses it to      *
 *                        compute statistic              *
 *      line_start -- output stat at the beginning of    *
 *                        a line                         *
 *      eof      -- output stat at the end of the file   *
 **********************************************************/
class stat {
    public:
        virtual void take_token(TOKEN_TYPE token) = 0;
        virtual void line_start(void) {};
        virtual void eof(void) {};
        // Default constructor
        // Default destructor
        // Copy constructor defaults as well (probably not used)
};


/**********************************************************
 * line_counter -- handle line number / line count       *
 *              stat.                                    *
 *                                                        *
 * Counts the number of T_NEW_LINE tokens seen and       *
 * outputs the current line number at the beginning      *
 * of the line.                                          *
 *                                                        *
 * At EOF it will output the total number of lines       *
 **********************************************************/
class line_counter: public stat {
    private:
        int cur_line;    // Line number for the current line
    public:
        // Initialize the line counter -- to zero
        line_counter(void) {
            cur_line = 0;
        };
        // Default destrctor
        // Default copy constructor (probably never called)

        // Consume tokens,  count the number of new line tokens
        void take_token(TOKEN_TYPE token) {
            if (token == T_NEWLINE)
                ++cur_line;
        }

        // Output start of line statistics
        // namely the current line number
        void line_start(void) {
            cout << setw(4) << cur_line << ' ' << setw(0);
```

Example 26-7. stat/stat.cc (Continued)

```
        }

        // Output eof statistics
        // namely the total number of lines
        void eof(void) {
            cout << "Total number of lines: " << cur_line << '\n';
        }
};

/************************************************************
 * paren_count -- count the nesting level of ()            *
 *                                                         *
 * Counts the number of T_L_PAREN vs T_R_PAREN tokens      *
 * and writes the current nesting level at the beginning*
 * of each line.                                           *
 *                                                         *
 * Also keeps track of the maximum nesting level.          *
 ************************************************************/
class paren_counter: public stat {
    private:
        int cur_level;          // Current nesting level
        int max_level;          // Maximum nesting level
    public:
        // Initialize the counter
        paren_counter(void) {
            cur_level = 0;
            max_level = 0;
        };
        // Default destructor
        // Default copy constructor (probably never called)

        // Consume tokens,  count the nesting of ()
        void take_token(TOKEN_TYPE token) {
            switch (token) {
                case T_L_PAREN:
                    ++cur_level;
                    if (cur_level > max_level)
                        max_level = cur_level;
                    break;
                case T_R_PAREN:
                    --cur_level;
                    break;
                default:
                    // Ignore
                    break;
            }
        }

        // Output start of line statistics
        // namely the current line number
        void line_start(void) {
            cout.setf(ios::left);
```

Example 26-7. stat/stat.cc (Continued)

```
            cout.width(2);

            cout << '(' <<  cur_level << ' ';

            cout.unsetf(ios::left);
            cout.width();
        }

        // Output eof statistics
        // namely the total number of lines
        void eof(void) {
            cout << "Maximum nesting of () : " << max_level << '\n';
        }
};

/************************************************************
 * brace_counter -- count the nesting level of {}          *
 *                                                         *
 * Counts the number of T_L_CURLY vs T_R_CURLY tokens      *
 * and writes the current nesting level at the beginning*
 * of each line.                                           *
 *                                                         *
 * Also keeps track of the maximum nesting level.         *
 *                                                         *
 * Note: brace_counter and paren_counter should           *
 * probably be combined.                                   *
 ************************************************************/
class brace_counter: public stat {
    private:
        int cur_level;          // Current nesting level
        int max_level;          // Maximum nesting level
    public:
        // Initialize the counter
        brace_counter(void) {
            cur_level = 0;
            max_level = 0;
        };
        // Default destructor
        // Default copy constructor (probably never called)

        // Consume tokens,  count the nesting of ()
        void take_token(TOKEN_TYPE token) {
            switch (token) {
                case T_L_CURLY:
                    ++cur_level;
                    if (cur_level > max_level)
                        max_level = cur_level;
                    break;
                case T_R_CURLY:
                    --cur_level;
                    break;
                default:
```

Example 26-7. stat/stat.cc (Continued)

```
                    // Ignore
                    break;
            }
        }

        // Output start of line statistics
        // namely the current line number
        void line_start(void) {
            cout.setf(ios::left);
            cout.width(2);

            cout << '{' <<  cur_level << ' ';

            cout.unsetf(ios::left);
            cout.width();
        }

        // Output eof statistics
        // namely the total number of lines
        void eof(void) {
            cout << "Maximum nesting of {} : " << max_level << '\n';
        }
};

/***********************************************************
 * comment_counter -- counts the number of lines           *
 *      with and without comments.                         *
 *                                                         *
 * Outputs nothing at the beginning of each line, but      *
 * will output a ratio at the end of file                  *
 *                                                         *
 * Note: This class makes use of two bits:                 *
 *      CF_COMMENT  -- a comment was seen                   *
 *      CF_CODE     -- code was seen                        *
 * to collect statistics.                                  *
 *                                                         *
 * These are combined to form an index into the counter    *
 * array, so the value of these two bits is very           *
 * important.                                              *
 ***********************************************************/
static const int CF_COMMENT = (1<<0);   // Line contains comment
static const int CF_CODE    = (1<<1);   // Line contains code
// These bits are combined to form the statistics
//
//      0                   -- [0] Blank line
//      CF_COMMENT          -- [1] Comment only line
//      CF_CODE             -- [2] Code only line
//      CF_COMMENT|CF_CODE  -- [3] Comments and code on this line

class comment_counter: public stat {
    private:
        int counters[4];        // Count of various types of stats
```

Example 26-7. stat/stat.cc (Continued)

```
        int flags;              // Flags for the current line
    public:
        // Initialize the counters
        comment_counter(void) {
            memset(counters, '\0', sizeof(counters));
            flags = 0;
        };
        // Default destructor
        // Default copy constructor (probably never called)

        // Consume tokens,  count the nesting of ()
        void take_token(TOKEN_TYPE token) {
            switch (token) {
                case T_COMMENT:
                    flags |= CF_COMMENT;
                    break;
                default:
                    flags |= CF_CODE;
                    break;
                case T_NEWLINE:
                    ++counters[flags];
                    flags = 0;
                    break;
            }
        }

        // void line_start(void) -- defaults to base

        // Output eof statistics
        // namely the total number of lines
        void eof(void) {
            cout << "Number of blank lines ................." <<
                    counters[0] << '\n';
            cout << "Number of comment only lines .........." <<
                    counters[1] << '\n';
            cout << "Number of code only lines ............." <<
                    counters[2] << '\n';
            cout << "Number of lines with code and comments " <<
                    counters[3] << '\n';
            cout.setf(ios::fixed);
            cout.precision(1);
            cout << "Comment to code ratio " <<
                float(counters[1] + counters[3]) /
                float(counters[2] + counters[3]) * 100.0 << "%\n";
        }
};


static line_counter line_count;             // Counter of lines
static paren_counter paren_count;           // Counter of () levels
static brace_counter brace_count;           // Counter of {} levels
static comment_counter comment_count;       // Counter of comment info
```

Example 26-7. stat/stat.cc (Continued)

```
// A list of the statistics we are collecting
static stat *stat_list[] = {
    &line_count,
    &paren_count,
    &brace_count,
    &comment_count,
    NULL
};


/*********************************************************
 * do_file -- process a single file                     *
 *                                                       *
 * Parameters                                            *
 *      name -- the name of the file to process          *
 *********************************************************/
static void do_file(const char *const name)
{
    input_file in_file(name);   // File to read
    token token;                // Token reader/parser
    TOKEN_TYPE cur_token;       // Current token type
    class stat **cur_stat;      // Pointer to stat for collection/writing

    if (in_file.bad()) {
        cerr << "Error: Could not open file " << name << " for reading\n";
        return;
    }
    while (1) {
        cur_token = token.next_token(in_file);
        for (cur_stat = stat_list; *cur_stat != NULL; ++cur_stat)
            (*cur_stat)->take_token(cur_token);
#ifdef DEBUG
        cout << "    " << TOKEN_NAMES[cur_token] << '\n';
#endif /* DEBUG */

        switch (cur_token) {
            case T_NEWLINE:
                for (cur_stat = stat_list; *cur_stat != NULL; ++cur_stat)
                    (*cur_stat)->line_start();
                in_file.flush_line();
                break;
            case T_EOF:
                for (cur_stat = stat_list; *cur_stat != NULL; ++cur_stat)
                    (*cur_stat)->eof();
                return;
            default:
                // Do nothing
                break;
        }
    }
}
```

Example 26-7. stat/stat.cc (Continued)

```
main(int argc, char *argv[])
{
    char *prog_name = argv[0];   // Name of the program

    if (argc == 1) {
        cerr << "Usage is " << prog_name << "[options] <file-list>\n";
        exit (8);
    }

    for (/* argc set */; argc > 1; --argc) {
        do_file(argv[1]);
        ++argv;
    }
    return (0);
}
```

UNIX *Makefile for CC (Generic Unix)*

Example 26-8. stat/makefile.unx

```
#
# Makefile for many UNIX compilers using the
# "standard" command name CC
#
CC=CC
CFLAGS=-g
OBJS= stat.o ch_type.o token.o

all: stat.out stat

stat.out: stat
        stat ../calc3/calc3.cc >stat.out

stat: $(OBJS)
        $(CC) $(CCFLAGS) -o stat $(OBJS)

stat.o: stat.cc token.h
        $(CC) $(CCFLAGS) -c stat.cc

ch_type.o: ch_type.cc ch_type.h
        $(CC) $(CCFLAGS) -c ch_type.cc

token.o: token.cc token.h ch_type.h
        $(CC) $(CCFLAGS) -c token.cc


clean:
        rm stat stat.o ch_type.o token.o
```

UNIX *Makefile for g++*

Example 26-9. stat/makefile.gnu

```
#
# Makefile for the Free Software Foundations g++ compiler
#
CC=g++
CFLAGS=-g -Wall
OBJS= stat.o ch_type.o token.o

all: stat.out stat

stat.out: stat
        stat ../calc3/calc3.cc >stat.out

stat: $(OBJS)
        $(CC) $(CCFLAGS) -o stat $(OBJS)

stat.o: stat.cc token.h
        $(CC) $(CCFLAGS) -c stat.cc

ch_type.o: ch_type.cc ch_type.h
        $(CC) $(CCFLAGS) -c ch_type.cc

token.o: token.cc token.h ch_type.h
        $(CC) $(CCFLAGS) -c token.cc


clean:
        rm stat stat.o ch_type.o token.o
```

Turbo C++ *Makefile*

Example 26-10. stat/makefile.tcc

```
#
# Makefile for Borland's Turbo-C++ compiler
#
CC=tcc
#
# Flags
#       -N  -- Check for stack overflow
#       -v  -- Enable debugging
#       -w  -- Turn on all warnings
#       -ml -- Large model
#
CFLAGS=-N -v -w -ml
OBJS= stat.obj ch_type.obj token.obj

all: stat.out stat.exe

stat.out: stat.exe
```

Example 26-10. stat/makefile.tcc (Continued)

```
        stat ..\calc3\calc3.cpp >stat.out

stat.exe: $(OBJS)
        $(CC) $(CCFLAGS) -estat $(OBJS)

stat.obj: stat.cpp token.h
        $(CC) $(CCFLAGS) -c stat.cpp

ch_type.obj: ch_type.cpp ch_type.h
        $(CC) $(CCFLAGS) -c ch_type.cpp

token.obj: token.cpp token.h ch_type.h
        $(CC) $(CCFLAGS) -c token.cpp


clean:
        erase stat.exe stat.obj ch_type.obj token.obj
```

Borland-C++ Makefile

Example 26-11. stat/makefile.bcc

```
#
# Makefile for Borland's Borland-C++ compiler
#
CC=bcc
#
# Flags
#       -N  -- Check for stack overflow
#       -v  -- Enable debugging
#       -w  -- Turn on all warnings
#       -ml -- Large model
#
CFLAGS=-N -v -w -ml
OBJS= stat.obj ch_type.obj token.obj

all: stat.out stat.exe

stat.out: stat.exe
        stat ..\calc3\calc3.cpp >stat.out

stat.exe: $(OBJS)
        $(CC) $(CCFLAGS) -estat $(OBJS)

stat.obj: stat.cpp token.h
        $(CC) $(CCFLAGS) -c stat.cpp

ch_type.obj: ch_type.cpp ch_type.h
        $(CC) $(CCFLAGS) -c ch_type.cpp

token.obj: token.cpp token.h ch_type.h
        $(CC) $(CCFLAGS) -c token.cpp
```

Example 26-11. stat/makefile.bcc (Continued)

```
clean:
        erase stat.exe stat.obj ch_type.obj token.obj
```

Microsoft Visual C++ Makefile

Example 26-12. stat/makefile.msc

```
#
# Makefile for Microsoft Visual C++
#
CC=cl
#
# Flags
#        AL -- Compile for large model
#        Zi -- Enable debugging
#        W1 -- Turn on warnings
#
CFLAGS=/AL /Zi /W1
OBJS= stat.obj ch_type.obj token.obj

all: stat.out stat.exe

stat.out: stat.exe
        stat ..\calc3\calc3.cpp >stat.out

stat.exe: $(OBJS)
        $(CC) $(CCFLAGS)  $(OBJS)

stat.obj: stat.cpp token.h
        $(CC) $(CCFLAGS) -c stat.cpp

ch_type.obj: ch_type.cpp ch_type.h
        $(CC) $(CCFLAGS) -c ch_type.cpp

token.obj: token.cpp token.h ch_type.h
        $(CC) $(CCFLAGS) -c token.cpp


clean:
        erase stat.exe stat.obj ch_type.obj token.obj
```

Programming Exercises

Exercise 26-1: Write a program that checks a text file for doubled words.

Exercise 26-2: Write a program that removes four-letter words from a file and replaces them with more acceptable equivalents.

Exercise 26-3: Write a mailing list program. This program will read, write, sort and print mailing labels.

Exercise 26-4: Update the statics program presented in this chapter to add a cross-reference capability.

Exercise 26-5: Write a program that takes a text file and splits each long line into two smaller lines. The split point should be at the end of a sentence if possible, or at the end of a word if a sentence is too long.

27

From C to C++

> *No distinction so little excites envy as that which is derived from ancestors by a long descent.*
>
> —François De Saliganc De La Mothe Fénelon

Overview

C++ was built on the older language C, and there's a lot of C code still around. That's both a blessing and a curse. It's a curse because it means you'll probably have to deal with a lot of ancient code. On the other hand, there will always be work for you. This chapter describes some of the differences between C and C++ as well as how to migrate from one to the other.

K&R-Style Functions

Classic C (also called K&R C after its authors, Brian Kernighan and Dennis Ritchie) uses a function header that's different from the one used in C++. In C++ the parameter types and names are included inside the () defining the function. In Classic C, only the names appear. Type information comes later:

```
int do_it(char *name, int function)    // C++ function definition
{
    // Body of the fucnction

int do_it(name, function)              // Classic C definition
char *name;
int function;
{
    // Body of the function
```

485

When C++ came along, the ANSI C committee decided it would be a good idea if C used the new function definitions. However, because there was a lot of code out there using the old method, C++ accepts both types of functions.

Classic C does not require prototypes. In many cases, prototypes are missing from C programs. A function that does not have a prototype has an implied prototype of:

```
int funct(...);    // Default prototype for Classic C functions
```

Also, Classic C prototypes have no parameter lists. They merely consist of "()," such as

```
int do_it();    // Classic C function prototype
```

This tells C that `do_it` returns an `int` and takes any number of parameters. C does not type-check parameters, so the following are legal calls to `do_it`:

```
i = do_it();
i = do_it(1, 2, 3);
i = do_it("Test", 'a');
```

C++ requires function prototypes, so you have to put them in. There are tools out there such as the GNU *prototize* utility that help you by reading your code and generating function prototypes. Otherwise, you will have to do it manually.

struct

In C++, when you declare a `struct`, you can use the structure as a type name. For example:

```
struct sample {
    int i, j;    // Data for the sample
};
sample sample_var;  // Last sample seen
```

C is more strict. You must put the keyword `struct` before each variable declaration:

```
struct sample sample_var;  // Legal in C
sample sample_var;         // Illegal in C
```

malloc and free

In C++, you use the `new` operator to get memory from the heap and use `delete` to return the memory. C has no built-in memory-handling operations. Instead, it makes use of two library routines: `malloc` and `free`.

The function `malloc` takes a single parameter—the number of bytes to allocate—and returns a pointer to them (as a `char *` or `void *`). But how do we know how big a structure is? That's where the `sizeof` operator comes in. It returns the number of bytes in the structure. So to allocate a new variable of type `struct foo` we use the code:

```
foo_var = (struct foo *)malloc(sizeof(struct foo));
```

Note that we must use a cast to turn the pointer returned by `malloc` into something useful. The C++ syntax for the same operator is much cleaner:

```
foo_var = new foo;
```

Suppose we want to allocate an array of three structures. Then we need to multiply our allocation size by 3, resulting in:

```
foo_var = (struct foo *)malloc(sizeof(struct foo) * 3);
```

The C++ equivalent is:

```
foo_var = new foo[3];
```

The function `calloc` is similar to `malloc` except that it takes two parameters: the number of elements in the array of objects and the size of a single element. Using our array of three `foos` example, we get:

```
foo_var = (struct foo*)calloc(3, sizeof(foo));
```

The other difference is that `calloc` initializes the structure to zero. Thus the C++ equivalent is:

```
foo_var = new foo[3];
memset(foo_var, '\0', sizeof(foo) * 3);
```

Programs can freely mix C-style `malloc`s and C++ `new` calls. The C memory allocators are messy, however, and should be converted to C++ whenever possible.

There are a number of traps concerning C-style memory allocation. Suppose we take our structure `foo` and turn it into a class. We can but shouldn't use the C memory routines to allocate space for the class:

```
class foo {...};
foo_var = (struct foo *)malloc(sizeof(struct foo)); // Don't code like
                  this
```

Because C++ treats `struct` as a special form of `class` most compilers won't complain about this code. The problem is that our `malloc` statement allocates space for `foo` and *that's all.* No constructor is called, so it's quite possible that the class will not get set up correctly.

C uses the function `free` to return memory to the heap. The function `free` takes a single character pointer as a parameter (thus making a lot of casting necessary):

```
free((char *)foo_var);
foo_var = NULL;
```

In C++ this would be:

```
delete foo_var;
foo_var = NULL;
```

for a simple variable and:

```
delete [] foo_array;
foo_array = NULL;
```

when foo_array points to an array.

Again, you must be careful when turning foo into a class. The free function just returns the memory to the heap. It does not call the destructor for foo.

C-style memory allocation is messy and risky. When converting to C++ you probably should get rid of all malloc, calloc, and free calls whenever possible.

WARNING

According to the ANSI C draft standard, memory allocated by malloc must be deallocated by free. Similarly, memory allocated by new must be deallocated by delete. However, most of the compilers I've seen implement new as a call to malloc and delete as a call to free. In other words, mixing new/free or malloc/free calls will *usually* work. To avoid errors, you should follow the rules and avoid missing C and C++ operations.

Turning Structures into Classes

Frequently when examining C code you may find a number of struct statements that look like they should be classes. Actually, a structure is really just a data-only class with all the members public.

C programmers frequently take advantage of the fact that a structure only contains data. One example of this is reading and writing a structure to a binary file. For example:

```
a_struct struct_var;    // A structure variable

// Perform a raw read to read in the structure
read_size = read(fd, (char *)&struct_var, sizeof(struct_var));

// Perform a raw write to send the data to a file
write_size = write(fd, (char *)&struct_var, sizeof(struct_var));
```

Turning this structure into a class can cause problems. C++ keeps extra information, such as virtual function pointers, in a class. When you write the class to disk using a raw write, you are outputting all that information. What's worse, when you read the class in you overwrite this bookkeeping data.

For example, suppose we have the class:

```
class sample {
    public:
        const int sample_size;      // Number of samples
        int cur_sample;             // Current sample number
        sample(void) : sample_size(100) {} // Set up class
        virtual void get_sample(); // Routine to get a sample
};
```

Internally, this class consists of *three* member variables: a constant, `sample_size` (which C++ won't allow you to change); a simple variable, `cur_sample`; and a pointer to the real function to be used when `get_sample` is called. All three of these are written to disk by the call:

```
sample a_sample;
// ...
write_size = write(fd, (char *)&a_sample, sizeof(a_sample));
```

When this class is read, *all three members* are changed. That includes the constant (which we aren't supposed to change) and the function pointer (which now probably points to something strange).

C programmers also make use of the `memset` function to set all the members of a structure to zero. For example:

```
struct a_struct { ... }
a_struct struct_var;
// ...
memset(&struct_var, '\0', sizeof(struct_var));
```

Again, be careful when turning a structure into a class. If we had used the class `a_sample` instead of the structure `struct_var`, we would have zeroed the constant `sample_size` as well as the virtual function pointer. The result would probably be a crash if we ever tried to call `get_sample`.

ssetjmp and longjmp

C has its own way of handling exceptions through the use of `setjmp` and `longjmp`. The `setjmp` function marks a place in a program. The `longjmp` function jumps to the place marked by `setjmp`.

Normally `setjmp` returns a zero. This tells the program to execute normal code. When an exception occurs, the `longjmp` call returns to the location of the `setjmp` function. The only difference the program can see between a real `setjmp` call and a fake `setjmp` call caused by a `longjmp` is that a normally `setjmp` returns a zero. When `setjmp` is "called" by `longjmp,` the return value is controlled by a parameter to `longjmp`.

The definition of the setjmp function is:

```
#include <setjmp.h>

int setjmp(jmp_buf env);
```

where:

env

is the place where setjmp saves the current environment for later use by longjmp

Returns

0

Normal call

Nonzero

Non-zero return codes are the result of a longjmp call.

The definition of the longjmp call is:

```
void longjmp(jmp_buf env, int return_code);
```

where:

env

is the environment initialized by a previous setjmp call

return_code

is the return code that will be returned by the setjmp call

Figure 27-1 illustrates the control flow when using setjmp and longjmp

There is one problem here, however. The longjmp call returns control to the corresponding setjmp. *It does not call the destructors of any classes that are "destroyed" in the process.*

In Figure 27-1 we can see that in the subroutine we define a class named a_list. Normally we would call the destructor for a_list at the end of the function or at a return statement. However, in this case we use longjmp to exit the function. Since longjmp is a C function it knows nothing about classes and destructors and does not call the destructor for a_list. So we now have a situation where a variable has disappeared but the destructor has not been called. The technical name for this situation is a "foul-up."

When converting C to C++, change all setjmp/longjmp combinations into exceptions.

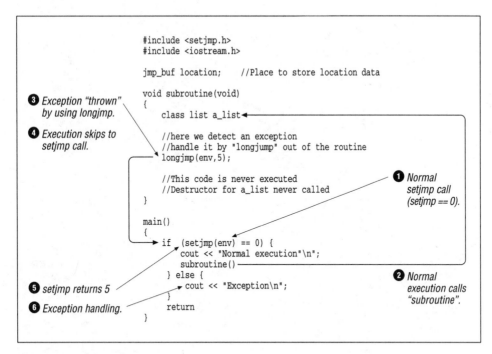

Figure 27-1. setjmp/longjmp control flow

Summary

What you *must* do to get C to compile with a C++ compiler:

1. Change K&R-style function headers into standard C++ headers.

2. Add prototypes.

3. Change setjmp/longjmp calls into catch/throw operations.

Following these two steps you have a C+$\frac{1}{2}$ program. It works, but it's really a C program in C++'s clothing. To convert it to a real C++ program you need to do the following:

4. Change malloc into new.

5. Change free into delete or delete [] calls.

6. Turn printf and scanf calls into cout and cin.

7. When turning struct declarations into class variables, be careful of read, write, and memset functions that use the entire structure or class.

Programming Exercise

Exercise 27-1: There are a lot of C programs out there. Turn one into C++.

28

C++'s Dustier Corners

There be of them that have left
a name behind them.
—Ecclesiasticus XLIV, 1

This chapter describes the few remaining features of C++ that are not described in any of the previous chapters. It is titled *C++'s Dustier Corners* because these statements are hardly ever used in real programming.

do/while

The `do/while` statement has the following syntax:

```
do {
        statement
        statement
} while    (expression);
```

The program loops, tests the expression, and stops if the expression is false (0).

NOTE

This construct always executes at least once.

`do/while` is not frequently used in C++ because most programmers prefer to use a `while/break` combination.

goto

All the sample programs in this book were coded without using a single `goto`. In actual practice I find I use a `goto` statement about once every other year. For those rare times that a `goto` is necessary, its syntax is:

```
goto label;
```

where *label* is a statement label. Statement labels follow the same naming convention as variable names. Labeling a statement is done as follows:

```
label: statement
```

For example:

```
for (x = 0; x < X_LIMIT; ++x) {
    for (y = 0; y < Y_LIMIT; ++y) {
        if (data[x][y] == 0)
            goto found;
    }
}
cout << "Not found\n";
exit(8);


found:
    cout << "Found at (" << x << ',' << y << ")\n";
```

Question 28-1: *Why does Example 28-1 not print an error message when an incorrect command is entered? Hint: There is a reason I put this in the* goto *section.*

Example 28-1. def/def.cc

```
#include <iostream.h>
#include <stdlib.h>

main()
{
    char  line[10];

    while (1) {
        cout << "Enter add(a), delete(d), quit(q): ";
        cin.getline(line, sizeof(line));

        switch (line[0]) {
        case 'a':
            cout << "Add\n";
            break;
        case 'd':
            cout << "Delete\n";
            break;
        case 'q':
            cout << "Quit\n";
            exit(0);
        defualt:
            cout << "Error: Bad command " << line[0] << '\n';
            break;
        }
    }
    return (0);
}
```

The ?: Construct

The ? and : operators work much the same as if/then/else. Unlike if/then/else, the ?: operators can be used inside of an expression. The general form of ?: is:

(expression) ? expr1 : expr2

For example, the following assigns to **amount_owed** the value of the balance or zero, depending on the amount of the balance:

```
amount_owed = (balance < 0) ? 0 : balance;
```

The following macro returns the minimum of its two arguments:

```
#define min(x, y) ((x) < (y) ? (x) : (y))
```

NOTE

It is better to define **min** as an inline function instead of as a parameterized macro. See Chapter 10, *The C++ Preprocessor*, for details.

The Comma Operator

The comma operator (,) can be used to group statements. For example:

```
if (total < 0) {
    cout << "You owe nothing\n";
    total = 0;
}
```

can be written as:

```
if (total < 0)
    cout << "You owe nothing\n", total = 0;
```

In most cases, {} should be used instead of a comma. About the only place the comma operator is useful is in a for statement. The following for loop increments two counters, **two** and **three**, by 2 and 3:

```
for (two = 0, three = 0;
     two < 10;
     two += 2, three += 3)
        cout << two << ' ' << three << '\n';
```

Overloading the () Operator

The "()" operator can be overloaded for a class to give the class a "default" function. For example:

```
class example {
    public:
```

```
        int operator () (int i) {
            return (i * 2);
        }
};
// ....
    example example_var;

    j = example_var(3);    // j is assigned the value 6 (3 * 2)
```

Overloading the ( ) operator is rarely done. Normal member functions can easily be used for the same purpose but have the advantage of providing the user with a function name.

Pointers to Members

The operator `::*` is used to point to a member of a class. For example, in the following code we declare `data_ptr` as a "pointer to an integer in sample":

```
class sample {
    public:
        int i;    // A couple of member variables
        int j;
};

int sample::* data_ptr;
```

Now `data_ptr` can point to either the `i` or the `j` member of `sample`. (After all, they are the only integer members of `sample`.)

Let's set `data_ptr` so it points to the member `i`:

```
    data_ptr = &sample::i;
```

An ordinary pointer identifies a single item. A member pointer identifies a member but does not identify an individual variable. All we've done is set `data_ptr` to a member of `sample`. `data_ptr` does not point to a particular integer.

To use `data_ptr` you need to tell it which class you want:

```
sample a_sample; // A typical sample
sample b_sample;

cout << a_sample.*data_ptr << '\n';
cout << b_sample.*data_ptr << '\n'
```

The line:

```
    cout << a_sample.*data_ptr << '\n';
```

tells C++ that we want to print an element of the variable `a_sample`. The variable `data_ptr` points to an integer member of `sample`. (The members `i` and `j` are our only two integer members.)

There is a shorthand notation for use with class pointers as well:

```
sample *sample_ptr = &sample1;

cout << sample_ptr->*data_ptr << '\n';
```

The syntax for pointers to members is a little convoluted and not terribly useful. I've only seen it used once by an *extremely* clever programmer. (The first maintenance programmer who got the code immediately ripped it out anyway.)

Vampire Features

This section discusses features that have been defined in the draft C++ standard[*] but have not yet been implemented in any of the currently available compilers.[†] "Vampire features" are those features of a language that have yet to see the light of day.

Because I've been unable to actually use these features, the information presented here is a bit sketchy.

bool

    Boolean type that can be either true or false

const_cast

    A new version of a cast that makes the result constant

dynamic_case

    A new casting operator that makes use of runtime-type information to allow safe casting between types

false

    New constant for use with the `bool` type

mutable

    Modifier that indicates that a member of a constant instance of a class can be changed

namespace

    This keyword allows the program to better divide up the program into different name spaces or sorts of modules

reinterpret_cast

    A cast that helps the programmer safely cast from a base class to a derived class

---

[*] *Working Paper for Draft Proposed International Standard for Information Systems—Programming Language C++* (20 September 1994), American National Standards Institute.

[†] Turbo-C++, Borland C++ Version 4.5, SunPro CC Version 4.0, g++ Version 2.5.8.

static_cast

Another new casting operator

true

New constant for use with the `bool` type

typeid

Allows the programmer to get type information from inside the program at runtime

NOTE

Many header files define macros for "bool," "true," and "false." This does not present a problem with compilers that have not yet implemented the `bool` type. However, as soon as the compiler makers catch up with the standard, such macros will cause problems.

Answers to Chapter Questions

Answer 28-1: The compiler didn't see our default line because we misspelled "default" as "defualt." This was not flagged as an error because "defualt" is a valid `goto` label. That's why when we compile the program we get the warning:

```
def.c(26): warning: defualt unused in function main
```

which means we defined a label for a `goto`, but never used it.

29

Programming Adages

Second thoughts are ever wiser
—Euripides

General

- Comment, comment, comment. Put a lot of comments in your program. They tell other programmers what you did. They also tell you what you did.

- Use the "KISS" principle (Keep It Simple, Stupid). Clear and simple is better than complex and wonderful.

- Avoid side effects. Use ++ and -- on lines by themselves.

- Never put an assignment inside a conditional. Never put an assignment inside any other statement.

- Know the difference between = and ==. Using = for == is a very common mistake and is difficult to find.

- Never do "nothing" silently.

```
// Don't program like this
for (index = 0; data[index] < key; ++index);
// Did you see the semicolon at the end of the last line?
```

Always put in a comment.

```
for (index = 0; data[index] < key; ++index)
        /* Do nothing */;
```

- Practice coding. Practice is crucial for people involved in almost every other profession that requires a significant level of skill and creativity (e.g., artists, athletes). Help others learn to program. It makes good practice for you to go over what you already know, or think you know.

Design

- If you come to a choice between a relatively "quick hack" or a somewhat more involved but more flexible solution, always go for the more flexible solution. You're more likely to reuse it or learn from it. You're also more likely to be thankful later on when requirements shift a little and your code is ready for it.

- Never trust any user input to be what you expect. What would your program do at any given point if a cat walked across the keyboard, several times?

- Watch out for signed-unsigned conversions and over/underflow conditions.

Declarations

- Put variable declarations one per line and comment them.

- Make variable names long enough to be easily understood, but not so long that they are difficult to type in. (Two or three words is usually enough.)

- Never use default return declarations. If a function returns an integer, declare it as type `int`.

switch *Statement*

- Always put a default case in a `switch` statement. Even if it does nothing, put it in:

```
switch (expression) {
    default:
        /* Do nothing */;
        break;
}
```

- Every case in a `switch` should end with a `break` or a `* fall through */` statement.

Preprocessor

- Always put parentheses, (), around each constant expression defined by a pre-processor `#define` directive:

```
#define BOX_SIZE (3 * 10) /* Size of the box in pixels */
```

- Put () around each argument of a parameterized macro:

```
#define SQUARE(x) ((x) * (x))
```

- Surround macros that contain complete statements with curly braces:

```
// A fatal error has occurred.  Tell user and abort
#define DIE(msg) {(void)printf(msg);exit(8);}
```

- When using the `#ifdef`/`#endif` construct for conditional compilation, put the `#define` and `#undef` statements near the top of the program and comment them.

- Whenever possible, use `const` instead of `#define`.

- The use of **inline** functions is preferred over the use of parameterized macros.

Style

- A single block of code enclosed in {} should not span more than a couple of pages. Split up any bigger blocks into several smaller, simpler procedures.

- When your code starts to run into the right margin, it's about time to split the procedure into several smaller, simpler procedures.

- Always define a constructor, destructor, and copy constructor for a class. If using the C++ defaults, "define" these routines with a comment such as:

```
class example {
    public:
        // Example -- default constructor
```

Compiling

- Always create a *Makefile* so others will know how to compile your program.

- When compiling, turn on all the warning flags. You never know what the compiler might find.

The Ten Commandments for C++ Programmers

By Phin Straite

1. Thou shalt not rely on the compiler default methods for construction, destruction, copy construction, or assignment for any but the simplest of classes. Thou shalt forget these "big four" methods for any nontrivial class.

2. Thou shalt declare and define thy destructor as virtual such that others may become heir to the fruits of your labors.

3. Thou shalt not violate the "is-a" rule by abusing the inheritance mechanism for thine own twisted perversions.

4. Thou shalt not rely on any implementation-dependent behavior of a compiler, operating system, or hardware environment, lest thy code be forever caged within that dungeon.

5. Thou shalt not augment the interface of a class at the lowest level without most prudent deliberation. Such ill-begotten practices imprison thy clients unjustly into thy classes and create unrest when code maintenance and extension are required.

6. Thou shalt restrict thy friendship to truly worthy contemporaries. Beware, for thou art exposing thyself rudely as from a trenchcoat.

7. Thou shalt not abuse thy implementation data by making it public or static except in the rarest of circumstances. Thy data are thine own; share it not with others.

8. Thou shalt not suffer dangling pointers or references to be harbored within thy objects. These are nefarious and precarious agents of random and wanton destruction.

9. Thou shalt make use of available class libraries as conscientiously as possible. Code reuse, not just thine own but that of thy clients as well, is the holy grail of OO.

10. Thou shalt forever forswear the use of the vile `printf/scanf`, rather favoring the flowing `streams`. Cast off thy vile C cloak and partake of the wondrous fruit of flexible and extensible I/O.

Final Note

Just when you think you've discovered all the things C++ can do to you — think again. There are still more surprises in store.

Question 29-1: *Why does Example 29-1 think everything is two? (This inspired the last adage.)*

Example 29-1. not2/not2.cc

```
#include <iostream.h>

main()
{
    int number;

    cout << "Enter a number: ";

    cin >> number;

    if (number =! 2)
        cout << "Number is not two\n";
    else
        cout << "Number is two\n";

    return (0);
}
```

Answers to Chapter Questions

Answer 29-1: The statement (`number =! 2`) is not a relational equation, but an assignment statement. It is equivalent to:

```
number = (!2);
```

(Because 2 is nonzero, `!2` is zero.)

The programmer accidently reversed the not equals `!=` so it became `=!`. The statement should read:

```
if (number != 2)
```

VI

Appendixes

IV

Appendixes

A

ASCII Table

Table A-1. ASCII Character Chart

Dec.	Oct.	Hex.	Char.		Dec.	Oct.	Hex.	Char.
0	000	00	NUL		23	027	17	ETB
1	001	01	SOH		24	030	18	CAN
2	002	02	STX		25	031	19	EM
3	003	03	ETX		26	032	1A	SUB
4	004	04	EOT		27	033	1B	ESC
5	005	05	ENQ		28	034	1C	FS
6	006	06	ACK		29	035	1D	GS
7	007	07	BEL		30	036	1E	RS
8	010	08	BS		31	037	1F	US
9	011	09	HT		32	040	20	SP
10	012	0A	NL		33	041	21	!
11	013	0B	VT		34	042	22	"
12	014	0C	NP		35	043	23	#
13	015	0D	CR		36	044	24	$
14	016	0E	SO		37	045	25	%
15	017	0F	SI		38	046	26	&
16	020	10	DLE		39	047	27	'
17	021	11	DC1		40	050	28	(
18	022	12	DC2		41	051	29	)
19	023	13	DC3		42	052	2A	*
20	024	14	DC4		43	053	2B	+
21	025	15	NAK		44	054	2C	,
22	026	16	SYN		45	055	2D	-

Table A-1. ASCII Character Chart (Continued)

Dec.	Oct.	Hex.	Char.	Dec.	Oct.	Hex.	Char.
46	056	2E	.	82	122	52	R
47	057	2F	/	83	123	53	S
48	060	30	0	84	124	54	T
49	061	31	1	85	125	55	U
50	062	32	2	86	126	56	V
51	063	33	3	87	127	57	W
52	064	34	4	88	130	58	X
53	065	35	5	89	131	59	Y
54	066	36	6	90	132	5A	Z
55	067	37	7	91	133	5B	[
56	070	38	8	92	134	5C	\
57	071	39	9	93	135	5D	]
58	072	3A	:	94	136	5E	^
59	073	3B	;	95	137	5F	_
60	074	3C	<	96	140	60	`
61	075	3D	=	97	141	61	a
62	076	3E	>	98	142	62	b
63	077	3F	?	99	143	63	c
64	100	40	@	100	144	64	d
65	101	41	A	101	145	65	e
66	102	42	B	102	146	66	f
67	103	43	C	103	147	67	g
68	104	44	D	104	150	68	h
69	105	45	E	105	151	69	i
70	106	46	F	106	152	6A	j
71	107	47	G	107	153	6B	k
72	110	48	H	108	154	6C	l
73	111	49	I	109	155	6D	m
74	112	4A	J	110	156	6E	n
75	113	4B	K	111	157	6F	o
76	114	4C	L	112	160	70	p
77	115	4D	M	113	161	71	q
78	116	4E	N	114	162	72	r
79	117	4F	O	115	163	73	s
80	120	50	P	116	164	74	t
81	121	51	Q	117	165	75	u

Table A-1. ASCII Character Chart (Continued)

Dec.	Oct.	Hex.	Char.
118	166	76	v
119	167	77	w
120	170	78	x
121	171	79	y
122	172	7A	z
123	173	7B	{
124	174	7C	|
125	175	7D	}
126	176	7E	~
127	177	7F	DEL

B

Ranges

Tables B-1 and B-2 list the ranges of various variable types.

Table B-1. 32-bit UNIX Machine

Name	Bits	Low Value	High Value	Accuracy
int	32	−2,147,483,648	2,147,483,647	
short int	16	−32,768	32,767	
long int	32	−2,147,483,648	2,147,483,647	
unsigned int	32	0	4,294,967,295	
unsigned short int	16	0	65,535	
unsigned long int	32	0	4,294,967,295	
char	8	System Dependent		
unsigned char	8	0	255	
float	32	−3.4E+38	3.4E+38	6 digits
double	64	−1.7E+308	1.7E+308	15 digits
long double	64	−1.7E+308	1.7E+308	15 digits

Table B-2. Turbo-C++, Borland C++, and Most Other 16-bit Systems

Name	Bits	Low Value	High Value	Accuracy
int	16	−32,768	32,767	
short int	16	−32,768	32,767	
long int	32	−2,147,483,648	2,147,483,647	
unsigned int	16	0	65,535	

Table B-2. Turbo-C++, Borland C++, and Most Other 16-bit Systems (Continued)

Name	Bits	Low Value	High Value	Accuracy
unsigned short int	16	0	65,535	
unsigned long int	32	0	4,294,967,295	
char	8	−128	127	
unsigned char	8	0	255	
float	32	−3.4E+38	3.4E+38	6 digits
double	64	−1.7E+308	1.7E+308	15 digits
long double	80	−3.4E+4932	3.4E+4932	17 digits

C

Operator Precedence Rules

Practical Subset of the Operator Precedence Rules

Table C-1. Practical Operator Precedence Rules

Precedence	Operator		
1	* (multiply)	/	%
2	+	−	

Put parentheses around everything else.

Standard Rules

Table C-2. Standard C++ Precedence Rules

Precedence	Operators				
1	( )	[]	->	.	
	::	::*	->*	.*	
2	!	~	++	--	(type)
	- (unary)	* (de-reference)			
	& (address of)	sizeof			
3	* (multiply)	/	%		
4	+	-			
5	<<	>>			
6	<	<=	>	>=	
7	==	!=			
8	& (bitwise AND)				

Table C-2. Standard C++ Precedence Rules (Continued)

Precedence	Operators			
9	^			
10	|			
11	&&			
12	||			
13	?:			
14	=	+=	-=	etc.
15	,			

D

Computing sine Using a Power Series

This program is designed to compute the sine function using a power series. A very limited floating-point format is used to demonstrate some of the problems that can occur when using floating point.

The program computes each term in the power series and displays the result. It continues computing terms until the last term is so small that it doesn't contribute to the final result. For comparison purposes, the result of the library function `sin` is displayed as well as the computed sine.

The program is invoked by:

```
sine value
```

where *value* is an angle in radians. For example, to compute sin(0) we use the command:

```
% sine 0
x**1      0.000E+00
1!        1.000E+00
x**1/1! 0.000E+00
1 term computed
sin(0.000E+00)=
   0.000E+00
Actual sin(0)=0
```

And to compute sin(π) we use the command:

```
% sine 3.141
x**1      3.141E+00
1!        1.000E+00
x**1/1! 3.141E+00
   total    3.141E+00

x**3      3.099E+01
3!        6.000E+00
```

```
x**3/3! 5.165E+00
   total   -2.024E+00


x**5     3.057E+02
5!       1.200E+02
x**5/5! 2.548E+00
   total  5.239E-01


x**7     3.016E+03
7!       5.040E+03
x**7/7! 5.985E-01
   total  -7.457E-02


x**9     2.976E+04
9!       3.629E+05
x**9/9! 8.201E-02
   total   7.438E-03


x**11    2.936E+05
11!      3.992E+07
x**11/11! 7.355E-03
   total   8.300E-05


x**13    2.897E+06
13!      6.227E+09
x**13/13! 4.652E-04
   total   5.482E-04


x**15    2.858E+07
15!      1.308E+12
x**15/15! 2.185E-05
   total   5.263E-04


x**17    2.819E+08
17!      3.557E+14
x**17/17! 7.927E-07
   total   5.271E-04


x**19    2.782E+09
19!      1.217E+17
x**19/19! 2.287E-08
   total   5.271E-04


x**21    2.744E+10
21!      5.109E+19
x**21/21! 5.371E-10
11 term computed
sin(3.141E+00)=
  5.271E-04
Actual sin(3.141)=0.000592654
```

Makefile

Makefile for UNIX

Example D-1. sin/Makefile

```
sine: sine.cc
        g++ -g -Wall -o sine sine.cc -lm

clean:
        rm sine
```
Makefile for Turbo-C++
[File: sin/Makefile.dos]
```
#
# Makefile for Borland's Turbo-C++ compiler
#
CC = tcc
#
# Flags
#       -N  -- Check for stack overflow
#       -v  -- Enable debugging
#       -w  -- Turn on all warnings
#       -ml -- Large model
#       -A  -- Force ANSI compliance
#
CFLAGS = -N -v -w -ml -A
#
sine.exe: sine.c
        $(CC) $(CFLAGS) -esine sine.c
```

Program: sine.cc

Example D-2. sine/sine.cc

```
/*********************************************************
 * sine -- compute sine using very simple floating      *
 *      arithmetic                                       *
 *                                                       *
 * Usage:                                                *
 *      sine <value>                                     *
 *                                                       *
 *      <value> is an angle in radians                   *
 *                                                       *
 * Format used in f.fffe+X                               *
 *                                                       *
 * f.fff is a 4-digit fraction                           *
 *      + is a sign (+ or -)                             *
 *      X is a single-digit exponent                     *
 *                                                       *
 * sin(x) = x   - x**3 + x**5 - x**7                     *
 *              -----   ----   ----  . . . .             *
 *                3!      5!     7!                       *
 *                                                       *
```

Example D-2. sine/sine.cc (Continued)

```
 * Warning: This program is intended to show some of      *
 *       problems with floating point.  It is not         *
 *       intended to be used to produce exact values for  *
 *       the sine function.                               *
 *                                                        *
 * Note: Even though we specify only one digit for the    *
 *       exponent, two are used for some calculations.    *
 *       This is due to the fact that printf has no        *
 *       format for a single-digit exponent.              *
 **********************************************************/
#include <iostream.h>
#include <stdlib.h>
#include <math.h>
#include <stdio.h>

main(int argc, char *argv[])
{
    float    total;    // Total of series so far
    float    new_total;// Newer version of total
    float    term_top;// Top part of term
    float    term_bottom;// Bottom of current term
    float    term;    // Current term
    float    exp;     // Exponent of current term
    float    sign;    // +1 or -1 (changes on each term)
    float    value;   // Value of the argument to sin
    int      index;   // Index for counting terms

    char     *float_2_ascii(float number);  // Turn floating point to ASCII
    float    fix_float(float number);       // Round to correct digits
    float    factorial(float number);       // Compute n!

    if (argc != 2) {
        cerr << "Usage is:\n";
        cerr << "   sine <value>\n";
        exit (8);
    }

    value = fix_float(atof(&argv[1][0]));

    total = 0.0;
    exp = 1.0;
    sign = 1.0;

    for (index = 0; /* Take care of below */ ; ++index) {
        term_top = fix_float(pow(value, exp));
        term_bottom = fix_float(factorial(exp));
        term = fix_float(term_top / term_bottom);
        cout << "x**" << int(exp) << "      " <<
                float_2_ascii(term_top) << '\n';
        cout << exp << "!        " << float_2_ascii(term_bottom) << '\n';
        cout << "x**" << int(exp) << "/" << int(exp) << "! " <<
                float_2_ascii(term) << "\n";
```

Example D-2. sine/sine.cc (Continued)

```
        new_total = fix_float(total + sign * term);
        if (new_total == total)
                break;

        total = new_total;
        sign = -sign;
        exp = exp + 2.0;
        cout <<"  total   " << float_2_ascii(total) << '\n';
        cout <<'\n';
    }
    cout << index +1 << " term computed\n";
    cout << "sin(" << float_2_ascii(value) << ")=\n";
    cout << "  " << float_2_ascii(total) << '\n';
    cout << "Actual sin(" << atof(&argv[1][0]) << ")=" <<
            sin(atof(&argv[1][0])) << '\n';
    return (0);
}
/***********************************************************
 * float_2_ascii -- turn a floating point string          *
 *      into ASCII                                         *
 *                                                         *
 * Parameters                                              *
 *      number -- number to turn into ASCII                *
 *                                                         *
 * Returns                                                 *
 *      pointer to the string containing the number        *
 *                                                         *
 * Warning: Uses static storage, so later calls            *
 *              overwrite earlier entries                  *
 ***********************************************************/
char *float_2_ascii(float number)
{
    static char result[10];     // Place to put the number

    sprintf(result, "%8.3E", number);
    return (result);
}
/***********************************************************
 * fix_float -- turn high-precision numbers into           *
 *              low-precision numbers to simulate a        *
 *              very dumb floating-point structure         *
 *                                                         *
 * Parameters                                              *
 *      number -- number to take care of                   *
 *                                                         *
 * Returns                                                  *
 *      number accurate to 5 places only                   *
 *                                                         *
 * Note: This works by changing a number into ASCII and    *
 *      back.  Very slow, but it works.                    *
 ***********************************************************/
```

Example D-2. sine/sine.cc (Continued)

```
float fix_float(float number)
{
    float   result;     // Result of the conversion
    char    ascii[10];  // ASCII version of number

    (void)sprintf(ascii, "%8.4e", number);
    (void)sscanf(ascii, "%e", &result);
    return (result);
}
/********************************************************
 * factorial -- compute the factorial of a number      *
 *                                                      *
 * Parameters                                           *
 *      number -- number to use for factorial           *
 *                                                      *
 * Returns                                              *
 *      factorial(number) or number!                    *
 *                                                      *
 * Note: Even though this is a floating-point routine,  *
 *       using numbers that are not whole numbers        *
 *       does not make sense                             *
 ********************************************************/
float factorial(float number)
{
    if (number <= 1.0)
        return (number);
    else
        return (number *factorial(number - 1.0));
}
```

Glossary

^   Symbol for the bitwise exclusive OR operator.

~   Symbol for the bitwise complement operator. Inverts all bits.

!   Symbol for the logical NOT operator.

!= Not-equal relational operator.

{} *See* curly braces.

| Symbol for the bitwise OR operator.

|| Symbol for the logical OR operator.

%   Symbol for the modulus operator.

&   1. Symbol for the bitwise AND operator.

    2. A symbol used to precede a variable name (as in &x). Means the address of the named variable (address of x). Used to assign a value to a pointer variable.

    Used to declare a reference variable.

&& Symbol for the logical AND operator (used in comparison operations).

*   1. Symbol for the multiply operator.

    2. Symbol used to precede a pointer variable name that means get the value stored at the address pointed to by the pointer variable. (*x means get the value stored at x.) Sometimes known as the de-referencing operator or indirect operator.

+   Symbol for the add operator.

++ Symbol for the incrementation operator.

–   Symbol for the subtract operator.

`--`   Symbol for the decrementation operator.

`->`   Used to obtain a member from a class or structure pointer.

`->*` Indicates the item pointed to by a "pointer to member."

`/`   Symbol for the divide operator.

`<`   Less-than relational operator.

`<<`   1.Symbol for the left shift operator.

    2.Used by the `iostream` package for output.

`::`   Scope operator. Used to indicate which class a particular identifier belongs to.

`::*` Used to declare a pointer to a class member.

`<=`   Less-than-or-equal-to relational operator.

`==`   Equal relational operator.

`>`   Greater-than relational operator.

`>=`   Greater-than-or-equal-to relational operator.

`>>`   1.Symbol for the right shift operator.

    2.Used by the `iostream` package for input.

`'\0'`
    End-of-string character (the NULL character).

`#define`
    A C++ preprocessor directive that defines a substitute text for a name.

`#endif`
    The closing bracket to a preprocessor macro section that began with an `#ifdef` directive.

`#ifdef`
    Preprocessor directive that checks to see whether a macro name is defined. If defined, the code following it is included in the source.

`#ifndef`
    Preprocessor directive that checks to see whether a macro name is undefined. If it is currently undefined, the code following is included in the macro expansion.

`#include`
    A preprocessor directive that causes the named file to be inserted in place of the `#include`.

`#undef`
    A preprocessor directive that cancels a `#define`.

_ptr

A convention used in this book. All pointer variables end with the extension _ptr.

abstract class

A class containing one or more pure virtual functions.

accuracy

A quantitative measurement of the error inherent in the representation of a real number.

address

A value that identifies a storage location in memory.

AND

A Boolean operation that yields 0 if either operand is 0 and 1 if both operands are 1.

ANSI C

Any version of C that conforms to the specifications of the American National Standards Institute Committee X3J.

ANSI C++

Any version of C++ that conforms to the specifications of the American National Standards Institute. At the time of this writing, the standards exist only in draft form and there are still a lot of details to be worked out.

array

A collection of data elements arranged to be indexed in one or more dimensions. In C++, arrays are stored in contiguous memory.

ASCII

American Standard Code for Information Interchange. A code to represent characters.

assignment statement

An operation that stores a value in a variable.

auto

A C++ keyword used to create temporary variables.

automatic variable

See temporary variable.

base class

A class that is used as the base for a derived class.

bit

Binary digit; either of the digits 0 or 1.

bit field

A group of contiguous bits taken together as a unit. This C++ language feature allows the access of individual bits.

bit flip

The inversion of all bits in an operand. *See also* complement.

bit operator

See bitwise operator.

bitmapped graphics

Computer graphics where each pixel in the graphic output device is controlled by a single bit or a group of bits.

bitwise operator

An operator that performs Boolean operations on two operands, treating each bit in an operand as individual bits and performing the operation bit by bit on corresponding bits.

block

A section of code enclosed in curly braces.

Borland C++

A version of the C++ language for personal computers developed by Borland. This is the high-end version of Borland's Turbo-C++ product.

boxing (a comment)

The technique of using a combination of asterisks, vertical and horizontal rules, and other typographic characters to draw a box around a comment in order to set it off from the code.

`break`

A statement that terminates the innermost execution of `for`, `while`, `switch`, and `do/while` statements.

breakpoint

A location in a program where normal execution is suspended and control is turned over to the debugger.

buffered I/O

Input/output where intermediate storage (a buffer) is used between the source and destination of an I/O stream.

byte

A group of eight bits.

C

A general-purpose computer programming language developed in 1974 at Bell Laboratories by Dennis Ritchie. C is considered to be a medium- to high-level language.

C++

A language based on C invented in 1980 by Bjarne Stroustrup. First called "C with classes," it has evolved into its own language.

C++ code

Computer instructions written in the C++ language.

C++ compiler

Software that translates C++ source code into machine code.

C++ syntax

See syntax.

call by reference

A parameter-passing mechanism where the actual parameter is not passed to a function, but instead a pointer is used to point to it. (*See also* call by value.)

call by value

A procedure call where the parameters are passed by passing the values of the parameters. (*See also* call by reference.)

`case`

Acts as a label for one of the alternatives in a `switch` statement.

cast

To convert a variable from one type to another type by explicitly indicating the type conversion.

`cerr`

Standard error stream for C++. (Corresponds to C's `stderr`.)

CFront

A program to translate C++ code into C code. This program was the basis for the first C++ compilers. Currently not used for most compilers, as many native C++ compilers now exist.

CGA

Color graphics adapter. A common color graphics card for the IBM PC.

`char`

A C++ keyword used to declare variables that represent characters or small integers.

`cin`

Character in. Standard input stream for C++. (Corresponds to C's `stdin`.)

`class`

A data structure consisting of different data types, protections for the members, and functions to manipulate them.

class (of a variable)
> *See* storage class.

clear a bit
> The operation of setting an individual bit to zero. This is not a defined operation in C++.

clog
> Standard log file for C++.

code design
> A document that describes in general terms how the program is to perform its function.

coding
> The act of writing a program in a computer language.

command-line options
> Options to direct the course of a program, such as a compiler, that are entered from the computer console.

comment
> Text included in a computer program for the sole purpose of providing information about the program. Comments are a programmer's notes to himself and future programmers. The text is ignored by the compiler.

comment block
> A group of related comments that convey general information about a program or a section of program.

compilation
> The translation of source code into machine code.

compiler
> A system program that does compilation.

compiling
> *See* compilation.

complement
> An arithmetic or logical operation. A logical complement is the same as an invert or NOT operation.

computer language
> *See* programming language.

conditional compilation
> The ability to selectively compile parts of a program based on the truth of conditions tested in conditional directives that surround the code.

continue

A flow control statement that causes the next execution of a loop to begin.

control statement

A statement that determines which statement is to be executed next based on a conditional test.

control variable

A variable that is systematically changed during the execution of the loop. When the variable reaches a predetermined value, the loop is terminated.

conversion specification

A C string used by the `printf` family of functions that specifies how a variable is to be printed.

cout

Standard output for C++ programs. (Corresponds to C's `stdout`.)

curly braces

One of the characters { or }. They are used in C++ to delimit groups of elements to treat them as a unit.

debugging

The process of finding and removing errors from a program.

decision statement

A statement that tests a condition created by a program and changes the flow of the program based on that decision.

declaration

A specification of the type and name of a variable to be used in a program.

default

Serves as a case label if no case value match is found within the scope of a `switch`.

define statement

See `#define`.

delete

A directive that returns a class or variable created by **new** to the heap.

de-referencing operator

The operator that indicates access to the value pointed to by a pointer variable or an addressing expression. *See also* *.

derived class

A class built on top of another, base class.

directive
> A command to the preprocessor (as opposed to a statement to produce machine code).

double
> A C++ language keyword to declare a variable that contains a real number. The number usually requires twice as much storage as type `float`.

double linked list
> A linked list with both forward and backward pointers. *See also* linked list.

double quotation mark
> ASCII character 34. Used in C++ to delimit character strings.

EGA
> Enhanced graphics adapter. A common graphics card for the IBM PC.

else
> A clause in an `if` statement specifying the action to take in the event that the statement following the `if` conditional is false.

enum
> A C++ keyword that defines an enumerated data type.

enumerated data type
> A data type consisting of a named set of values. The C++ compiler assigns an integer to each member of the set.

EOF
> End-of-file character defined in *stdio.h*.

escape character
> A special character used to change the meaning of the character(s) that follow. This is represented in C++ by the backslash character, \.

exclusive OR
> A Boolean operation that yields 0 if both operands are the same and 1 if they are different.

executable file
> A file containing machine code that has been linked and is ready to be run on a computer.

exponent
> The component of a floating-point number that represents the integer power to which the number base is raised in order to determine the represented number.

exponent overflow
> A condition resulting from a floating-point operation where the result is an exponent too large to fit within the bit field allotted to the exponent.

exponent underflow

A condition resulting from a floating-point operation where the result is an exponent too large in negative value to fit within the bit field allotted to the exponent.

`extern`

C++ keyword used to indicate that a variable or function is defined outside the current file.

fast prototyping

A top-down programming technique that consists of writing the smallest portion of a specification that can be implemented that will still do something.

`fclose`

A function that closes a file. From the old C-style I/O package *stdio*.

`fflush`

A routine to force the flushing of a buffer. From the old C-style I/O package *stdio*.

`fgetc`

A function that reads a single character. From the old C-style I/O package *stdio*.

`fgets`

A stream input library function that reads a single line. From the old C-style I/O package *stdio*.

`FILE`

A macro definition in *stdio* that declares a file variable. From the old C-style I/O package *stdio*.

file

A group of related records treated as a unit.

`float`

A C++ keyword to declare a variable that can hold a real number.

floating point

A numbering system represented by a fraction and an exponent. The system handles very large and very small numbers.

floating-point exception (core dumped)

An error caused by a divide-by-0 or other illegal arithmetic operation. It is a somewhat misleading error because it is caused by **integer** as well as floating-point errors.

floating-point hardware

Circuitry that can perform floating-point operations directly without resorting to software. In personal computers, it is found in the math coprocessor. More advanced processors such as the 80486 have floating-point units built in.

fopen

A function that opens a file for stream I/O. From the old C-style I/O package *stdio.*

fprintf

A function to convert binary data to character data and write it to a file. From the old C-style I/O package *stdio.*

fputc

A function that writes a single character. From the old C-style I/O package *stdio.*

fputs

A function that writes a single line. From the old C-style I/O package *stdio.*

fread

A binary I/O input function. From the old C-style I/O package *stdio.*

free

A C function that returns data to the memory pool. Obsolete in C++. This has been replaced by the C++ **delete** operator *See also* **malloc**.

Free Software Foundation

A group of programmers who create and distribute high-quality software for free. Among their products are the editor *emacs* and the C++ compiler *g++.* Their address is: Free Software Foundation, Inc., 675 Massachusetts Ave., Cambridge, MA 02139, (617) 876-3296.

friend

A function that although not a member of a class is able to access the private members of that class.

fscanf

An input routine similar to **scanf**. From the old C-style I/O package *stdio.*

fstream.h

The C++ package for file I/O.

function

A procedure that returns a value.

fwrite

A binary I/O output function. From the old C-style I/O package *stdio.*

generic pointer

A pointer that can point to any variable without restriction as to type of variable. A pointer to storage without regard to content.

Ghostscript
> A Postscript™-like interpreter that is freely available from the Free Software Foundation.

global variables
> Variables that are known throughout an entire program.

guard digit
> An extra digit of precision used in floating-point calculations to ensure against loss of accuracy.

header file
> *See* include file.

heap
> A portion of memory used by **new** to get space for the structures and classes returned by **new**. Space is returned to this pool by using the **delete** operator.

hexadecimal number
> A base-16 number.

high-level language
> A level of computer language that is between machine language and natural (human) language.

I/O manipulators
> Functions that when "output" or "input" cause no I/O, but set various conversion flags or parameters.

IEEE floating-point standard
> IEEE standard 754, which standardizes floating-point format, precision, and certain non-numerical values.

if
> A statement that allows selective execution of parts of a program based on the truth of a condition.

implementation dependence
> The situation where the result obtained from the operation of computer or software is not standardized because of variability among computer systems. A particular operation may yield different results when run on another system.

include file
> A file that is merged with source code by invocation of the preprocessor directive #include. Also called a header file.

Inclusive OR
> *See* OR.

index
A value, variable, or expression that selects a particular element of an array.

indirect operator
See de-referencing operator.

information hiding
A code design system that tries to minimize the amount of information passed between modules. The idea is to keep as much information as possible hidden inside the modules and make information public only if absolutely necessary.

instruction
A group of bits or characters that defines an operation to be performed by the computer.

`int`
C++ keyword for declaring an integer.

integer
A whole number.

interactive debugger
A program that aids in the debugging of programs.

invert operator
A logical operator that performs a NOT.

iostream.h
Standard C++ I/O package.

left shift
The operation of moving the bits in a bit field left by a specified amount and filling the vacated positions with zeros.

library
A collection of files.

linked list
A collection of data nodes. Each node consists of a value and a pointer to the next item in the list.

local include files
Files from a private library that can be inserted by the preprocessor at the directive `#include "filename"`.

local variable
A variable whose scope is limited to the block in which it is declared.

logical AND

A Boolean operation that returns true if its two arguments are both true. When used on integers, each bit is operated on separately.

logical operator

A C++ operator that performs a logical operation on its two operands and returns a true or a false value.

logical OR

A Boolean operation that returns true if any one of its two arguments is true. When used on integers, each bit is operated on separately.

long

A qualifier to specify a data type with longer than normal accuracy.

machine code

Machine instructions in a binary format that can be recognized directly by the machine without further translation.

machine language

See machine code.

macro

A short piece of text, or text template, that can be expanded into a longer text.

macro processor

A program that generates code by replacing values into positions in a defined template.

magnitude (of a number)

The value of a number without regard to sign.

maintenance (of a program)

Modification of a program because of changing conditions external to the computer system.

make

A utility of both UNIX and MS-DOS/Windows that manages the compilation of programs.

Makefile

The file that contains the commands for the utility make.

malloc

A C procedure that manages a memory heap. This function is now obsolete. The C++ operator new supersedes this function.

mask

A pattern of bits for controlling the retention or elimination of another group of bits.

member
> An element of a class or structure.

module
> One logical part of a program.

MS-DOS
> An operating system for IBM personal computers developed by Microsoft.

new
> C++ operator to get a new variable from the heap.

new-line character
> A character that causes an output device to go to the beginning of a new line.

nonsignificant digits
> Leading digits that do not affect the value of a number (0s for a positive number, 1s for a negative number in complement form).

normalization
> The shifting of a floating-point fraction (and adjustment of the exponent) so there are no leading nonsignificant digits in the fraction.

NOT
> A Boolean operation that yields the logical inverse of the operand. NOT 1 yields a 0 and NOT 0 yields a 1.

not a number
> A special value defined in IEEE 754 to signal an invalid result from a floating-point operation.

NULL
> A constant of value 0 that points to nothing.

null pointer
> A pointer whose bit pattern is all zeros. This indicates that the pointer does not point to valid data.

object-oriented design
> A design methodology where the programmer bases his or her design on data objects (classes) and the connections between them.

octal number
> A base-eight number.

ones complement
> An operation that flips all the bits in a integer. Ones become zeros and zeros become ones.

operator
> A symbol that represents an action to be performed.

OR

A Boolean operation that yields a 1 if either of the operands is a 1 or yields a zero if both of the operands are 0.

overflow error

An arithmetic error caused by the result of an arithmetic operation being greater than the space the computer provides to store the result.

packed structure

A data-structure technique whereby bit fields are only as large as needed, regardless of word boundaries.

pad byte

A byte added to a structure whose sole purpose is to ensure memory alignment.

parameter

A data item to which a value may be assigned. Often means the arguments that are passed between a caller and a called procedure.

parameterized macro

A macro consisting of a template with insertion points for the introduction of parameters.

parameters of a macro

The values to be inserted into the parameter positions in the definition of a macro. The insertion occurs during the expansion of the macro.

permanent variable

A variable that is created before the program starts, is initialized before the program starts, and retains its memory during the entire execution of the program.

pixel

The smallest element of a display that can be individually assigned intensity and color. From **Picture Element**.

pointer

A data type that holds the address of a location in memory.

pointer arithmetic

C++ allows three arithmetic operations on pointers:

1. A numeric value can be added to a pointer.

2. A numeric value can be subtracted from a pointer.

3. One pointer can be subtracted from another pointer.

pointer variable

See pointer.

Portable C compiler
> A C compiler written by Stephen Johnson making it relatively easy to adapt the compiler to different computer architectures.

precision
> A measure of the ability to distinguish between nearly equal values.

preprocessor
> A program that performs preliminary processing with the purpose of expanding macro code templates to produce C++ code.

preprocessor directive
> A command to the preprocessor.

`printf`
> A C library routine that produces formatted output. From the old C-style I/O package *stdio*.

`private`
> A C++ keyword indicating that the members that follow are to be accessible only from inside the class or by **friends** of the class.

procedure
> A program segment that can be invoked from different parts of a program or programs. It does not return a value (function of type `void`).

program
> A group of instructions that cause a computer to perform a sequence of operations.

program header
> The comment block at the beginning of a program.

program specification
> A written document that states what a program is to do.

programmer
> An individual who writes programs for a computer.

programming (a computer)
> The process of expressing the solution to a problem in a language that represents instructions for a computer.

programming language
> A scheme of formal notation used to prepare computer programs.

`protected`
> A C++ keyword indicating that the members that follow are accessible inside the class, inside the class's **friends**, or inside any derived classes, but are not accessible to the outside world.

pseudocode
A coding technique where precise descriptions of procedures are written in easy-to-read language constructs without the bother of precise attention to the syntax rules of a computer language.

`public`
A C++ keyword indicating that the members to follow are accessible outside the class.

pure virtual function
A virtual function that does not have a default body. The class containing a pure virtual function cannot be used directly but must be the base for another class. (*See also* derived classes *and* abstract classes.)

qualifier
A word used to modify the meaning of a data declaration.

radix
The positive integer by which the weight of the digit place is multiplied to obtain the weight of the next higher digit in the base of the numbering system.

real number
A number that may be represented by a finite or infinite numeral in a fixed-radix numbering system.

recursion
Recursion occurs when a function calls itself directly or indirectly. (For a recursive definition, *see* recursion.)

redirect
The command-line option >`file` allows the user to direct the output of a program into a file instead of to the screen. A similar option, <*file*, exists for taking input from a file instead of the keyboard.

reduction in strength
The process of substituting cheap operations for expensive ones.

relational operator
An operator that compares two operands and reports either true or false based on whether the relationship is true or false.

release
The completion of a programming project to the point where it is ready for general use.

replay file
A file that is used instead of the standard input for keyboard data.

return statement

> A statement that signals the completion of a function and causes control to return to the caller.

revision

> The addition of significant changes to the program.

right shift

> The operation of moving the bits in a bit field right by a specified amount.

round

> To delete or omit one or more of the least significant digits in a positional representation and adjust the part retained in accordance with some specific rule, e.g., minimize the error.

rounding error

> An error due to truncation in rounding.

save file

> A debugging tool where all the keystrokes typed by the user are saved in a file for future use. *See also* replay file.

scanf

> A library input function that reads numbers directly from the keyboard. Hard to use. In most cases an **fgets/sscanf** combination is used. From the old C-style I/O package *stdio*.

scope

> The scope of a variable is the portion of a program where the name of the variable is known.

segmentation violation

> An error caused by a program trying to access memory outside its address space. Caused by de-referencing a bad pointer.

set a bit

> The operation of setting a specified bit to 1. This is not a defined operation in C++.

setw

> An I/O manipulator to set the width of the next output.

shift

> The operation of moving the bits in a bit field either left or right.

short

> An arithmetic data type that is the same size as, or smaller than, an integer.

side effect

> An operation performed in addition to the main operation of a statement such

as incrementing a variable in an assignment statement: `result = begin++ - end;`.

significand

The most significant digit of a floating-point number without regard to placement of the radix point.

significant digit

A digit that must be kept to preserve a given accuracy.

single quotation mark

ASCII character 39. Used in C++ to delimit a single character.

`sizeof`

Operator that returns the size, in bytes, of a data type of variable.

source code

Symbolic coding in its original form before it is translated by a computer.

source file

A file containing source code.

specification

A document that describes what a program does.

`sprintf`

Similar to `fprintf` except it uses a string output. From the old C-style I/O package *stdio*.

`sscanf`

A library input routine. From the old C-style I/O package *stdio*.

stack

An area of memory used to hold a list of data and instructions on a temporary basis.

stack overflow

An error caused by a program using too much temporary space (stack space) for its variables. Caused by a big program or by infinite recursion.

stack variable

See temporary variable.

`static`

A storage class attribute. Inside a set of curly braces, it indicates a permanent variable. Outside a set of curly braces, it indicates a file-local variable. For class members it denotes a variable or function that is instance independent. See Table 14-1 for a complete list of uses.

`stderr`

Predefined standard error file. From the old C-style I/O package *stdio*.

`stdin`
> Predefined input source. From the old C-style I/O package *stdio*.

stdio.h
> The old C-style I/O package.

`stdout`
> Predefined standard output. From the old C-style I/O package *stdio*.

storage class
> An attribute of a variable definition that controls how the variable will be stored in memory.

string
> A sequence of characters or an array of characters.

`struct`
> A C++ keyword that identifies a structure data type.

structure
> A hierarchical set of names that refers to an aggregate of data items that may have different attributes.

style sheet
> A document that describes the style of programming used by a particular company or institution.

Sunview
> A graphics and windowing system available on SUN workstations.

`switch`
> A multiway branch that transfers control to one of several case statements based on the value of an index expression.

syntax
> Rules that govern the construction of statements.

syntax error
> An error in the proper construction of a C++ expression.

temporary variable
> A variable whose storage is allocated from the stack. The variable is initialized each time the block in which it is defined is entered. It exists only during the execution of that block.

test a bit
> The operation of determining whether a particular bit is set. This is not a defined operation in C++.

test plan
> A specification of the tests that a program must undergo.

text editor
> Software used to create or alter text files.

translation
> Creation of a new program in an alternate language logically equivalent to an existing program in a source language.

tree
> A hierarchical data structure.

truncation
> An operation on a real number whereby any fractional part is discarded.

Turbo-C++
> A version of the C++ language for personal computers developed by Borland.

typecast
> *See* cast.

`typedef`
> A operator used to create new types from existing types.

typing statement
> A statement that establishes the characteristics of a variable.

unbuffered I/O
> I/O in which each read or write results in a system call.

`union`
> A data type that allows different data names and data types to be assigned to the same storage location.

UNIX
> A popular multiuser operating system first developed by Ken Thompson and Dennis Ritchie of the Bell Telephone Laboratories.

`unsigned`
> A qualifier for specifying `int` and `char` variables that do not contain negative numbers.

upgrading (of a program)
> Modification of a program to provide improved performance or new features.

value
> A quantity assigned to a constant.

variable
> A name that refers to a value. The data represented by the variable name can, at different times during the execution of a program, assume different values.

variable name
> The symbolic name given to a section of memory used to store a variable.

version

> A term used to identify a particular edition of software. A customary practice is to include a version number. Whole numbers indicate major rewrites. Fractions indicate minor rewrites or corrections of problems.

virtual

> A C++ keyword indicating that a member function can be overridden by a function in a derived class.

void

> A data type in C++. When used as a parameter in a function call, it indicates there is no return value. void * indicates that a generic pointer value is returned. When used in casts, it indicates that a given value is to be discarded.

volatile

> A C++ keyword that indicates that the value of a variable or constant can be changed at any time. This attribute is used for memory-mapped I/O, shared memory applications, and other advanced programming.

while

> An iterative statement that repeats a statement as long as a given condition is true.

X Window System

> A graphics and windowing system, available from the X Consortium, that is currently running on many computing systems.

zero-based counting

> A system of counting where the first object is given the count zero rather than one.

Index

About the Author

Steve Oualline wrote his first program when he was eleven. It had a bug in it. Since that time he has studied practical ways of writing programs so that the risk of generating a bug is reduced. He has worked for Motorola and Celerity Computing, and is currently a special consultant for Hewlett Packard, working in the research department of their Ink-Jet division.

Colophon

The animal on the cover of **Practical C++ Programming** is an Eastern chipmunk, a striped ground squirrel found mostly in eastern North America. Eastern chipmunks have five dark and two light stripes on their backs, extending from head to rump, and two stripes on their long, bushy tails. They are distinguished from other ground squirrels by the white stripes above and below their eyes. The coloration of chipmunks throughout North America varies, but is quite uniform within regions.

Chipmunks often make their homes in sparse forests or farms, where they can build the entrances to their lodges in stone walls, broken trees, or thick underbrush. The lodges consist of a maze of tunnels leading to a large leaf-lined nest. Chipmunks spend most of the daylight hours outdoors, but head for their lodges before nightfall. Although they are excellent climbers, chipmunks live primarily on the ground.

Chipmunks eat nuts, seeds, insects, and occasionally birds' eggs. Like all ground squirrels, they have large cheek pouches, sometimes extending as far back as their shoulders, in which they can store food. They collect and store nuts and seeds through the summer and fall. When the weather starts to get cool, all the chipmunks in a region will suddenly disappear into their lodges where they begin hibernation. On warm winter days one can often see chipmunk pawprints in the snow, as they will sometimes wake up and leave their lodges for brief periods when the temperature rises.

Mating season for Eastern chipmunks is mid-March to early April. The gestation period is 31 days, after which a litter of three to six is born. Baby chipmunks leave the lodge after one month, and are mature by July.

The chipmunk most likely got its name from the noise it makes, which sounds like a loud "cheep." You can occasionally see a chipmunk hanging upside down from a tree branch "cheeping" its call.

Edie Freedman designed the cover of this book, using a 19th-century engraving from the Dover Pictorial Archive. The cover layout was produced with Quark XPress 3.3 using the ITC Garamond font.

The inside layout was designed by Edie Freedman, with modifications by Nancy Priest, and implemented in FrameMaker by Mike Sierra. The text and heading fonts are ITC Garamond Light and Garamond Book. The illustrations that appear in the book were created in Aldus Freehand 5.0 by Chris Reilley and Michelle Willey. This colophon was written by Clairemarie Fisher O'Leary.

Programming

UNIX, C and MULTI-PLATFORM

Books from O'Reilly & Associates, Inc.

Fall/Winter 1995-96

C Programming Libraries

Practical C++ Programming

By Steve Oualline
1st Edition September 1995
584 pages, ISBN 1-56592-139-9

Fast becoming the standard language of commercial software development, C++ is an update of the C programming language, adding object-oriented features that are very helpful for today's larger graphical applications.

Practical C++ Programming is a complete introduction to the C++ language for the beginning programmer, and also for C programmers transitioning to C++. Unlike most other C++ books, this book emphasizes a practical, real-world approach, including how to debug, how to make your code understandable to others, and how to understand other people's code. Topics covered include good programming style, C++ syntax (what to use and what not to use), C++ class design, debugging and optimization, and common programming mistakes. At the end of each chapter are a number of exercises you can use to make sure you've grasped the concepts. Solutions to most are provided.

Practical C++ Programming describes standard C++ features that are supported by all UNIX C++ compilers (including *gcc*), DOS/Windows and NT compilers (including Microsoft Visual C++), and Macintosh compilers.

C++: The Core Language

By Gregory Satir & Doug Brown
1st Edition October 1995
228 pages, ISBN 1-56592-116-X

A first book for C programmers transitioning to C++, an object-oriented enhancement of the C programming language. Designed to get readers up to speed quickly, this book thoroughly explains the important concepts and features and gives brief overviews of the rest of the language. Covers features common to all C++ compilers, including those on UNIX, Windows NT, Windows, DOS, and Macs.

Porting UNIX Software

By Greg Lehey
1st Edition November 1995
480 pages (est.), ISBN 1-56592-126-7

This book deals with the whole life cycle of porting, from setting up a source tree on your system to correcting platform differences and even testing the executable after it's built. It exhaustively discusses the differences between versions of UNIX and the areas where porters tend to have problems. The assumption made in this book is that you just want to get a package working on your system; you don't want to become an expert in the details of your hardware or operating system (much less an expert in the system used by the person who wrote the package!).

Programming with Pthreads

By Bradford Nichols
1st Edition February 1996 (est.)
350 pages (est.), ISBN 1-56592-115-1

The idea behind POSIX threads is to have multiple tasks running concurrently within the same program. They can share a single CPU as processes do, or take advantage of multiple CPUs when available. In either case, they provide a clean way to divide the tasks of a program while sharing data. This book features realistic examples, a look behind the scenes at the implementation and performance issues, and chapters on special topics such as DCE, real-time, and multiprocessing.

POSIX.4

By Bill Gallmeister
1st Edition January 1995
570 pages, ISBN 1-56592-074-0

A general introduction to real-time programming and real-time issues, this book covers the POSIX.4 standard and how to use it to solve "real-world" problems. If you're at all interested in real-time applications—which include just about everything from telemetry to transaction processing—this book is for you. An essential reference.

POSIX Programmer's Guide

By Donald Lewine
1st Edition April 1991
640 pages, ISBN 0-937175-73-0

Most UNIX systems today are POSIX compliant because the federal government requires it for its purchases. Given the manufacturer's documentation, however, it can be difficult to distinguish system-specific features from those features defined by POSIX. The *POSIX Programmer's Guide*, intended as an explanation of the POSIX standard and as a reference for the POSIX.1 programming library, helps you write more portable programs.

"If you are an intermediate to advanced C programmer and are interested in having your programs compile first time on anything from a Sun to a VMS system to an MSDOS system, then this book must be thoroughly recommended." —*Sun UK User*

Practical C Programming

By Steve Oualline
2nd Edition January 1993
396 pages, ISBN 1-56592-035-X

C programming is more than just getting the syntax right. Style and debugging also play a tremendous part in creating programs that run well. *Practical C Programming* teaches you not only the mechanics of programming, but also how to create programs that are easy to read, maintain, and debug. There are lots of introductory C books, but this is the Nutshell Handbook®! In this edition, programs conform to ANSI C.

Using C on the UNIX System

By Dave Curry
1st Edition January 1989
250 pages, ISBN 0-937175-23-4

This is the book for intermediate to experienced C programmers who want to become UNIX system programmers. It explains system calls and special library routines available on the UNIX system. It is impossible to write UNIX utilities of any sophistication without understanding the material in this book.

Programming with curses

By John Strang
1st Edition 1986
76 pages, ISBN 0-937175-02-1

Curses is a UNIX library of functions for controlling a terminal's display screen from a C program. This handbook helps you make use of the curses library. Describes the original Berkeley version of curses.

Understanding and Using COFF

By Gintaras R. Gircys
1st Edition November 1988
196 pages, ISBN 0-937175-31-5

COFF—Common Object File Format— is the formal definition for the structure of machine code files in the UNIX System V environment. All machine code files are COFF files. This handbook explains COFF data structure and its manipulation.

C Programming Tools

Microsoft RPC Programming Guide

By John Shirley & Ward Rosenberry, Digital Equipment Corporation
1st Edition March 1995
254 pages, ISBN 1-56592-070-8

Remote Procedure Call (RPC) is the glue that holds together MS-DOS, Windows 3.x, and Windows NT. It is a client-server technology—a way of making programs on two different systems work together like one. The advantage of RPC is that you can link two systems together using simple C calls, as in a single-system program.

Like many aspects of Microsoft programming, RPC forms a small world of its own, with conventions and terms that can be confusing. This book is an introduction to Microsoft RPC concepts combined with a step-by-step guide to programming RPC calls in C. Topics include server registration, interface definitions, arrays and pointers, context handles, and basic administration procedures. This edition covers version 2.0 of Microsoft RPC. Four complete examples are included.

Power Programming with RPC

By John Bloomer
1st Edition February 1992
522 pages, ISBN 0-937175-77-3

RPC, or remote procedure calling, is the ability to distribute the execution of functions on remote computers. Written from a programmer's perspective, this book shows what you can do with RPCs, like Sun RPC, the de facto standard on UNIX systems. It covers related programming topics for Sun and other UNIX systems and teaches through examples.

lex & yacc

By John Levine, Tony Mason & Doug Brown
2nd Edition October 1992
366 pages, ISBN 1-56592-000-7

Shows programmers how to use two UNIX utilities, lex and yacc, in program development. The second edition contains completely revised tutorial sections for novice users and reference sections for advanced users. This edition is twice the size of the first, has an expanded index, and covers Bison and Flex.

Applying RCS and SCCS

By Don Bolinger & Tan Bronson
1st Edition September 1995
528 pages, ISBN 1-56592-117-8

Applying RCS and SCCS is a thorough introduction to these two systems, viewed as tools for project management. This book takes the reader from basic source control of a single file, through working with multiple releases of a software project, to coordinating multiple developers. It also presents TCCS, a representative "front-end" that addresses problems RCS and SCCS can't handle alone, such as managing groups of files, developing for multiple platforms, and linking public and private development areas.

Programming with GNU Software

By Mike Loukides
1st Edition TBA 1996 (est.)
250 pages (est.), ISBN 1-56592-112-7

This book and CD combination is a complete package for programmers who are new to UNIX or who would like to make better use of the system. The tools come from Cygnus Support, Inc., a well-known company that provides support for free software. Contents include GNU Emacs, gcc, C and C++ libraries, gdb, RCS, GNATS, and make. The book provides an introduction to all these tools for a C programmer.

UNIX Systems Programming for SVR4

By Dave Curry
1st Edition December 1995 (est.)
600 pages (est.), ISBN 1-56592-163-1

Presents a comprehensive look at the nitty gritty details on how UNIX interacts with applications. If you're writing an application from scratch, or if you're porting an application to any System V.4 platform, you need this book. It thoroughly explains all UNIX system calls and library routines related to systems programming, working with I/O, files and directories, processing multiple input streams, file and record locking, and memory-mapped files.

Software Portability with imake

By Paul DuBois
1st Edition July 1993
390 pages, ISBN 1-56592-055-4

imake is a utility that works with *make* to enable code to be compiled and installed on different UNIX machines. *imake* makes possible the wide portability of the X Window System code and is widely considered an X tool, but it's also useful for any software project that needs to be ported to many UNIX systems.

This Nutshell Handbook®—the only book available on *imake*—is ideal for X and UNIX programmers who want their software to be portable. The book is divided into two sections. The first section is a general explanation of *imake*, X configuration files, and how to write and debug an *Imakefile*. The second section describes how to write configuration files and presents a configuration file architecture that allows development of coexisting sets of configuration files. Several sample sets of configuration files are described and are available free over the Net.

Managing Projects with make

By Andrew Oram & Steve Talbott
2nd Edition October 1991
152 pages, ISBN 0-937175-90-0

make is one of UNIX's greatest contributions to software development, and this book offers the clearest description of *make* ever written. It describes all the basic features of *make* and provides guidelines on meeting the needs of large, modern projects. Also contains a description of free products that contain major enhancements to *make*.

Checking C Programs with lint

By Ian F. Darwin
1st Edition October 1988
84 pages, ISBN 0-937175-30-7

The *lint* program is one of the best tools for finding portability problems and certain types of coding errors in C programs. This handbook introduces you to *lint*, guides you through running it on your programs, and helps you interpret *lint's* output.

Fortran/Scientific Computing

Migrating to Fortran 90

By James F. Kerrigan
1st Edition November 1993
389 pages, ISBN 1-56592-049-X

This book is a practical guide to Fortran 90 for the current Fortran programmer. It provides a complete overview of the new features that Fortran 90 has brought to the Fortran standard, with examples and suggestions for use. Topics include array sections, modules, file handling, allocatable arrays and pointers, and numeric precision.

"This is a book that all Fortran programmers eager to take advantage of the excellent features of Fortran 90 will want to have on their desk." —*FORTRAN Journal*

High Performance Computing

By Kevin Dowd
1st Edition June 1993
398 pages, ISBN 1-56592-032-5

Even if you never touch a line of code, *High Performance Computing* will help you make sense of the newest generation of workstations. A must for anyone who needs to worry about computer performance, this book covers everything, from the basics of modern workstation architecture, to structuring benchmarks, to squeezing more performance out of critical applications. It also explains what a good compiler can do—and what you have to do yourself. The author also discusses techniques for improving memory access patterns and taking advantage of parallelism.

Another valuable section of the book discusses the benchmarking process, or how to evaluate a computer's performance. Kevin Dowd discusses several of the "standard" industry benchmarks, explaining what they measure and what they don't. He also explains how to set up your own benchmark: how to structure the code, how to measure the results, and how to interpret them.

ORACLE Performance Tuning

By Peter Corrigan & Mark Gurry
1st Edition September 1993
642 pages, ISBN 1-56592-048-1

The Oracle relational database management system is the most popular database
system in use today. Oracle offers tremendous power and flexibility, but at some
cost. Demands for fast response, particularly in online transaction processing
systems, make performance a major issue.
With more organizations downsizing
and adopting client-server and distributed
database approaches, performance tuning
has become all the more vital. Whether you're a manager, a
designer, a programmer, or an administrator, there's a lot you
can do on your own to dramatically increase the performance of
your existing Oracle system. Whether you are running RDBMS
Version 6 or Version 7, you may find that this book can save you
the cost of a new machine; at the very least, it will save you a lot
of headaches.

"This book is one of the best books on Oracle that I have
ever read.... [It] discloses many Oracle Tips that DBA's and
Developers have locked in their brains and in their planners....
I recommend this book for any person who works with
Oracle, from managers to developers. In fact, I have to keep
[it] under lock and key, because of the popularity of it."
—Mike Gangler

ORACLE PL/SQL Programming

By Steven Feuerstein
1st Edition September 1995
916 pages, Includes diskette, ISBN 1-56592-142-9

PL/SQL is a procedural language that is
being used more and more with Oracle,
particularly in client-server applications.
This book fills a huge gap in the Oracle
market by providing developers with a
single, comprehensive guide to building
applications with PL/SQL—and building
them the right way. It's packed with
strategies, code architectures, tips,
techniques, and fully realized code.
Includes a disk containing many examples
of PL/SQL programs.

DCE Security Programming

By Wei Hu
1st Edition July 1995
386 pages, ISBN 1-56592-134-8

Security is critical in network applications
since an outsider can so easily gain network
access and pose as a trusted user. Here lies
one of the greatest strengths of the Distributed
Computing Environment (DCE) from the Open
Software Foundation (OSF). DCE offers the
most complete, flexible, and well-integrated
network security package in the industry. The
only problem is learning how to program it.

This book covers DCE security requirements, how the system fits
together, what is required of the programmer, and how to figure
out what needs protecting in an application. It will help you plan
an application and lay the groundwork for Access Control Lists
(ACLs), as well as use the calls that come with the DCE security
interfaces. Using a sample application, increasingly sophisticated
types of security are discussed, including storage of ACLs on disk
and the job of writing an ACL manager. This book focuses on
version 1.0 of DCE. However, issues in version 1.1 are also
discussed so you can migrate to that interface.

Guide to Writing DCE Applications

By John Shirley, Wei Hu & David Magid
2nd Edition May 1994
462 pages, ISBN 1-56592-045-7

A hands-on programming guide to OSF's
Distributed Computing Environment (DCE)
for first-time DCE application programmers.
This book is designed to help new DCE
users make the transition from conventional,
nondistributed applications programming
to distributed DCE programming. In addition
to basic RPC (remote procedure calls),
this edition covers object UUIDs and basic
security (authentication and authorization).
Also includes practical programming examples.

"This book will be useful as a ready reference by the side of the
novice DCE programmer." —*;login*

Distributing Applications Across DCE and Windows NT

By Ward Rosenberry & Jim Teague
1st Edition November 1993
302 pages, ISBN 1-56592-047-3

This book links together two exciting technologies in distributed computing by showing how to develop an application that simultaneously runs on DCE and Microsoft systems through remote procedure calls (RPC). Covers the writing of portable applications and the complete differences between RPC support in the two environments.

Understanding DCE

By Ward Rosenberry, David Kenney & Gerry Fisher
1st Edition October 1992
266 pages, ISBN 1-56592-005-8

A technical and conceptual overview of OSF's Distributed Computing Environment (DCE) for programmers, technical managers, and marketing and sales people. Unlike many O'Reilly & Associates books, *Understanding DCE* has no hands-on programming elements. Instead, the book focuses on how DCE can be used to accomplish typical programming tasks and provides explanations to help the reader understand all the parts of DCE.

Multi-Platform Code Management

By Kevin Jameson
1st Edition August 1994
354 pages, Includes two diskettes, ISBN 1-56592-059-7

For any programming team that is struggling with build and maintenance problems, this book—and its accompanying software (available for 15 platforms, including MS-DOS and various UNIX systems)—can save dozens of errors and hours of effort. A "one-stop-shopping" solution for code management proplems, this book shows you how to structure a large project and keep your files and builds under control over many releases and platforms. Includes two diskettes that provide a complete system for managing source files and builds.

Encyclopedia of Graphics File Formats

By James D. Murray & William vanRyper
1st Edition July 1994
928 pages, Includes CD-ROM
ISBN 1-56592-058-9

The computer graphics world is a veritable alphabet soup of acronyms; BMP, DXF, EPS, GIF, MPEG, PCX, PIC, RIFF, RTF, TGA, and TIFF are only a few of the many different formats in which graphics images can be stored. *The Encyclopedia of Graphics File Formats* is the definitive work on file formats—the book that will become a classic for graphics programmers and everyone else who deals with the low-level technical details of graphics files. It includes technical information on nearly 100 file formats, as well as chapters on graphics and file format basics, bitmap and vector files, metafiles, scene description, animation and multimedia formats, and file compression methods. Best of all, this book comes with a CD-ROM that collects many hard-to-find resources. We've assembled original vendor file format specification documents, along with test images and code examples, and a variety of software packages for MS-DOS, Windows, OS/2, UNIX, and the Macintosh that will let you convert, view, and manipulate graphics files and images.

Understanding Japanese Information Processing

By Ken Lunde
1st Edition September 1993
470 pages, ISBN 1-56592-043-0

Understanding Japanese Information Processing provides detailed information on all aspects of handling Japanese text on computer systems. It brings all of the relevant information together in a single book and covers everything from the origins of modern-day Japanese to the latest information on specific emerging computer encoding standards. Appendices provide additional reference material, such as a code conversion table, character set tables, mapping tables, an extensive list of software sources, a glossary, and more.

At Your Fingertips—

A COMPLETE GUIDE TO O'REILLY'S ONLINE SERVICES

O'Reilly & Associates offers extensive product and customer service information online. We invite you to come and explore our little neck-of-the-woods.

For product information and insight into new technologies, visit the O'Reilly Resource Center

Most comprehensive among our online offerings is the O'Reilly Resource Center. You'll find detailed information on all O'Reilly products, including titles, prices, tables of contents, indexes, author bios, software contents, and reviews. You can also view images of all our products. In addition, watch for informative articles that provide perspective on the technologies we write about. Interviews, excerpts, and bibliographies are also included.

After browsing online, it's easy to order, too, with GNN Direct or by sending email to **order@ora.com**. The O'Reilly Resource Center shows you how. Here's how to visit us online:

☞ *Via the World Wide Web*

If you are connected to the Internet, point your Web browser (e.g., **mosaic, netscape,** or **lynx**) to:

http://www.ora.com/

For the plaintext version, **telnet** to: **www.ora.com** (login: **oraweb**)

☞ *Via Gopher*

If you have a Gopher program, our Gopher server has information in a menu format that some people prefer to the Web.

Connect your **gopher** to: **gopher.ora.com**
Or, point your Web browser to:
gopher://gopher.ora.com/
Or, you can **telnet** to: **gopher.ora.com**
(login: **gopher**)

A convenient way to stay informed: email mailing lists

An easy way to learn of the latest projects and products from O'Reilly & Associates is to subscribe to our mailing lists. We have email announcements and discussions on various topics, for example "ora-news," our electronic news service. Subscribers receive email as soon as the information breaks.

☞ *To join a mailing list:*

Send email to:
listproc@online.ora.com

Leave the message "subject" empty if possible.

If you know the name of the mailing list you want to subscribe to, put the following information on the first line of your message: **subscribe** "listname" "your name" **of** "your company."

For example: **subscribe ora-news Kris Webber of Fine Enterprises**

If you don't know the name of the mailing list, listproc will send you a listing of all the mailing lists. Put this word on the first line of the body: **lists**

To find out more about a particular list, send a message with this word as the first line of the body: **info** "listname"

For more information and help, send this message: **help**

For specific help, email to: **listmaster@online.ora.com**

The complete O'Reilly catalog is now available via email

You can now receive a text-only version of our complete catalog via email. It contains detailed information about all our products, so it's mighty big: over 200 kbytes, or 200,000 characters.

To get the whole catalog in one message, send an empty email message to: **catalog@online.ora.com**

If your email system can't handle large messages, you can get the catalog split into smaller messages. Send email to: **catalog-split@online.ora.com**

To receive a print catalog, send your snail mail address to: **catalog@ora.com**

Check out Web Review, our new publication on the Web

Web Review is our new magazine that offers fresh insights into the Web. The editorial mission of Web Review is to answer the question: How and where do you BEST spend your time online? Each issue contains reviews that look at the most interesting and creative sites on the Web. Visit us at **http://gnn.com/wr/**

Web Review is the product of the recently formed Songline Studios, a venture between O'Reilly and America Online.

Get the files you want with FTP

We have an archive of example files from our books, the covers of our books, and much more available by anonymous FTP.

ftp to:

ftp.ora.com (login: **anonymous** – use your email address as the password.)

Or, if you have a WWW browser, point it to:

ftp://ftp.ora.com/

FTPMAIL

The ftpmail service connects to O'Reilly's FTP server and sends the results (the files you want) by email. This service is for people who can't use FTP—but who can use email.

For help and examples, send an email message to:

ftpmail@online.ora.com

(In the message body, put the single word: **help**)

Helpful information is just an email message away

Many customer services are provided via email. Here are a few of the most popular and useful:

info@online.ora.com
> For a list of O'Reilly's online customer services.

info@ora.com
> For general questions and information.

bookquestions@ora.com
> For technical questions, or corrections, concerning book contents.

order@ora.com
> To order books online and for ordering questions.

catalog@online.ora.com
> To receive an online copy of our catalog.

catalog@ora.com
> To receive a free copy of *ora.com*, our combination magazine and catalog. Please include your snail mail address.

international@ora.com
> Comments or questions about international ordering or distribution.

xresource@ora.com
> To order or inquire about *The X Resource* journal.

proposals@ora.com
> To submit book proposals.

info@gnn.com
> To receive information about America Online's GNN (Global Network Navigator).™

O'Reilly & Associates, Inc.

103A Morris Street, Sebastopol, CA 95472
Inquiries: **707-829-0515, 800-998-9938**
Credit card orders: **800-889-8969** (Weekdays 6 A.M.- 5 P.M. PST)
FAX: **707-829-0104**

O'Reilly & Associates—
LISTING OF TITLES

INTERNET

CGI Scripting on the World Wide Web
(Winter '95-96 est.)
Connecting to the Internet:
An O'Reilly Buyer's Guide
Getting Connected (Winter '95-96 est.)
HTML Handbook (Winter '95-96 est.)
The Mosaic Handbook for
Microsoft Windows
The Mosaic Handbook for
the Macintosh
The Mosaic Handbook for
the X Window System
Smileys
The USENET Handbook
The Whole Internet User's
Guide & Catalog
The Whole Internet for Windows 95
Web Design for Designers
(Winter '95-96 est.)
The World Wide Web Journal
(Winter '95-96 est.)

SOFTWARE

Internet In A Box ™ Version 2.0
WebSite™ 1.1

WHAT YOU NEED TO KNOW SERIES

Using Email Effectively
Marketing on the Internet
(Winter '95-96 est.)
When You Can't Find Your
System Administrator

HEALTH, CAREER & BUSINESS

Building a Successful Software Business
The Computer User's Survival Guide
Dictionary of Computer Terms
(Winter '95-96 est.)
The Future Does Not Compute
Love Your Job!
TWI Day Calendar - 1996

USING UNIX

BASICS

Learning GNU Emacs
Learning the bash Shell
Learning the Korn Shell
Learning the UNIX Operating System
Learning the vi Editor
MH & xmh: Email for Users &
Programmers
SCO UNIX in a Nutshell
UNIX in a Nutshell: System V Edition
Using and Managing UUCP
(Winter '95-96 est.)
Using csh and tcsh

ADVANCED

Exploring Expect
The Frame Handbook
Learning Perl
Making TeX Work
Programming perl
Running Linux
Running Linux Companion CD-ROM
(Winter '95-96 est.)
sed & awk
UNIX Power Tools (with CD-ROM)

SYSTEM ADMINISTRATION

Building Internet Firewalls
Computer Crime:
A Crimefighter's Handbook
Computer Security Basics
DNS and BIND
Essential System Administration
Linux Network Administrator's Guide
Managing Internet Information Services
Managing NFS and NIS
Managing UUCP and Usenet
Networking Personal Computers
with TCP/IP
Practical UNIX Security
PGP: Pretty Good Privacy
sendmail
System Performance Tuning
TCP/IP Network Administration
termcap & terminfo
Volume 8 : X Window System
Administrator's Guide
The X Companion CD for R6

PROGRAMMING

Applying RCS and SCCS
C++: The Core Language
Checking C Programs with lint
DCE Security Programming
Distributing Applications Across DCE
and Windows NT
Encyclopedia of Graphics File Formats
Guide to Writing DCE Applications
High Performance Computing
lex & yacc
Managing Projects with make
Microsoft RPC Programming Guide
Migrating to Fortran 90
Multi-Platform Code Management
ORACLE Performance Tuning
ORACLE PL/SQL Programming
Porting UNIX Software
POSIX Programmer's Guide
POSIX.4: Programming for
the Real World
Power Programming with RPC
Practical C Programming
Practical C++ Programming
Programming with curses
Programming with GNU Software
(Winter '95-96 est.)
Programming with Pthreads
(Winter '95-96 est.)
Software Portability with imake
Understanding and Using COFF
Understanding DCE
Understanding Japanese Information
Processing
UNIX Systems Programming for SVR4
(Winter '95-96 est.)
Using C on the UNIX System

BERKELEY 4.4 SOFTWARE DISTRIBUTION

4.4BSD System Manager's Manual
4.4BSD User's Reference Manual
4.4BSD User's Supplementary Docs.
4.4BSD Programmer's Reference Man.
4.4BSD Programmer's Supp. Docs.
4.4BSD-Lite CD Companion
4.4BSD-Lite CD Companion: Int. Ver.

X PROGRAMMING

THE X WINDOW SYSTEM

Volume 0: X Protocol Reference Manual
Volume 1: Xlib Programming Manual
Volume 2: Xlib Reference Manual
Volume 3: X Window System
User's Guide
Volume. 3M: X Window System
User's Guide, Motif Ed.
Volume. 4: X Toolkit Intrinsics
Programming Manual
Volume 4M: X Toolkit Intrinsics
Programming Manual, Motif Ed.
Volume 5: X Toolkit Intrinsics
Reference Manual
Volume 6A: Motif Programming Man.
Volume 6B: Motif Reference Manual
Volume 6C: Motif Tools
Volume 8 : X Window System
Administrator's Guide
PEXlib Programming Manual
PEXlib Reference Manual
PHIGS Programming Manual
PHIGS Reference Manual
Programmer's Supplement for Release 6
The X Companion CD for R6
X User Tools (with CD-ROM)
The X Window System in a Nutshell

THE X RESOURCE

*A QUARTERLY WORKING JOURNAL
FOR X PROGRAMMERS*

The X Resource: Issues 0 through 15

TRAVEL

Travelers' Tales France
Travelers' Tales Hong Kong (12/95 est.)
Travelers' Tales India
Travelers' Tales Mexico
Travelers' Tales Spain
Travelers' Tales Thailand
Travelers' Tales: A Woman's World

O'Reilly & Associates—
INTERNATIONAL DISTRIBUTORS

Customers outside North America can now order O'Reilly & Associates books through the following distributors. They offer our international customers faster order processing, more bookstores, increased representation at tradeshows worldwide, and the high-quality, responsive service our customers have come to expect.

EUROPE, MIDDLE EAST, AND AFRICA
(except Germany, Switzerland, and Austria)

INQUIRIES
International Thomson Publishing Europe
Berkshire House
168-173 High Holborn
London WC1V 7AA, United Kingdom
Telephone: 44-71-497-1422
Fax: 44-71-497-1426
Email: itpint@itps.co.uk

ORDERS
International Thomson Publishing Services, Ltd.
Cheriton House, North Way
Andover, Hampshire SP10 5BE, United Kingdom
Telephone: 44-264-342-832 (UK orders)
Telephone: 44-264-342-806 (outside UK)
Fax: 44-264-364418 (UK orders)
Fax: 44-264-342761 (outside UK)

GERMANY, SWITZERLAND, AND AUSTRIA
International Thomson Publishing GmbH
O'Reilly-International Thomson Verlag
Königswinterer Straße 418
53227 Bonn, Germany
Telephone: 49-228-97024 0
Fax: 49-228-441342
Email: anfragen@ora.de

ASIA *(except Japan)*
INQUIRIES
International Thomson Publishing Asia
221 Henderson Road
#08-03 Henderson Industrial Park
Singapore 0315
Telephone: 65-272-6496
Fax: 65-272-6498

ORDERS
Telephone: 65-268-7867
Fax: 65-268-6727

JAPAN
O'Reilly & Associates, Inc.
103A Morris Street
Sebastopol, CA 95472 U.S.A.
Telephone: 707-829-0515
Telephone: 800-998-9938 (U.S. & Canada)
Fax: 707-829-0104
Email: order@ora.com

AUSTRALIA
WoodsLane Pty. Ltd.
7/5 Vuko Place, Warriewood NSW 2102
P.O. Box 935, Mona Vale NSW 2103
Australia
Telephone: 02-970-5111
Fax: 02-970-5002
Email: woods@tmx.mhs.oz.au

NEW ZEALAND
WoodsLane New Zealand Ltd.
21 Cooks Street (P.O. Box 575)
Wanganui, New Zealand
Telephone: 64-6-347-6543
Fax: 64-6-345-4840
Email: woods@tmx.mhs.oz.au

THE AMERICAS
O'Reilly & Associates, Inc.
103A Morris Street
Sebastopol, CA 95472 U.S.A.
Telephone: 707-829-0515
Telephone: 800-998-9938 (U.S. & Canada)
Fax: 707-829-0104
Email: order@ora.com

Here's a page we encourage readers to tear out...

O'REILLY WOULD LIKE TO HEAR FROM YOU

Please send me the following:

❏ *ora.com*

O'Reilly's magazine/catalog,
containing behind-the-scenes
articles and interviews on the
technology we write about, and
a complete listing of O'Reilly
books and products.

Which book did this card come from?

_____

Where did you buy this book?
   ❏ Bookstore   ❏ Direct from O'Reilly
      ❏ Bundled with hardware/software   ❏ Class/seminar
Your job description: ❏ SysAdmin   ❏ Programmer
   ❏ Other_____

Describe your operating system: _____

_____

Please print legibly

Name   Company/Organization Name

Address

City   State   Zip/Postal Code   Country

Telephone   Internet or other email address (specify network)

Nineteenth century wood engraving
of raccoons from the O'Reilly
& Associates Nutshell Handbook®
Applying RCS and SCCS.

PLACE
STAMP
HERE

NO POSTAGE
NECESSARY IF
MAILED IN THE
UNITED STATES

BUSINESS REPLY MAIL
FIRST CLASS MAIL   PERMIT NO. 80   SEBASTOPOL, CA

Postage will be paid by addressee

O'Reilly & Associates, Inc.
103A Morris Street
Sebastopol, CA 95472-9902